Advance Praise for Douglas Sadownick and *Sex Between Men*

"In all, this is an ambitious book . . . a serious and eminently readable treatment of late 20th century homo-eros."
      —Ian Young, *Torso*

"Sadownick's work is exhaustive and groundbreaking . . . chock-full of graphic, first-hand sexual accounts and steeped in archetypal psychology. . . . I found *Sex Between Men* immensely enjoyable, intelligent, and accessible, and I recommend it to anyone interested in exploring the inner life of developing gay sexuality."
      —Tom Maroney, *Bay Area Reporter*

"It's odd that no one has written this book before now. It's . . . interesting to this reader to learn what the O Boys' parties in Los Angeles are all about, or what goes on in one of Joseph Kramer's Body Electric workshops. What stays in the mind after reading *Sex Between Men* is not the history, or even the psychologizing, but things like Arnie Kantrowitz's realization in the Mineshaft one day that he had gone there not to have sex, but just to get out of his apartment."
      —Andrew Holleran, *The Harvard Gay & Lesbian Review*

"Sadownick's emphasis on the dynamics of the unconscious mind is purposeful and clear throughout the book. . . . Serves the reader best as a provocative philosophy of gay male desire."
      —Daniel R. Mullen, *Gay People's Chronicle*

"Two things stand out about Douglas Sadownick's new book, *Sex Between Men*: It is a work of considerable scholarship, and it doesn't read at all like a scholarly book."
      —Brian Caffall, *Philadelphia Gay News*

"A frank and admirably un-whitewashed exploration. Ultimately, this book goes where none has gone before, so I grant it its flaws and read it with relish."
      —Al Cotton, *Southern Voice*

"An erotocentric history of gay male self-awareness—history, sociology, psychology, politics. Sadownick puts the *sex* right back into the heart of *homosexual*, and tells how we've sought out and found not just each other, but ourselves."
      —Jack Fertig, *San Francisco Bay Times*

"*Sex Between Men* is much more than just another book about male sexuality. It is a space shuttle, packed with investigative data. Any gay man who dares to call himself knowledgeable about sexual matters needs the directionals this extraordinary book provides."
      —Jack Nichols, *TWN News Magazine*

"In *Sex Between Men*, Douglas Sadownick is boldly determined to, as he puts it, 'value the subjective in the individual lives of gay men over and beyond anything else.' But it will not surprise this gifted writer's legions of admirers to learn that his investigation of the sex lives of gay men since World War II is as objective in documenting, overviewing, and giving spiritual dimension to this experience as it is thoroughly engrossing and exquisitely honed as a work of literature and art."

—Lawrence D. Mass, author of *Confessions of a Jewish Wagnerite: Being Gay and Jewish in America*, cofounder, Gay Men's Health Crisis

"For all our flaunting of sexuality, gay men rarely get beyond the stilted clichés of porno dialogue and talk honestly about sex. Doug Sadownick's *Sex Between Men* provides a refreshingly candid look at the ways in which gay men get physical. Filled with heartfelt confessions and insights, the book reads like a communal diary of our recent lives."

—Michael Lowenthal, editor of *Flesh and the Word 3* and *Friends and Lovers: Gay Men Write About the Families They Create*

"Doug Sadownick is smart enough to know the truth, and brave enough to tell it. His book will drive people crazy in all the best ways: it's prickly, nosy, sexy, blunt, caressing, and insightful."

—John Weir, author of *The Irreversible Decline of Eddie Socket*

"A remarkable overview of contemporary history using personal witness and anecdote to provide a fascinating look at the role sex played—and continues to play—in the lives of gay men. Douglas Sadownick displays his exhaustive scholarly research with a light touch while his passionate engagement draws the reader in, making *Sex Between Men* a consistently involving and rewarding experience."

—Patrick Merla, editor, *Boys Like Us: Gay Writers Tell Their Coming Out Stories*

"Sadownick has taken on nothing less than the entire modern history of gay love—and life—its gnarled roots and its glossy surfaces, and he has succeeded in limning it with a sharp, yet always compassionate understanding of our unique, spiral path."

—Felice Picano, author of *The New Joy of Gay Sex* and *Like People in History*

sex between **men**

sex between men

an intimate history
of the sex lives of
gay men postwar
to present

douglas sadownick

HarperSanFrancisco
An Imprint of HarperCollins*Publishers*

Permissions appear on page 263 and constitute a continuation of this copyright page.

[A TREE CLAUSE BOOK] HarperSanFrancisco and the author, in association with The Basic Foundation, a not-for-profit organization whose primary mission is reforestation, will facilitate the planting of two trees for every one tree used in the manufacture of this book.

HarperCollins Web Site: http://www.harpercollins.com
HarperCollins®, ■®, and HarperSanFrancisco™ and A TREE CLAUSE BOOK®
are trademarks of HarperCollins Publishers Inc.

FIRST HarperCollins PAPERBACK EDITION PUBLISHED IN 1997
Book design by Ralph Fowler
Set in Electra

Library of Congress Cataloging-in-Publication Data
Sadownick, Douglas.
Sex between men : an intimate history of the sex lives of gay men postwar to present /
Douglas Sadownick. — 1st ed.
Includes index.
ISBN 0–06–251268–4 (cloth)
ISBN 0–06–251269–2 (pbk.)
1. Gay men—United States—Sexual behavior. 2. Homosexuality—United States—History—
20th century. I. Title.
HQ76.2.U5S33 1996
306.7'08'6642—dc20   95-25895

97 98 99 00 01 ❖RRD 10 9 8 7 6 5 4 3 2 1

contents

acknowledgments

Despite the prevailing prejudice about Los Angeles as the culturally vacu-
ous home to Hollywood, Los Angeles has played a key historic role in the evolution of gay consciousness. The first lasting efforts to organize gay men politically (the Mattachine Society) and spiritually (the Radical Faeries) have their
roots in Los Angeles. Gay elders and visionaries like Harry Hay and Jim Kepner
still live and work in Los Angeles and offer historical perspective. As well, a group
of people engaged in gay-centered inner-work and depth psychology can be
found here. I'm grateful to these dedicated individuals in this new and promising
field, a few of whom include Mitch Walker, Mark Thompson, Chris Kilbourne,
Wendell Jones, Matt Silverstein, Sandra Golvin, Hassan Moinzadeh, Chad
Mitchell, Leng Leroy Lim, and Felipe Hernandez. This book could not have
been written without their support and wisdom and is the fruit of much hard
work on both the community and individual levels.

I wish to thank my editor at Harper San Francisco, Kevin Bentley, who as a
gay man, not to mention a fine editor and writer, played a powerfully creative
role in bringing this book about. With caring, hard work, and a sense of humor,
he helped me balance theory with fact.

The seeds of this book were planted by my agent, Charlotte Sheedy. It is
rare to find a person of such high ethical and intellectual standards these days.

The International Gay and Lesbian Archives, based in Los Angeles, and
now part of the One Institute, proved a resource without which I could not have

written this book. John O'Brien and Pat Allen provided exhaustive help in tracking down hard-to-find letters, manuscripts, brochures, and posters. They also shared their own observations of gay sexual life over the last twenty years: invaluable material.

I have taught writing to several hundred gay men in Los Angeles, many from different cities and even countries. Some have been kind enough to contribute their observations and journal entries to this book. The artists and board members at Highways/The 18th Street Arts Complex have, over the last seven years, provided a place for me as a board member and artist to provide a forum for discourse on the issues of sexuality.

I have interviewed more than a hundred individuals for this book, many of whom gave such extensive interviews that they took up entire afternoons and often had to be continued on an additional day. These people told me the most private things anyone could tell another and I am indebted to them for their heroic honesty: Alan Bell, Michael Bronski, Scott C., Larry Cain, the late Michael Callen, Rob A. Cambell, Tom Cendejas, Stan Coffin, the late Steven Corbin, Jordi Cosentino, Bob Davis, Sean Early, David Ehrenstein, Ross H. Farley, Jack Fritscher, Allan Gassman, Dean Goishi, Ronald D. Hardcastle, Simon Harvey, John Francis Hunter, Dredge Byung'chu Kang, Arnie Kantrowitz, Jim Kepner, Robert Kindred, Herb King, Stephan Korsia, Leng Leroy Lim, Marshall O-Boy, Dr. Walt Odets, Dr. Lawrence D. Mass, Patrick Merla, Tim Miller, Douglas Mirk, Chad Mitchell, Hassan Moinzadeh, Mike Moreno, Fakir Musafar, Hung Nguyen, Connie Norman, Scott O'Hara, Oscar Penagos, Felice Picano, Greg Scott, Matt Silverstein, Steven G. Solberg, Michael Spillers, David Stein, Jöel B. Tan, Duncan E. Teague, Mark Thompson, Rob Vargas, Martin Weich, Chuck Williams, Michelangelo Signorile, Phill Wilson, and Vince O-Boy!

There are others whose insights have proved invaluable: Luis Alfaro, Eric Arimoto, Victoria Baker, Hannah Bleier, Malcolm Boyd, the late Chris Brownlie, Peter Cashman, Ken Yamaguchi Clark, Douglas Crimp, Paul Daniels, Robert Dawidoff, Bill Dobbs, Martin Duberman, Richard Dworkin, Richard Elovich, Larry Ewing, Rob Ford, Ganymede, Steven Greco, Eloise Klein Healey, the late Essex Hemphill, Keith Hennessey, Richard Isay, the late Wayne Karr, Michael Kearns, Kevin Koffler, Richard La Bonte, the late Barry Laine, Michael Lassell, Michael Lowenthal, Brian Miller, the late Paul Monette, Marcus Kuiland Nazario, Roland Palencia, Jordan Peimer, Phranc, the late James Carroll Pickett, Robin Podolsky, Jeff Richardson, Eric Rofes, David Roman, Gabriel Rotello, Richard Rouilard, the late Asotto Saint, David Schweizer, Lewis Segal, Dr. Charles Silverstein, Kevin Spicer, Michael Weinstein, John Weir, Neon Weiss,

Nicole Werner, Winston Wilde, Richard Wolf, Terry Wolverton, Norman Wong, Carla Wood, and Urvashi Vaid.

Kit Rachlis (formerly of the *L.A. Weekly*) helped hone material that was written for the *L.A. Times* and later appeared in this book; so did the *Weekly*'s current editor, Sue Horton, who published material of mine on the crisis in AIDS prevention as I wrote it for her. The same for Kevin Koffler (now of *Out*, formerly of *Genre*). Michael Denneny, who edited *Sacred Lips of the Bronx*, gave good feedback too.

Mark Thompson, Joel B. Tan, Ken Yamaguchi Clark, Sandra Golvin, and Tim Miller read the manuscript and offered valuable suggestions. Jack Fritscher, John Francis Hunter, Mark Thompson, and Jim Kepner opened their hearts and archives to me. I also wish to thank Stanley Siegal for his support and good will. He and I had an idea for a more comprehensive sociology book on gay sex that didn't work out, but all the same led to this more eccentric approach.

Chad Mitchell, Leo Garcia, and Alistair McCartney provided editorial assistance.

Faculty members and colleagues at Antioch University's MA program in Clinical Psychology, where I'm now a full-time student, continue to provide a supportive foundation for the deeper exploration of the psychological themes relating to gay sex and gay love.

And finally, thanks to my "soul buddy" of the last thirteen years, Tim Miller, who continues to teach me much about the transforming spirit of gay love.

sex between **men**

introduction: **foreplay**

We're cruising the Meatrack—a maze of tar-black glory holes in seedy Hollywood. U2 is being blasted so you can't hear a single sweet nothing. *Haven't found what I'm looking for.* It's Saturday night. With the bars closed, this place could give a sardine claustrophobia. Which isn't great for the elders or the heavy-set. They get elbowed by the two buds in Raider's caps who might as well be modeling SS gear, what with their lack of empathy, never mind body fat. This tried-but-true hellhole may reek of piss and poppers, but it draws Grade A cuts from West Hollywood's gyms and talent agencies.

Still, no one is that unique when it comes to sex. Here the collective rules almost as much as size—individuality, like sobriety, a real drag. For despite the L.A. particulars—crystal-tweaked laddie-boys in buzz cuts and Doc Martens—we could be at New York's Zone DK or San Francisco's Blow Buddies or Miami's Paragon. In other words, absent a lover or a fuck buddy, or in spite of them, or in search of them, men who want a tango with an apparition have no place to go but here, "here" being any public place where you can meet a man to touch without getting drunk—or bashed.[1]

Home isn't an option, really. So you invest your last bucks in sex clubs. With the closing of the baths and the hardening of love's arteries from so much AIDS and so much unexpressed grief, backroom sex clubs have made a come-back in the roaring '90s. Half the community's got HIV and the other half knows about condoms, right?[2] *So why hold back?*

It's hard to regard sex objectively, because, well, as queer theorist Jeffrey Weeks tells us, sex is one of the few purified subjective experiences left in an oh-so-extroverted Boys' Town.[3] And Weeks is right. The men who come to this club are looking for more than just to get off, explains AIDS prevention activist Hung Nguyen, who dispenses safer-sex info here. Otherwise they wouldn't linger till dawn. "People are hunting," he says, "looking for treasures. I have no judgment about it, as long as they do it safely." Sure, a man *shoots* — but only if he's been pushed off a cliff by the delirium of a tongue kiss (or an inner voice that nags: *This is the best you're going do tonight, he's under fifty . . .*). There is a paradox to desire: one loves what one lacks and does not yet possess. Getting it on ends the hunt. Hence the endless circling around a man one thinks one craves — yet fears having.[4]

This game isn't just a way to avoid contact with life. It's the closest homosexual men have to fingering a rosary. In fact, this backroom roaming reminds one not a little of that famed twelfth-century Sufi, Ibn 'Arabi, who, wandering about a certain temple, came upon a curly-haired youth — an Angel who was also the spitting image of the Sufi himself. Seated on a throne, the boy-god said, "The Temple which contains me is your heart." One doesn't know if the Sufi got his way with his divine Alter Ego, but it's safe to say he found *his* Mr. Right.[5]

That's all well and good, but Nguyen says that despite the adventuresome wags here tonight, many younger gay men worry that going to a sex club confirms society's worst views of gay men — that they have so much more sex than straights and that sex and love mix like water and vinegar. It is instructive, Nguyen insists, to remind gay men that heteros indulge in public erotic acts all the time, from touching to kissing to holding hands. Gay men lack places to bring a sense of togetherness and affection to bear on public life.

Hearing this, you are reminded of the work of writer/editor John Preston, who believed that the gay world had failed at providing a sense of bonding and meaning for its members outside of AIDS. Besides coming out, there are so few rites of passages. If one looks at the controversial word *religion*, not as a social creed, but as a private *attitude* about life and one's bond to history, it could be seen as the missing link in gay life. But gay men, being either militantly materialistic or attached to established creeds (or New Age slogans), balk at seeing their erotic impulses as coming from a profound inner source, unique to them.

"If," Preston maintained, "as the masculinists pronounce directly, and even Freudian and Jungian thinkers say less frankly, the male needs a rite of social initiation, it becomes obvious that the gay man needs it all the more. Since he has been denied access to the more run-of-the-mill initiations, too weak to accomplish transformation no matter who is performing them, the gay man has had to create coming-out scenarios of his own."[6]

For reasons gay politicos or social services workers don't dare address, neither rainbow flags nor twelve-step programs get to the heart of the gay matter. But what, exactly, might this heart be? Some say it's love. Others say sex. Panache? Anarchy? Masculinity? Androgyny? Call it what you may, for many it all boils down to homo eros, the creative principle of relatedness.

Speaking of which, an African American man posing in a corner lets himself laugh a little at your detachment, even if it's connection you intellectualize over. You do a double take. Bingo!—you realize that he's your "evanescent youth": a tall man with a shaved head, sporting lean muscles "cut" into precision with either Gold's Gym barbells or hard labor. You want to touch his "six pack," but you hold back. If you're so magnetized by his sneer that you can't think or act, what does that make you—a monster, a naïf, a worshipper of Forms?

He slides up against your wall. In a standoff in which you breathe each other's cigarette breath (you don't smoke, but everyone is getting lung cancer from a lack of circulation) you decide you won't hurt each other too badly. Then you're two Lestats crowding into a coffin-of-a-booth and there's some doglike sniffing and finger-trailing and although he's taller than you, there's a mutual appreciation society forming: a call-and-response, a "Yeah," a "You like that, doncha?" This mirroring touches a raw nerve; you want to cry. But you bite your tongue. There's nothing worse than being embarrassed when someone sees who you really are. Your voice goes too high or you say something stupid about "Newt" or "Freud." A come-close-stay-away protocol must be adhered to: an eyeing of the nipple; a graze at the Adam's apple stubble; a manhandling of the *huevos* through the jeans. And if a third person zeroes in, you broadcast your best "Don't call us, we'll call you" lip purse.

And then a kiss becomes fertile with a salty translucence that you hope isn't another person's cum. Belts unbuckle. You're on your knees.

You're not a Catholic, but you do believe for now in the spirit-as-flesh business. And there's even that sacrifice, because you *do* wonder for a moment if this is the act that will make you die for your sins. But despite the word on the street—that pre-cum may have more HIV than semen[7]—your safer-sex guidelines have been slipping a bit lately, yes? Last month you let that Leave-It-To-Beaver type from Venice Beach jostle it in—just for a minute!—*sans* latex. You shake your head now to take your mind off your guilt (which is tied up with your fear that you will be punished for your pleasure) and regard this man's family jewels.

"Excuse," he says, pulling you up to your feet.

He scratches his head. "Damn," he says. "This is hard."

You convey to him that you're used to hard things.

"I'm HIV-positive."

After some silence, you inform him that you see no risk in licking his balls. He spits on his hand and you return to your place.

"You like those balls, don't you?"

Although your mouth is full, you manage to convey your admiration.

"I'm sorry," he says in a voice that's part Ivy League, part inner city, pulling you up again.

For the first time, you caress his shoulder blade, although you have no idea what he's hiding there.

"This goes against my program," he says.

He says his name is Joel. He's thirty-three and attends Sexual Compulsives Anonymous meetings. While it's been relatively easy to give up anonymous sex, it's been terribly hard to give up the bonhomie of the Meatrack. He explains that, as a poet and all, being around so many men inspires. He's been trying to be with his "authentic feelings"—not to have sex from an "acting out kind of place." In other words, he's experimenting with his sexual instinct, as if it were manna from heaven. Rather than eat it all at once, or starve himself silly, he's trying to see the sustenance for what it is.

You tell him you're sympathetic, but an authentic part of you feels like you're getting shafted.

"Wanna come on over for a cup of tea?" he asks. "I live down the street."

Welcome to sex in the 1990s, where the question of the street is a bit perplexing, a bit paradoxical, a bit off-putting. Not a few gay men are asking themselves how is it possible to be a vital being—to live and breathe man-to-man love and connection—without having to have sex to prove one's worth, identity, or attractiveness? Apart from all the socially ingrained moral issues, or questions relating to promiscuity (is it a path to intimacy or an escape?) for better or for worse, fate has made sexuality into a problem.[8]

Part of the problem is AIDS. To be sure, traditional AIDS education, pioneered by safer-sex cocreator Michael Callen in 1983, has resulted in a drastic reduction in AIDS cases in the gay community. But activists also look with alarm at new statistics among gay men, especially those who are younger, especially those of color. An increasing number of gay men are now finding that unfailing condom use is impossible to maintain for a lifetime. And while some have turned to alternative practices, others have given up hope.

But the problem also extends beyond AIDS. Condoms haven't removed *all* of the headaches of being a sexual person these days. Those men into promiscuous cocksucking often find little support for their exploits from friends and lovers. And those who want virginal courtships with Mr. Right find it difficult meeting anyone who isn't into either repressive frigidity or immediate gratification.

In fact, gay men remain as confused as ever as to how to cope with the clamoring call that comes sometimes from out of the blue, sometimes as a constant hum, to find a beautiful man to touch, love, or marry (or all of the above). For every man who says that sexuality ought to be as basic a human constant as eating and breathing, another man can't help but seek to entertain a more objective attitude toward his dominant appetites. One man wonders what that weird and terrifying affect grabbing his balls is (one moment he's scrambling eggs, the next he is dreaming of a prodigious cock in his mouth). One man never wonders at all: the moment that affect comes, he's dialing 976-MEET. Then there are men who entertain contradictory views about sex. They like it rough but not too rough; they use sex to snare men, but they find such behavior compulsive. Rational thinking, which some gay men have perfected as a tool for living almost second to sex, is no help when it comes to understanding sex. Sex often is a matter for the unconscious, which, by virtue of its name, is positively irrational.

Most confounding of all, a few gay men have used sex as a way either to act in cahoots with the authorities or to defy them. In 1994, a New York City activist group, concerned about rising AIDS cases, called for New York City to shut down backrooms if the city's health codes (which prohibit all oral and anal sex with or without condoms) weren't adhered to. Another group coped with the same problem by holding safer-sex parties around Manhattan. After some ugly brawls, the two groups disbanded.

In the midst of this political infighting, something almost grand is taking place. A new attitude about relating to sexual life seems to be emerging not from any kind of conscious "strategic planning" in the manner of gay movement politics, but rather from a deeply rooted place in people's hearts and unconscious life processes. Although the new attitude is vague, its outline can be traced.9

Contemporary gay sexual life can be understood as the tension between a variety of powerful opposites whose pattern and design are just now becoming clear to gay men. These Olympian forces or opposites are not mere effects of cultural conditioning, but, as one man put it, forces of nature, "like the ebbing and flowing of waves." They are epitomized by the attitudinal differences between the '70s and '80s. For example, the '70s introduced to homosexual men the experience of the "Dionysian," a hot sexy dive into instinctual gratification, the sensual breaking loose of the unbridled dynamism of animal and divine passions. The '80s demanded an "Apollonian" emphasis on thinking things through, a need to objectify feelings, and an attempt at establishing limits, sobriety, and boundaries.[10]

But by no means are these two separate impulses appendages from a bygone era. They are as alive and well in any given gay man now as they have ever been. The question of the time is deceptively simple: how to bring these opposites together without canceling out one or the other?

If the '70s suggested that *sexuality ought to be creatively expressed* with the surefire help of poppers, MDA, the Mine Shaft, the flourishing of open relationships, and maybe a little leather, the '80s put forward the notion that *sexuality ought to be creatively contained* either through the use of latex barriers, twelve-step programs, monogamous relationships, or a little leather. The '90s offer gay men an opportunity to view these opposing values *simultaneously*, operating as systole and diastole in the same individual. The '90s have become a decade not so much of new discoveries, or new sexual feats, but of integrating the accelerated changes of the past in a symbolic and literal way.[11] Some gay men have intuited a self-regulating sexual system of values that offers a way out of the bind between "feast" or "famine." This book is written, in part, to report on their findings.

The current moment marks a shift in perspective. It's been twenty-five years since the Stonewall Riots, and the resulting sexual liberation that galvanized gay life and shook it free from the respectful efforts of the homophiles of the '50s and '60s. Half of the time has been spent in ecstatic experimentation; the other half in recovery and depression. Modern gay life seems sometimes less about sex than about the opposites that constellate around the great energy system alternately called sex, romance, or love. Since Stonewall, gay men have found themselves poised between two divergent time periods: one upbeat and one sad. A lot of ink has been spilled to make sense out of these symbolic extremes from a political point of view.[12]

Sex, however, has been left out of this effort—an odd phenomenon given that homosexual identity has largely been predicated on same-sex love. The story of sex—the way in which sex creates consciousness and community—has rarely been told. This book reports on gay men trying to put the sex—and the feelings around sex—back in homosexual, arguing that same-sex eros is the engine behind gay identity—a view that has had its political ups and downs in the age of

AIDS, assimilation, and civil rights agendas. Combining personal testimony with archival material, *Sex Between Men* aims to show how and why the sexual behavior of gay men has been influenced by historical and sociological changes since World War II. However, it is unnecessary, and in fact, ill-advised, to take the "soul" out of gay sociology. Or put another way, behind the need for men to connect erotically one finds more than a biologic drive or even a "social construction." What this something is, who can really say? Some refer to an awareness, or "sensibility," inside themselves that they see as different from the ego. Some call this source of life the "self" (a middle ground between conscious and unconscious life). It is a private place, but it can be realized only through intimacy with others.[13]

Previously, sex has been paradoxically too close to home and yet too saturated in shame to be examined. Gay men have been so protective of their hard-won sexual freedoms that efforts to pull back from sex in order to try and regard it more neutrally were dismissed as homophobic. "To be open-minded in regard to the challenges of life and to be open sexually to men were synonymous," recalls Felice Picano, coauthor of *The New Joy of Gay Sex*, of his Fire Island days. "To see a blemish in sex was to cast yourself as an uptight person — not Pines material at all."

Some gay men have realized, especially with AIDS, that to see something or someone clearly, one has to step away from it. This can be hard to do. Just as it requires a Herculean effort for a man to leave his mother's home prematurely, gay men did not wish to overanalyze what felt so good — to try to make a clear distinction between themselves and the contents of their own minds. After all, science — physics, depth psychology — has only recently turned its focus to the place from which it comes in the first place: the mind, the world of the living psyche. So it stands to reason that gay people have only recently begun an objective conversation about sex and their instinctual lives. ("Who would have thought that empathy implied separation?" asked the African American man from the Meatrack, who had just moved out of the house he shared with his lover.)[14]

In dozens of interviews, men who considered their sexual identities the ontological ground on which they stood now say that there are other floors below ground level. Sexual frustration, as opposed to sexual scoring, has had the effect of imploding the libido inward.[15] Just as a person can be introverted or extroverted, so too can libido be withdrawn or projected out, sometimes consciously, mostly by the force of unlucky circumstances. For a few, the introverting effect hasn't been entirely devastating; subbasement floors were discovered that contained layers of feelings, images, thoughts, and associations heretofore unexplored.[16] Not that sexual frustration is anything new to gay people; aging, married life, or just plain boredom have always imposed themselves as enemies to the sexual athlete. But AIDS offered its frustrations in a collective and sudden way. After fourteen years of coping with this massive intervention on sexual freedom, it seems safe to say that a new level of awareness has evolved, a new attitude to the sexual drive that had previously been equated with the personality as one and the same thing.

"When you pull back from something that had once possessed you so completely, you can begin to see the extremes it has been comprised of," said the late Steven Corbin, a New Yorker. To him, gay life could be summed up as a problem of antithetical: the culture of desire versus the culture of containment; the culture of respectability versus the culture of outlaws; the culture of Dionysus versus the culture of Apollo; the culture of Adonises versus the culture of aging queens.

The dilemma can be understood outwardly as the struggle between the '70s and the '80s. It can be understood inwardly as the tension between thinking and feeling—between the mind and the heart; between spontaneity and reflection; between being overcome and overcoming. On the one hand, you have the Dionysian liberation of instinct in which the intoxicated individual is merged ritually with the collective through orgasm. This gives a person a certain oneness with the world. On the other, you have the Apollonian subjugation of everything wild and natural through the process of objectification—the "god of individual and just boundaries."[17] This can give a person a certain breathing space from the collective.

Despite the fact that the individual thinks he alone suffers this antagonism between fucking-with-abandon and fucking-with-caution, these are everyday problems with an ancient ring to them. Enough history has gone by for some gay men to say that they see once and for all what is really happening to them. "From a gay perspective," writes psychologist Mitch Walker, "being gay is a matter of having a gay-identified ego, and not one of sexuality per se. Sexuality in gays, rather, serves the development of personality just as it does for persons whose libido is heterosexually organized."[18] This is a radical notion. It suggests that the myth that has been on imposed on homosexuals through the late-nineteenth-century medical models—that being gay is just about sex—is too limited a definition. Sex accelerates consciousness. Sex is in the service of the gay personality—not vice versa.

Just as through slow and patient scrutiny one might see a pattern emerging in one's dreams, so too gay men see an almost natural cycle emerging in sexual life.[19] One man hypothesizes that gay men are living through a new myth—the birth of a people who are just now emerging from forty years of wandering in the desert.[20] Another suggests that sex, and quite a bit of it, as usual, precedes birth. Each bases his theory on the only thing that matters when it comes to sex: personal experience.

Sex is always a matter of individual heart. But sexuality, the discourse around sexual practices, is a more political thing. History—and history books—bear this out.[21] Before 1950, there were no organized homosexual political organizations in existence and certainly no thoughtful magazines and few books. The few meeting places that homosexual people frequented were subject to routine police busts and vicious entrapment efforts. An aura of paranoia and self-loathing afflicted even the most well adjusted, who considered themselves "handicapped."

In a mere half-century, an entire civilization was born and grew to almost full maturity. By the '70s, a cult of sex grew up in urban centers that rivaled any in the history of mankind in terms of sophistication and accessibility. That period of physical and spiritual emancipation, however limited or fruitful it seems in retrospect, was short-lived. In the '80s, the ascent toward the ecstatic turned into its opposite: the deflation that resulted from AIDS and the corresponding moral confusion that tainted gay male sexuality. In the '90s, a new appraisal seems to be evolving from the up-and-down seesaw of homosexual sex. It may be as groundbreaking as any the sexual revolution has seen thus far.

I first began this book under a hypothesis—that sex is the *sine qua non* of homosexuality—that I now see as faulty. For every gay man for whom sex is the highest value in his life, there is another for whom love reigns supreme. Then there are gay men who don't need either lovers or sex companions. Their first love is their work or their friends. But you would risk offending them if you told them they were not gay, or homosexual.

I have been forced, therefore, to revise my position and to argue instead that sex isn't the bedrock of gay life. It may just be a fluke of history that gay men had, for a time, fucked their brains out. We must see this sexual revolution more as a feature of repression or else a kind of Big Bang that created the gay universe or a combination therein. To see the sexual revolution as the goal to which gay society ought to evolve is to fail to understand the philosophical lessons of any health crisis, which apart from the obvious homophobia the culture has inflicted on gays, have to do with balance, and an appreciation of the opposites, and the development of personality, gay personality.

The little sociological data we have on gay sex supports this view, although it is hard to draw firm conclusions from the piecemeal data that's available.

As a measure of how truly little information we have on gay lovemaking, *The 1994 Advocate Survey of Sexuality and Relationships* marks the first such national survey of gay sexuality. (Most surveys of gay male sex have been prompted by AIDS and are conducted in a few large cities.) True, the survey suffers from its own limitations. Only every fourth survey was tabulated; mostly educated men responded (those who enjoy writing about their sexual practices, are out of the closet, and belong to a gay organization). All the same, the results—there were a staggering thirteen thousand respondents, an 18 percent return—refute many stereotypes. These gay men (only 3 percent say they're bi) want love more than sex.

A whopping 85 percent of those responding say they prefer hugging, caressing, and snuggling to any other kind of physical contact, with kissing coming in at a close second. Eighty percent of the men said that if they had to live without sex or love, they'd sacrifice sex. When it comes to sex per se, most say they go for the oral variety—both giving and receiving—with less than half giving their highest marks to anal intercourse and with many giving anal sex of any variety low grades. Not only are the vast majority vanilla, most haven't had more than four partners in the last year.

Such data do not discount many people's hunch that gays have more sex than straight. However, it's difficult to make comparisons between how often straight Americans have sex and how often gay Americans do based on the current figures. The most recent reports only *imply* that heterosexuals may have less frequent sex.[22]

The Chicago researchers of the 1994 *The Social Organization of Sexuality* concede that it was hard to get the skinny on homosexual sex. "This is a stigmatized group," says Stuart Michaels of the Chicago team. "There is probably a lot more homosexual activity going on than we could get people to talk about."[23] It's that much harder to get information about subgroups within the population, let's say gay Latinos. The studies bias heterosexuals, in part because there are more of them and in part because it's easier to admit to being one. Nearly 40 percent of married people say that they have sex twice a week, compared to 25 percent for singles, according to the Chicago researchers. And 83 percent of those heterosexuals interviewed have one or zero sexual partners a year. To some gay men, those statistics make them happy they're gay.

We simply don't know how often homosexual men have gay sex, in part because most men who have sex with men don't identify as homosexual, never mind gay. Americans underestimate the social stigma that still exists around homosexuality. Most people who answer survey questions lie, sometimes because they're afraid of being found out, sometimes because they'd rather not admit to themselves just how often they think about getting it on with another guy. The locker rooms of sports clubs are filled with men who admire male bodies and who sometimes touch them; but these men don't see themselves as homosexual. Then there are others who do admit to "going all the way." I spoke with dozens of these men—hustlers, bodybuilders, corporate workers—who enjoy having a male fuck buddy on occasion but show the world a hetero face and resist any inclination to affiliate themselves with gay causes. Part of this stigma comes from AIDS. Part of it may not be about stigma, but may result from the fact that, as Alfred Kinsey pointed out, people have sex in ways that don't jive with their identity. We only have to recall the success of Kinsey's groundbreaking 1948 study, *Sexual Behavior in the Human Male*, which sold 250,000 copies and spent six months on the *New York Times* best-seller list, to remember that homosexual sex remains of great interest to many Americans, perhaps because they privately like it but publicly have to hate it.[24] Over a third of the adult males interviewed by Kinsey said they had engaged in homosexual experience. As historians John D'Emilio and Estelle Freedman put it, "Taken together, Kinsey's statistics pointed to a vast hidden world of sexual experience sharply at odds with publicly espoused norms."[25]

To cope with the gap in information, some useful books came out in the '70s that tried to classify sociologically how American homosexuals live. Martin S. Weinberg and Colin J. Williams's *Male Homosexuals: Their Problems and Adaptations*, for instance, concluded that heterosexuals have less trouble than homosexuals not because homosexuality is inherently problematic but because heterosexuality is more rewarded, but the book still treats homosexuality as a dilemma. Other scientific studies include, Masters and Johnson's *Homosexuality in Perspective* and two Bell and Weinberg Kinsey Institute studies. Karla Jay and Allen Young's *The Gay Report*, written by queers for queers, evolved from answers to written questionnaires submitted by thousands of anonymous men and women. The exhaustive book explores childhood issues, promiscuity, courtship, sex between men and boys, living arrangements, self-esteem, bottom/top roles, fetishes, and every aspect of sexuality. This book signaled an important shift: gays and lesbians began to place less credibility on medicine and psychiatry and turned to the direct testimony of gays and lesbians, a movement exemplified by

Dr. Lawrence D. Mass' seminal two volume work, *Dialogues of the Sexual Revolution*, which included interviews with Charles Silverstein, Thomas Szasz, John Boswell, Ned Rorem, and many others. These groundbreaking books made little effort to say whether gays have more sex than straights, in part, because they could have cared less.[26]

Despite the lack of official information, many gay men intuit that gay-identified gay men have more sex with each other than heterosexuals do with each other. If this is true, which no one can yet prove, it may be because it is physically easier for two openly homosexual gay men to have sex with each other (to, say, get each other off in a men's room) than it is for a man and a woman. Or there may exist an erotic poise that comes with sameness. In other words, the otherness that attracts a straight woman to a straight man may also repel—an otherness that is reduced in male-to-male same-sex love. (All that testosterone.) Of course, it's hard to make global assessments about people one doesn't know. Paleoanthropologists talk about the "essential" wandering tendency of men and the "essential" gathering tendency of women,[27] a theory rejected by cultural constructionists—and many feminists. Feminists talk about the cultural restraints that patriarchy imposes on female sexual experimentation and promiscuity, a theory rejected by Camille Paglia. The truth, if such a thing as "truth" can be found to exist in sexual life, may lie in a combination of factors.

Whether or not gay men have more sex than straight men, I have discovered that gay men in the '90s are nothing if not confused about how to go about getting touched by someone they're attracted to. As the movies *Jeffrey* and *Sex Is* point out, sex is vexing, weird, problematical, sometimes blissful, often more trouble than it's worth. Of course, people live for it, but chances are they do a good deal more fantasizing than they do acting. Fantasy can be a much richer experience than tricking in part because the imagination is no mere figment but a real thing—a fact no less real than cumming. It is fantasy that motivates a man to have sex in the first place—that disturbs his sleep, that distracts him.

So I have changed my hypothesis—that sex is the *sine qua non* of homosexual life—to state that homosexual libido (one's vital energies) is the motivating energy that informs this book and informs, at least from my perspective, gay life. It is largely an error in judgment (and one from which I have suffered) that sees sex as the defining principle of this libido. I would argue instead that sex is an effect of libido, or the extroverted end result of it. A great many unconscious processes take place before the performance of sex, processes we can know more about if we so choose. In some cases, the backstage dramas may be as entertaining. A person doesn't see a great performance and not think, for a moment, of the hours of behind-the-scenes preparation it took for an actor to become a virtuoso.

This book arises from four different impetuses: ten years of journalistic writing and interviewing on the subject of sex and desire; five-years-plus as a gay writing teacher; my encounter with gay-centered depth psychology; and my experience in taking care of safer-sex cofounder Michael Callen during the last year of his life. Callen moved to Los Angeles to spend his remaining time making music. Our friendship was founded on a common interest in sexuality. "Why have gay men never developed a theory and defense of sex the way the lesbian feminists did in the '80s?" he asked. He thought gay men at a painful loss of theoretical tools to put sexual compulsion and sexual health in perspective. "Gay people are at the forefront on calling the central bluff of Western culture," he told me, "that uses sex to sell everything from toothpaste to cars, but heaven forbid you should admit to actually having it." He gave me a crash course in feminist thought and literature. Like the radical lesbians he so admired, he wanted to know the ways in which sex offered both pleasure and danger and he wanted to create a "practical homosexual ethic" along such lines.

As he started to die, I saw that there was a level to his experience feminism had denied him. Yes, he experienced profound feelings, but they seemed of an alien nature. They were mostly masculine. He wanted a potent and almost transpersonal healing with his father and his "former, current lover" (who with his love of baseball and complete absence of feminine affectation made a good father surrogate). While Mike mastered a brokered peace with the two, his need for them remained as desperate as it was interchangeable. It wasn't merely that Callen had a "father complex." Rather he seemed to project onto his dad and lover a rather potent and mysterious figure, a figure, it seemed, who must have resided first in his own mind *a priori*. It seemed his father was the recipient of this powerful romantic imagery, not the cause of it. Likewise with his lover. I saw this with my own eyes. So did the others, for the electric charge was unmistakable.

And yet so strange. The father and the lover—flawed humans like all the rest of us—bore little resemblance to the demigods Mike's imagination concocted—a fact he, in all his queenlike clarity, knew all too well. I had the honor of asking Mike about this driven need to settle scores with the men in his life. Lucid until his final moment, the staunch materialist noticed, to his shock, something almost profound in his longing. He knew of the word *projection* but it seemed too clinical to describe what he was feeling. "Musta been that morphine the FABULOUS doctors are giving me," was his explanation. A few days before his death, he told me he was going to try to "take it back." He was too out of it for conversation, but I think I understood his drift.

The experience convinced me to try to write the book Callen wanted (his feminist sexual politics; his historical review) as well as to incorporate what I learned when he was dying (that *unconscious* life deserves at least as much respect and attention as *conscious* life when it comes to understanding sex). I couldn't help but wonder whether or not the intense unconscious projection with which he saddled the men he loved were also what drove him to seek so many sexual contacts during the '70s. He literally personified the "soul" as a father and a lover and a brother and cinematically jutted this stuff out on an available hot stud. He, like so many gay men, dared not fully "own" these split-off, part-selves until he began to die. With death so close at hand, he talked easily about promiscuity, and the theories behind it. A product of the Midwest at heart, he shrugged his shoulders at one point and said, "I was always looking for love and I did not ever feel myself worthy of it so sex was the next best thing." All the same, he went out of his way to defend sex-for-sex's sake as a way to repair wounded pride and self-esteem. "It should be seen as a wholesome need, like eating or taking a walk."

We talked about all the books that were needed both to chart a theory of gay sex as well as to simply defend it. Although it was obvious that a review of changing sexual attitudes in the manner of George Chauncey's historical opus, *Gay New York*, did not yet exist, and was sorely needed, the urgency of the current moment demanded that such a book be as much about the future as about the past. Sex is interesting in and of itself, but what makes it remarkable is how it pulls people out of inertia, how it makes people move in vast migrations from city to city, how it creates consciousness and identity, how it causes both bliss and pain. And because I am a journalist and not a historian, I wanted to write a book about what was newsworthy about people's changing attitudes toward sex in the '90s.

At the same time, no appreciation for the evolving changes in consciousness can take place outside of a historical review. The future makes no sense unless gay people understand the incredibly cruel and vicious stigma placed on all aspects of homosexual lovemaking, from the most carnal to the most chaste, before the '70s and especially in the '50s. To feel the burden of this ancient shame is almost too much for most people; and it is no wonder that gay men, when given an opportunity to react against the strictures of society, did so with so much urgency and sexual panache. But a serious inquiry into the sexual lives of gay men shows that what is repressed often returns, in one distorted form or another. A few years before AIDS, gay men suffered enormous depression as well as a slew of venereal diseases—and drug burnout. No one predicted an intervention as cruel and government-abetted as AIDS, but many predicted that the sexual paradise could not last.

It is the task of this book to show that a series of strong forces—they may be called archetypes or simply stages or just ups-and-downs—stand in natural relation to each other and that their succession determines the growth of consciousness. In the course of development, the individual must pass through the same stages that determine the evolution of his community. Very often, an individual's growth can stand for his community's and vice versa.

To point this out, I have tried to tell a certain history—an "intimate" history—of the changes gay sexual life has undergone since World War II. Even a modest effort to represent some of the cum shot since 1945 over other men's torsos and buttocks sketches an epic story, almost biblical—or at least Faustian—in its dramatic swings. These dramas point to the present moment and that which is to come. It is as if new indigenous soil, psychological mulch, has been tilled in the gardens of the instincts and is now bearing fruit (so to speak).

To tell this story, we start with the modern birth of homosexual eros with World War II in the chapter called "What Did You Do in the War, Daddy?" A chapter called "Toward Democracy" provides some historical background on the social clamping down on homosexuality that took place in the '50s after the lessening of restraints in the '40s.

The book's focus is on the sudden swings of postmodern gay sexual history, from the years 1969 to the present. In the two chapters that explore the sexual revolution, "So, You Say You Want a Revolution?" and "Trouble in Paradise," I identify what seems to be the purposive extroversion of libido. The next chapter, entitled "The Great Depression," deals with the introversion of libido and covers the years 1981 to 1990. Two final chapters, "The Second Sexual Revolution?" and "Condom Meets Crystal Meets Individuation," survey some of the efforts at synthesis taking place in the '90s.

The issue of cultural and racial diversity poses problems for this project, given my interest in the world of archetypes and my abiding fascination in the life of the unconscious. How can one presume to speak of gay community symbols when some individuals in that community reject the very notion of common citizenry?

Make no mistake about it: this book departs from the current materialist rage in gay academic circles, which sees gay identity as a "social construction." The book posits instead that gay identity begins on the inside of the individual and gets only in part shaped (or crushed) through its encounter with life.

As such, sex cannot be understood merely by analyzing its surface "signs," but must first be acknowledged as having symbolic depth, a depth as vast and as mysterious as the unconscious itself. Interviews with a hundred men tell me that the basic core symbolic issues that shape gay male identity—a search for a double; the treacherous affiliation with mother; the hunger to be seen and loved; the pent-up rage at father—remain not so terribly different from culture to culture. Everyone experiences feelings of inferiority, rage, unfinished family business, and hurt, not to mention sexual wishes.

And yet one would be a fool and a racist to overlook the way in which class and race vicissitudes shape homo eros, never mind the way in which society stamps its privileged white vise-grip on diverse forms of gay love. These days, the minute one tries to represent oneself as "other," one is silenced, as Richard Fung has noted: "Speaking as gay, as Asian or as a gay-Asian man is a tricky proposition. For one thing, speaking as any one thing too often implies not being listened to on any other."[28] Or as gay Latino playwright and AIDS activist Luis Alfaro puts it, "Belonging to multiple communities can sometimes leave you feeling schizophrenic. It's not a matter of allegiance, it's a matter of recognizing the identities in you as one. *Ni de aqui, ni de alla*. Neither here, not there."[29] Leng Leroy Lim, a gay Christian priest, puts his predicament this way when being asked to describe his sexual identity: "For Chinese gay men and lesbians, familial and hence ethnic identity may be perceived to be much stronger and more useful than reductionist sexual categorization." In other words, even the emphasis on sex with which I write is saturated in Western biases, as is the notion of the individual and "individual choice" I put forward.

I have coped with this problem by trying to do two things at once: by (1) honoring the poignancy of stories that all point to patterns experienced by most gay men as a matter of course in sex and in love; while also (2) being as respectful of difference as I can be, given my own limitations as a Jewish writer from working-class roots. It can't be stated enough that the monolithic term *gay community* excludes as much as it includes. In the words of AIDS activist Jöel B. Tan, "The Rainbow Flag does nothing for me," a reference to the way in which the mainstream can resemble a melting pot that tries to fit everyone into a niche. The niche undermines individuality and crushes idiom.

Gay men of color, for example, sometimes negotiate their sexual practices from within the white gay community, but many don't. For every gay Pacific Islander who is proudly nationalistic and avoids one-night stands with white men there is another who conscientiously chooses friends (and fashions) from the Chelsea Gym. Within that category, there is the man who maintains the primacy of his ancestral roots while still another thinks nothing of changing his name and resembling a darker-skinned Marky Mark all the while threatening to deck a friend who chastises him as "colonized."

"Nowadays," adds Alfaro, "you can't walk into Mickey's without noticing the sea of Asian, Anglo, Latino and African-American heads bobbing to the same delicious beat. But still there are differences. Gay Latinos tend to live in the neighborhoods we're raised in. Sometimes it's pure economics, sometimes it's compounded with a cultural reality."[30]

Add to this the racial tensions that exist in any mixed-race environments, such as the sexualized "macking" Philipino who may be perceived as too pushy and "latinized" by a Korean American. (*Macking* is street slang for "sweet talking a guy" into bed.) Or an African American queer man might mistake the same Philipino for a bottom due to Western stereotypes that feminize Asians. Racial projections inform sex at least as much as the presumably simple wish to be touched (which is never simple).

The gay world is thus made up of "worlds." And while the facts of gay social history—the emergence of the Mattachine Society, the Stonewall Rebellion, the development of venues like the Mine Shaft, the murder of Harvey Milk, the appearance of the AIDS epidemic, the leadership of the Bayard Rustin, publication of books like *The Joy of Gay Sex*, the influence of magazines like *The Advocate*— not only affect men of color but may be the result of actions by men of color (as in the case of men and drag queens who stood up to police at the Stonewall Inn), the historical artifacts become the assets of white gay America.

How to cope with the problem of representation is currently being been tackled by a group of academics in gay theory programs across America. But most of these thinkers are trapped in proto-Marxist-Feminist-Freudian materialist dogma. There discourse limits the discussion. Virtually no authentic dialogue about sex and desire is possible on their terms, because their terms often spurn the real world of "feeling." How can you talk sensibly about sex without addressing feeling? Moreover, social constructivism can never get to the heart of gay people's experience around sex because it fails to address spiritual issues.

For the dirty secret of human life is plain: people are hungry to lose their minds, to forget their worries, and to return (as if in a state of permanent incest) to Mother Nature. Gay academic theorists go a long way in showing how different people fall in love differently. But because they often posit nothing greater at play in an individual's life than cultural forces, they don't touch sufficiently on the "over your head feeling" of falling in love. Social constructivists treat the notion of gay soul dismissively. (So do homophobes.)

But the reason need not be demonized. One can inquire into matters of the irrational parts of the psyche through "scientific" means. One can treat each feeling—hurt, desire, rage, love—as a fact. Of course, we are a long way from slowing down our actions to actually turn attention in a fair and square way to the emotions—some of them quite overwhelming—that bubble under the surface of life. Many individuals still suffer an inner split of which they remain unaware.

For this reason, this book values the subjective in the individual lives of gay men over and beyond any thing else. And while it springs from my own passionate concerns, I have done my best to inhibit my own impulses toward overvaluing my own subjectivity and have gone "out" to interview others and to conduct archival research. To be sure, there are failings in my approach. I couldn't help but value men who had more interesting sex stories than those who didn't. Moreover (and unfortunately), this book does not touch on the concerns of the elderly or the transgendered or even effeminate as much as it should. Although I have tried to challenge my own limitations in dealing with issues around race and color, I can't help but see that I could have done better, been even more inclusive of diversity, been more aware of the difficulties of a white person asking people of color personal questions. And, most confounding of all, I detailed people's sex stories to get at the heart of what lay beyond them; and yet there is no way to say what "psyche" is but to point to its effect, which, in this case, is sex.

So the book ends up reading much more graphically sexual than I had intended. It gives the impression that people are fucking much more than they are, when, truth be told, I believe they are yearning and fantasizing and courting and hunting much more than anything. Make no mistake about: the imagination is the most active sexual organ, a fact that should not be overlooked in reading this book. What you will be reading here are the end results of great efforts of gay men's minds as they spin homosexual fantasy and imagery and hopes and dreams on a frequent and subliminal basis. Sex is one effect of libido and not necessarily its most consistent one.

Despite my efforts to be objective, I did end up reading books and monographs with my own eyes and listening to men talk with my own ears. The material has been either amplified or corrupted by my involvement. So this is really the book about one man's way of seeing the world, of trying to put into perspective the most problematic of issues of sexuality because they, at bottom, seem to point to even more central concerns. What those are I cannot really say. No one I've talked to has ever once been able to define to me exactly what being gay is, for it eludes purely materialistic or reductive definitions; homosexuality, or same-sex sex, remains an easier thing to describe. And while I remain convinced that gay sex does not begin to answer the question, the notions of "gay-centeredness" or of "homosexual libido" put forward in this book may bring some new conceptual tools to our primitive understanding of sex, love, feelings, survival, and potential. I hope the reader will open this book knowing that while the book tries to be objective it can't help but be limited by the strengths and weaknesses of one writer. Given that prefatory note, there is the hope that the readers can pick and choose something of value for their own uses. Any book that values the individual as the beginning and end of all questions related to the mystery of life may serve to empower rather than to confound.

what did you do in the war, daddy?

one man's story: holding it all in

In 1942, Herb King was a blond, nearly six-foot-tall lieutenant on his way overseas to fight in the North African campaign against the Axis powers. Raised in a Boston, Jewish burb, with straight A's to spell "normalcy," he nonetheless felt a monkey on his back. At night, King would take a girlfriend out to the movies, but when he closed his eyes to neck, he'd fantasize instead of a buddy.

It was the duty he felt to fight in World War II that freed King from his duty to be a husband.

Stationed in Chicago before going overseas, King met a married officer who took a shine to him. The older man provoked the young ingenue into a wrestling match that didn't stop at "uncle." As King puts it, "It was an obnoxious experience you could call rape." The bourbon-induced "quickie" might have been "for the birds," but it opened King's eyes. "I had no idea that someone who was married could be so interested in another guy," he remembers. The oral sex didn't impress him, but his feelings afterward did. King remembers his awakening this way:

> It became clear to me, somewhere between the North African campaign and the Italian campaign, between the years 1942 and 1945, that I was strongly attracted to other men. This was taking place at the time when I was promoted from a second lieutenant to a major—commander of a battalion. But I was very careful about not showing my true feelings. They did, however, permeate my actions. To

be frank, I didn't know homosexuals existed. The only time I heard of homosexuality in the service was in the case of a particular officer who was brought before the board and released. I was to learn later on that he received quite lenient treatment, compared to enlisted men.

King says that "being in an all-male environment, sleeping together and eating together while in dangerous situations for many months" brings most men intimately together, whether they're homosexual or not. So he didn't fret too much about his open heart. "I was a nice middle-class Jewish boy," he says, "and we weren't supposed to do things like lust after men." King enjoyed socializing with women, mostly nurses. He grew very close to his men.

He actually fell in love with them. He didn't so much sublimate his feelings as he contained them, thus giving new meaning to platonic love. Sexual feelings saturated the time and space during which the company provided munitions and supplies to frontline fighters. Images burnt through sleep: tall, thin young men, lying half-naked on tanks during those hot Mediterranean evenings, smoking cigarettes in the humid dusk.

"That's when my identity began to form," King recalls. "I was concerned about the welfare of the men in a certain way that saved many a man's life. I was one of the more respected of officers." Later, it dawned on him that it was this homosexual love that kept his unit so cohesive, so courageous.

King eventually found himself in a troubling situation. When King was a first lieutenant, a captain—"a real Southern bigot"—came onto the scene who acted in a callous way to the younger servicemembers. Many of the enlisted men came to King to talk over their sore feelings. "This led to an uncomfortable situation," King reminisces—"the enlisted men spoke to me in a personal manner." The only solution was to transfer to another organization. There King became the commanding officer.

The new men also looked up to him. For many years afterward, they kept up correspondence. Because King's sexual awakening took place synchronously with his initiation as a man and a soldier, it helped him feel good, eventually, about coming out as gay—even though not a single role model, not a single serious magazine, not a single organization existed in the mid-'40s to promote a positive understanding of King's self-discovery.[1]

passion plus patriotism equals fantastic sex

Herb King loved men with a passion easily confused with patriotism. His emblematic story stands as boundary in historical time between two different gay worlds: a covert and disguised series of prewar subcultures (what sociologist Laud

Humphreys calls "a satellite culture") versus the slow emergence of a postwar identity. The war galvanized the forces that enabled King, and many others like him, to create the conscious awareness of the interlocking connection between sexual need and identity that led to the modern gay community.

Todd Grison, an African American soldier, recalls that it was next to impossible to turn down the advances of certain beautiful men:

> There was a drill sergeant who did have a beautiful body. He used to come into the supply room—my private quarters were in the back. I guess I was gay then and didn't know it because I had them all fixed up. You know, the iron bunk beds? Well, I had mine all boxed in, real fancy. Anyway, this drill sergeant had to come back to my quarters to turn in his pistol and he would always hang around and bullshit. At that age we were playing, horsing around and shit like that. This guy was about twenty-two. Once I threw him and pinned him and there was no way I could have done that, me at a hundred and twenty-five pounds and him with a great body like that! I pressed against him and all at once I could feel something, something real hard, and I jumped up and said, "Oh, come on, let's quit this horsing around."[2]

The affectionate exchanges weren't isolated to that one time. "He used to tell his wife he was protecting me from the other guys," Grison continues. "Hell, he was protecting me for himself. Another time I was drunk and I remember him bringing me home, undressing me, putting me in bed and kissing me, kissing me on the cheek. He was so good-looking."[3]

As Alan Bérubé points out in his ground-breaking *Coming Out Under Fire*, GIs made their first gay pals on military bases. Or they made friends with pock-marked lads and burly men during first-time excursions to big cities where sailors and marines, crowded into port cities, combed neon-lit streets, round the clock. In port cities, where there were no parents to supervise, and more money than Dust Bowl babies had so far seen, men shared beds at YMCAs and slept together in parks or movie theaters.[4]

"It was my experience," writes Gore Vidal brazenly in his *Palimpsest*, "that just about everyone, either actively or passively, was available under the right circumstance."[5] Recruits being transferred from one camp to another were placed in Pullman cars where they shared beds. Bob Thompson's first same-sex experience in the Navy took place on a troop train from San Diego to Madison, Wisconsin, in a little compartment. ("So it was something at night when we closed that door.") Another man, a chief petty officer in the Navy, recalls that when he first got into the recreation hall, there'd be "this subtle eye contact kinda thing." An entire network of friends developed via this nuanced cruising, which bespoke a new idiom.[6]

These epiphanies took place as men served their country. All this proved to soldiers that they could be "real" men while also becoming "gay men." Improved self-esteem created more men willing to come out and take chances; quick gropes evolved into makeout scenes, then affairs—then cliques. In psychological terms, what took place was a public sense of "mirroring," a psychic kind of "holding" that takes place when any new sense of consciousness is being raised up from baby steps.

some stories from the war: the cult of masculinity

It is strange to think that it took the American military to stage a national coming out experience for gay men. Imagine: the crowning achievement of the United States government, the proud moment that made the world safe for democracy, the mobilization that ended the Great Depression, the liberation of the concentration camps, the emergence of the military-industrial complex of the postwar years—all this provided the conditions for more gay sex than Christian culture had ever seen. As Bérubé puts it, World War II was as significant to gays in the '40s as Stonewall was to a later generation. "Their experiences in the military and on the assembly line, their discovery of gay nightlife in cities, and their struggle to survive the postwar antigay crackdowns all helped to lay the groundwork for gay life as we know it today."[7]

The war uprooted tens of millions of people, and placed them in a nonfamilial, same-sex setting that encouraged male bonding. John Nichols remembers the milieu this way:

> Looking back, World War II was not all blood, sweat and tears. For many a gay guy who did not participate on the raw, raging battlefront, it was a time of high excitement, a chaotic atmosphere and a tomorrow-you-may-be-dead attitude. There was plenty of gay action available and although by today's living standards we certainly were not emancipated, we were not bored nor living in a closet either.[8]

Never had so many Americans at once been forced to leave their homes in a vast migration to cities. Most were people young, white, single, and male, but many were African American and of Asian and Latino origin. Young adults who would have gone from their parents' homes into youthful marriages cascaded into an all-male military culture that was supposed to stand for heterosexual values but that teemed with homosexual subtext. Cities, especially ports like San

Francisco, became electric, charged, sultry meccas for the greenest of lads liberated from the destiny of their parents:

> Soldiers, sailors and Marines enjoyed a wartime prominence and respect never since equalled. Civilians bought them drinks, talked to them, offered them rides; anything to ease their way. . . .
>
> Possibly because of their revealing, body-hugging uniform with its 13 fly-buttons, bulging baskets and flare pants, sailors came to represent gay sex with a capital "S." One of the first signs of spring was when you spotted your first sailor in whites after seeing him all winter in his Navy blues.
>
> A more uncommon sight was a Marine. They represented virility, manliness and a challenge. Although their traditional uniform was no match for the Navy, a Marine's entrance with his crew-cut hair and determined chin could bring every bar to attention.[9]

Reports in diaries, letters, and personal accounts show men in strange cities collectively experiencing enormous shifts that rocked their psychic households. A sudden intimacy took place through the threat of death. Warm embraces at night kept two guys from freezing in the winter frost. "During the years that I was with my army unit," recalls Bob Basker, a New York man who enlisted in 1941, "of the four hundred men in it I must have had sex with a hundred of them."[10]

Imagine the shock for the young, sheltered, and sexually confused man. One day, he'd be in Detroit, eating ribs with his bickering mom and dad, the next day he'd find himself surrounded by young, physically fit naked men in the shower and bathroom. There was no privacy in these stalls, but a lot of testosterone. "My God!" explained Ben Small, who at eighteen enlisted in the Army Air Corps. "This is what I am. How do I cope?" Greg Aarons, who got the call from the draft board while working at a shipyard, recalls that "Suddenly I find myself on the third floor of the old P.E. station and there is a sea of cocks."[11]

These men woke up to the fact that they had been barely living above the collective level. Desire helped them climb out of that fishbowl into something more individual. Inertia, the old enemy of men (and women), was felled once again by the sexual instinct. "Certainly, things were pretty open in the Pacific Islands," adds Vidal, "where on one, no doubt mythical, island an entire marine division paired off." If someone was the least bit latent—and horny—the service drew that out. "During the time I was stationed in Antwerp," recalls Bob Basker, "I became acquainted with an older group of gay men. . . . Pierre not only had an apartment in Antwerp, he had one in Brussels, too. . . . We were very compatible . . . he loved to fuck and I loved being fucked. And the guy was just insatiable at fifty-one."[12]

Some men remember a gentle understanding that settled on a combat area; men hugged one another in moments of fear or during a unexpected reunion. As Bérubé tells it, when Ted Allenby's friend Barrett ran into him on board ship after thinking he had been shot dead, he "grabbed hold of me," Allenby recalled, "hugged me, and couldn't let go," crying uncontrollably. Allenby remembers that had these two men embraced so lovingly on the streets of San Diego, they would have been smeared as a "couple of queers."[13] Combat soldiers were allowed to respond to each other's personal losses with a respect and understanding that carried a homoerotic charge to it. Jim Warren, whose boyfriend was shot while doing his best to dislodge a machine gun nest in Saipan, tells this poignant story:

> They brought him back and he was at the point of death. He was bleeding. He had been hit about three or four times. I stood there and he looked up at me and I looked down at him and he said, "Well, Jim, we didn't make it, did we." And tears were just rolling down my cheeks. I don't know when I've ever felt such a lump and such a waste. And he kind of gave me a boyish crooked grin and just said, "Well, maybe next time." And I said, "I'm going to miss you. And I'll see your mother." There were people standing around, maybe seven or eight people standing there, and I was there touching his hand and we were talking. Somebody said later, "You were pretty good friends," because I had been openly crying and most people don't do this.[14]

One is reminded of the agonizing cries made by Gilgamesh at the death of his beloved Enkidu. One also hears echoes of the farewells made by lovers during AIDS when the late Paul Monette wrote elegiac love poems to his now dead friend, Rog. The "love of sames," when it is experienced between two men, does not offer the contrasexual attributes provided in the erotic love experienced between a man and a woman. It does, however, provide a man with a missing piece of his personality. The loss of such a lover is thus experienced as an inner death. An individual has projected his unconscious treasures onto the hero in question.

Of course, not all combat teams were comprised of men who made passionate love to each other on lonely evenings or who wept when they lost such lovers. Some servicemembers, so wary of being found out as gay, never touched another man in any but the most neutral manner. In his memoirs, *For You Lili Marlene*, Robert Peters gives an impression of coded conversations, where gay men flirted and that's all, and where touches meant friendship. A certain corporal, who says he can "almost taste the cum as I mozey through the barracks," calls Peters on his guarded approach. ("I know what jiggles your tits, Peters. . . . So, don't hide from me, Mary.") Peters seems rather less open, and a bit more self-divided:

> I was ignorant of real sex with either men or women and was secure only with my own masturbatory fantasies. I dread that the CO might order me to investigate Jackson as "queer" and "undesirable." If that happened, my rational self would follow orders, even if it meant a dishonorable discharge. What a hypocrite! While I hungered for Jackson, I felt self-hatred and vowed to God that I would never sin again.[15]

does every man have a homosexual side?   Strange, but as some soldiers and sociologists report, the homosexual tendencies that came about from so many homosocial cliques affected almost everyone, not just the men who otherwise might have been gay. They experienced what psychologist Mitch Walker calls the archetype of the "Double." As in the case of Huck and Jim (and Jonathan and David), the archetype may include "a tendency to homosexuality, but is not necessarily a homosexual archetype. Rather the double embodies the *spirit* of love between those of the same sex." In other words, ". . . the double is a soulmate of intense warmth and closeness."

Vidal puts the "double" experience this way: "Although the traditional hysteria about same-sexuality ran its usual course in the well-policed army camps Stateside (to categorize is to control), bars like the one on the ground floor of the Astor Hotel throve. At any time of day or night, hundreds of men would be packed six-deep around the long oval black bar within whose center bartenders presided."[16] Adds Robert Peters, talking about a straight buddy, in his memoirs about World War II, "Mike sleeps with an arm over my chest."[17]

As if to cultivate homo eros, the army cultivated a "buddy system" that to many gay men seemed as romantic as anything gay culture might have later cooked up. The 1922 song "My Buddy" became one of the most popular songs of World War II. It was okay, in fact in some ways it was mandated, that guys fall in love with each other. According to Scott C., it was as if the war gave "permission to all men to get with their homosexual side, which most of the time had been hidden away with lots of other crap."

The pages of gay male pornography bristle with stories of straight Army dudes having sex with gay ones.[18] While clichéd, these stories appeal to gay men in part because they do represent a patriarchal world in transition, a world in which manhood was threatened not just by the new freedoms being experienced by women, but as well by the ways in which automation and technology had begun to make men feel inferior. With all these changes in gender roles, homosexuality acted as both a threat to manhood and a way to ensure it. Erotically charged glances directed at a straight male hunk of a buddy who might then deflect them touched the gay male father complex at a romantic edge.

Homosexual men experience Oedipal incest regarding their fathers, not their mothers, a psychological phenomenon psychologist Mitch Walker calls the "Uranian Complex." So men with "Uranian Complexes" really had a field day in the war. They got the male bonding and even erotic entanglements so hungered for with men who sometimes shared likeness with their fathers. Some veterans say they had powerful reminisces of their father while at war. And no wonder. The "Uranian Complex" suggests that the gay boy, born homosexual, is programmed to search for a masculine outer figure on whom to project romantically powerful inner symbolism. The earliest such figure is likely to be his father. Then, he wishes (unconsciously) to erotically marry his father, an effort that gets frustrated by the incest taboo (often abetted by a rejecting dad) in a highly charged and vibrational manner. The frustration creates ego-consciousness, but when there is an absent or rejecting father, it creates terrible defenses against the homosexual wishes lodged in his "id" or unconscious. These overwhelming defenses can block the emerging personality. A gay man is thus wounded and yet dissociated from the source of his wounding; he experiences an inner war. Odd, but it took an outer war to break loose some of these defenses and bring some inner peace to gay men. What a trick of history that the emergence of modern gay identity would take place just when the patriarchy was about to peak or climax.

During the war, enforced intimacy with the same sex sometimes led to sex whether both men were "gay" or not. A straight man who got drunk and fucked his buddy did not feel at risk for being pegged "queer." Gay men, perhaps feeling more emotionally receptive, helped egg the situation on. This provided a perfect opportunity for an emerging gay male to feel both virile and vulnerable, a highly charged numinous romance that leather men and Castro men tried to bottle and clone, as it were, years later. As Basker recalls:

> Sex was on an individual basis, in the shower room, in different ways. There were a few gay ones among them, but most of them were straight yet willing to play. How it worked was you'd get in the shower, around one o'clock in the morning after you'd been out on the town, taking a shower before you went to bed. My technique was to say to the guy next to me, "Hey, would you do me a favor and

soap my back?" And the guy would soap my back and I'd say, "Thanks," and then I'd say, "Here, let me do your back." I wouldn't ask, I'd just assume, and start to soap his back. If he didn't flinch, I'd start soaping his chest and if he didn't flinch then, I'd start soaping his stomach. Then I would do one leg, then the other, then start soaping his balls, then maybe his ass. Generally, by this time, they'd have a hard on. If they flinched anywhere along the line, they'd say, "Thanks," and move away. Only one time did someone come to me who must have heard something from someone else and approached me to have sex. Other than that I never had any problems. [19]

Not a few gay men exploited this user-friendly situation, especially if it kept them warm at night or helped stave off the fear of impending battle. In Bérubé's book, Jim Warren gives a classic explanation of coming on to a charged-up hetero buddy. "You start talking," he says, "and you don't say, 'I'm straight' or anything, but you say, 'Gee, it sure gets lonely around here without girls.'" (Apparently, the effect of this cat-and-mouse game increases if a hard-on can be detected.) Afterward, one thing leads to another and the guys become buddies, hang out all the time, and go to the movies together. "And then later you decide to take a walk somewhere and [say] 'Let's sit down' and from there your hand [is] resting or his hand resting [on your leg], then you're in business."[20] Other men report resorting to similar measures to blur the line between hetero and homo in a militantly homosocial environment.

For the more closeted of men, the war loosened constraints that kept a man fighting his crushes and his fantasies in civilian life. At home, the first awareness of homosexuality may have taken place around a bar in a seedy part of town, or a reference to an old man who was not married. In the military, the men were young and beautiful, thus breaking down some of the stereotypes that kept some homosexuals from admitting their fantasies to themselves.

the cracking of the container When a person's defenses against integrating homosexual feelings are so strong, only a massive intervention in the form of fate or a trauma can dislodge formidable barriers. "The war provided just such a kick in the butt to peoples' resistances," Scott C. says. Men remember being possessed by a seizure of images not unlike Proust's *petit madeleine* or Dante's Beatrice; it took a psychic revolt of near-nuclear magnitude to allow sheltered, prejudiced men to admit their attraction to other men.

For Will Whiting, his transformation was accompanied by vaguely mystical imagery:

*When I turned eighteen I enlisted. The service did a lot for me. I had a girlfriend
I wrote to every day. I had no homosexual friends in the service at all, none.
Which astounds me today because, boy, it was there. But I was macho and
straight, never thought of myself as being gay though I had my cock sucked a few
times, no big thing. That's all it was and it was fun. I never gave it any thought
until after I got shot up pretty bad and lay in the hospital. I got to thinking, re-
membering when I was a youngster and fantasized about one of the kids on the
basketball team. How I wished he would get sick so I could take care of him!
That's gay thinking, right? I started to put it all together. I could never forget
him. He was a beautiful boy, blond, and I had a thing for blonds. Anyway, after
I got wounded I moved back to Indiana in the middle of winter and there were
blizzards all the time and I thought "To hell with it, no way am I going to live
in this part of the country."*[21]

One has to read in between the lines (somewhere between "blonds" and
"anyway") to get the psychic switch that gets turned on when Whiting remembers the beauty of the blond basketball player. But it not terribly hard to see in
Whiting's resolve to leave the blizzards—"To hell with it, no way am I going to
live in this part of the country"—a clear decision to thaw a frozen place in his
heart.

Such thawing isn't dissimilar from what Herb King experienced, albeit
more platonically.

Jim Kepner, who did not serve in the war, but kept up an active correspondence with gay service members, recounts scores of letters in which men had
similar awakenings about a secret, almost imaginal life. "I would read letters in
which men were falling in love over and over again with 'the man of my dream,'
or 'Mr. Right' or 'a beautiful youth,' or 'an Angel,'" recalls Kepner. "Then they
would experience this terrible loss, either through a friend dying, or marrying, or
plain old losing touch." There was an inflation of spirit, followed by a crash—an
extroversion of libido, followed by its painful withdrawal.

It was as if, in the process of creating consciousness, a young homosexual
man were thrown back and forth between opposing moods and attitudes—between Dionysian and Apollonian, between merger and then loss—so as to learn
how to experience opposite viewpoints simultaneously.

"This convinced me," recalls Kepner, "even at this early stage of gay history, of the creative and transforming nature of homosexual sex." For Kepner, it
was as if love and sex had become a person's highest calling, thus filling up the
vacuum now left in social life from the slow but continual breaking down of religious meaning since the rise of capitalism after the Reformation. This realiza-

tion—that Western society no longer had a viable myth besides the economic one—seemed to be taking place for Kepner just at the moment that he discovered that homosexual men were unearthing something new about their bodies, hearts, and desires. This discovery around the profound mythic potential of homo eros led Kepner to devote his life to gay letters, gay archiving, and gay activism.

War—indeed a crisis of any kind—has a way of suspending stereotypes and accelerating the speed by which myths and symbols are rewoven into the tapestry of an individual's spirit. Moving one's eyes from World War II, if just briefly, one sees how *Leaves of Grass* bard Walt Whitman witnessed similarly powerful epiphanies during the Civil War around the "love of comrades." On June 18, 1863, the poet-cum-nurse encountered Thomas Haley, a "regular Irish boy, a fine specimen of youthful physical manliness," shot in the lung, on his death bed. As Whitman tells the story, Haley—who "lies with his frame exposed above the waist, all naked for coolness"—takes on a near hallowed value, personifying for a moment Whitman's libido:

> I often come and sit by him in perfect silence; he will breathe for ten minutes as softly and evenly as a young babe asleep. Poor youth—so handsome, athletic, with profuse, beautiful, shining hair. One time, as I sat looking at him while he lay asleep, he suddenly—without the least start—awakened, opened his eyes, gave one clear, silent look, a slight sigh, then turned back and went into his doze again. Little he knew, poor death-stricken boy, the heart of the stranger that hovered near.[22]

The notion of homosexual libido put forward here by Whiting, Kepner, and Whitman seems rooted in an inborn quality, linked to a person's subjectivity. "Subjectivity" here is another way of saying what a person feels intensely and powerfully—or, stated another way, what intensity and power one worships. One generally attributes the word "worship" to monotheistic religions. This shows a limited awareness of how a person can live within his own myth. The propensity to attach an extraordinarily high value to an object exists in every human psyche—as romantic love demonstrates. A gay man projects his soul-complex onto another, and then mistakes what is actually an operation of his own soul for an outside object. In letters written to and by gay veterans they say that they, at times, "loved" or "obsessed on" or "went crazy" or "fell hard for" or "went head over heels for" a pal, a buddy, a captain, a pirate.[23]

As Randy Shilts tells us, this is not remarkable. All wars promise to do at least one thing: to take a boy and make him a man. This requires that he look up to men who are his superiors and even surrender his life to men who are his peers, a homosocial hierarchy with implicit homosexual undertones. What's different about World War II is that this implicit veneration of men became explicit. And more than that, it became a form of new consciousness.[24]

the background behind king's ability
to become his own monarch

This valorization of gay life in World War II isn't meant to suggest that men did not have their share of hot gay sex before Pearl Harbor, as documented by historian George Chauncey in his epic *Gay New York*. During the Roaring Twenties, "fairies" and "wolves," as well as lower-class "queers" and middle-class "gays," fashioned an extensive, organized and highly visible gay world in saloons, dancehalls, YMCAs, and drag balls from Harlem to Greenwich Village. An industrial society mushroomed just as millions of immigrants, fleeing persecution and poverty, flocked to the "gold-paved" streets of urban capitals. Cities exploded with sweatshops. Bachelors crammed into tenements. Speakeasies provided entertainment. Harlem boasted a Renaissance. People who had been reared in the claustrophobic embrace of tribal cultures and the idiom of ethnic collectivity experienced an unprecedented awareness of their own individuality. Millions became anonymous overnight.[25]

In the 1920s, as Chauncey reports, so many guys cruised and gathered on the open lawn in Central Park that they nicknamed it the "Fruited Plain." One stretch of the park was called "Vaseline Alley" and "Bitches' Walk." In the late 1930s, according to Chauncey, "Mayor Fiorello La Guardia had closed most of New York's gay bars in a pre–World's Fair crack-down"; so the parks and streets offered a place to socialize on warm summer evenings. "The nance element holds regular conventions in Paddies Lane," went one report in *Variety* in 1929. In an era before air conditioning, beaches on both coasts attracted male bathers who loved the sight of each other. Some men blended in with their ethnic clans, while others congregated *ensemble*, putting on flamboyant shows with odd hats, not to mention swishes up and down the boardwalk.[26]

This new appreciation for the body and its public display made its way into social life just as Americans began to cotton to a vulgarized Freudianism that showed the sexual instinct as a drive that a person had to pay at least some attention to. "The urge is there, and whether the individual desires or no, it always manifests itself," wrote one American psychologist in, of all places, *Good Housekeeping*. "It will never be stopped except with satisfactions."[27] Sexologist Havelock Ellis, a British contemporary to Freud, gave to sexuality the power of individual self-definition, "penetrating," as it were, the whole person. Writing in 1910, Ellis went so far as to question monogamy and marriage as an adequate response to human sexual life. Moreover (departing from Freud), he stressed the inborn nature of homosexuality for "inverts"; yet (joining with Freud) he considered a limited spectrum of homosexual behavior a normal feature of psychosexual development for all people.[28]

The hard work of feminists, in particular Margaret Sanger, made effective contraception accessible to American women, thus effectively detaching sexual activity from the goal of procreation. Even Anthony Comstock's brutal attack on Sanger couldn't stop the public from coming to grips with the new energies released in orgasms that weren't produced for the sake of progeny. "Sexual expression was moving beyond the confines of marriage, not as the deviant behavior of prostitutes and their costumers, but as the normative behavior of many Americans," write the authors of *Intimate Matters*. America had entered a new era that marked, if not the demise of nineteenth-century prescriptions about continence and self-control, then a reappraisal of their stranglehold.[29]

This new sexual liberalism trickled down to men who enjoyed sex with men. In Harlem, you had your drag balls and late-night clubs. In San Francisco you had your rooming houses, hotel-salons, and automats. On the East Coast, you had a bustling cafeteria society. In Louisiana, you had your speakeasies. In Newport, Rhode Island, you made a point of bumping into the guys who sat around the YMCA at night if you wanted to bump and grind. In New York, bars patronized exclusively by men who wanted other men appeared. Private Russian and Turkish baths numbered fifty-seven by the 1920s. Gay-tolerant baths sprung up. Two baths—Stauch's and Claridge's—were infamous for homosexual tête-à-têtes. Immigrants, shop owners, bootleggers, dandies, and Central Park strollers crossed class lines as never before in steamrooms where idioms fell by the wayside, with shirts and ties.[30]

At the YMCA, as Chauncey tells it, one did not "come out" as gay to the straight world (as one does nowadays) but rather, one was "brought out" into gay society. Some gay New Yorkers literally rented rooms (and assumed aliases) at the immense Sloane House just to catch some tail; the fifteen-hundred-roomed albatross, offering accommodations to transient young men, provided rich opportunities. The West Side Y, located on Sixty-third Street, was no less serviceable. All you needed was a shower and a bar of soap—a clever way of breaking the ice, as far as Donald Vining was concerned.[31] Although one wonders if the folklore of the Ys as a precursor of the sexual revolution isn't a bit overexaggerated, gay elders do reminisce that the letters Y M C A used to stand for "Why I'm So Gay." As Chauncey puts it:

Grant McGree arrived in the city in 1941, not knowing anyone, intimidated by the size of the city, and full of questions about his sexuality. But on his first night at the Y as he gazed glumly from his room into the windows of other men's rooms he suddenly realized that many of the men he saw sharing rooms were couples; within a week he had met many of them and begun to build a network of gay friends.[32]

Neither were the signals so obtuse at the famous Horn and Hardart cafeteria. Over a plain donut and a steaming five-cent cup of coffee you could catch the eye of a businessman lighting a cigarette. Next thing you knew, you might be renting a room at the Men's Residence Club on West Fifty-sixth Street.

This "gay world" was no Mardi Gras. People were broken by the necessities of living double lives. The aliases, the lingo, the changing of voices, the masks — all these posed terrifying dangers. "Forget the giggles, girl, he's jam," Jim Kepner remembers telling a queen-of-a-friend who was coming on to a man who, though pretty and delicate, was a straight man ("jam") known for his violent rejection of advances.

This "gay world" that George Chauncey maps in his *Gay New York* was also terribly underground, often riddled with paranoia and terror, according to men like Kepner, Scott C., King, and Harry Hay. It took the sex-segregated nature of the armed forces during World War II to raise homosexuality closer to the surface of public life as never before.

the shadow side of gay life in world war II

World War II may have jump-started the gay movement, but it did so at great cost to many homosexuals who were humiliated and destroyed by surveillance, imprisonment, discharge, and ridicule.[33] There were too many mixed messages, too much shame, for anything but a guarded sense of awakening to take place for most homosexuals. "There was this constant threat of being found out," remembered Stuart Loomis, "and being cashiered out of the service"[34] Sissy men found it hardest of all to fit in, unless they turned their effeminacy into seductiveness; but that sometimes went against their own moral code. Jim, one such sissy (nicknamed "Cherry"), saw his flirtatious behavior as a "defense mechanism" to survive the pressures of being different:

> *So I developed only a very aggressive method of sex while playing a very passive role in the sense of cruising. They'd think they were gonna get me, but I was always the one that finally got them, which is strange. It was done with a kind of*

coldness that was totally unsatisfactory because there was no emotional, roman-tic attachment to the affairs at all. It was like mutual masturbation, primarily to gratify me. I was aware of that, but I didn't know what else to do.[35]

The military knew what to do.

It had a problem on its hands: a lot of homosexual servicemembers who were also deeply conflicted about such "tendencies." No census was taken of the gay men who entered the military. But if Alfred Kinsey's statistics apply as much to the military as to the civilian population, that would mean at least a million soldiers were gay. So just as the war provided a coming out experience par excel-lence for homosexuals, it also enabled the state to identify, and control, the new threat of deviance.[36]

As gay people came of age during World War II, so did the once-dismissed science of psychiatry. With the war, psychologists, some of them gay, saw a way to legitimize themselves by formulating elaborate screening processes and then a series of complex regulations that banned deviants. In 1942, the military began discriminating between "normals" and those "persons habitually or occasionally engaged in homosexual or other perverse sexual practices." In 1943, regulations banned homosexuals from all branches of the military. Some army psychiatrists pushed for reform; others insisted homosexuality could not be changed; others spoke about it in a progressive fashion.[37]

It is an irony of history that the military's brutal treatment of homosexual men helped jump-start early gay organizing. Patriotic gay soldiers felt infuriated when thrown in locked wards with people suffering genuine mental illness. Groups of men who had received "blue discharges" banded together. Veterans felt a heightened sense of legitimacy as citizens. Those who had been discharged preferred striking out on their own in gay enclaves rather than returning home in disgrace. They had little to lose. The army had radicalized a group of gays, many of whom went on to start the first openly gay organizations in America.

Thus a social identity formed: through a complex series of setbacks and gains; through freedom and then the state's reaction to that freedom; through classification and then reform against such scientific taxonomy; through the ac-knowledgment on the part of the Secret Service of the importance of homosex-ual men in the military (through a lax recruitment policy) and then later on through the acknowledgment of the dangers of too many homosexuals serving in the military (resulting in the creation of a bureaucratic apparatus to manage ho-mosexual personnel); through the forced confessions (which made men come out irrevocably); through the arrests (which allowed men to band together);

through the discharges (thus giving GIs a cause and a target to attack); and through broadening social discourse on the subject of homosexuality.

This suggests that it is not through mere freedom or a linear progress that an identity is formed.

the creation myth?

Historians attribute the emergence of modern homosexuality largely to economic and social factors. Industrial capitalism dealt a blow to the structures of family. Urban culture pushed people off farms into bustling cities. Apartment living gave a new anonymity to bachelor life. The women's suffrage and civil rights movements challenged prevailing social mores.

"Only when individuals began to make their living through wage labor," writes John D'Emilio, "instead of as parts of an independent family unit, was it possible for homosexual desire to coalesce into a personal identity—an identity based on the ability to remain outside the heterosexual family and to construct a personal life based on attraction to one's own sex."[38]

Some gay thinkers see a more purposive element to homosexual libido than what the prevailing post-Marxist, postfeminist models allow, and a few, like Ian Young or Mark Thompson, refer to thinkers like Walt Whitman, Edward Carpenter, Gerald Heard, and Harry Hay to speak about homosexuality as being "inborn." Edward Carpenter, a British socialist and a contemporary of Whitman's, rejected explanations of love that were too rational and mechanistic. He used the Lamarckian concept of "exfoliation" to talk about homosexuals (whom he called "Uranians") as an evolution inspired from within nature—a plant emerging from the soil of obscurity, a seed growing into an oak. Exfoliation, not so different from C. G. Jung's concept of individuation, suggests that the purpose of a human life is a development of individual personality from its own unknown depths. Jung used the term *self* to point to the center of psychic awareness that transcends ego consciousness that includes parts of the psyche that are unconscious. It would seem as if Carpenter presaged the modern awareness of this self.

Carpenter saw gay people as making an important contribution to the development of culture; for gays, as a new social force, could referee the ancient feud between tradition and the individual. "Only go far enough, deep enough, into your own nature and you are sure to haul up something which will get you into trouble with the world," he writes.[39] In those days, gays still believed in the numinous power of natural forces.

Sociologists today attribute the explosion of sexuality to the evolution of liberal and democratic societies in Western Europe and North America, shaking up class, gender, and race lines. It seems a bit "retro" to harken back to the mythopoetic Carpenter. But his little known "myth" has not been exhausted. Carpenter invites his reader to entertain the notion that the psyche or the imagination has more possibilities than Western science gives it credit for. As he puts it, life is an adventure that seeks to transform the adventurer: "Our union with Nature and humanity is a *fact*, which — whether we recognize it or not — is at the base of our lives; slumbering, yet ready to wake in our consciousness when the due time arrives."[40]

Obscuring our ability to benefit from unorthodox and psychical views on homosexuality is the fact that rarely has homosexuality ever been called by one name. (*Gay* is a relatively recent invention; *Uranian* hardly stuck; neither did *adhesiveness* or *homophile*.) Moreover, most gay men forget how recent a development modern homosexuality is and how quickly attitudes about it have changed. Before World War II, for example, there was relatively little stigma attached to a married man having his dick sucked because, as historian George Chauncey points out, "Heterosexuality had not yet become a precondition of gender normativity in early-twentieth century working-class culture." The effeminacy assigned to the fairy allowed more masculine working-class toughs and businessmen alike to engage in homosexual activity without losing their status as normal.[41] It's hard to believe, but, according to thinkers like George Chauncey, Jeffrey Weeks, and Jonathan Ned Katz, one's sexuality was simply not defined by one's heterosexuality or homosexuality, as it is so often is these days. The term *homosexuality* wasn't even invented until 1869.[42]

But some gay "essentialists" argue that we do homosexuality a disservice if we continue to see it entirely as a performative behavior, as the "social constructions" call it, and less as an exfoliation whose potential and meaning has yet to become clear. Carpenter's belief in the sense of unity (first with oneself, then with others and nature) shows sex as a bridge to self-understanding. No great cynic, Carpenter thought Uranians to be "students of life and nature, inventors and teachers of arts and crafts . . . revealers of the gods and religion."[43] But he also saw this so-called learning process as just beginning:

> *The youth, deeply infected with the sex-passion, suddenly finds himself in the presence of Titanic forces — the Titanic but sub-conscious forces of his own nature. "In love" he feels a superhuman impulse — and naturally so, for he*

identifies himself with cosmic energies and entities, powers that are preparing the future of the race, and whose operations extend over vast regions of space and millennial lapses of time.[44]

The concept hasn't been forgotten by contemporary gay thinkers like Michael Bronski and Ian Young. "So at the time of the creation of modern homosexuality," writes Ian Young, "its greatest spokesmen and prophets saw it not as a barren, meaningless variation, or as a minority taste to be confined in an officially prescribed alternative lifestyle, but as a necessary step in evolution, a means of development (and consequently, perpetuation) of the human species and the earth itself. The view recalls the Platonic and alchemical myth of the androgyne, symbol of reconciliation and wholeness."[45]

It would seem, then, too mechanistic to look at the Herb King story—the emergence of homosexuality from an implicit fact to an explicit one during World War II—as a result of economic and social changes alone.

motherfuckers   Although the mobilization of men away from their families was not understood consciously as a gay masculine initiation, it served as such for many men who had previously led sheltered lives in the bosom of domesticity. Many saw their attachment to comfort as powerful a force as their attachment to cock and would have sacrificed great sex for great peace. "Only by rending me away from my mom did my tour of duty help me to see that I didn't need her to grow up," one officer from New Jersey says.

But many gay men neither could nor wanted to get away from the feminine so easily. Some found a way to express this femininity—whether of a bitchy variety or a more empathic nurturing variety—even in the Army.

army drag: a compensation for all the masculinity

Performing sambas in a costume of red fabric may not have been as daring as storming the beaches of Normandy, but some gay servicemembers thought their Carmen Miranda routine had its place in the war effort. As Bérubé tells it, Robert Fleischer convinced his commanding officer to approve an all-male, all-soldier variety show. And why not? He noticed, after all, that a lot of guys in his outfit (the 473d Antiaircraft Artillery Batallion) happened—surprise!—to be not only from Manhattan but from the world of *theater*. Fleischer thought they'd make *fabulous* singers, dancers, set designers, stage managers—chorus girls, too.

After enough moiling and toiling with his superiors, he did manage to get permission to do a musical comedy, *The Colonel Wants a Show*. His fellow servicemembers—some rather butch types—donned dresses and tutus and high heels, shifting gears and genders.

He wasn't alone. "Gay GIs who performed in drag acted on many levels at once," writes Bérubé. "They boosted soldier morale, played with gender roles, secretly entertained each other with coded signals, met kindred spirits, and created opportunities to be physically affectionate with other men, all the while pressing against the boundaries that would keep their routines safely heterosexual."[46]

In 1942, Special Services personnel, along with the American Red Cross and the USO, went so far as to organize soldier show workshops to train men in scriptwriting, costume and set design, stage managing, directing, and the application of makeup. A soldier handbook, for example, published and distributed by Army Special Services, had more than eight pages of dress patterns for soldier drag in the show *Hi, Yank*. Compensating for all the masculine energy the war provoked, American GIs put on all-male revues and musicals for one another that included female impersonation.

Camp has always proved a useful way for the homosexual to reveal himself to others while satirizing rigid gender roles. But it provides something more—an identification with an inner feminine. Here the feminine is not projected as the soul-figure, as it is with a man whose libido is organized heterosexually, but rather constellates as a "sisterly" aid, and performs the task of being receptive to feelings—and other men. Gay GIs tell stories about jumping into officers' laps, kissing men—and then, later on, being propositioned! Fleischer relates this story about how his drag routine got a bit out of hand:

> What started to happen is the tough guys in the outfit started to tease me quite often. I didn't know quite how to handle it. Sometimes they would show up in the hutment after hours and literally sit on my bed and try to play with me— half-heartedly joking and half serious. You couldn't tell whether they really wanted to have sex or they were just being teasing and showing how macho they [were].[47]

Soldier shows gave gay GIs an opportunity to hook up with other gay men as buddies, which, as some GIs point out, marked the first time in their lives that they enjoyed a full-fledged friendship as an out homosexual. And with coded words and made-up faces they also experienced pride in the efforts. "You are entertaining soldiers," General Eisenhower said once to an all-male cast in Algiers that featured some female impersonators. "You are not fighting with machine guns, but your job is just as important."[48]

affective splits

World War II showed up two different types in homosexual life: a cult of masculinity, and a more hermaphroditic, feminine personality. Along this sexually charged continuum, one can place two nineteenth-century visionaries who identified, classified, and paved the way for the full expression of these roles in modern life. Walt Whitman is the exemplar of a certain homoerotic faith that stresses athletic youths, strong sinews, American health, immigrant feistiness, manly affection, and fierce wrestlers—these are Whitman's icons of homosexuality. It's virtually impossible to overlook the generating power of *phallos* in his words:

> The butcher-boy puts off his killing clothes, or sharpens his
> knife at the stall in the market,
> I loiter enjoying his repartee and his shuffle and break-down.
> Blacksmiths with grimed and hairy chests environs the
> anvil,
> Each has his main-sledge, they are all out, there is a
> great
> heat in the fire.[49]

On the other side of the spectrum sits Karl Heinrich Ulrichs, the first self-proclaimed homosexual—or "Urning"—to speak out publicly on the rights of homosexuals in Germany. Magnus Hirschfield, the founder of the first homosexual rights organization in 1897, saw Ulrichs not only as a researcher into "Uranismus" (Ulrich's term for homosexuality), but as a fighter for it too.[50] Ulrichs asserted the existence of individuals who have male bodies but who at the same time feel sexual love for men as a female might. This "special sexual class of people" he called Urnings, or "a third sex coordinate with that of men and women."[51] To Ulrichs, the effeminate man is usually not attracted to like kind, but rather a "Dioning," or a heterosexual:

> Blond fellow with dark blue glance
> From your eyes like violets
> You have robbed me of my rest
> Give me back again my peace[52]

Ulrichs tried to prove that Uranian love and its feminine characteristics were "inborn." He relied on Plato for the notion of a natural, archetypal realm that wasn't created by culture but rather acted as the mother of all culture. Ulrich's distinctions between Dioning and Urning come from a speech in Plato's *Symposium*. Pausanias argues that there are two different ways to love people because there are two different kinds of Aphrodite. Aphrodite-Uranus, more heavenly and older, is aroused when men go crazy for men. Aphrodite-Dione, more common and vulgar, gets men all hot and bothered over women.

Later in his life he found cases of rugged, masculine men who loved men and he tried his best to amend his "Third Sex" categories to include them. Despite the presence of straight-acting gay guys, as it were, his theory—that Uranians are born with a woman's soul but a man's body—became widely popular among gays who saw it as justification against persecuting people whose sexual orientations were natural.[53]

lonely civilians

And then there are gay men who boast both characteristics: masculine *and* feminine.

Around the beginning of World War II, Jim Kepner was a shy, lanky, twenty-year-old science fiction aficionado from Texas who had moved to San Francisco with his father—and he was horny as all hell. Lonely too. And in 1941 terribly inexperienced about meeting men. Based on recollections from his past—a man simply lifted him up from the ground when he was five and put him on his shoulders, and he never forgot the heat, the vibration, the hardness—Kepner knew he loved men. But how to find them?

Kepner got advice from a woman friend that cruising gays wore gabardine raincoats draped over their shoulders, underneath which they hid copies of *The Well of Loneliness* or *Strange Brother*. They also walked a certain effeminate walk that came utterly natural to them. Kepner did just that—up and down Market Street one night. "The recommendation," he recalls, "did not include hiding the books so thoroughly under the raincoat that the dustjacket didn't show at all." But the mincing hardly came naturally at all:

> I tried practicing and finally almost tripped myself up. Then one night, walking this crazy way, I locked eyes in that special way that I didn't understand yet with a guy who didn't seem particularly attractive. After a few minutes I decided the guy—his name was Nile—was nicer and nicer looking. Short. Plain. Thin, but

thick lips—erotic looking. I thought he couldn't possibly be gay because from what I had read, gays were recognizably effeminate or terribly loathsome old men who just had drool coming out and all sorts of growths, cancerous growths all over them. So he didn't look gay. But that lock had been established, so we paraded up and down the street for an hour or two, looking in windows. I finally asked him if he had a cigarette and we stopped at one corner to wait to cross. There was no light there. He started to hand me a cigarette and then I got the giggles and said I didn't smoke.

Kepner had adopted the persona of the fairy because it was the only one the culture had provided to him as the proper gender role for receiving affection from a man. But although he was hardly macho, the fairy routine wasn't right either:

Well I had no idea about how to move on from here and I'd decided he wasn't gay, but I was still pretty hooked. So he said he had a room nearby which he shared with three or four friends who were out of town and that it was much too late for me to go home and get up in time to go to work, so I could get a few hours of sleep in that room. And so, I went to his cruddy little room. We undressed and lay in bed together for an hour and a half—just with the undershorts. Nothing happened. We both tried to go to sleep.

At this point, Kepner felt himself almost at a loss, a little dejected, fearing abandonment, and yet, at the same time, back to some boyish place in himself. In the midst of this cyclone of feeling, and during which each man pretended to snore several times, Nile rolled over and put his arm over Kepner. "Let's get this show on the road," Nile said. "You haven't done this before, have you?" Nile proceeded to teach Kepner the ABCs of lovemaking, which in this case amounted to just some kissing and rubbing and tussling about in the bed. "Sex has always remained pretty much the same," reminisces Kepner in that discreet way characteristic of men who survived the '40s and '50s with their gay pride intact. "There's the front, and the rear, and there's up and there's down, and there's around the world." Once the passions grew hot, Nile guided Kepner's head down to his cock. Nile reciprocated. Kepner recalls no interest in wishing to penetrate Nile.

Although Kepner tended toward the more passive side of things, the sex proved to be mutual. Still, Kepner found himself unable to enjoy receptive anal intercourse with Nile. "If [anal sex] was done right, and I maintained some control, it could be very exciting. But then most guys who are doing it to you don't want you to be maintaining control. They want you to be bouncing on it and whether it hurts or not seems irrelevant to them. Nile was much more careful, of course. He didn't force anything. And oh God, because of his gentleness, did I fall in love with him. He recommended books about gay life and he gave me some pointers—keep up your ideals; don't get involved with trash; you can get arrested if you're not careful—and pretty much set me on my way." Kepner fell head over heels for Nile, but Nile was a merchant marine and had to ship out to China the next day. Like many gay men, Kepner's major coming out experience was greeted by tears.

Alone again, Kepner resumed his fairy act, but it wasn't right. He did his best to cavort with his pal Henrietta, escorting him/her to a famous gay wedding at the Mark Hopkins Hotel—a high point of San Francisco social life circa 1943. Coming from a working-class background, Kepner felt intimidated by the gala. "I was not a practiced escort, after all," he claims. The groom was a prominent local attorney. The bride was a handsome blond. The gay crowd who usually frequented the Top of the Mark gathered tonight around the circular bar and the inner row of tables. But it wasn't the class problem that unhinged Kepner as much as the swish routine, which Kepner felt unable to ape. And to make matters worse, Kepner was cajoled into performing the wedding. The minister—"known as 'Evil Mary,' a foul-mouthed thing"—didn't show up. Kepner had made the error of once telling Henrietta that he was a student of ministry.

"If you called yourself gay," Kepner reminisces, "you were supposed to be a swish." What a bore. "The bars in those days were dominated by queens," he adds. "I'd constantly get the sort of thing, 'Well, Jimmy, if you're gay, act gay.' And I tried. I put on a little cosmetics and nearly rubbed my skin off trying to see that it didn't show. And I would try to swish but my hips just didn't swivel right, although I think I learned how to do it better than I will admit to." So to perform the service he did his best to camp it up. "Thank God, Evil Mary eventually showed up and relieved me," he remembers.

With this act, Kepner not only witnessed the marriage of two men, but he came out publicly. "I mean," he says, "it was like heaven. I was looking for a community, and here it was."

But not every night was so fabulous. Kepner found himself back at the Top of the Mark a few days later all over again. And despite the fact that he met great guys at bars throughout the city—there was a sensuous Russian ballet dancer; there were those sailors at Lipo's where even the butches sang "The Man I Love"—he found gay life hard and lonely.

Kepner went back in the closet in 1943, for a number of reasons: because of the expectation that if he defined himself as gay he should act like a queen;

because the police grew quite vicious about crackdowns; because he had his heart broken; because he wasn't terribly forward or aggressive once in the bars; because during lively sex he got tired and wanted to rest for a few minutes ("A real turnoff to most"); because he learned that there were real hot individuals whom he couldn't stand to be with for more than a few minutes at a time; because one-night stands talked about wanting love before they made their way into your room, but were up and out of the door the moment they came ("They had to take a leak and never came back"); because most men who he picked up were married and felt crushing guilt once the sex was over; because the bars, if they got too much pressure from the police, turned from gay to straight overnight.

"You could just get arrested for acting the least bit effeminate," he recalls. "It was very, very hard to feel good about yourself. Most of us really believed we had a handicap that one day we might overcome." The notion of gay pride didn't exist at all, although it seemed to burn as a secret truth in Kepner's heart. In fact, he didn't stay in the closet for long. When the police cracked down hard on San Francisco gay life, Kepner moved to Los Angeles. After a decade of hardship, one-night stands, and loneliness, he took a rare and dangerous step: he became a gay leader. He became a member of the Mattachine Society—the first lasting attempt to organize homosexuals politically in America—and he wrote for *One Magazine*, the first serious gay publication.

chapter two

toward
democracy

On a spring day in 1955, he walks into his favorite Central Park public rest room. Empty, it smells of ammonia and dried piss. He approaches the middle urinal—it offers a bird's-eye view of the other urinals and the main stall. He forces a few drops out. After five minutes, another man enters. The first man risks more: after shaking some imaginary pee from his dick, he shoots a look at the other man. When the second man returns the gaze, the first stares at the floor. He takes a step back. He reveals a hint of his half-hard hard-on. He fights the urge to let the smile creep across his face, for he feels the payoff coming. He grabs his own member, and as hearts beat, the door opens and the men furtively return to the urinal, as if dying to pee.[1]

The new man, an older gentleman in a three-piece gray business suit, absorbing the electricity, takes his sweet time washing his hands. The white hand towel hanging from the rusty dispenser is too stained, so he wrings his hands. One man recognizes the newcomer: the older fellow has played lookout before. Lighting a Lucky Strike and peering out a broken side window, he lets the two men know with a slight nod that the coast is clear with a stream of smoke sailing from just-pursed lips. He keeps watch in case a cop, a hoodlum, or a horny underage youth approaches. For the moment, the three men have little, presumably, to fear.

The first man stares down at the second man's cock, which looks similar to his own: smooth and long but on the thin side, with a posture that announces intentions. The man puts a firm hand on the younger man's shoulder, as if to push him to his knees. Our hero has fought off this kind of demand throughout his entire tearoom career, but, with the older man standing guard and the younger looking so needy and impatient, he thinks twice about his reasons for being so averse to serving another. He recalls a line his father used to say when they went out to dinner in Chicago: *You might as well try anything, at least once.* He also recalls that the Kinsey report, which had just come out, suggested that 37 percent of adult men had had some form of homosexual sex as adults. This gave a few men permission to see that their sexual transgressions proved them neither terribly deviant nor terribly exceptional.[2]

public settings for private acts

If the World War II years announced the possibility of a gay identity emerging from a mass of hidden and repressed feelings, the years following showed how difficult the formation of such an identity would be without structure or gradients through which the energies could flow and shape themselves. A growing ego, much like a growing child, needs mirroring to emerge as intact. Some argue that the evolution of urban gay communities is nothing but a structure to provide such mirroring on a grand, public scale.

Before 1950, there were no organized homosexual political organizations and certainly no thoughtful magazines. Only a handful of books could be found. Gay bars and saloons did exist before World War II, especially in the relatively visible gay world of New York in the 1920s. But it was rare to find a gay man who did not lead a double life. Gay fads came and went, but the closet remained constant. A member of the Society for Individual Rights, looking back to the '50s, explained the small ranks of gay activists this way: "Why should you come up front and risk anything when you can play this game of a dual identity? In spite of all our activities, we were still closeted. It was a collective closet, but it was still a closet."[3]

The halting steps made to open the door sometimes had the effect of closing further. The one positive book that emerged in 1951—Donald Webster Cory's *The Homosexual in America*—painted an unappealing picture of a world of law-abiding felons, their spirits crushed by social stigma and self-imposed secrecy. "Do the pick-ups and the one-night stands engender a sense of shame, an overwhelming guilt, that prevents each of the individuals from facing the other on a second occasion?" Cory asks. "Or are the participants in these fly-by-night arrangements fearful lest their gay friends discover this phase of their activities? Or are these particular homosexuals so promiscuous, so adventurous, so unable to combine sex with fidelity, that only the unknown, the untasted, the uncharted are attractive to them?"[4]

Quoted and worshiped by the homophiles of the '50s, Cory's book tried to find a middle ground between condoning gay life and apologizing for it. "If homosexuals are arrested under rather sordid circumstances," he mused, "seeking sexual partners in places forbidden by public law, shall society not stop to ask whether the cause of this action is the banishment of their pursuits from so many of the accepted pathways of life?" His book isn't just self-flagellating. Quoting W. E. B. DuBois — "The worst effect of slavery was to make Negroes doubt themselves and share in the general contempt for black folks" — Cory takes the onus off homosexuals and puts it back on the discriminating society.[5]

The sharp disparity in attitude between the '50s and '90s might serve as an indication of how quickly gay life transformed itself in fifty years. Yet some argue that we are closer to the attitudes of the '50s than we think. "If you pierce through the veneer of muscled homosexual men who live in the gay ghettoes of the '90s," says one gay veteran, "you might discover a resistance to living the fullness of gay energies not so terribly different from what we experienced in the '50s." It's just, as he puts it, that the shame has been transferred from a conscious attitude toward gay life to the unconscious, where it exacts a price.

instant sex

Chuck Williams remembers now: he went crazy for men who looked like *he* wished he looked: blond, 5'10", clean-shaved, hazel-eyed men in their mid-twenties who looked like they were on the high school Varsity team but who listened to Benny Carter and read the Beats. (And it wasn't so easy to get your hands on such stuff. It was 1957, the year the San Francisco police department seized copies of Allen Ginsberg's *Howl* from City Lights Bookstore and charged owner Lawrence Ferlinghetti with selling obscene material.) Come to think of it, Chuck had no idea what was in the minds (or books) of men who sucked him off in a minute or two at his favorite Central Park tearoom. He had only chatted with a man here or there since he started hanging out seeking "release" in bathrooms eight years ago. Rarely did anyone speak to anyone else in a tearoom — no "Thank you," or "Take it easy." Conversations came as a warning of a disturbance — or as a result of one.

One day in '59, five or six red-haired Chicago street kids cornered Chuck and four other men, "with one guy pulling a knife and the others making fists and throwing out a few ugly names," before the sound of a distant siren broke up the melee. "We thought the police were going to show up so we ran out after our assailants into the parking lot. But the police never came. Me and the guys were pretty shaken. We talked and smoked cigarettes and, for once, the tension broke and we got to know each other as people. One guy was a married lawyer, another, who I was thought was rough trade, was actually kinda nelly."

Chuck knew that danger was part of the tearoom game, but when he got a taste of real trouble, he fine-tuned his intuition and reduced his nighttime attendance in parks. But he never stopped going completely, even during the five-year period when he went so far as to get engaged to "a real nice Italian girl," who came from a conservative family but who "had a spark in her. . . . She caused a real stir when she went for me instead of another Catholic guy. Truth is, her mother was right. She deserved a helluva lot better than me." During the late '50s and early '60s, he looked for college boys at safer locales, City College, the public tearoom not far from the Central Park Zoo. ("There was too much activity for hoodlums but not enough for the police to make but one or two arrests a year.")

Chuck first learned the art of public sex in tearooms and parks back home, in Illinois. If some men experienced psychological education of the heart, coming out as homosexual after years of getting quick service, Williams limited his education to the refinement of technique. He learned how to hold a dick to ward off a thrust that might cause gagging. He learned how to wait until his "friend" washed his hands and departed before spitting out the cum. (He often knew if people were drinking by the taste of the cum.) He learned that once his hair started to thin, he—a swaggering top—had no choice but to become a "cocksucker" if he wanted action. "The competition," he says, "got brutal right around the time I turned thirty-five."

He also learned that when men had tearoom sex, both parties had to refine their sensation functions, because talking was out of line. If they wanted to slow a man down to prolong sex, or to pull away before the ejaculation so as not to drink the cum, it made sense to use the hands to monitor muscle tension. In this way, Chuck learned how to predict when a man was about to shoot in his mouth.

The best places lurked off the highway. They were easily accessible, easily recognized by those in the know and yet not frequented often by normals—and hardly at all visible to the public. In this way, a tearoom was both a very public setting, and yet, for the homosexual, relatively private. The best provided fast action with just as many men—and as little remorse—as possible.

The sex remained autoerotic and impersonal. Chuck never had a boyfriend. He did feel attached, however, to certain locales. "I felt more fond and sentimental about a specific tearoom," he recalls, "than an individual I met there." Years later, Chuck would read of similar accounts in Laud Humphreys' classic study of the field, *Tearoom Trade*, marveling at how analagous the description of the mating games, sexual techniques, and eye-winks described in Humphreys' sociological work seemed to Chuck's experience. (Humphreys reports in his 1970 book that the basic foot-tapping routine doesn't change much from state to state, nor from tearoom to tearoom.) Just as a woman might express an autoerotic relationship to a man whom she just desired for the purpose of giving her children, gay men like Chuck allowed themselves to become the tool of libido. But this was an advance over many men who simply repressed the cries from the world of instinct.[6]

nettling twins: hunger and contrition

This wrestling match between need and guilt continued from World War II to Stonewall. Men like Chuck Williams and Jim Kepner attest to a confusing world of sexual need and self-loathing twinned like two dark and light brothers. The activists of the period, who called themselves "homophiles," contributed to the psychological split by begging for acceptance. When a psychiatrist told a conference of gay activists that 80 percent of male homosexuals were curable, and the audience booed him, a Mattachine officer scolded the rowdy attendees: "Surely a professional psychiatrist has every right to disapprove of homosexual practices." Men who lived through the '50s describe a vicious and shaming sexual milieu in which a man caught by a cop with his pants down often felt that he deserved the arrest he experienced.[7]

survival tactics

Diary entries from gay New Yorker Donald Vining show a homosexual man living life in some ways very like that of a gay man in the '90s. He experiences a love-hate relationship with his mother and enjoys going to the theater. He suffers classic love problems ("Woke up with a dreadfully empty feeling in my chest, as tho a great hollow had been scooped out, and wondered for a while if I could bear to give Ken up"); deals with the problems intimacy brings to a sexual relationship ("Ken said that sex with me wasn't repulsive but that he had developed an aversion, my word, not his, to it that must be physical"); and worries how to make ends meet[8] ("It seemed that my unhappiness with my job and my unhappiness about the end of my affair with Ken were too much for me to bear at once").[9] What he lacks in gay social venues, he makes up for in beautiful diary writing (his idea, at the time, was to provide positive reinforcement for younger gays). His attitude toward finding sex—at first explosively vital—becomes more objective, jaded:

> Was cruised by a gigantic fellow. I hadn't anything like that in mind at that time but his following and looking put it in my mind. He virtually invited himself home with me, about which I wasn't too enthusiastic because I wasn't sure when Ken would arrive home. He pulled that old corny gag about giving me a massage, which no one has used on me in years. He had really quite depraved tastes, even wanting me to urinate in his mouth.[10]

One-night stands depress him. If the '70s would see the separation of sex from intimacy as an evolution, men of the '50s like Vining see it as a dead end:

> I had a shower as soon as he'd left, then settled down to wait for Ken's return. I'm so tired of sex and so hungry for love, which is ten times more enjoyable. Once I was bored with tributes to my mind and wanted interest in my body. Now I am bored with compliments on my figure, my tan, my genitalia, and want admiration for my character and person.[11]

The answer for Vining doesn't come from the inside, but from adapting oneself to outside concerns: "The answer, I suppose, lies in making myself a pleasant and lovable person just as I worked to make my body muscular, symmetrical and attractive." But given the fact that there is really no viable "outside"—no real community or network outside of park cruising and a small society of friends—one wonders for whom exactly Vining is seeking to change. One callow trick or another? "Gay pride" has hardly yet become a community standard. Caught in a limbo land between "a hollow whole in my chest," and a hit-and-miss social scene, Vining demonstrates the uphill battle gay people faced in finding meaning in a world that considered their simple needs as criminal.

the survival instinct   When life feels difficult and unfriendly, especially in the area of desire, the unconscious produces libido and erotic symbolism as a compensation—a kind of SOS to a person's bad humor, despite efforts at repression. People reach out with a certain drive and communities are formed almost as underground cells. Herb King recalls the Boston of the '50s as a wonderful place to come out, as long as a certain discretion was observed:

> The Napolean was quite a decent place. They had a piano bar and people behaved well. I never went to Sporters. I heard it was a trade bar. There was Parker House, and the Cliff House, a regular hotel with a bar and lounge, and the

Copley Plaza, which was a common situation. I learned that places like the Copley were not exclusively gay but you could see pickups there. If a straight person wandered in by accident, it wouldn't make a difference. People behaved in an appropriate way. You could go there and not realize what was going on.

King lived in the upscale Back Bay. Like gay men in cities throughout America, he negotiated the difference between his public life and private self so that the two finally began to blur:

I had a circle of friends and we had dinner parties and all very tasteful. Some of the people took great pride in culinary art, really putting on a fancy meal, and providing cocktails. That was the casual gay life. A fairly large group of people who knew each other—several dozen people who circulated but who never gathered together at once. It was really social . . . mainly well-educated people with good jobs who lived in nice apartments in Back Bay and Beacon Hill.

One man remembers "a happy-go-lucky time" of bar-hopping in Los Angeles and in Chicago—despite the occasional discrimination he says he suffered for being black. "If you were a clean-cut looking fellow and knew which bars to go to, chances were that you didn't have to spend too many lonely nights at home if you didn't want to." Likewise Scott C. lived with his lover throughout the '50s, cultivating as friends a circle of gay couples who enjoyed fine food, good music, and each other's company.

"My friend and I weren't entirely suburban either," he warns:

We had a couple of bathhouses in L.A. in those days and sometimes he and I went there together to bring a little spice into our life. As much as we were lovers—we did everything with each other, kissing, around the world, you name it—we were also each other's best friends. And we created our life without a hint of the militancy you see these days that can really grate on a person.

Men outside of the major urban centers describe a less easy time being gay and social. One Cleveland man says that "these meeting places existed not so much because we wanted them, of course, but because bar owners knew that we needed them and that they could make high profits selling us liquor":

There was, in fact, gratitude at just having the space where one could relax and be with one's own kind. That curious combination of exploitation and liberation helped define the mood in gay bars then as it does now, though perhaps both elements were more extreme in those days.[12]

He mentions that guys liking rough trade would "sometimes drop in one Mac and Jerry's, not a gay bar, but a hangout of spot-laborer workers and minor hoods." He reports that two murders and many fatal beatings of gays have been traced to those pickup joints, opposite the Cleveland Hotel:

> There were other gay bars in the downtown area during the late 1940s, but most were desperation moves. As the postwar boom faded and the straights got married and moved to the suburbs, downtown bars would "go gay" for a month or two before finally being forced to close.[13]

Despite George Chauncey's claim that the personal cost of passing was minimal for some gay New Yorkers in the years before World War II, many attest to a far more gloomy picture of gay life in those years. "Living in a gay world," rants Cory. "What gay world, and where, and which one? The world of the street corner, or of a special and well-known path in the park, or the lonely and dark street on the breezy lake front, or the banks of a river in one of America's largest cities?"[14] Just walking in a swishy manner could get men busted in the streets of Los Angeles and San Francisco, according to gay archivist Jim Kepner. Bars were subjected to routine police busts. Entrapment awaited men in rest rooms. A sense of paranoia, at best, and self-loathing, at worst, afflicted many gay men. "What kind of life can we have in this room," the main character asks Giovanni in James Baldwin's *Giovanni's Room*, "this filthy little room. What kind of life can two men have anyway?"[15]

discretion is the better part of valor?   Men took pains not to look or act themselves, equating authenticity with punishment or rejection. "You could get arrested, anywhere in the country, for looking gay," recalls Jim Kepner. The charge? Indecent behavior. Kepner recalls a party at an attorney's home being raided by the police with the lawyer arrested on the charge that he wore women's clothing. "He was wearing a shirt that was buttoned the wrong way was all," Kepner recalls. Guilt infiltrated sexual activity:

> I picked up many a guy who insisted that they weren't "that way." They just did this and that because their wife was on the rag and they were horny. And that I usually found to be a total turn off. But if I was caught in bed with them already, I went ahead and did whatever they wanted to do, and I was happy when they left. This one very slender, very prissy sort insisted on the use of condoms. He explained that he didn't want to get a goiter. But he saved the condoms!

Duplicity took its toll. Kepner might pass a man in the street who'd he slept with the night before and the trick would act as if he'd never known Kepner.

"You'd know better," he recollects, "but you'd take the rejection personally." Being in the homophile movement didn't improve matters. "There'd be a movement event and everything would be wonderful and you'd trade names and so on, but then you'd see them at their place of work, and they wouldn't come near you." Kepner recalls that the highest compliment you could pay to another gay in the '50s was to be discreet.

you will meet a stranger

Two youths—one pale-skinned, the other Mediterranean—stroll in opposite directions down New York City's Avenue of the Americas during rush hour. Their sultry, swollen eyes meet, lock for a split second, dart away, then join again. The first man, clearly the younger, slows down his pace. He stops in front of a women's lingerie store, glaring mindlessly at the window display until it occurs to him that he is eyeing a corset.

So he turns on his heels and notices that the other youth is right behind him, nodding his head at the arrangement of bras, as if to suggest, "Not a bad display for Gimbels."

One man asks for the time. Or maybe he says something about the weather. Or he asks for a light. The faces approach as the burning match is cupped to keep out the autumn wind.

Each looks for a word or a sign in the quick interchange. This is the moment of truth. If the fellow is too feminine—well, that's a turnoff. But if he's too macho, that's a sign that sex may not be a possibility. What's needed is a middle ground between effeminacy and straight-acting distance—a suggestion or a mannerism whereby each lets the other know that no trap or cruel ploy is at hand.

"Watcha up to?" asks one man.

"Just taking in some night air," the other answers, repressing the desire to end the statement with the word "doll."

natural opposites

Many gay men remember closeted and secretively coded dialogue as so cruelly imprinted on their natures it never left their systems and ultimately left them feeling great shame. Later, when the '60s brought more bonhomie to openly gay bathhouses and house parties, many felt positively out of place when everyone else let their hair down. "We required so much from those very first words," recalls Scott C. "It wasn't like phone sex these days, where another caller waits on the line if someone hangs up on you. If you found a man who you thought was your type, and he looked nice and safe, you didn't want to fuck it up with too nelly a phrase or too distant an approach. You didn't want to look desperate, but neither did you want to look too cool so as to be mistaken for a cop or trade."

This is how Cory comments on a similar interchange, where, through a code word or a mannerism, the ice has been broken:

> The word *has been uttered, and the rapport has now been established. From that moment on, there is no doubt as to the direction of the evening. They stop at a bar for a glass of beer, and there we shall leave them. Back to the street we go, while they make their way to an evening of adventure. Adventure? Pleasure? Happiness? It would not be at all unusual if, many hours later, one of these youths might fall asleep in the stranger's bed, happy as he thinks of the partner at his side, and contented with the release from the tension that had gripped him. He had enjoyed the moments after sex as much as the moments during the heights of passion; and in sleep he finds a restful satisfaction.*

These men are the lucky ones. The orgasmic bliss and subsequent cuddling bring an almost infantile satisfaction—long overdue. "It was as if one were reunited with the World Parents, a kind of primal Adam and Eve," recalls a veteran of the '50s who hungered for any opportunity not so much "to suck off a man, but to hold him as he slept afterwards."

Luck, however, did not always win out over Fate. Most of the time, the sexual experience, if it was drawn out for more than a few minutes, split into emotional opposites.[16] The trick was both beautiful and balding; he slept like a baby and he snored; he was too clingy by night yet so withdrawn by day. The fairy tale of Beauty and the Beast took on a new level of pathos when the men were not just gay, but closeted:

> But it would be not at all unusual, at the same time, if the partner were to rise, cleanse himself with care and shake his head as he sees his image in the mirror. He would lock his watch and wallet in a desk drawer, hide the key, and creep into bed, burdened by a guilt that, within him, always follows sex. Only the hospitality demanded of the host, only the wish not to hurt the other as he himself had often been hurt, might restrain him from awakening his companion and asking him to leave.[17]

Given the wobbly social condition in which gay men hunted for love and sex, some were not able to easily integrate the organic opposites that naturally make up any powerful sexual and romantic experience.[18] Most of the time, men from the '50s say they blamed themselves or their tricks for the negative feelings that popped up after sex. These resulted in a sour mood, a feeling of annoyance, a desire to be suddenly alone. For this reason, the sexual act that did *not* take much time was valued over the one that did. Apart from the obvious practical purposes—invasion from law enforcement, harassment by thugs—brevity served a psychological purpose. "Quickies" kept the emotional highs and lows from overwhelming a person. Gay men had no tools, psychological or otherwise, to make sense of the opposites. One was less likely to crash in a fit of disappointment in a tearoom than one's bedroom, where so much more was at stake.

For this reason, public rest stops and street corners provided the community setting homosexuals, whether married or not, needed without too great a risk of rejection or exposure. "While the agreements resulting in 'one-night-stands' occur in many settings," writes Evelyn Hooker, one of the first psychologists to conclude that there was no connection between homosexuality and psychopathology, "the bath, the street, the public toilet—and may vary greatly in the elaborateness or simplicity of the interaction preceding culmination in the sexual act, their essential feature is the expectation that sex can be had without obligation or commitment."[19] The tearoom provided the best venues for what sociologist Laud Humphreys called "instant sex."[20]

cold war, cold hearts

It was the height of the cold war, a time when the Soviet Union had the A-Bomb (presumably because of United States spies), a time when a little-known senator from Wisconsin—Joseph R. McCarthy—scapegoated gays and communists as leading to the downfall of the country, a time when no homosexual man in his right mind made gay waves. Queers, especially those in the State Department, were seen as a security risk no less threatening than the red menace. "Already believed to be morally enfeebled by sexual indulgence," write historians D'Emilio and Freedman, "homosexuals would readily succumb to the blandishments of the spy and betray their country rather than risk exposure of their sexual identity."[21]

Inflammatory remarks against the "enemy within" caught on around the country. In 1950, the Senate authorized an inquiry into the governmental jobs of homosexuals and other "sex perverts." The 81st Congress Senate Document proclaimed that "the lack of emotional stability which is found in most sex perverts and the weakness of their moral fiber, makes them susceptible to the blandishments of the foreign espionage agent."[22] The report used language—"One homosexual can pollute a government office"—that reminded some gay World War II veterans of Nazi propaganda.

The situation went downhill. Gay witch-hunts took place in many federal departments. The post office monitored those men who ordered physique magazines in the mail (and did so until 1966). The 1953 executive order barring gay men and lesbians from all federal jobs—as well as the gay-baiting McCarthy hearings of 1954—sent the message that homosexuals deserved no protection from the government.[23]

Even heterosexuals suffered backlash. Some of the sexual innovations that came from the rise of coeducational institutions persisted. And the experiments in dating and petting that the car and the drive-in provided also continued apace. But the unprecedented opportunities for premarital heterosexual sex provided by World War II—the move to cities, fresh economic freedoms, the lessening of adult supervision, the rise of professional vocations for women—reached a peak around 1945 and began tapering off. As Kinsey noted in his 1948 study, American couples of the '50s were having sex less often than their parents.[24]

This stigmatizing of homosexuals as depraved national security risks trickled down to all levels of the social system. The emergence of bars and cruising areas for the large numbers of gays liberated by the war only made gay men more obvious and therefore vulnerable to vicious attacks by the police. A Kinsey Institute survey showed that 20 percent of the homosexual respondents reported serious trouble with law enforcement. Middle-class white America, experiencing prosperity, dared not look below the surface of suburban calm, perhaps because they intuited trouble ahead. Anyone who seemed guilty of exposing the hotbed of racial dissatisfaction, sexual ambiguity, and intellectual boredom that threatened to pierce the veneer of penny loafers and Dinah Shore songs faced punishment.[25]

a crippled feeling function

Sexually speaking, men learned how to make the most of the limitations. With no phone lines, bulletin boards, classified ads, or magazines, they had but few options. Some men sought more than sex, looking for companionship, conversation, and romance. But the full emotional dimension of the rising libido could not be trusted. "A person cannot live in an atmosphere of universal rejection, of widespread pretense," writes Cory, "of a society that outlaws and banishes his activities and desires, of a social world that jokes and sneers at every turn, without a fundamental influence on his personality."[26]

Shame made one man kick tricks out of his YMCA room as soon as they climaxed. A nagging voice made another unable to sleep with even the most ravishing of hustlers. A fear of the police barging into his hotel room and stealing his "black book" made one man burn the addresses of homosexual lovers and friends he had known for over a decade. Suburban propriety made one Long Island man call an annoying man he met at a bar one night, "Miss Mattachine."

One man explains his neurotic self-division this way: "It was as if I was besieged by two different and yet opposing voices every time I went out looking for a man to have sex with. On one hand, there was a nagging internal voice telling me what a cheap slut I was pursuing some young boy. And on the other, there was another voice telling me that the man I was pursuing wasn't good enough for me, that I could 'do better.'"

No wonder he spent many nights home alone.

The feeling function of most American men had been squashed by American life. While the overemphasis of masculine proficiency reached its peak during World War II, most men in the '50s adhered to the old Christian myth. The surfaces of suburban life offered no escape from the dying American Empire; so the fact of its dying was covered up. In the late nineteenth century, Victorian women came to Sigmund Freud with neurological ailments that revealed a psychological cause: the sexual life force had been driven underground in a world of symptoms. When they free-associated, these women revealed sexual "wishes" and the defenses that imprisoned them. Gay men must be seen as the inheritors of this madness, for their inner feeling function had been rendered dysfunctional too. And they had no one to talk to. For psychiatry pathologized them. A new system of emotional valuing, ready to explode in the '60s, had not yet become apparent. Sissy men were suspect. They reminded heterosexual men of their own unexplored yet dynamic inferior functions: their feeling function and their inner femininity. These areas had been so violently repressed that they loaded up with energy in a shadow area. Instead of being integrated, this demonic shadow, as is the case with anything unconscious, was projected—in this case—onto the loathsome homosexual.

To make matters worse, homosexual men were not immune to the effects of their own crushed feeling function. Despite the mythos attached to some homosexual men about being more sensitive than straights, very few were able to do more with their hurt feelings than snuff them out. "Most of the time," recalls one man, "we took our hurt out on each other. I don't mean to give drag queens a hard time—for about six months I was one myself—but a lot of us needed an outlet for bitchiness. We made the *Boys in the Band* look tame by comparison."

In fact, gay people were at a terrible disadvantage in navigating the treacherous world of feelings, due in part to the way in which feelings of sin, sickness, and criminality were so internalized. So to begin to feel at all, one felt shame—unbearable! Worse yet, the tools psychologists discovered for encouraging people to look inside were being used against gay people by antigay shrinks. In 1962, Dr. Irving Bieber published a well-publicized report that homosexuality was an acquired illness that could be cured. In 1964, the New York Academy of Medicine confirmed that view. The emergence of "gay and proud" psychologists in the '70s, such as the pioneer Don Clark, allowed gays to separate internalized homophobia from desire, a process a few militants had begun in the '60s.

Because there was so little psychological valuing of the symbolic place of longing and need, a community of homosexual men began to make objective "scoring" into a high art. For gays believing in society's "Myth of the Homosexual" (i.e., that the homosexual was nothing by a sexual classification), libido became understood as an objective "act" rather than a subjective "feeling." This was a necessary stage in the evolution of gay consciousness for it at least allowed men to gather erotically. It also marked a limitation. This strategy did not address with any dignity the repressed functions hiding away in the unconscious. That the inferior function might figure as *the* source of creativity is a paradox gay culture would not be able to entertain until it had exhausted itself in more extroverted ways.

sex leads one man into ethics

Born in England in 1912, Harry Hay was raised by American parents in Los Angeles. A respected Marxist teacher, Native American–rights activist, musicologist, a married family man and actor (he and Will Geer were an item in the '30s), Hay did not see anything wrong with eyeing a handsome man in the moonlight and necking with him behind some bushes. But it began occurring to him that he could not longer compartmentalize his homo eros. Rather, it ran up and down his body and mind as if it were the whole—or the center—of who he was. True, he was married, so a certain level of secrecy was in order. But the Kinsey Report, which had just come out, suggested that 37 percent of adult men had had some form of homosexual sex as adults. This figure implied a minority who could be organized for political action, especially to help elect Henry Wallace, who was running for presidency on the Progressive ticket.

Hay, a consummate extrovert, thought that there must be a way to translate this centering force of homosexual desire into a political statement. To Hay's mind, homosexuals conformed to two of Stalin's principles of a minority—they shared the same language and culture—and he called his new group "International Bachelors Fraternal Order for Peace & Social Dignity." He appealed to higher levels of law than that of the state for fair treatment. ("The idea of reassessing ourselves by a more modern and humane standard of law was the logical approach," he'd say in retrospect.) But despite Hay's groundbreaking desire for unprecedented political involvement, the text of his "call" shows how much internalized distrust even gay visionaries like Harry Hay had to overcome:

> WE, THE ANDROGYNE OF THE WORLD, HAVE FORMED THIS RESPONSIBLE CORPORATE BODY TO DEMONSTRATE BY OUR EFFORTS THAT OUR PHYSIOLOGICAL AND PSYCHOLOGICAL HANDICAPS NEED BE NO DETERRENT IN INTEGRATING 10% OF THE WORLD'S POPULATION TOWARD THE CONSTRUCTIVE SOCIAL PROGRESS OF MANKIND.[27]

Beginning with a group of five men, Mattachine began as an attempt to create a "highly ethical homosexual culture" and proved itself the first successful attempt to organize homosexuals politically in America. Hay adapted the name from *Les sociétés joyeuses*, a medieval group of itinerant French dancers who dressed in masque as women and did not marry. The name of the society suggested that a refined homosexual culture, however suppressed and implicit, flourished just at the time two important Western myths—the Holy Grail and Tristan and Isolde—fomented the new spiritual and romantic freedoms being enjoyed by individuals.

Hay asked provocative philosophical questions at a time when no safe identity for homosexuals existed: "Who are gay people? Where have we been in history? What might we be here for?" The organizing took place at the height of McCarthyism, and Hay worried that one wrong move might jeopardize the movement for years to come. As Hay explains it, "We were speaking the dream of marvelous brotherhood . . . but we were still being rather amorphous and indefinite." The Mattachine Society was essentially a series of what would be called consciousness-raising groups. "We were talking about the right of self-respect and to appreciate that we are a strong, not a weak people," he recalls, "that a sissy means a stubborn person who's put up with an awful lot. A lot of people were saying, 'My God, I never thought of that.'"

Out of such conversations emerged an analysis of homosexuals as an oppressed cultural minority. Mattachine members asked themselves whether or not homosexuality was a psychopathology because they could not help but notice that so many of their friends and associates seemed disturbed. They decided that the imposition of the "heterosexual ethic" on the homosexual person to force "empty imitation" resulted in "self-deceit, hypocrisy" and a sense of being "disturbed, inadequate and undesirable." The chief problem was that most homosexuals seemed unaware that they constituted a "social minority imprisoned within a dominant culture."

To protect the Mattachines, Hay conceived of an official front: to foster public dialogue of concerned citizens, based on the 1948 Kinsey Report that 20 million homosexuals existed in the country. Unofficially, gays were identified covertly and separated into subgroups of ten, to ensure that no individual knew the identities of more than ten others should there be a police raid.

With its cell-like structure, the organization was so underground that people like Harry Hay remained virtually anonymous. But the desire for more public events could not be stifled. "The 1950s was the decade of the 'organization man,'" writes Michael Bronski, in analyzing why the homophile movement took off. "This was as true for homosexuals as heterosexuals. By organizing and defining themselves, homosexuals reassured straight people terrified by the *Kinsey Report*: they were visible. Clearly recognizable homosexuals implicitly guaranteed the boundaries of heterosexuality." In 1951, Mattachine hosted a "community" public dance. Hay recalls four street toughs standing in the doorway, weeping at the sight of sixty men waltzing together.[28]

The notion of being a well-adjusted homosexual was unheard of. "Even those of us who felt halfway at home with loving men understood that we were psychologically handicapped," explains Kepner. "We were not ready to believe we were normal without the support of psychologists, who were mostly against us. At the very most, we agreed that one day we ought to pull ourselves up by our bootstraps and get married to a woman."[29]

harlem is gay

As historian Barbara Smith tells it, black gays and lesbians have been the unacknowledged leaders of gay liberation and culture. One has but to look at the main players of the Stonewall Rebellion, or the Harlem Renaissance, to see the role women and men of color have played in trying to unlock the vise-grip of attitudes that sees gays, women, and people of color as "other" or "subhuman." The obstacles to creating a homosexual identity from the mass of resistances and compressed unconscious particles was formidable. The Harlem Renaissance did much to differentiate new cultural and sexual energies around homosexuality. It is unlikely that the Stonewall Riots could have mattered as much without the work of Langston Hughes, Bessie Smith, Richard Bruce Nugent, Countee Cullen, or other gay trailblazers of Jazz Age Harlem.

The combination of minority sexual identity with outside racial status had explosive effects on artistic creation and sexual expression. Social historian Michael Bronski attributes great power to the role black blues and jazz played in the formation of a gay identity: "A black woman singing about unhappiness in love with the consciousness that she was outcast because of her race, was sure to attract the attention and empathy of gay men."[30]

in the life　The histories of white gay sexual liberation and black gay sexual liberation don't occupy the same time lines.[31] If white gay men had to leave their native cities to become gay, many black gays did the opposite and stayed close to home. "I was real nelly in my family," says a man who grew up in Atlanta in the '50s and never left:

> There was no question that I wasn't one of the boys and that I would grow up a bachelor. I was my grandmother's favorite and no one bothered me. Once when I was caught playing doctor with another twelve-year-old, my mother shrugged and, talking to God, said "Lord, you work in mysterious ways." She shooed my friend home, but no mention was made of the event. I never came out to my family per se but I have never lied. I've had two long-term lovers in my life, very butch, masculine men, mind you, and each was included as part of the family during holidays and weddings and funerals and such. I don't talk about my lifestyle, but I think I got a better deal than some of my white friends who have no relationship to their parents. My father, a generally silent man, was, until his death in the late '70s, nothing but a gentleman to me.

For an elderly black gay man, bohemianism and homosexuality went together like cheese and crackers during the Harlem Renaissance literary moment of the 1920s. A migration of Southern blacks before, during, and after World War I made Harlem into the most populous African American community in the United States. By the Roaring Twenties, Harlem became a cultural center of black American music, literature, and art—and homosexuality.

Drag balls rocked the Savoy ballroom. Gladys Bentley impersonated a man at Harry Hansberry's Clam House. A speakeasy on 126th Street and Seventh Avenue attracted both rough trade and men who "swished better than Mae West." Apartments were converted into sex clubs. Fairly nonjudgmental articles on homosexuality appeared in black publications. A look at a few song titles from the

'20s show some overt homosexual references: George Hannah's "The Boy in the Boat," Bessie Jackson's "BD Women's Blues." Most of the major players of the Harlem Renaissance—Langston Hughes, Countee Cullen, Claude McKay, Richard Bruce Nugent, and Alan Locke, to name a few—were either gay or bisexual.[31]

The Harlem Renaissance, as well as the black civil rights movement, gave gay liberation its moral footing. Many of the early GLFers identified more strongly with Malcolm X than they did with any single homophile leader. During the pre–World War II years, an elaborate network of black gay culture had developed in more identifiable ways than white gay culture.[32] "Let me tell you," describes Ira L. Jeffries, who came out in Harlem in the 1940s, "Harlem's lesbian and gay community was *thriving* until certain white business men realized the money we generated and wanted to tap into it. Starting in the 1960s, our clubs were either systematically closed or mysteriously burned down. Finally, there was nothing left, so we were all forced go to downtown."[33]

am i the only asian gay man in the world?

Dean Goishi grew up in a sheltered Japanese American rural community in central California. Achieving in school and developing trustworthy friends overshadowed the need to satisfy the most private of homosexual feelings flourishing like a dream in his imagination. Unlike many Christian families, Goishi's Buddhist family never used spirituality to condemn either the flesh or homosexuality. On the other hand, sex was rarely broached. His mother, all the same, did promote a certain progressive line. When he got accepted to Berkeley in 1961, she told him not to think all his learning was going to take place in the classroom. Little did she know how she blessed his sentimental education.

In his freshman year, the thought did dawn on him, "I am gay, I would like to find men." But how to proceed? A college counselor did nothing to point him in the right direction of new friends, responding to Goishi's need for direct answers with "nebulous and subjective" psychological theories that sought to obscure the keen charge in his loins. He found appreciation at a burlesque theater in San Francisco. But if he was looking for naked men, he must have felt disappointed. "I loved watching the women striptease," he said, "from an artistic standpoint, that is." The Burlesque adventure did, however, open his eyes to the fact that San Francisco had already earned its reputation as Sodom by the Sea. Walking around one bar "located on the nicer side of Polk Street" over and over again until his feet ached, he found the courage to take the dive:

I can't remember if the jam-packed place was called Pink Cloud or Cloud 9 but what I do recall is that I was the only Asian. The place was totally white. I don't remember feeling as if that situation was wrong—I didn't have that conscious- ness then. But I do remember feeling that I did not receive a lot of attention in those places. I was 5'4" and I was not at all assertive. If someone didn't approach me, I would usually go home alone. I didn't mind that. I went to these places to relax, to be with other men, to learn about the gay world and, then, if I were lucky to have sex. I saw immediately what I liked: rugged men, blue collar men, men who lived in the outdoors, blond men and men who were taller with a lot of facial hair and chest hair. Someone who could smother me. We have a word for this masculinity in Japanese. It's Otoko Rashi. I suppose I also became some- thing of a size queen. I also found myself mysteriously drawn to the leather bars: The Ramrod and FeBes. I never liked S&M, but I did love passing the time at a leather bar. I saw the experience—the beer drinking, the conversation, the groping, the chatting, the camaraderie—as stress reduction. The idea of being around a group of men who had let down their facades was just so liberating, so new. I never once felt at all bad about being gay, although I do remember not feeling very attractive. I suppose I had poor self-esteem in those days and I also suppose that it was difficult in those days to pick up a man who wanted an Asian partner. I used to wonder if I was the only gay Asian in the world. I knew it couldn't be true, but I saw no signs.

That would change, in part due to Goishi's efforts in helping to create a vi- brant political gay Asian community in Los Angeles in years to come. For now, circa 1962, Goishi found himself a pioneer. And for two reasons. He was gay in a newly emerging gay community and he was Asian during a time before Asian gays organized to empower themselves in a sea of white racism. He also had to battle many of his own internalized feelings that the only way to be gay was to be feminine: "Take the passive side in the sexual relationships, do flower arrange- ments, play the Koto." As he explains it, gay men *are* accepted in some Asian cul- tures as long as they allow themselves not to claim masculine privilege. Then they are dismissed as "can't be helped."

Goishi instead, like most gays of the '50s, compartmentalized his gayness. By day, he made good money in insurance and passed. By night, he trekked down to Folsom Street to the Levi and leather bars. "I was neither homosexual nor heterosexual," he says. He joined ROTC and became an officer, serving in South Korea. On his return back to San Francisco, he resumed his life of picking people up at the baths, once or twice taking someone home, and making a good living by day. "Sex was the primary objective in the '70s," he recalls. "It never occurred to me that I should live with another man. I loved to be thinking that I am the person who is going to get this person off," he recalls. "I always liked taking the passive role, and actually found that I didn't like, at the time, sucking or getting fucked. I preferred a kind of intense physical contact, a kind of rolling around." It wasn't till a move to Seattle that he developed the "emotional maturity," to see that "some of the men who were interested in me sexually wanted to become lovers. I suppose we were all reacting from the intense secrecy of the '50s."

"gay is very american"

No history of sexual attitudes in America can overlook the role race played in establishing systems of segregation and repression. Nor can it minimize the influence native cultures had on sexual growth and transformation. Lesbian author Judy Grahn makes a case that America is a "gay" country because the people who lived here originally honored same-sex unions as divinely ordained.[34]

There is plenty of evidence from a variety of observers—missionaries, explorers, trappers, traders, settlers, and anthropologists—that some Native American tribes did not share the European disgust for sodomy. Although the reportage is contaminated by Western biases, the accounts demonstrate that Native people were not presumptuous enough to shame natural impulses. "The sin of sodomy prevails more among them than in any other nation," writes Pierre Liette after a four-year sojourn in Chicago in 1702, "although there are four women to one man. . . . There are men who are bred for this purpose from their childhood."[35]

In other words, the boy who goes to a doll, instead of the toy machine gun, is seen as having a few extra spirits in his life:

> When they [the effeminate boys] are seen frequently picking up the spade, the spindle, the axe, but making no use of the bow and arrows, as all the other small boys do, they are girt with a piece of leather or cloth which envelops them from the belt to the knees, a thing all the women wear. Their hair is allowed to grow and is fastened behind the head. They also wear a little skin like a shoulder strap passing under the arm on one side and tied over the shoulder on the other. They are tattooed on their cheeks like the women and also on the breast and the arms, and they imitate their accent, which is different from that of the men.[36]

In the report of Spanish explorer Cabeza de Vaca's five-year captivity among the Indians of Florida from 1528 to 1533, he saw enough to flip his skirt: "During the time that I was thus among these people I saw a devilish thing, and it is that I saw one man married to another. . . ."[37] He seems unhinged by the Indian way of integrating the unusual: a person has a few more spirits, that's all. In other words, as Grahn points out, when the spirits, through dreams and visions, tell a person to marry a person of the same sex, it would be a breach of culture and spirituality not to do so.[38] "Although sexuality might be embedded within a spiritual context," write D'Emilio and Freedman, "as in the case of puberty rituals, menstrual seclusion, or the visionary call to cross-dress—sexual intercourse and reproductive functions rarely evoked shame or guilt for Indian men or women."[39]

For this acceptance of premarital intercourse, polygamy, or institutionalized homosexuality, native tribes were decimated. Walter Williams, author of *The Spirit and the Flesh*, shows how the sadistic Spanish conquistadors of the sixteenth century used the fact that the indigenous people engaged in sodomy as rationale for genocide. Nineteenth-century artist George Catlin, who lived among the Native Americans, describes the "Dance to the Berdashe," as a funny and amusing scene:

> which happens once a year or oftener, as they chose, when a feast is given to the "Berdashe," as he is called in French (or I-coo-coo-a, in their own language), who is a man dressed in woman's clothes, as he is known to be all his life, and for extraordinary privileges which he is known to possess, he is driven to the most servile and degrading duties, which he is not allowed to escape. . . . It is looked upon as medicine and sacred.[40]

During the initiation, a few young men of the tribe dance toward him and make their sexual moves. Catlin found the ritual disgusting and hoped it would be extinguished before too long. He didn't have to wait long at all.

gay meccas import straight racism

Race provided a pivot on which the history of sexual regulation turned. White segregationists concerned themselves with issues related to marriage and procreation; between 1907 and 1917, more than a dozen states passed laws that would prevent reproduction of those deemed as undesirable. "Jim Crow," a highly elaborate legal and cultural system of social segregation that gave blacks a pariah-like caste status, was meant to keep white women from black men. It didn't help sweeten relations between gay men of different races either. "For us black gays," explained one African American New Yorker now in his sixties, "either a deep fear of the mixing of races or a deep attraction around it colored, as it were, all of our interchanges. It made any kind of objective seeing of each other next to impossible, which of course, became altogether exhausting if you wanted to do something else besides educate or mollify."

exchange rates

Underscoring the profound color line cleaving the gay world in two, the gay-specific physical culture magazines that sprouted up in the '50s depicted exclusively white athletes and models. They also revealed the rigid class lines most Americans, whatever their orientation, preferred denying. The average model, for example, received from five dollars to a hundred, depending on his so-called skills. "Besides the obvious exceptions," reports Clark P. Polak, in what seems like the first review of physique photography in a 1965 volume of the magazine *Drum*, "models are from lower socio-economic levels." Men from this stratum are considered more sexually flexible—less defended by middle-class mores and education. Most insist that the rationale for becoming a "cover boy" is the money.

"It was a heady experience seeing my pictures plastered wherever I went," recalls one ex-star. "But I still told myself I was doing it for the money. Now that I have a stable of young bucks and my personal posing days are over, I realize the money was the least of it."[41]

strength and health

A scan through some of the erotic literature and film and video pornography over the last seventy years shows that while the basic repertory of sexual behaviors don't change, the attitudes do. Drag acts as a key element in erotic art films and documentaries from the '20s to the '60s (*Flaming Creatures*, *The Queen*). But the drag queen is absent from the porn of the '70s—that is, unless you want to consider the well-oiled Joe Gage in *Kansas City Trucking* a kind of butch drag.[42]

In the stag and porn films before 1940, sexual passes between men are mostly contained within straight films. In *Picolo Pete* (1935) and *Monkey Business* (1935), it's okay for a stud to help a buddy out as long as a girl lingers nearby. Other films incorporate active anal sex as part of an authoritarian world, where discipline and penetration are interchangeable. In *The Exclusive Sailor* (1923), for example, a man and a woman are caught having sex by an officer, who demands to fuck them both as punishment.

But it's mostly static pictures, not moving ones, that galvanized homosexual men before the '60s. With magazines becoming the first visual mass medium in the nineteenth century, editors saw that pictures sell well. In the early teens, rising wages and a shrinking work week gave men more time for sports. In this climate, men's magazines flourished. Some publications narrowed their categories from sports publications to body building magazines. Two former "male beauty pageant" winners, Charles Atlas and Joe Wieder, devoted themselves to "building up the muscles of the young of the world." By 1965, total sales of physique magazines were estimated at nine million a year, a large portion of these subscribers no doubt gay.[43]

Gay entrepreneurs saw a vacuum and a niche. "Homosexuals masturbate more than any other group of males," argues one editor of a muscle magazine, "and physique inspired phantasies contribute a large measure to this satisfaction."[44] By the mid-'60s, only a few magazines—*Drum*, *The Vikings*, *The Young Physique*, and *Muscle Boy*—specifically addressed homosexual readers. The editors of *Drum* prided themselves on bringing artistic panache together with gay eros:

> The most that can be said for [the body building publication] Tomorrow's Man *is that it is never offensive.* Physique Pictorial, *reputedly the magazine with the largest circulation, substitutes generous gobs of sado-masochistic text and illustrations for exposed genitalia, but rarely publishes a notable picture.*[45]

Few photographers can lay as much claim to boosting gay consciousness as Bob Mizer, a young amateur Hollywood photographer. He took pity on all the Errol Flynn wannabes and formed an agency, The Athletic Model Guild. He used his family garage as AMG Central, where he took photos and created résumés. Men stripped gladly for Mizer, especially the street punks. Taking out ads for his work, Mizer had no lack of customers by 1948 (the year the post office began to censor mail-order advertisements). He solved the problem by creating a magazine of his own, *Physique Pictorial*. Some of the covers, painted by Quaintance, show an image of archetypal, even daemonic, male eros no one could have possibly understood at the time. (In one painting, two loin-clothed indigenous-style men are laying prostrate side-by-side with blood-dripping arrows in their backs. In the foreground glows a mandala in which a warrior man is bound by his legs to a bright sun.)

What made Mizer's work so stunning was his lack of shame about loving male beauty. Previously, well-oiled lads may have been gorgeous, but their job was to sell soap or vegetable juice. Now there was nothing to sell. "These images celebrated the male body with a directness that had not been seen since the collapse of the Roman Empire."[46] Such boldness took courage. Obscenity laws and post office surveillance made the physique art militantly vanilla.

Despite the intellectual content of *One*, a magazine that grew out of the homophile movement, it had a painfully small readership. (*Physique Pictorial* and *Tomorrow's Man* sold over 40,000 copies each per issue all around the country. *One* magazine reached a top circulation of 3,500, mostly in New York, San Francisco, and Los Angeles.) Mizer's magazines, and those that followed, such as Joe Wieder's *Adonis* in 1954, were really the first magazines whose images let gay men know their desire for other men was shared by others. These magazines helped closeted gays feel less alone in an alien world, less ashamed of their attraction, in part because the men were so exquisite.[47]

Images from the late '50s and early '60s show young guys clowning around in the most innocent of ways ("It's like they took this white skinny kid, put a windbreaker on him, and posed him in Reseda," comments one vintage porn aficionado). Later on, the men look more tough. The Athletic Model Guild grew famous for its images of young, tattooed, leather-booted, motorcycle Jimmy Dean-clones. In retrospect, the images conjure a mythic age of innocence where being gay was implicit.[48]

fireworks on demand

Shuttling from one antigay shrink to another, driven to compensate for his lonely hunger for another man's touch by overachieving in his academic career, Martin Duberman found an outlet at Times Square hustler bars. It gave him the immediate gratification he desired ("Unfit for intimacy? Okay, let's go for fireworks instead") as well as a certain superiority and entitlement ("Let's get that excitement *now* and on my terms"). And, for once, in a world where looks rivaled cash in importance, he felt handsome. He describes his experience this way in his autobiography, *Cures:*

> I could even guarantee [in a hustler bar], as I could not in a gay bar, that I would be a star attraction; my youthful good looks in startling contrast to the other patrons, the odds were high that I would be noticed and courted. For someone who liked controlling attention and writing the script, who lusted after straight-seeming, butch young men but hated wasting time wooing them, the cash-and-carry ethic of a hustler bar had a persuasive appeal.[49]

Duberman doesn't act immediately on his impulses. He has good reason to be wary. His antigay shrinks had filled him up with doubt about his crushes. Also, he had the police to fear. He recalls one situation where a member of a foreign delegation to the U.N. was arrested by a cop posing as trade.

Eventually Duberman gets up his courage at the Wagon Wheel and, as he recounts in *Cures*, meets an eighteen-year-old "struggling artist" who takes Duberman's breath away: "Since physical culture was not in the sixties an established art form, I couldn't imagine at which temple of the imagination this astonishing-looking young man burned his devotional candles." Duberman got lucky with this hustler, who seemed more giving than most: "He had, quite simply, the most perfectly proportioned body I had ever seen, and he used it with an uninhibited passion rare in someone so beautiful." But the young creative genius was soon to leave Duberman's side and become a famous public figure. And Duberman found himself almost addicted to paying for love for "one wounded, tender man," after another.[50]

But despite the transactional quality to the affair, or perhaps because of it, a sweet intimacy seeped in:

> When I met him, Ned had been hanging out in the Port Authority men's room turning five-dollar tricks; after we met, Ned went right on turning tricks, in bathrooms and out of them. Fond though we grew of each other, we never talked the language of love or entertained anything like the notion of a commitment. Even I, a born romantic, knew truly terrible odds when I saw them, and I was able to resist Ned's periodic urging that I let him move in with me. But we did see each other fairly often, and over time Ned began to confide in me.[51]

The string of affairs ended in 1968, with Duberman's negative review in *Partisan Review* of Mart Crowley's *Boys in the Band*.[52] Duberman, while head over heels for one lying loser of a hustler, objected to Crowley's play, which showed the extent of duplicity by intelligent men caught in the double bind of desire and shame, for romanticizing the "unlucky hand" Fate had dealt homosexuals; he disliked the way in which Crowley celebrated the bravery and wit shown by the Boys. He thought the play dangerous because it would "help to confirm homosexuals in the belief that theirs is merely a different not a lesser way."[53]

shirking the shrinks   Duberman would one day repudiate the review as a "ferocious attack on my own humanity." No doubt about it: the climate of the times made him into a man more sinned against than sinning. He tried everything to change himself ("Unlikely to admit, even to myself, my lack of lust for women, I kept trying to substitute will power").[54] But his high-octane libido would win the day ("Then, in my junior year, drunk and desperate, I groped another equally drunk twenty-year-old outside a fraternity house—and barely escaped a nasty fight"). Like many men of his class and upbringing, he sought relief from his homosexuality in many years of relentless Freudian psychotherapy geared toward making him straight. His book *Cures* stands as a robust attack on the perverted psychology of the time that failed to see homo eros as anything but pathological and "narcissistic." The autobiography makes essential reading for anyone at all curious why the gay movement distrusts authority, and why, despite the twelve-step lingo one often hears in gay ghettoes, many gays remain skeptical of psychological thinking as a way of making meaning out of gay life.

The bias against psychology, which was also a bias against too much self-exploration, shows how little maneuvering ground gays had to explore the mid-point between sex and identity. The only behavior "The Myth of the Homosexual" permitted gays was quick sex, which both accelerated the development of a movement (because it did bring people together) and also tended to overload sex with importance. "For homosexual couples," writes Duberman, "social values serve further to underscore, rather than counteract, interpersonal difficulties; being called 'sick' and 'degenerate' hardly gives one the needed psychic support for sustaining a relationship."

Gays were so oppressed that they dared not acknowledge the oppression. To admit to self-hatred was to be overwhelmed by it. To admit to dick-lust was to be a slave to it. If they had sex, they felt "loose." If they didn't have sex, they felt "uptight."

Here, for example, is a wrenching account of the first time Duberman heard that a "large park abutting the Yale campus" acted as a hangout for fairies:

> That very same night, having gotten myself so drunk I felt conveniently mud-dled, I headed toward the Green. It was dark and looked empty, but as my eye-balls focused, I saw a very fat, middle-aged black man sitting quietly on a bench. I sat down on the empty bench opposite him. After a minute or two, he started whistling softly, tantalizingly in my direction. Fueled by liquor, I got up, reeled my way over, and stood boldly in front of him. He started playing with my cock, then took it out of my pants. Wildly excited, I started to fondle him.[55]

Duberman asks the man if he has a place the two can go when they hear laughter coming from undergraduates. Hysterical and ashamed, Duberman flees back to his dorm room: "I stayed in the shower for hours, cleaning, cleaning. I actually washed my mouth out with soap, though I hadn't used my mouth—other than a prayerful pact with God that if He let me off this time, I'd never, *never* go near the Green again."

god's opposites

If Duberman represents a man caught between the past and the present, a predicament that would eventually make Duberman into a visionary scholar of gay letters, Allen Ginsberg stands for those who put their bottom dollar on the future. And as such, he is more of a prophet than a historian.

So a nebbish Jewish intellectual from New Jersey with a paranoid schizophrenic for a mother and a overbearing lefty for a father was able to arrive at the campus of Columbia College and, by force of his personality, woo Jack Kerouac,

William Burroughs, and Neal Cassady. Ginsberg convinced them to join a movement dedicated to "A New Vision." He learned how to write in a pedestrian way, abandoning, with the encouragement of famed poet William Carlos Williams, meter and rhyme, and digging up phrases from old journals, cutting them into thirds, bringing a new argot to cultural life that had biblical, Faustian, Jobian, gnostic, and Dionysian sweeps.

Throughout the '50s, Ginsberg became a nerdy gay Anthropos, a Primal Gay Man who was also a Primal Doormat for the straight male god. With the mixing and matching of drugs, sex, cosmic thinking, and homo eros, he both foreshadowed the '60s and conjured them. Of course, the times—the straight Stanley Kowalski-football types for whom he fell—didn't allow him easy revelry. He was not always fulfilled. "If you want to know my true nature," he wrote to Kerouac, "I am at the moment one of those people who goes around showing his cock to juvenile delinquents." As biographer Barry Miles puts it:

> This was the winter when Allen became "more actively queer," trying to drown out the memory of Neal [Cassady] by haunting the gay bars in Greenwich Village and Times Square and on Seventy-second Street. It was while he was living on West Twenty-seventh Street that he was sometimes able to persuade Kerouac to have sex: "I remember one particular time, he was high on Benzedrine and so extremely horny, as you get with Benzedrine, but at the same time, he couldn't come for a long while. One time there, he blew me."[56]

In 1948, a few years before the libidinal gold rushes and shadow-laden prophetic rants of the epic poem *Howl* established Ginsberg as a queer-visionary with "a lot of new mind and eyeball kicks," Ginsberg had a mystical, initiatory experience with the opposites in his own mind. The experience was so magnificent and yet awesome that Ginsberg tried to recreate the alchemical meeting of light with dark for twenty years. Little did he know how much his experience would stand for the two most transformative decades of gay liberation: the '70s and the '80s.

He had just masturbated and ejaculated while reading the William Blake poem "Ah Sunflower!" ("Ah, Sunflower, weary of time,/Who countest the steps of the sun,/Seeking after that sweet golden clime/Where the traveller's journey is done.") Suddenly Ginsberg thought he heard Blake's deep voice shaking in his room. It arrived to him over the vault of time "with all the infinite tenderness and mortal gravity of a living Creator speaking to his son."[57] As if the poem had been written for the reader, Ginsberg saw that *he* was the sunflower. The realization became an initiation; everywhere he saw the evidence of a living hand. Then he read Blake's poem "The Sick Rose," apprehending "the inevitable beauty of doom." Immediately doubling his thinking process, Ginsberg read other poems, and saw too that the sunflower was his new mind. Ginsberg opened up the window to his apartment and screamed that he had found God. But opening up to unconscious energies also opens one up to their daemonic forces. Bliss only reflects the conscious attitude; there is still the other side to integrate. At one point, Ginsberg began dancing, asking the initiatory spirit (the spirit of Mercurius?) to dance with him. That's when the experience turned on him, and he encountered his shadow or rather he felt his own Faustian inner split come alive: "And then it started coming over me this big . . . creepy feeling, cryptozoid or monozoidal, so I got scared and quit."

Ginsberg later wrote that he was experiencing the great "unconsciousness that was running between all of us." This life-changing episode led him to think that the everyday pretensions of life were nothing but defenses to keep people from sharing great knowledge. But it wasn't knowledge for knowledge's sake — it was a deeply felt and lived ordeal, bringing the feeling function up to speed with the thinking. If it were a "God experience," it proved that it was composed of antimonies, the God and the devil, light and dark. According to Ginsberg's account, these comprise the unconscious divinity. It is up to the individual to synthesize these opposites — the sunflower and the shadow — in an ethical manner.

It is also no accident that Ginsberg had this experience just as he had orgasmed. The revelation explained much about the inherent dilemma of sex as a magical place where fiery antipodes meet head on, and, which for the naive individual, can cause quite a serious ethical dilemma.

a tale of two cities

The home feels immense to Allen K. Newly arrived in Los Angeles, the law student is impressionable and handsome and horny, which makes him a sitting duck for some of the less sensitive Angelinos in town. It's a good thing that Mr. S, an older gentleman, caught wind of him, and introduced him to the "A" group in L.A. These gentlemen didn't scour the streets for "trade" or "chicken" but lived respectful and discreet lives with their lovers in Hollywood and the mid-Wilshire area. Mr. S was proud of his social circle. As he told the young man, it was their greatest delight to entertain: hold barbecues, pool, and "introduce the newcomers to the old *veteranos*."

China. Dom Perignon. Paella. A black maid serving small dishes of pâté. Elvis Presley on the hi fi. Maria Callas. Two stories. Home movies from the latest vacation to Mexico taken by Mr. S and his older lover. Men in flowery ties and white button-down shirts smoking cigars, toasting each other. One man referring to another as "his wife." But the "wife" looking quite masculine and quite young.

"It's a good thing you bumped into the good sort," Mr. S told Allen after the dessert was served, referring, by implication, that these are not the kind of men who seek sex in bathrooms. "The Mattachine girls down the street criticize us for not getting involved, but the best thing is to not call attention to yourself and you'll be fine. Settling down makes the best sense."

But the notion of settling down unhinged Allen. Isn't that what his mother and father did forty years ago? A few weeks later, he'd hear a story about a man who got arrested in a tearoom. That man made history. He sounded more like Allen's cup of tea than the tea he drank at Mr. S's.

meanwhile . . .

Down the street, Dale Jennings wasn't buying the bourgeois line; neither was he buying the psychotherapeutic line that gay men were neurotic and that they had better get their appetites under control. He was lonely and out walking, looking for the kind of trouble that takes the edge off depression.

This is how Harry Hay recalls the drama:

Dale had just broken off with Bob Hull and was not, I know, feeling very great. He told me that he had met someone in the can at Westlake Park. The man had his hand on his crotch, but Dale wasn't interested. He said the man insisted on following him home, and almost pushed his way through the door. He asked for coffee, and when Dale went to get it, he saw the man moving the window blind, as if signaling to someone else. He got scared and started to say something, when there was a sudden pounding on the door, and Dale was arrested.[58]

After much debate, the Mattachines decided to fight the charges as a way to expose unethical police entrapment practices against homosexuals. (Most of the time, the police engaged in aggressive entrapment to the point of making the first advance. A joke at the time went, "It's been wonderful, but you're under arrest.") "These arrests created a victim in a victimless situation," writes Stuart Timmons in his biography of Hay, "and served as a controlling threat to all male homosexuals." To make matters worse, most lawyers wouldn't touch such cases.

At the trial on June 23, 1952, Jennings admitted he was a homosexual. He also admitted that he was not guilty of the charges against him. These statements, as courageous as they were unprecedented, did much to jump-start the fledgling homophile movement. Mattachine scored a victory when the district attorney's office decided to drop the charges. The success gave a huge boost to the fledgling organization. Mattachine grew to more than two thousand members by 1953.[59]

assimilationists *du jour*

But trouble loomed. Harry Hay pushed the idea of cultivating "highly ethical homosexual culture" that would seek its own emancipation through education, political protest, and social awareness. In the lingo of the '90s, Hay was the quintessential antiassimilationist. Chuck Rowland put his gay-centeredness this way: "We must disenthrall ourselves of the idea that we differ only in our sexual directions and that all we want or need in life is to be free to seek the expression of our sexual desire."[60]

But to younger, more conservative gay men, Hay and Rowland might have well been speaking Swahili. They wanted to be like everyone else. To Bob Bishop, of the Long Beach, California, Mattachine, gay men were "average people in all other respects outside of our private sexual inclinations." A San Francisco Mattachine pamphlet put its members' views this way: "Any organized pressure on lawmakers by members of the Mattachine Society as a group would only serve to prejudice the position of the Society. It would provide an abundant source of hysterical propaganda with which to foment an ignorant, fear-inspired antihomosexual campaign." That Hay and his gang were communists only made their vision more suspect—a serious liability.[61]

Finally, the initial framers of the Mattachine were pushed out. Recalls Rowland, "This group of conservative insurgents came up with this half-baked piece of shit [constitution] and it was obvious that they were going to pass it."[62] Radicals who had given Mattachine their lives now had nothing. Mattachine was now run by people who had no organizational skills. Young, handsome upstarts equated social progress with legitimacy in the eyes of educators, government officials, and psychologists. Veterans grew despondent. Hay became inaccessible. Bob Hull killed himself. Rowland became suicidal. Rudi Gernreich left politics, becoming a wealthy designer. The split between a radical vision and an accommodationist tactic would characterize gay movement politics to the present day.[63]

the jolts leading up to stonewall

Conditions did evolve—slowly. At a 1956 meeting of the American Psychological Association Evelyn Hooker presented her paper on the male overt homosexual, arguing "that gay men can be as well adjusted as straight men and that some are even better adjusted than some straight men."[64] A variety of progressive Supreme Court rulings on obscenity swept away the formidable legal barriers to the production and consumption of homosexually explicit material. In 1965, two magazines put male nudes on their covers.[65]

In addition, one or two militant voices emerged amidst the staid homophiles, demanding that gays follow the example of blacks and demand change. "We cannot ask for our rights," railed Frank Kameny of Washington, D.C.'s Mattachine in the early '60s, "from a position of inferiority, or from a position, shall I say, as less than WHOLE human beings."[66] One New York man—Randy Wicker—single-handedly mounted a Gay and Lesbian Alliance Against Defamation precursor, lambasting homophobic radio stations, encouraging mainstream newspapers and magazines.

A vicious police crackdown on San Francisco bars in the early '60s provoked Black Cat employee Jose Sarria into running for city supervisor. Known and loved for drag routines that combined social satire, gay camp, and operatic hysteria (he made attendees sing "God Save Us Nelly Queens"), Sarria's candidacy showed the powerful intersection between bar life and political life. In 1962, the representatives from several of San Francisco's most prominent gay bars formed the Tavern Guild to advocate for the rights of patrons. From this effort rose a politically active gay male membership organization: the Society for Individual Rights (SIR).[67]

By this time, the civil rights movement had radicalized various clergy members; San Francisco's homophile movement, along with minister Ted McIlvenna, held a four-day meeting between gay activists and Protestant ministers. In 1964, the two groups formed the Council on Religion and the Homosexual. In January 1965, the ministers held a press conference during which they assailed the police department for "deliberate harassment and bad faith."[68]

These actions brought the gay movement and the subculture of bars together—for once—and the movement tore down its walls of isolation. *Life* magazine labeled San Francisco the nation's gay capital—with good reason. It was as if San Francisco had been sending mescaline-induced quakes to New York City, soon-to-be the gay media capital of the world. But it would take almost a decade before its groundbreaking psychedelics and political shakedowns snowballed into the sexual revolution heralded by Stonewall.

chapter three

so, you say you want a revolution?

the age of innocence

love at the riots

Jordi Cosentino knew the Village—and its corrupt cops—like the back of his hand. His mother and father ran an Italian restaurant off Sixth Avenue. He studied art at Cooper Union college. He went to the Stonewall Inn with men like Nureyev. He indulged in sweet dope-glazed three-ways with Allen Ginsberg and Peter Orlovsky. So the twenty-two-year-old hustler-intellectual was really the last person to be fazed by rumors that the police intended to harass his favorite bar tonight.[1]

Cosentino doesn't remember exactly why he went to the Stonewall Inn that hot summer night. He may have had no place to live at the time (he had moved out of his parents' house with his sixteen-year-old boyfriend five years ago). Maybe he had to sell his body for a buck. Or maybe he just needed to be held. The Stonewall was the one place in which you could kill some time until you got up the courage to approach a cute guy and say, "Hey, I need a place to crash for the night."

Latter-day mythology would make the Stonewall out to be a dive frequented only by outsiders, drag queens, and street people. But that's not the whole story. True, drag queens had no place else to go but here (and maybe The Gold Bug). True, teenie-boppers came to this decrepit joint because the bar lacked a liquor license. (No one was carded, so once you paid your three dollars, you could hole up here all night.) But make no mistake about it: the Stonewall, infamous for its dance floor and acid-rock, attracted its share of the rich and famous.

With his quasi-Elvis, coal black locks and rail-thin Sicilian body, Cosentino had no trouble currying sexual favors from the upper crust. But although he had been having homo-romances in his native Bronx since he was a kid, he was, when it came to meeting a boyfriend, "shy-as-shit." His journal entries show how dancing rather than chatting breaks the ice:

> Sitting at the table near the dance floor, sipping my four-hour-old Tab. I enjoy being watched and glanced at by this dark man. He is about my age, fair-skinned, sharp features and long legs in skin-tight white jeans and white T-shirt, unusual for New York. He inches his way closer to me in the fifth hour, rubbing his leg against mine. Not saying a thing, we get up and dance slowly.

Cosentino goes on to describe the "love at first sight" surge that took place between the two men. Each likes the way the other smells and feels. Attraction burns away shyness like midtown heat. The men stare into each other's eyes, saying nothing, kissing delicately as the Beatles sing "Can't Buy Me Love."

At around midnight, Cosentino and his friend prepared to jet, only to be "slammed back and pushed down." A cop hovered over Cosentino, pulling his hair and lifting the young man off the ground. ("My new boyfriend cracked a beer bottle on the policeman's shoulder.") Cosentino opened his mouth to scream, but nothing came out. "I saw red," he says, "and ran after a policeman. He was smiling at me. I knew him from the neighborhood. I attacked. It was a full evening and a long one."

the defining ritual

On Friday, June 27, 1969, nine Manhattan plainclothes police detectives crashed the Stonewall Inn at 53 Christopher Street in Greenwich Village. Their goal was to close the bar for selling liquor without a license. The crowd, pissed off, gathered outside throwing beer bottles and bricks. Screaming "Pigs!," a group of nearly four hundred angry queens forced the cops to retreat to the bar, at which point one protestor tried to torch it. Protestors were beaten. "Some adorable butch hustler boy pulls up a *parking meter*," writes Edmund White in a letter to a friend, "mind you, out of the pavement, and uses it as a battering ram (a few cops are still inside the Wall, locked in). . . . Huge flashes of flame and billows of smoke."[2]

Every social movement tries to find a particular drama it can trace its birth to. "Today," Martin Duberman would write, more than twenty years later, in his classic *Stonewall*, "the world resonates with images of insurgency and self-realization and occupies a central place in the iconography of lesbian and gay awareness."[3] While not everyone agrees that the West Coast and East Coast movements ultimately shared the same historical time lines—Michael Bronski argues that San Francisco was further along pre-Stonewall than New York City—few would dispute Stonewall's claim to be the essence of modern gay political theater, what with its taunting line of tough chorus girls in front of the Stonewall Inn bar. "[The event] jolted awake," in the words of Donn Teal, author of *The Gay Militants*, "an only half-remembered outrage against straight society's bigotries in those older, generally conservative 'Boys in the Band' who had been out of town on the weekend of the 27th–28th–29th tanning their thighs at Cherry Grove and the Hamptons." The "forces of faggotry" had indeed arrived.[4]

"Sheridan Square this weekend, looked like something from a William Burroughs novel," wrote a *Village Voice* reporter, "as the sudden specter of 'gay power' erected its brazen head and spat out a fairy tale the likes of which the area has never seen. . . ."[5]

> *The scene became explosive. Limp wrists were forgotten. Beer cans and bottles were heaved at the windows and a rain of coins descended on the cops. . . . Almost by signal the crowd erupted into cobblestone and bottle heaving. . . . From nowhere came an uprooted parking meter—used as a battering ram on the Stonewall door. I heard several cries of "let's get some gas," but the blaze of flames which appeared in the window of the Stonewall was still a shock.*[6]

There were no more riots in the days that followed, remembers author Felice Picano, but instead organized demonstrations at the Sheridan Square subway station, where the riots had happened ("a blackened and abandoned Tara," according to historian Donn Teal). The entire area—really two triangles—were surrounded by fender-by-fender police buses and paddy wagons for five or six days following the riots. Within days, lesbians and gay men formed the Gay Liberation Front (GLF), a revolutionary organization with a new-left ideology, dedicated to rejecting "society's attempt to impose sexual roles and definitions of our nature." Additional GLF chapters spread to L.A. and San Francisco. Recalls Picano: "Marty Robinson and Vito Russo et al. had bullhorns and were exhorting us, 'What do we want?' (Answer: 'Gay Power') 'When do we want it?' (Answer: 'Now'). Onlookers like Picano remember this emboldening spirit as if it were yesterday, just as they remember the strained looks on the faces of older gays: "We couldn't believe how staunchly antagonistic and closeted so many of our gay elders were."[7]

The victims hadn't disappeared, they just identified less with their oppressors. Or in the words of poet Allen Ginsberg (who arrived at the scene of the Stonewall Riots flashing peace signs): "You know, the guys there were so beautiful—they lost that wounded look that fags all had 10 years ago."[8]

A radical, psychedelic, anarchic cum-spewing revolution had been building steam for the years preceding the famous Stonewall Rebellion. A police campaign against L.A. bars sparked the infamous Black Cat demonstrations of 1967 and gave rise to a mimeographed newsletter that would later become *The Advocate*. And before the Black Cat affair, homophile groups like the Mattachine Society and Daughters of Bilitis did much to prove that homosexuals were solid citizens; there were countless blood drives, letter-writing campaigns, and charity efforts in a long-term effort to educate society about the misunderstood homosexual. As activist and author Randy Wicker points out, contrary to public opinion about the homophiles, these mildly militant individuals actually paved the way for Stonewall.[9]

But if a picket line had previously been a last-ditch attempt for the more passive homophiles, now blatant militancy served as the bedrock of gay lib. As historian John D'Emilio points out, gay movement politics and homosexual subculture began to merge in the late '60s. A community began forming around a shared sexual orientation. Stonewall confirmed and catalyzed this phenomenon, allowing the community to say things that sounded so rational they were radical. "We have to realize that our loving each other is a good thing," wrote Carl Wittman in "Refugees from Amerika," considered the bible of gay lib, "not an unfortunate thing, and that we have a lot to teach straights about sex, love, strength and resistance."[10]

With blatant slogans ("Super Fag," "Fuck Forever," "Gay Is Good," "Gay Power"), gay lib looked like a revolution. Calling itself part of the "gay youth rebellion," the Gay Liberation Front formed in New York City in July 1969. That August, the fifth North American Conference of Homophile Organizations met in Kansas to form its first radical caucus. That same year, a complaint was filed in Alameda County Superior Court by San Francisco's Society for Individual Rights protesting police entrapment in tearooms. (The article about the complaint run in the newly born *Advocate* was entitled "Get the Pigs Out of the Pissoirs.") Exuberant "Gay-ins" (which were attacked by the police) were held in Los Angeles's Griffith Park. Chanting "Suck cock, beat the draft," and "Bring our boys home," GLF members joined a Washington, D.C., war protest and held a "nude-in" in the Lincoln Memorial reflecting pool.[11]

The sea change looked political, but its main drive was sexual. Or rather, libido blurred the lines between the political and the sexual. "It is easy to forget," writes Michael Bronski, "that the promise of Stonewall was (among other things) the promise of sex: free sex, better sex, lots of sex, sex without guilt, sex without repression, sex without harassment, sex at home and sex in the streets."[12]

Reminisces Cosentino, who moved to California with the man he met at the Stonewall Riots, "My memory of Silverlake [a gay neighborhood in L.A.] in the '70s is that it smelled like rancid Crisco."

it gets easier to get laid

During the '60s, gay men had resorted to anonymous sex often because nothing more long-lasting seemed available. Some lived with wives or parents or boyfriends; others simply needed immediate connection for the purpose of release. According to Michael Bronski, Stonewall didn't change the fact that gay men enjoyed public sex: "The change that came after Stonewall was not that men *stopped* having public sex, but that they stopped doing it furtively. They felt better about it, less guilty, and—most importantly—they felt it was their right."[13] Journal entries from the late '60s and early '70s show a slow, at first barely perceptible, shift in sexual attitudes from the '60s to the '70s. Former Marine Ron Hardcastle points to something like a "before Stonewall" and "after Stonewall" sexual psychology emerging in his sexual diaries.[14]

He writes that in the '60s, the place for public sex was the big john at State Beach in Santa Monica. At least three of the open stalls had large holes bored into the plywood—ideal for peeking and poking:

I arrived early, considering the cloudiness. The restrooms were still locked. Went down to the regular beach, which was boring. Went back, met a middle-aged fellow with a large cock, whom I did. Then he screwed me, first standing up and later at the end of the bench with my legs in the air. After he left, a smooth-bodied jogger arrived whom I had sucked once before, and I repeated it, although he came beating off in the urinal with me squeezing him tightly and tickling his nipples with my tongue. Later, Rocky arrived, looking fantastic and I sucked his incredible, incredible cock. Then he too screwed me, which is something I had only done twice in such a place in the past. . . . I was so satisfied that I returned to my sheet on the sand and just collapsed there, with my legs spread and my arms out like the wings of an airplane. . . .

The tranquility is short-lived:

Within the space of the next hour I had done a young kid who couldn't have been more than 16, as well as a 6'2" Adonis with a cock like a javelin (David

*from Phoenix) as well as miscellaneous sex with five other people, two of whom
we had all concluded earlier were very likely vice, though our fears were dispelled when both of them ejaculated into my mouth.*

Hardcastle's sexual investigation turns from tearooms to bars in the late
'60s and then to bathhouses in the early '70s. He admits that the transformation
to bathhouse sex demonstrates a certain evolution in attitude, a change that can
be seen reflected in pop culture. Gay writers heralded *Playboy*'s switch to total
nudity as well as "the message of sexual liberation and nudity" that was "carried
all over the world by the many road companies of *Hair*." In addition, the television broadcast of *That Certain Summer*—the story of a married man (played by
Mark Twain impersonator Hal Holbrook) with a fourteen-year-old boy who can't
resist his homosexual impulses (lover played by Martin Sheen) helped to alter
nelly stereotypes shared by both straights and gays. John Waters's cult film *Pink
Flamingos* introduced Divine, "the filthiest person alive," to the country the
same year that Representative Shirley Chisholm advocated on behalf of gay rights.
The East Coast radicals coalesced and zapped homophobic New York state and
city officials; in the spring of 1972, they led a march from Manhattan to Albany.
Gay writers and shit-kickers like Jack Nichols danced all night long at the Fire Island Ice Palace to Diana Ross. *The Advocate* and *Gay Sunshine* reached national
audiences, as did John Francis Hunter's comprehensive *The Gay Insider*. *The Advocate* at that time distinguished itself with articles trumpeting new sexual freedoms while also cautioning against cruelty against men in their forties who "laid
the groundwork for the present culture" but were now dismissed by the young
turks *both* in consciousness-raising groups *and* in the alleyways. Sociologists
Simon and Gagnon reported on "crisis of aging" already tearing apart the gay community.[15]

All these forces contributed, making the sexual pursuit a touch easier for
Hardcastle, humanizing it:

> *Throughout the '70s, there was the 1170 on Western just a block or two north of
> Santa Monica Boulevard. There would be furtive sex in the back corners and in
> the crowds but, for me at least, most of the sex occurred outside. . . . The sex a
> block north of Greg's Blue Dot Bar on Highland could sometimes be almost as
> plentiful as it was at the baths. Sometimes you'd find trucks parked there, and
> all variety of sex taking place. It you were good looking or good at sex (or a com-
> bination thereof), you could sometimes meet ten or more guys on a good night.
> I had many good nights back there, sometimes getting the guys to return to my
> apartment, although most of the men in the alley were looking for a quick sex*

scene, a quick orgasm, and cheerio-see-you-around. . . . Places like Los Angeles, and San Francisco and New York were incredible for meeting guys in the late '60s and '70s. Those were the days of my frequent gym workouts and religious trips to the beach, so I was as hard as I was golden, and I seemed to meet guys just about everywhere I went. It was an important part of my life.

Sex gave Hardcastle's life meaning at a time when he was struggling to find firm ground to stand on as a gay man. "I would trade all that casual and faceless sex in an instant for something with more substance," he wrote, characteristically hoping for love, yet gripped by the power he discovered. Hardcastle was never without friends, it seemed. His fuck buddies *did* make him feel less alone and suicidal than he had previously felt. Some of these trysts did evolve into romances. But he was like two men here: one looking for a man to love, another looking for a man to fuck.

For the first time ever, a community standard developed that transformed anonymous sex into a good thing—another choice on the broadening sexual palette. Casual sex encounters no longer took place simply because men needed to conceal their identities, but because it was considered hot to separate sex from intimacy. "When I first arrived in New York City in 1969," recalls Alan Bell, the African American publisher of *BLK*, "the freedom of sexual cruising really liberated me from being just my mother's son. It gave me a sense of powerful independence and I liked the fact that after a very passionate kiss with a man you didn't have to marry him." The more tricks one had, the more one helped to push the revolution along, according to editors at the Canadian gay magazine *The Body Politic*.

For many, the emerging new attitudes toward anonymous sex simply made it easier to get close to another man. It offered an excuse to create community. "How many of us go to a Gay bar," asked Craig Rodwell, "for the simple and very human purpose of being with people like us and interacting with them on many levels—social, intellectual, cultural, and yes, sexual?"[16] Because men lacked indigenous community spaces in which to come out, anonymous sex became the main route to explore one's gay identity, as this account from Steven Solberg's journal shows:

> *I was young and he was hungry. He wore leather. He led me from the street corner where I waited for him though we had never met. I knew I was waiting for something. Was it day or night? It was Silverlake in L.A. I can smell the leather. I had no experience yet with anonymous sex or any deliberate intentional sex for that matter. He led me into an open garage and lay me on the dirty cement floor.*

*I think he lay down a blanket. I was too green to be aggressive. He worked me
over, stripped me naked, behind the garage door. He licked me all over, me
moaning. I'd never been done by an experienced cock sucker before. Someone
who knew how to flick my balls with his tongue. I was completely naked now.
He lifted my legs over his shoulders, licking the crack of my ass, and darting his
tongue now and then into my rosy hole in deliberate circles. Rimming was not
even a word in my vocabulary yet. But "good" was. And it was good. And as I
came closer and closer, his timing was perfect. Snapping my first hit of poppers
under my nose — rushing and flushing and squirting in deep spasms down his
throat. Extending his hand, he helped me up to my feet, he handed me my
jeans and T-shirt, and, thanking me, split.*[17]

Not all rendezvous glimmered with such naïveté. In overcoming centuries
of repression, rebels like David Wojnarowicz and John Rechy were attracted to
situations that extracted the least amount of sentimentality from them and underscored the difficulties involved in moving toward emotional freedom in a culture that dismissed the feeling function in everyone, especially queers. "In the
warehouse just before dark," Wojnarowicz writes, describing a more shadow-laden
sexual milieu, "I passed along the hallways . . . in passing through a series of
rooms, saw this short fat man with a seedy mustache standing in a broken closet
filled with old wet newspapers and excrement and piss, standing with his hands
locked behind his head and with a hard-on poking out through his trousers from
beneath a grimy heavy overcoat." The man stabbed the air with his dick, whis-
pering, "Come in here . . . I'll make ya feel so goood . . . so good. . . ."[18]

While some men relied on anonymous sex as a method of coming out without the attachment of a relationship, as a way to strip sexuality of the clutches of
the emotional merge inherent in intimate touch, others, like Jordi Cosentino, relied on casual sex with strangers as a means of finding a relationship:

*I was mostly a serial monogamy kind of guy, but between relationships I'd get
horny or lonely or out of my mind with desire in that New York City I-gotta-
have-it way. I remember the Continental Baths when they had floor shows there.
How wild it was to see men dancing to Donna Summer in towels. I ran after tail.
I suppose I was an asshole queen. I loved fucking guys, holding them from behind, kissing their necks. I didn't know anyone who didn't have a lot of sex. But
I wasn't versatile like the rest, which was big in the '70s. Even though I loved
being held, I was always looking for a boyfriend. It was sometimes easier to find
someone to love at the baths than the bars, because with clothes off and a kiss
on the lips, a lot of attitudinal shit went by the wayside and people were a helluva lot more real with a dick in their ass.*

Men grew progressively less self-divided about relying on anonymous sex as a way to meet men. Michael Bronski muses on the thrill of breaking through the public sex barrier in the '70s. The possibilities seemed endless in Boston:

> In the mood for a fresh-air experience, one could always go to the Cambridge Bird Sanctuary as well as the Fenway and the Esplanade. For something a little more scholarly, Harvard presented endless venues: the basement men's rooms in Paine Hall, any number of places in Widener Library, the first floor at the now-defunct Burr Hall (rumored to have been torn down because the tearoom action was simply too notorious), as well as the recently infamous Science Center. But if you were just passing through Harvard Square the basement bathroom at ZumZums (now the Ms. Coop) was always busy and presented a wide range of trick.[19]

For some, the primary sexual meeting grounds shifted from unpredictable, heterogeneous environments such as tearooms to more overtly gay spaces such as bathhouses and sex clubs. But there were others who continued to stake out public streets and alleyways. Alleyways offered more than sleaze venues. They also worked as "containers" for emotion. The old alchemists identified as the missing piece of the Christian Trinity a fourth, rejected function (which included aspects of the flesh and the feminine). Throughout history, the fourth piece bubbled up from the depths. Only in modern times has its integration brought greater humanity to life. Researching this site can send one into the belly of Jonah's Whale. But with a successful integration of this "fourth," the so-called Trinity becomes a Square, an attitude suggesting wholeness.

new ways to do things the old way

Public sex wasn't limited to anonymous sex. Lovers cruised together, frequented baths together, and exploited the burgeoning public sex underground as a way to juice up the relationship's sex-charge, as this account from Bronski shows:

> It is a hot night and my lover Walta and I go for an after-dinner walk in the Victory Gardens. We do not plan to have sex but discover that the sight of two or three random coupling couples turns us on. At first we only neck but soon go down on one another, half hidden behind some scattered reeds close to the winding path that runs through the patchwork of gardens.[20]

Bronski hears an enemy police car beginning a "watchful ride" through the cruising grounds. Others flee, but he has no impulse to do so. "Not only am I enjoying my lover's cock in my mouth," he thinks to himself, "but in my erotic half-trance I do not see any illegality or even danger. After all, I would have told the police if questioned, this wasn't some illicit, promiscuous sexual encounter, this was my lover." It's interesting to watch the ways in which public sex acts as a political way for gay men to claim the streets that had once, in the '50s, exposed them to punishment. The added legitimacy provided by Bronski's relationship strengthens Bronski's conviction. Sex is no mere biological drive, but a political assertion and performance—proving to the world, proving to oneself, proving to one's lover that the right-to-make-love and the right-to-be-alive as a gay man are one and the same.

cocksucking as an act of revolution   Gay liberation marked one of the final radical causes to come out of the youth rebellion of the '60s. Like feminism, it was based on dismantling some of the ingrained inhibitions surrounding pleasure and the body. While feminism focused more on the erotic as a vehicle for patriarchal domination over the feminine,[21] gay men embraced it as a way to dismantle the controlling powers of the state. ("When the ass is licked clean, then come to me talking of 'revolutionary sensuality.' Then I will kiss your sweet tongue.")[22] With a clarity that would have made Walt Whitman and Edward Carpenter proud, a critique of repression blended with a critique of capitalism:

> We need to be indiscriminate [about having sex]. No one should be denied love because they are old, ugly, fat, crippled, bruised, of the wrong race, color, creed, sex or country of national origin. We need to copulate with anyone who requests our company; set aside all the false contraptions of being hard to get, unavailable—that is, costly on the capitalist market.[23]

Sex replaced money as the main commodity of the early days of gay liberation. But even that equation was criticized as coming from the straight white man's values.[24] Gay militants called for "a truly human revolution that will have as its aim an end to all oppression." Not only did this give gay men permission to fuck other gay men, it also gave a green light for fucking all men. These men didn't see gay liberation as a struggle for a particular minority, but an effort to free the homosexual in everyone.[25]

"In this context," wrote John Rechy, "the sexual outlaw flourishes. The pressures produce him, create his defiance. Knowing that each second his freedom may be ripped away arbitrarily, he lives fully at the brink. Promiscuity is his righteous form of revolution."[26]

Rechy's books allowed homosexual men to feel like insiders to each other about their outsider status, to feel good about saying "Fuck you" to society even as they fucked each other. His work showed an honoring of the whole body—a part-infantile, part-ritualistic glee about everything human that culture denies. To become a complete person meant to no longer remain blind to the *total* personality, even its excesses. The idea behind gay lib was to let the psyche lead with less of a fight than usual.

And the psyche did. "They lived only to bathe in the music," rhapsodized Andrew Holleran, "and each other's desire, in a strange democracy whose only ticket of admission was physical beauty—and not even that sometimes."[27] Carl Whitman's 1970 *Gay Manifesto* announced, "We are euphoric, high, with the initial flourish of a movement. . . ." Jack Fritscher, the former editor of *Drummer*, wrote that "much of San Francisco sex in those early first days was sanctuary sex. The war was on. Students protest in the streets. Nixon was president. The baths were safe haven from the world. There was no tomorrow. There was only the night. The music never stopped and there was no piper to pay."

Everything announced upward movement, as the title of Barry D Adams's history shows—*The Rise of a Gay and Lesbian Movement*. If gnostic writers suggested that the soul descended from the heavens to inherit astrological dispositions, gay men tried to reclaim their origins through newfounded efforts at ecstasy and liberation. Some men went so far as to announce a new era: "They were men, as bonded as ancient priests, assisting in the reincarnational birth of a kind of homosexual religion that predated Christianity. There was the night and the music and the drugs and the men. It was ritual. It was sex. It was raw male bonding."[28]

Others chalked up the endless sex to simple common sense. "If you tell people for two thousands years that they can't touch," says African American writer David Ehrenstein, "and then, all of sudden, someone says they can, you're going to see lots of action." Men didn't just experience Dionysus, they became him.

the personal gets political—and personal

Not every gay man felt comfortable being branded as a purely sexual creature whose spurting cum contained the revolutionary juice of the Boston Tea Party, the Freedom Rides, and the *Communist Manifesto* all rolled into one. Gay men put a great deal of their libido into politics—and intracommunity catfights.

Young student radicals, who had cut their teeth in the civil rights movements, admitted their homosexuality and promptly joined GLF. But some had never been to a gay bar. Others had never touched another man. Even so, they had little patience for the standards of behavior entertained by most gays. Lefties like Steve Dansky argued against gay bars, tearooms, baths, streets, and other cruising institutions because the "use of these institutions by GLF men must be seen as copping out to The Man's oppression of homosexuals." They wanted "encounter groups," a lot of relating, "revolution in the streets," and "the continuum of violent and non-violent confrontation." They wanted not just gay ghettoes, a gay Alternative Culture the likes of which no one had quite seen—in short, an ethical outgrowth of the hippie movement.[29]

The call for the building of a new, indigenous culture hit a nerve. Foreshadowing the militancy of '80s-style in-your-face groups like ACT UP and Queer Nation, GLF repudiated the previous generations' suit-and-tie tendencies. If the homophile groups of the '50s looked inward, focusing on themselves and their problems, gay groups in the early '70s looked outside themselves to explain the roots of their oppression.[30]

Two groups emerged to confront the problem. Charged up by revolutionary Black Panthers rhetoric, GLF argued that complete sexual liberation cannot come about unless existing social institutions are abolished. (The first GLF flyer proclaimed: "DO YOU THINK HOMOSEXUALS ARE REVOLTING? YOU BET YOUR SWEET ASS WE ARE.") The group picketed antisexual attitudes. They confronted Western and Delta Airlines about antigay employment practices. They joined in antiwar rallies and presented well-attended, high-spirited gay dances in New York, San Francisco, and Chicago, cities where men had previously been arrested for touching in public.

The first Gay Liberation Front dances held at Alternate U in the summer of 1969 attracted hundreds, despite the $1.50 fee. The notion of gays hosting gays was new and charged, as this newspaper account reveals: "On the third floor, in the not-so-dark, several hundred bodies pound to the sound of tape-deck rock and twirling light show slides, 95 percent men and boys, smiling, dancing, hugging, kissing, pinching, all as though no one had ever mentioned another sex!"[31]

But GLF meetings, a cross between Quaker meetings and informal rap sessions, unhinged those members who "wanted to get something done." As early as November 1969, activists Jim Owles and Marty Robinson, insisting that GLF was too anarchic, too obsessed with rhetoric to organize effectively, stormed out to create Gay Activists Alliance. GAA simply wanted to concentrate on the single issue of gay rights without diffusion into a hundred different left-leaning concerns. GLFers were aghast, condemning GAA's obsession with structure and elected leaders. "The movement," writes Adam, "was facing a transition experienced by so many others before it, when charisma and chiliasm give way to structure and institution." GLF soon exhausted itself. GAA, a hip political pressure group with a spirited penchant for organization—and zaps against New York City officials—lasted far longer and, to many, accomplished more.[32]

The internal split between a call for revolution and a call for getting things done would never go away, popping up each time the movement faced a life-and-death challenge. Following in GAA's footsteps, gay politics would focus mostly on issues of laws, fair employment, and civil rights. It would take ACT UP and Queer Nation to make the gay left popular again and to play out the tension between being single-issue or more revolutionary. Mostly, mainstream gay politics distanced itself from both culture and sexuality, leaving the discussion of sex to pornography, books, private conversations, and of course, the bathhouses.

sex develops personality   The sexual revolution wasn't necessarily the goal most gay activists worked toward: gay liberation was. Yet many worried that sex would be split off from its relationship to social change—in service of making another kind of change: money. Theodore Roszak, in his groundbreaking book, *The Making of a Counter Culture*, went so far as to warn against the enemies of the spirit: "It is the cultural experimentation of the young that often runs the worst risk of commercial verminization—and so of having the force of its dissent dissipated."[33] Sex was just a way to effect the larger revolution against the "technocracy." In the place of technocracy he suggested that "there must be a new culture in which the non-intellective capacities of the personality—those capacities that take fire from visionary splendor and the experience of human communion—become the arbiters of the good, the true and the beautiful."[34]

When R. D. Laing described the psychological death-and-rebirth that was needed to take place for the purpose of "true sanity," wasn't he describing the coming out experience for gay men par excellence? If anyone understood a "false self" it was a gay man growing up in a heterosexual home.[35] Sex shattered this false self. But did it create a new one?

a small group of trendsetters   What young gay men of the early '70s had going for them, as opposed to their predecessors of the early '60s and '50s, was a generational context that supported their endeavors. This adversarial Baby Boomer youth culture had smoked pot in college, read Allen Ginsberg, screamed at their uptight parents, demonstrated against the Vietnam War, took acid—or knew people who did. They came of age during the assassination of a president and the murder of a civil rights leader and witnessed the passage of the landmark Civil Rights Act of 1964. They went to concerts, demos, boycotts, sit-ins, love-ins, be-ins—or they read about them. The decade of crisis saw the Tet Offensive, the Chicago Democratic Convention, the trial of the Chicago Seven, and the student deaths at Kent State. To some gay observers, the conditions created a small group of gay men who not only engaged in the most "way out" forms of sexual expression, they made social commentary about these activities. Many of the gay sexual athletes of the '70s were its activists and were its writers and were its disco dancers and were its tastemakers, as Felice Picano recalls:

> You have to remember that not that many people were out in those days as gay. Yes, there were men who had sex with men. But in terms of those who were making a life of being gay, I think there were maybe two thousand to three thousand and we all pretty much knew each other. And because of our professions— music, clothing design, and home design—we were connected with the tastemakers of the culture. To me, this was profoundly important because gays exerted great direct influence over how everyone in society dressed, partied, loved (and lived) at the time. And we saw that we were having an immediate effect. We were a very cohesive group, yet actually quite diverse. The Flamingo had a distinctly Latino flavor because so many of its employees—DJs, lighting men, and decorators—were Latino. This Utopian gay Fire-Island/New York Paradise elevated everyone to an equal playing field. There were no color or race bars that I was aware of. If you were hot, good-looking, into sex, drugs, dancing, and the beach, you fit in easily.[36]

To Picano's mind, this world—a kind of Eden set apart from the mundane qualities of American life and vulgarity—was dependent on three social factors:

> Most important, we had very good dance music. In the summer of 1976, people weren't fucking in the Meat Rack [the sexual playing field on Fire Island, located between Cherry Grove and the Pines] but were dancing to the fabulous dance music. Second was the presence of easily available and cheap drugs. The drug dealers and manufacturers would come to the Pines and give out free samples so as to test out, say, Special K or a new version of speed or early xtc. And the third factor was that a lot of attractive men were having sex with each other all the time and as much as possible, which, of course, can now never be duplicated. We simply believed you could get to know someone very differently if you got into his pants than if you talked to him. Even though we were promiscuous, it's important to keep in mind that it was with this group of two thousand or three thousand men, all of whom knew someone who knew each other.

Picano bristles at the suggestion that he and his kind created yet another exclusive club. "If it sounds somewhat elite," he adds, "it's just that there were so few people out at the time."

As he sees it, his "Class of 1975," a group of college-educated men between the ages of 25 and 35, did much to raise gay life to a new level of "outness" and creative élan. This group feathered out to similar urban centers in San Francisco, Los Angeles, and Miami and through its early visibility in the media helped in the overall coming out process.

gender bending

Aiding in the coming out process were newspapers and books—some large-circulation, some fringe, all fairly sexy—written and published for and by gay people and really for the first time ever. "Not surprisingly," writes Mark Thompson, longtime *Advocate* editor, of his twenty-plus-year history with the magazine, "the publication itself germinated and took root in the darkness that so much of gay life inhabited a quarter of a century ago." Dated September 1967, the first issue was "clandestinely printed in the basement of ABC Television's Los Angeles headquarters by gay men working there." (The newspaper had existed in the '60s in the form of a newsletter called *PRIDE*, an L.A. homophile group, which featured writings by Jim Kepner.) By 1974, the magazine's print run increased to forty thousand copies per issue. David B. Goodstein, a New York millionaire investment banker, bought and remade the *Advocate* in 1974: "Gone was the jumbled newspaper format with its endless columns of dull type; readers now held a graphically sophisticated tabloid-style magazine on newsprint."[37]

While few publications could compete nationally with the *Advocate*, many others often did a good, if not better, job of walking the tightrope between bolstering gay pride and needling the community. These included *Fag Rag, Gay Community News, The Body Politic, Manroot Poetry Journal, Gay Sunshine, R.F.D.* Lige Clarke and Jack Nichols, self-professed former "homophile extremists" from the Mattachine Society of Washington, coedited *Gay*, a New York–based bi-weekly "life-style newspaper which points the way to new values." In the early '70s, the two lovers also wrote a column for *Screw* called "Homosexual Citizen."[38]

Though little remembered, the publication that provided some of the best political analysis, book review writing, and naked men posing was *QQ*. With views ranging from practical to whacky to kinky, *QQ* touched on sexual culture more voluminously and specifically than any other magazine did (or has since). Articles gave medical information ("Sex Has It's Ugly Side: VD"), fetish information ("It's Not Nice to Fool Mother Nature: The Folly of Increasing Phallic Size Through Silicone"), sociological information ("Glory Holes: A Piece of Vanishing America"), and disturbing information ("Sex & Cocaine: The Drug Called 'Powdered Champagne'").[39]

The gay sexual life guidebooks that emerged in the early '70s share a similar masculinist eccentricity. Angelo d'Arcangelo's *The Homosexual Handbook* reads like a sexual picaresque, offering sexual tips with a literary panache and a knowledge of world cultures and mythology. "Fetish nor no," writes the manic Joycean sex writer, "nothing will stop me from telling all

> *and I think it's about time to get down to cocksucking. There, that sounds easy enough, and truly, it is easy. One gets a vision of popping a joint into one's mouth and simply sucking it as one might suck, say, a peppermint stick. And that's just about right. But there's more to it if you believe that a thing worth doing is worth doing well. You know, I believe the reason we have so many frustrated irritable women in this country is that most men regard sex as a matter of sticking one's dick into something and rattling it around, like stirring soup with a wooden spoon.*[40]

Although gay to the max, d'Arcangelo doesn't think for a moment that the only people reading his book—and the only men having sex with men—are gay. "By revolution we mean a conscious return to a previously known and accredited liberty. . . . Having no longer to control the sexual drives of women, we are free ourselves to compete with them in pleasure. Thank heaven, that charade is over. I've always maintained that the best way to tell if you're hetero- or homosexual is to look carefully at the person you're in bed with. A simple and effective test. However, it's only pertinent for one encounter at a time."[41] D'Arcangelo shows himself as something of a behaviorist: being gay is a matter of action, not the inner culture of a person.

Not so for John Paul Hudson, who differentiates men whose only claim to homosexuality is that they like sex with men versus those men who saw their attraction coming from an immutable center of being that has as its source being gay. Hudson's immensely informative two guides—published under the pseudonym John Francis Hunter—*The Gay Insider* and *The Gay Insider/USA* build on d'Arcangelo's Swiftian style and amplify the literature with more contemporary takes on movement politics and personalities, such as Morris Knight, Jack Nichols, and Vito Russo, and analyses of books, such as Peter Fisher's *The Gay Mystique* and Dennis Altman's *Homosexual Oppression and Liberation*. To write *The Gay Insider/USA* Hudson journeyed crosscountry and in the manner of Edmund White's later masterpiece, *States of Desire*, took notes, jotted down his thoughts, and analyzed the sociology of gay life. Filled with hundreds of pieces of data about clubs, bars, venues—and lush with anecdotal narrative—it is a classic of gay literature and a measure of our cultural amnesia that it is no longer available or read.[42]

His *The Gay Insider: A Hunter's Guide to New York and a Thesaurus of Phallic Lore*, is, as its title says, more erotic and more New York. The narrator is a modern-day detective of eros: a Mercurius. Someone who throws himself right in the middle of a "Uranian" complex, a son sandwiched between a straight man and a queen of a mom. At the Tenth of Always, for example, located in Manhattan's Upper East Side, one found, for three dollars, "an extraordinary cross-section of low-life, including beautiful drag queens." The one who catches his eyes is aptly named Fellatia, a Hedy Lamar type with blond hair who, with a fashion model's body, "passes uptown for a woman." Hudson meets Fallatia with his heterosexual friend Kurt; Kurt frequents gay dives with Hudson to pick up what Hudson calls "fag hags" or "faggot's molls." Now and then Kurt digs femme men and he and Hudson successfully courted Fallatia. With a sculpted body and undergarments as flouncy and expensive as they come, she boasts succulent pecs that are hermaphroditic enough to drive both men wild. Hudson had expected his straight friend to be "a little turned off by Fellatia's substantial cock," but apparently the "Brooks Brother's–cut stud went down on the serpentining beauty with the flowing blonde hair," sucking without restraint. Finally, everyone collapsed in a frenzy of gender confusion about the lines between homo and hetero, a fact that can be appreciated only by one born to mediate between the sexes.[43]

Hudson shares with d'Arcangelo a masculinist approach, one that doesn't exclude heterosexuals. But he is more gay-centered.

baths

Arnie Kantrowitz prepared for his weekend jaunt to the Continental Baths as if he were going on vacation. He packed his "bath bag," filled with a bottle of wine, a tidy towel, a change of clothes, "moist towelettes for those emergency moments," the appropriate number of joints, a roach clip, and "a little thing" full of various pills, not to mention a much-used jock strap. At a certain point, the bag grew too heavy, and he couldn't forget that little red light bulb he'd screw in to get the atmosphere he needed.[44]

The Continental wasn't a place to go to lose his mind as much as it was one in which he found his Self. The schedule went this way: check-in Saturday afternoon at 5 P.M.; relax, massage, laps in the pool, then a light dinner in the restaurant. In the late evening—when the straights breezed in for the Bette Midler show in the tuxedos and Norma Kamali gowns—Kantrowitz would greet them in his towel. Then, it was time for dancing downstairs—which required a costume change: tight jeans, fish-scale belt, and platform shoes—"They were shit for walking, but you could move your body in these great ways when dancing," he reminisces.

With his shaved head, red glasses, "great big mustache heading down to the nipples," and newly slenderized body, Kantrowitz would feel like a dancing, tripping "outlaw" among the hets, luxuriating in the colliding dimensions. "I always had the urge," he recalls, "to go up to these very nicely attired people and say, 'Hi, my name is Professor Kantrowitz and I teach at the College of Staten Island,' to give them another dimension."

For he was getting a look at another dimension, and not just of the world, but of his own personality. The idea wasn't just to have a good time, or be decadent, but to unearth new layers of libido—just as an archaeologist might excavate a buried city in an effort to learn of its true history. So much of Kantrowitz's '50s middle-class upbringing had been a lesson in how to fear his deepest nature. In his case, a heroic attempt was made to react against the perpetual hesitations of the modern man—especially one raised in a middle-class Jewish home in New Jersey. Passion, whether sexual or romantic, is understood here as a challenge to upbringing. Who knew at that time—a time before coming out, a time before AIDS—that a challenge to Fate can never be undone?

The sex at the baths was wonderful, because it was highly taboo, challenging each man to go one step further in unsheathing something heretofore banned about his desires. "I was rimming somebody," one man recalls, "and all of a sudden I felt something entering my mouth. It turned out to be a piece of Goldenberg's Peanut Chews, chocolate covered, that my partner had so thoughtfully inserted."

If there was such a thing as a sexual envelope, the men at the baths felt compelled to push as far into it as possible. There was, for example, such a thing as "felching," an activity that takes place when you drink the cum out of someone's ass—a special thing because the cum had been planted by a stranger. Others did the same thing with urine. These acts weren't considered base. They were "a community sacrament."

the bathhouses create a container   Bathhouses provided opportunities for sexual consummation under relatively safe and comfortable conditions. There was simply less chance of being bashed in a bathhouse than in a tearoom. And for some men, bars, with their emphasis on drink, and endless sizing-up, inhibited sexual freedom and crippled self-esteem. "If the last thing a guy wanted was to be brushed off, a bar was not the place to go," recalls Kantrowitz. "At least in a bathhouse you could go into the orgy room, or you could have yourself a luxurious massage."

Some nights, the Everhard resembled a clubhouse. Remembers one man, "It was fun to meet friends at the Everhard, to catch up on old gossip and to even talk some politics, while catching one's breath between men." Gay men required a venue in which to have fast, easy sex without class or style issues getting in the way. They liked having this kind of sex while being witnessed by each other. After Stonewall, the baths married the need for community with the need for touch in a new way.

They grew so well established in the '70s, that one chain, operated by the Mafia, offered membership in twenty cities. Some New York City baths, like the Continental, offered entertainment; others, like the Everhard, provided a man-sized swimming pool; another boasted a gymnasium. Different baths each boasted a unique character and clientele. At the Wall Street sauna, businessmen got off during lunch. At the Beacon, East Side executives undid shirts and ties, and met messenger boys. Students went for the ten-story Man's Country on Fifteenth Street; admission cost eight dollars. The St. Mark's Baths drew Third World and East Village types as well as executives. Mount Morris served Harlem. S&Mers opted for the New Barracks, especially on Thursday, known affectionately as "Dollar Dick" days.

"Everard was a haven where I could stare at crotches in dimly lit hallways," reminisced the late author Arthur Bell, "wander the steam room, which smelled of sweat and Lysol, and screw with a cast of thousands, who, like the extras in *Quo Vadis* were faceless and nameless." In a word, the baths represented freedom—"a place where I could have sex without plodding through the required conversation of a bar, where points are given for social status and artistic tastes and deducted for . . . staying in the wrong borough."[45]

They provided a vessel for the psychic transformations that come with multiple orgasms during a weekend evening. Yet the sign language was as old as the hills: "If one's towel is knotted in the back, sodomy is the order of the night. Lying on one's back in a cot, legs ajar, is an open call for fellatio. And one doesn't have to be an Einstein to know what lying on one's stomach means." Politesse, not always the status quo, is all the same not thrown out with the bath water: "Common practice is for a hand to crawl into your room, travel up your leg, hit a vital organ, rest for a moment, then, just as quickly, travel out. If, by chance, that hand feels it has hit gold, and you don't care for the arm behind it, you plead exhaustion. White lies are permissible among gentlemen."[46]

If some resorted to the baths to be touched in the simplest of ways, others flocked there to find an Idol, an embodiment of the soul-complex at its most ideal manifestation. And yet in the embrace, the possession of the love object seemed to elude such a man, due partly to the intensity of the experience itself. Drunk with passion, he could not understand that his absorption had less to do with his beloved than with what his own soul was doing to him:

Under overhead lights, on a raised platform in a hallway niche, a heroically buffed exhibitionist bodybuilder posed. He stroked his penis. He rubbed his hands over his well-greased muscles. He teased the nipples of his huge pecs. He played to the kneeling, adoring crowd of men.[47]

Sometimes, one even found religion:

They jerked off to his muscular build with one hand. With their other hand, like Israelites kneeling before the golden idol in The Ten Commandments, *they reached toward him like a god. He shot his load across the rolling fields of their open mouths.*[48]

Others found a First-Aid kit; the floors in too many bathhouses were slick and not everyone, as Arthur Bell points out, had strong calves.

public sex gets a new level of respectability

Before *Rolling Stone*, with its articles on Bette Midler, made the Continental world famous, bathhouses were understood by the gay and straight public alike as licensed men's health clubs that provided a setting for impersonal homosexual sex. They could be sleazy. "Traditionally," writes one sociologist, "baths offered little to the patrons except sex. Most of the owners were not themselves homosexuals, and they were generally lax about the upkeep or development of facilities."[49]

Continental bathhouse owner Steve Ostrow brought the baths above ground by starting up its cabaret shows. Between Bette Midler singing to the audience and *Rolling Stone* covering the phenomenon, almost more straight people flocked to its portals than homosexual men (who began to feel resentful about being ogled). While the Continental lost its edge around 1974, it had helped make the bathhouse scene respectable. Bob Kohler, a former CORE activist and early member of the Gay Liberation Front, was credited with making the Club Baths the Howard Johnson's of bathhouse sex. For a time, the Club Baths offered a VD clinic on its premises; the inebriated were turned away. Rooms at the Club were clean, replete with wood-paneling and light dimmers.

Despite the differences in clientele and accommodation offered by a variety of venues, the essential qualities seemed to remain unchanged, as one sociologist makes clear:

The whole bath is extremely crowded, with all facilities—bar discotheque, TV—utilized. The hallways around the private rooms are full of people, and it is difficult to circulate because sexual activity has begun in one of the corridors. Group sex involving at least five persons has also begun in another corridor, and the covey of spectators makes passage even more difficult. Few words are spoken, but the air is filled with grunts and moans, exacerbated by a great deal of sexual activity going on in a concentrated space.

The orgy room is equally crowded. Two males are engaging in anal intercourse on a central bed, surrounded by some 15–20 spectators. Throughout the room, cruising and sexual activity are taking place. When they come into the room, patrons move clockwise around the room, squeezing through the crowd. The room is very hot and humid, with a great deal of traffic and no conversation.

Upstairs in the discotheque, an audience of towel-clad males roar their appreciation of an elderly female burlesque star doing a strip-tease.[50]

The best San Francisco baths were located in newly renovated blue-collar motels South of Market. The first of the early baths were located near Folsom, behind the Red Star Saloon. The Barracks, a four-story maze of fantasy sex, perfected sport fucking. Everyone, writes Fritscher, went there, after stopping at the Red Star for a cheap beer, relaxing to the sounds of Creedence, Janis Joplin, and the Doors: "In its long narrow corridors, men stripped down to combat boots and jockstraps. Most carried a white towel over one shoulder and a bottle of poppers tucked in their gray wool socks topped with red and green stripes. They paraded the halls and stairwells bumping into newer and newer flesh arriving in those early days. They cruised the open doors of the hundred rooms."[51]

Kicking back to the sounds of "It's a Beautiful Day," men invited the bright, inflated positivity of sex into their lives:

It was a golden time, those first post-Stonewall years with their Haight-Ashbury glow; everyone seemed young, because everyone was. Drugs were for going up; there was no coming down. No one had yet overdosed or burnt out. There wasn't the cannibalistic hunger one reads about in stereotyped accounts of gay baths that always end up seeming like the scenario for Suddenly Last Summer. *The only diseases were euphemized as social and they were few considering the shenanigans. Banners of LOVE, PEACE, JOY hung over the City. John and George and Paul and Ringo sang about me being he and him being me and us being all together.[52]*

What emerged on a Saturday night at the St. Mark's Baths was an esprit de corps. Not every rejection was brutal; sometimes a man gently removed another's hand with a smile. Not every fuck was quick; sometimes a man made love to a stranger as if they had agreed to a temporary marriage. Not every brush against a stranger in a dark hall was stone-faced and anonymous; sometimes a sweet smile crossed the faces of two men as they felt themselves to be in the midst of one of the twentieth century's greatest social experiments.

A similar community spirit emerged in other sexual venues. Felice Picano and Alan Bell recall how each used to take turns with other men to keep watch against hoodlums or the fuzz at the docks near Christopher Street as men had sex with each other in deserted trucks. But the baths could, at times, draw out an extra level of good-feeling than the trucks, in part, because the social hierarchy that comes with clothes had been stripped away by nakedness. "The baths invited men to think of their bodies as Temples," recalls Michael Callen, "not merely as pedestrians in a sexy alleyway or clients with a hustler or drinkers in a bar." With gyms, whirlpools, saunas, and quiet time in bedrooms, the baths helped equate sex not just with pleasure, but with a somewhat healthy effort at honoring the body and treating it right.

the downside of the baths

Many gay men developed a love for bathhouse sex not at the expense of bar attendance or even more traditional dating experiences. Bathhouse sex was simply another choice on an expanding palette of sexual tastes and options. There was an unredeemable side too. For Dennis Altman, the baths fed off homosexual oppression; highly priced, they relied on the closetedness of homosexuals who couldn't greet each other in social life.

Often, damp, poorly ventilated venues became sites for rejection, depression, and crashing out on bad acid. Men tweaked on speed, hungry for the touch they didn't get, headachy from amyl, became sexual predators. Mattresses were damp. Cigarette butts littered the floor. Light bulbs blinked on and off. Attendants barked their irritation. Some gay men behaved in brutally rude ways to each other. Men deemed too fat or too old were treated as pariahs; they in turn could be seen to paw younger men without permission. Those whose dicks did not measure up perhaps suffered worst of all.

For every bonus there lurked a minus. "Yet the glitter [of the Continental's floor shows] feeds off the rest of the baths," wrote Altman, "a dark complex of lockers and small half-lit rooms with thin floor mattresses, reminding me of the rabbit warren complexes one finds sometimes in old houses, retired to hold migrants and old age pensioners."[53]

libido creates a city   By the '70s the Castro had become *the* most active cruising strip in the country. By day, hundreds of young men cruised the bars (Midnight Sun, Toad Hall, Bear Hollow), bookshops (Paperback Traffic), and restaurants (the Castro Cafe). Some men experienced their first invitation to move to San Francisco while reading *Life* magazine. It was Chuck Arnett's mural, spread across two pages, that showed images of bikers and muscle men. Men arrived in 1970, via Greyhound, at the height of the Castro's post-beat, post-hippie transformation from lazy old neighborhood to funky revival. "It was a scene right out of Maupin," one African American man recalls. "Only I wasn't naive. I knew what I wanted."

A vast migration of sexual-athletes-in-training contributed to making San Francisco one of the gayest of metropolises, in part because it was so economically depressed. By the '60s, the port had lost its business to Oakland and its industrial base to other Californian sites. Manufacturing moved to the suburbs; blue-collar workers followed their union jobs out of the city. "Amid great promises of urban renewal," writes Randy Shilts, "the city bulldozed giant tracts of the black Fillmore neighborhood."[54] The promised new housing was never built. The city's ethnic neighborhoods died as City Hall put its attention on downtown and tourism, turning San Francisco into a poor minority city on one hand and a rich white-collar city on the other. Large vacuums existed in Haight-Ashbury and the Castro.[55]

It was in this sociological climate that the gay population soared. "It would have been harder to find a segment of the population more suited to fill the thousands of new jobs in the skyscraper corporate headquarters and tourist industries," adds Shilts. Cheap homes in the Mission, Fillmore District, and the Castro were "ideal for the tribes of sixties children who came to live on the fringes of the economy."[56] And while it would take till 1975 for gays to begin to consolidate political power — by 1971 the San Francisco police were arresting an average of about twenty-eight hundred gay men a year on public sex charges — there was no question that by the early '70s, many of America's urban centers had a distinctly gay flavor.

The first migration of men and women during World War II did bring many homosexuals together; but it wasn't a conscious or explicit gathering. And while the influence of homosexual Beat poets like Allen Ginsberg, Robert Duncan, and Jack Spicer should not be underestimated during the '50s, it was limited to a minority of Beats and self-professed "freaks." This second migration, during the '70s, was an infinitely more intentional gathering of men for the purpose of homosexual union. Thousands of gay men left the interior of the country and flocked to the metropolitan coastline to find either Mr. Right or legions of his nameless equivalents in bushes in Buena Vista Park. "There were no reliable statistics," writes Frances FitzGerald in her Pulitzer-winning *Cities on a Hill*, "but the movement was clearly national, and in many cities on a scale to be of some significance to city planner and politicians." As she says, the concentration of gay men and women in the Bay Area probably had no parallel in history.[57]

White gay men found it easier to become part of the new culture than did men of color, who faced resistance from within the black community for being gay and from the white gay establishment for being black. But the problem was not isolated to San Francisco. Some Chicagoans who, like Joel Hall, were pulled between allegiances as well, felt angry that members of the Black Panther party used the term *faggot* to denote psychological castration. When Black Panthers began relating to homosexuals, Hall became a revolutionary too. But the idea was to remain uniquely gay. "I'm really struggling right now with developing my own gay consciousness," he said in 1973, with quintessential revolutionary vitality. "I think that most of the people in Third World Gay Revolution and in Gay Liberation are developing their own consciousness, and trying to relate to other consciousness-raising issues."[58] While some African Americans sought lovers who were also men of color, others preferred to see African American gay men as *bristers*, a combination of "brother" and "sister," and felt less incest taboo with white lovers: "Whenever I'd touch Chris," reminisces Phill Wilson, a gay black Los Angeles AIDS activist, about his late lover, "I felt safe, at home: He showed me how two bodies could become one."

For whatever race you felt drawn to ascribed to or whatever books you read in whatever city you lived, coming out in the early '70s meant pretty much the same to just about everyone: casting off self-hatred. "Long-deferred dreams were made real with heady charm and glee," writes Mark Thompson. "Even more important, painful secrets were now at last being exposed, given up, and healed. The guilt and shame that belonged to previous generations of gay folk were consumed in celebration. The San Francisco sun seemed to burn away more than just the morning's dank and predictable fog."[59] In many cases, sex returned to men a stolen inner life: "When I think of the men I loved," mused David Einstein, "I feel terribly lonely and yet oddly at peace."

While coming out was essentially a personal exercise, it had public implications too—and not all of them good. Gay visionary Carl Wittman, a student of history, saw that ghettoes breed self-hatred and maintain defensive systems. A person can get warped by oppression and can feed on self-exploitation:

> San Francisco is a refugee camp for homosexuals. We have fled here from every part of the nation, and like refugees elsewhere, we came not because it was so great here, but because it was so bad there. By the tens of thousands, we fled small towns where to be ourselves would endanger our jobs and any hope of a decent life; we have fled from blackmailing cops, from families who disowned or

"tolerated" us; we have been drummed out of the armed services, thrown out of schools, fired from jobs, beaten by punks and policemen.

And we have formed a ghetto, out of self-protection. It is a ghetto rather than a free territory because it is still theirs. Straight cops patrol us, straight legislators make our laws, straight employers keep us in line, straight money exploits us. We have pretended everything is OK, because we haven't been able to see how to change it—we've been afraid. . . . [60]

As books like Felice Picano's *The Lure*—a novel about a gay-related murder—makes clear, the ghetto didn't glitter. "Bars, discos, and sex clubs were located in high-crime neighborhoods," writes Rofes in *Reviving the Tribe*. "The drug culture of the '70s, now sentimentalized as ebullient and harmless, was laced with breakdown from bad acid and deaths from overdoses." Rofes also recalls tenacious intestinal parasites, deadly hepatitis that spread "madly and killed many," and "sex-related battering and murder."[61]

As Allen Ginsberg's light-and-dark experience with the Blake poem revealed, an experience of wholeness presents a man with not just the positive side of life. The conscious "I" prefers to split off the "good" from the "bad" and repress the former. But these distinctions don't apply in the unconscious. The bad won't forever stay repressed.

But without a crisis like AIDS, the daily crises of life appeared arbitrary and most remained hopeful about living a completely gay life in a non-gay city. Scores of lavender- and beige-painted houses as well as the shirtless, flirting, flower-buying denizens of Folsom, Polk, and Haight Streets bespoke optimism. By the mid-'70s, it was estimated that one out of every three or four San Francisco voters was gay. There were almost one hundred gay bars, almost twice as many gay organizations and social services, a half-dozen gay newspapers, and three gay Democratic clubs. In retrospect, it's easy to see the shadow brewing in loneliness, alcoholism, and inertia. It's also easy to see why, after so much oppression, gays wanted to focus almost exclusively on the positive; no matter how ultimately destructive that one-sided attitude would turn out to be. For a time, fucking seemed nothing but healing.

the recrudescence of greek culture

As Karla Jay and Allen Young point out in their groundbreaking study of the '70s, *The Gay Report: Lesbians and Gay Men Speak Out About Sexual Experiences and Lifestyles*, a bit of baggage accompanies the activity of anal intercourse. In the Commonwealth of Massachusetts, for example, the coming together of the penis and the anus is known as "the abominable and detestable crime against nature." It's amazing how quickly gay men tried to dismantle that taboo. Jay and Young found that there are "innumerable men who find nothing but delight in anal intercourse," which is also referred to as "ass-fucking," "butt-fucking," "cornholing," and the now old-fashioned term, "browning."

One interviewee tells a story of the journey he and his lover take in which anal sex is the goal of the sex act itself. The setting is an apartment. The interest in having sex is expressed in words through appreciation of the two men's bodies. Soon enough, they're clothed yet supine in bed, making out. Slowly clothes come off. Lying naked, they rub their bodies together, "groin to groin," so that "cocks touch." With a free hand, one man gently touches the cock of another, using plenty of spit for lube. With hands full, kissing resumes a new intensity. One man then lowers himself down to his partner's belly, whereupon he gently licks and sucks the cock and balls. The other partner pushes his friend gently aside to reciprocate. This activity takes anywhere from fifteen to twenty minutes.

For another fifteen or twenty minutes, they shift into a "69" position, with each man lying "with one leg raised, bent at the knee," with the other leg flexed so that each partner can "rest his head on the other man's thigh while sucking." This arrangement gives the best exposure to what appears now to be the main focus of sex: cock and balls. But the focusing of attention is soon to shift. For both men consider oral sex not to be an end in and of itself, but rather a stepping stone to reaching orgasm:

> When we disengage from the 69 position, one of us asks the other, "Want to fuck?" and we reach for the lubricant. Most of the time we use K-Y, occasionally Vaseline. We lie loosely in each other's arms, each with one hand free, and start loosening up each other's asshole with finger-fucking. We usually finger-fuck each other simultaneously, but the man who is going to get fucked first, usually me, gets more attention.

What's striking about the account is the sweetness of attitude combined with a relatively primal sense of urgency. A technical precision has combined with empathy. Here two powerful yet different instincts have met their match—the drive to fuck like an animal, and the drive to open the heart in love:

> First the outer rim of the asshole is rubbed with K-Y, then a finger is gently inserted and moved slowly until the asshole is loosened up. The finger is withdrawn, more lubricant applied, and the finger is inserted as deeply as it will comfortably go. Then the whole procedure is repeated, this time with two fingers. When two fingers can be inserted comfortably, my ass is ready for my lover's

cock. I lie on my side, and with my hand I guide his cock into me. (Previously
I have lubricated his cock with K-Y and masturbated it gently until his hard-on
is good and stiff.) When my lover's cock in inside me, I relax, concentrate on the
good feelings, and he starts fucking me, gently. He works his cock in deep, turns
me over on my stomach, and fucks me for a while in that position. Then we dis-
engage, put more lubricant in my asshole and on his cock, and I lie on my back,
a towel underneath me, my legs up, knees bent, my feet resting on his shoulders.
He reinserts his cock—by now my asshole is really loosened up and he can do
anything he wants with me. This is the part of getting fucked I enjoy the most:
with his cock in me, my lover can lean forward and kiss me, and play with my
nipples, cock, and balls. He fucks me slowly and rhythmically, and I like to feel
him as deep inside me as possible as long as he does not thrust too hard. The
speed of his thrusts increases as he reaches his climax. We cling together, kissing
and moaning. Slowly we disengage, kiss some more, then lie together quietly.[62]

Gay men in the early days of gay liberation placed a higher premium on versatility than men would a few years later. These two men, for example, strive for equality. After the two men have rested, the man who was fucked begins to play with his friend's asshole. Here the fucking is more gentle because one man seems less oriented to being penetrated than the other.

bars to sex?

In Philadelphia you had the P.B.: Clug at 204 South Quince Street or the Boom-Boom Room on 1330 Walnut Street, between Juniper and Broad Streets. In San Diego you had the Barbary Coast on 2341 Pacific Coast Highway (or Mothers at 2501 Kettner). In San Francisco you had the Bolt at 1347 Folsom (formerly the No-Name). Especially before Stonewall, bars served an important function for homosexual men in a world where it wasn't safe to gather publicly. They allowed anonymity as well as a meeting place for those who liked to see friendly faces.

Bars served much the same function in the '70s, with one added difference: They weren't the only place to go to meet another homosexual in public. A man could allow himself a range of choices at a bar. He could have a drink. He could have a cigarette. Or he could have on-site sex:

There must be fifteen men crammed into the unlit women's room at the back of
the bar. I am against the back wall, nearly unable to breath as my hands move
from crotch to crotch looking for a half-opened zipper, a half-hard dick, some
pubic hair. Hands roam over my pants as the smells of leather, poppers, and

beer transform this mundane group grope into a transfigured queer picnic. Lust coexists with breathing as we shift back and forth, moving almost as one, making small spaces to pull or pinch, probe or pummel. My body is crushed against the wall as the group shifts and reestablishes itself. Just as I catch my breath someone puts a bottle of poppers under my nose and for a second, maybe two, I am out of my body and suspended in the natural state of pure lust.[63]

Much of the gay left, however, was horrified by lily-white venues that went so far as to card men of color. They criticized the bars for promoting gay sex with Mafia-like greed. However, some radicals, such as Allen Young, understood bars as a necessary evil:

While fully recognizing the oppressive nature of dimly-lit bars in out-of-the-way streets such as Greenwich Street in New York and Folsom Street in San Francisco, we will continue to preserve the bars as temporary gay turf where there is at least minimal freedom for gay people. This campaign goes on simultaneously with attempts to provide alternative meeting grounds, such as coffee houses and community centers. Such places, along with gay liberation meetings, communal houses and apartments, already offer such an alternative to thousands of gays in nearly 100 localities.[64]

The tug-of-war between all-inclusive politics and the hierarchy of beauty was to cause many a gay man to confront an inherit contradiction between movement politics and individual need. Arthur Bell recalls Gay Liberation Front meetings where men, who called each other "brother," exhorted each other not to use each other as sex objects. Yet after these meetings, he'd "bump into these same preachers sulking in their beers at backroom bars or stalking the corridors of the tubs."[65]

stonewall's ripple

In the first years following the Stonewall Rebellion, gay organizations emerged in major cities; the American Sociological Association became the first professional organization to take a stand against institutional homophobia; openly gay delegates spoke at the 1972 Democratic National Convention; the smash-hit film *Cabaret*, one of the first big-screen validations of homosexual longing, showed sympathetically the betrayal of a handsome bisexual, in the figure of Michael York; college bulletin boards displayed notices for emerging gay student unions. The TV show *Laugh-In*, a barometer of popular culture, featured about one joke per program on gay liberation.

While most younger gay men and teenagers weren't affected in any but a subliminal way, homosexuality was in the air. As Jack Hart says, gayness emerged as something one could be:

> For the first time, it was common to know a happy, healthy, open homosexual. College students, in particular, had many opportunities to see old stereotypes shattered. For some, this made coming out easier. It helped erase the myth that being gay would condemn them to a life of loneliness.

Not everyone benefited. Increased visibility made it harder to fool around innocently. "Unless you were quite adept at self-deceit," adds Hart, "your first man-to-man sex brought an awareness that you were gay. For some, it was too big a package to swallow all at once."[66]

Some guys were lucky enough to have a family member show them the ins and outs:

> John's dark eyes fixed on me; he smiled, he turned toward me. "What men and women do with each other," he murmured with all the savoir faire of a grown up. Blood rushed in my ears. "Didn't anyone ever tell you that?" I shook my head, I was lying, but could he tell? I turned on my stomach because the raging hard-on was forcing itself at right angles from my body.

> It seemed as if I watched us from above, or in the reflection of the tilting bureau mirror, because as my cousin told me the forbidden things about what exactly men and women did, I saw him remove his shirt, saw his brown chest and its first wild swirls of black curly hair; and then his pants came off, and then he helped me with mine. "We have to be quiet." I saw his cock standing up, pulsating, against the sunset-brightened window shades; I watched his face tighten in some strange convulsion, and felt something wet on the bedsheets.[67]

In the early '70s a few gay-oriented films and books did trickle into pop culture. In *Kathleen and Frank: The Autobiography of a Family*, Christopher Isherwood discussed his homosexuality. W. W. Norton published *Maurice*, E. M. Forster's novel about a young man in Edwardian England struggling to come to terms with his homosexuality. John Schlesinger's 1971 film *Sunday, Bloody Sunday* featured a gay doctor and a divorcee sharing the same male lover.

But for many gay teens, it was just as hard as ever to feel good about being gay. On January 27, the New York City Council vetoed a gay rights ordinance that would have prohibited discrimination in employment, housing, and public accommodations. To make any kind of real dent in the psyche, the means of communication had to be sexual. Wakefield Poole's 1972 cutting-edge gay porn flick, *Boys in the Sand*, did more to help younger gay men feel good about loving other guys than any city ordinance. Some remember sneaking into New York City's Fifty-fifth Street Playhouse as adolescents to see the twenty-eight-year-old, blue-eyed Casey Donovan getting sucked off in some of the finest camera work ever done on a porn movie. The film, about a group of handsome men cruising Fire Island for quick sex, boasts the infamous line, "There are no more closets."

the heritage of pornography   By the mid-'70s, porn reached a level of respectability, an effective tool not just for erotic stimulation, but for mirroring changing sexual attitudes. Jack Stillman, a starving twenty-eight-year-old actor, danced on stage between porn films in L.A.'s Paris Theater. That's where he got his break. Lacking both the muscle-clad body of a gay porn icon and the baby-faced dimples of an ingenue, he had what so few porn stars could lay claim to: an authentic love of male-to-male sex. He became known as Jack Wrangler. Whether grabbing another man's dick in *The Boys from Riverside Drive* or jerking himself off in his first film, *Ranch Dudes*, he showed a certain talent for blending masculinity with overt homosexual impulses, urges, and instinctual drives. He wasn't some straight guy getting off with another "dude" while his girlfriend was out of town.

This still didn't keep some gay radicals from criticizing the imagery. "The most successful makers of 8-mm male pornographic movies for home projection," railed Allen Young in the '70s, "such as Brentwood and Falcon, peddle their wares by setting up situations where masculinity is portrayed, relationships are spared or anonymous and emotional aspects down played (emotion = femininity)." Young's psychological critique didn't take into account gay male psychology. Oppressed or not, many homosexual men lusted after men who symbolized the "masculine archetype" as it filtered through their feelings for their fathers. It bothered Young that masculinity was affirmed by having models portrayed as athletes or hard-hats.[68]

He wasn't alone in criticizing the cultural prejudices around race, age, body type, and penis size that most porn films seemed guilty of. While some activists agreed with Young, many were wary of taking porn on in the same way radical feminists did. "It seemed unhealthy to attack fantasies of any kind," reminisced one gay New York editor, "even if the fantasies seemed unhealthy." His generation of gay men did not want to shame already shamed people. The fantasy life of gay men was deemed off limits to political correctness. If there was a critique, it was gentle and put in a larger context.

By the mid-'70s, porn was just getting off the ground, transforming itself from its mail-order underground to commercial respectability. The year 1975 showed the publication of both *Drummer* and *Blueboy* as preeminent skin magazines. *Drummer,* a slick, forty-page publication, devoted itself to S&M, bondage, water sports, and leather. *Blueboy,* published by a former advertising representative for the gay-inflected *After Dark,* combines nudes with erotic fiction and articles on gay culture.

But it was Fred Halsted's film *Sextool,* replete with fist-fucking, nipple piercing, forced anal sex, bondage, and hustler action, that invited *Variety* to dub Halsted the "Ken Russell of S&M homoerotica." Beautifully edited, with a charged acid-rock sound track, *Sextool* distinguished itself from the poorly made, slow-paced gay porn films of the previous ten years. According to one observer, the level of care and refinement that came to porn in the late '70s showed an increased appreciation among gay men for how homosexuality was depicted. "The basic postures," he says, "never changed. But the lighting and direction did." He refers to a moment in Wakefield Poole's *Boys in the Sand,* when Casey Donovan approaches the crotch of a man with a slowness and delicacy that had not been seen before.

Pat Rocco's movies of the late '60s characterized sex as a celebration, with a great deal of kissing. But it took Wakefield Poole and Fred Halsted to bring a level of cinematic elegance to the beauty of naked bodies fucking. And while it's hard to equate these mid-'70s films as art forms, porn connoisseurs see them as a cut above most skin flicks. They paved the way for the seamless edge characterized by the sexiest of Falcon movies.

a little theory on extroversion

In providing cultural and historical information about sexual life during the '70s, some of the men interviewed feared that they would be judged harshly by men who came of age during AIDS. "Staying rational is more cherished now than it was in the '70s," explains one man. "You have to understand that we were trying to find another way to be besides 'staying rational.'" To his mind, people were trying to lose themselves in the inflationary aspect of sexuality for the purpose of actually finding themselves. "No one knew at the time," he adds, "that the real 'finding' would take place with the downside of things."

"There was something distinctly cosmic going on for me in the midst of all this groping," comments Arnie Kantrowitz. Gay sexual pioneers like Kantrowitz suggest that this incredibly rich and precarious dance with Dionysian energies was not merely a way to redeem a lost god, but was an accelerated effort for gay men to encounter a psychological fact, namely that there are two autonomous centers of psychic being. Just as Copernicus discovered that the sun does not revolve around the earth, thus challenging the egocentrism that considered this planet to be the center of the universe, gay men discovered that life does not revolve around the conscious mind. Some other seemingly implacable hunger bubbling up from the unconscious showed itself as a force to be reckoned with. This force would not be willed away. It had to be integrated as part of the personality.

"Eons have passed," writes one of the characters in Fritscher's novel, "waiting for this specific convergence of so many old souls to worship the Old God who predates Christianity. Our spirits have been harvested from time older than time, collected here and now out of all uncounted ages of men for this reincarnation in unison. I have no father, no brother, no son more than these men gathered here in this time, in this flesh, in this space more auspiciously than any of us realized at first."[69]

Despite the lack of irony in that account, it does correspond to many efforts during that time to attribute more than arbitrary meaning to the sex taking place. What, after all, *is* the difference between an orgy and a ritual? "Never on this planet," adds the writer, "have so many men of such similar mind gathered together to fuck in the celebration of pure, raw, priapic, manhood. If the mythic St. Priapus has never been canonized by the Catholic Church, then he has been made a saint in San Francisco in these halls, in the temples of our conjoined bodies, tangled in passion, slick with sweat and glazed with seed."[70] Fritscher suggests that gay men have a hero guarded in the back of their own minds. An autonomous complex, it is one's own Patrocolus, but it lives in the shadows. This is nothing new. The old religions that valued such symbols of the collective psyche were born of the human soul. But gay men had abandoned those religions (because they had, after all, abandoned gays). In other words, gay men, feeling the heat of this heroic force in the psyche, did not believe the heat came from within. They projected it outward. A man is supposed to be a master of his own house. Perish the thought that he'd have to share his abode with a complex, not to mention one more hot than he.

on body worship   In reminiscing about the '70s, some gay men suggest that the archetypal need to worship, which had been dying a slow death in Christian culture since the Enlightenment, was rekindled in the act of public homosexual sex.

"Some people really got off on having you worship them," Kantrowitz recalls. "That was their drawing card. I would often stay for hours on my knees, in the doorway, signaling that people could come in for a certain kind of headtrip, or adventure. This was not good for the knees. It may have been very good, however, for the spirit. Think back to some of those Christian ascetics. They would kneel on the gravel, so why can't I kneel on a bathhouse floor? We're all disciplining our bodies to deal with a higher purpose, no?"

Jack Fritscher's novel about gay life in the '70s, *Some Dance to Remember*, epitomizes the kind of idolatry some men sought from each other. The protagonists bumps into a muscled god wearing a HP jacket and wool shirt. Ryan kneels in front of Kick. His right hand he uses on himself. His left, "as if for all my life I had been saving a virgin hand for stroking [Kick's] hardpumped muscle, palmed the contours of his body. I ram my left hand up [Kick's] . . . calves and thighs not daring to touch his hard rod for fear the muscle worship would revert to purely genital sex." Falling into a litany of verbal appreciation, Ryan mentions how much he worships Kick's energy, and Kick shoots rivers of seed on the prostrated man's face.[71]

The account points to a phenomenon that emerged in the mid-'70s and which has been recouped from the '50s: body worship or muscle sex. "I think that the ultimate ritual act of worship in the twentieth century," says one man in *Some Dance to Remember*, "is a grown man, stripped, naked, stoned on grass, with poppers by his side and clamps on his tits, greasing up his dick, kneeling on the floor with his face four inches from the video screen, masturbating to glorious close-ups of bodybuilders flexing and posing."[72]

As gay life matured in urban centers, many men returned to a masculine style of dress formerly abandoned by gays attracted to the hippie image or the androgynous, *un*developed body as epitomized by pop idols Mick Jagger and David Bowie. Either out of an appreciation for the archetypal male form or because of an nagging insecurity that homosexual men were inherently *not* male, gay urban culture of the mid-'70s saw the emergence of the hypermasculine gay guy. For the first time in history, gay men were able to fall in love with straight-acting men who were very open about being gay. These men struck a pose; they were Tarzan; they were one's father; they were Lou Ferigno; they were Tony Sansone — "idealized visions of perfection unconnected with the world around them."[73]

It's easy to reduce muscle worship to a psychological referendum on the poor self-esteem of gay men. "Some men opened their hearts best when they felt like doormats," quipped one sexual athlete of the '70s. "In their masochism, in their not-being, they found an escape from life." But Kantrowitz and Fritscher argue for a deeper analysis. Here the man being adored is the recipient of the worshiper's projection of an inner sense of wholeness, calm, and beauty.

Gay libbers, weaned on the lesbian feminism of Jill Johnston and Mary Daly, posited that adorations of masculine perfection were taught to gay men by a violently male culture.[74] With their glorification of militaristic styles, the infamous skin magazines published by the American Model Guild were criticized as part of the problem. But by the mid-'70s, this feminist critique of the body-as-phallus had lost its power. The gay clone, with his flannel shirts and blue jeans, had triumphed over androgyny as the object of men's crushes. "The clone dress," explains one gay archivist, "was really a folk dress, an affordable, masculine outfit accessible to everyone." Edmund White was less kind, describing the look as

> a strongly marked mouth and swimming, soulful eyes (the effect of the mustache): a V-shaped torso by metonymy from the open V of the half-buttoned shirt above the sweaty chest; rounded buttocks squeezed in jeans, swelling out from the cinched-in waist, further emphasized by the charged erotic insignia of colored handkerchiefs and keys . . . legs moulded in perfect, powerful detail; the feet simplified, brutalized and magnified by the boots.[75]

Whatever one's view of the "clone" was, everyone agreed that the uniform provided a socially recognizable way for the gay man to "fit in" as a man in his community. But it also showed something else: that the symbol—the masculine double—had not yet been differentiated by the individual.

When a symbol of the collective unconscious remains projected into the world, and not owned by the ego, it stays locked in place out in the social world, as it were. A person mistakes his own most private thoughts as a piece of external reality. A person can't tell the difference in this condition; the ego is unconscious of its own psyche and thus is actually in a state of unconscious merger with the projected contents. Anthropologists call this *participation mystique*. People who see a lover as nothing but an extension of their own secret wishes are engaging in a merger as are any number of people who sacrifice their own individuality for the "good of the group." To pull away from this *participation mystique* is difficult and is the subject of many world myths (*Prometheus Bound*, Adam and Eve, the stories of Jesus and Buddha).

This understanding of "differentiation" suggests a way of working with unconscious, symbolic material so as to discover its reality within and thereby form an individual relationship to it rather than a merely collective (and, thus ultimately anonymous) participation. This is how a symbol is transformed. Historically speaking, the collective soul symbol of the gay male community hadn't been seen for what it was: the result of what happens when a vast number of people project their soul image in the world. As such, the symbol cannot yet possess an inner presence for the ego.

This happens because the sexual instinct first expresses itself globally as an insatiable need to merge with another human being on an immediate soul-sex level. Our relations with unconscious contents start with projections. At this level of awareness, there are no tools to do otherwise. Just as a person acts from collective instinct, so the image that motivates him is also collective. If the love object becomes too human—if it loses his symbolic mystery, impersonal character, and archetypal charge—it loses its heat. The relationship cannot continue outside the participation mystique. A transformation of attitude is in order. A person might consider owning his projections. Or Fate will force him to.

In the '70s, people experienced nuclear, frequent, and immediate soul epiphanies without a manageable and indigenous container that could support reowning of projections. Heterosexual male culture has had millennia to differentiate its feminine soul figure (Earth Goddess; Mother Mary; Mary Magdalene; one's own mother; Madonna). Gay male culture has had to do this work in record time, and with no assistance. Men had immediate crushes. There was not time to think about what was going on. One had to satisfy one's crush, if that meant creating a community—so be it.

That's reasonable enough. After all, the power of the sexual crush is almost mind-boggling, so much so that some gay men did their best to have it often. "Sex enabled me to both look for and find a 'crush' on a nightly basis," says Ross Farley. "And if one 'crush' didn't work out, you could console yourself with the notion that there were other men who would do, especially with the lights turned down." The reality underlying the search for the crush could not be dismissed.[76]

Men like Mark Thompson, Kantrowitz, and Fritscher suggested the idea of looking at the search for these crushes psychologically. If a gay man were secretly crushed inside, if fate (or his father) had hurt him, then chances are the hunger for wholeness through sex would be all that more pressing. When archetypal demands press themselves upon a person who suffers a serious wound, the energies for connection will spring from that wound. This is the basic message of the Wounded King in the Grail Legend: how to return to the wound so as to avail oneself of new sources of life. Homo eros lives in one's heart, one's broken heart. For this reason, any man might find himself attracted to someone who reflects (or complements) the condition of his soul. A man might look for a strong daddy—or a wounded boy or an effeminate man (or a man who seems to contain all those attributes) to magically (and quickly) heal the Fisher King's wound. Even in a brief suck-session, the projection of the soul complex (or some version therein) could be the psychological event behind the "quickie."

But the autonomous "soul complex" is rarely felt as a personal and imme-diate reality inside. It is not owned. Rather it is encountered in a suitable object. That continual projecting spells trouble. While men hunger for a feeling of sexy completeness through the "other," such a one-sided attitude conjures its oppo-site in their own hearts: emptiness, lack, hunger. Remember, there is a wound associated with yearning. If the projections aren't consciously returned home, a person may be left feeling worthless and exhausted indefinitely. He may be left with nothing but his shadow, his uniquely crushed and revenging gay shadow.

This duality—feelings of worthlessness and feelings of selfhood—is rarely seen as the puzzle behind sexual attraction. This marks a tragic limitation in our one-sided thinking and feeling. To know both is to be whole. Eros seeks what it lacks and is therefore ugly. No wonder "wholeness" can be unbearable to feel over a long period of time and with a single man, for it includes integrating con-sciously one's inferiorities. So the search gets repeated—and with strangers. The soul figure is not differentiated, is not loved for itself. Neither is the flesh-and-blood beloved.

Gay thinkers who present these views don't mean to condemn the way most people, gay men included, have loved. The idea is to value projective ef-forts in a historical sense as the initial means by which gay personality gets devel-oped. We simply can't discover an unconscious content *unless* it is projected first. To go to the next step, then, one must begin to recollect the process. We must separate our ego from the symbol of our fiercest yearning, the masculine soul-double. The idea is to objectify the soul as an actual being in his own right, as a living daemon, as a spirit within, the personification of homosexual libido.

Fritscher, in his '70s novel *Some Dance to Remember*, paints a picture of a mythic Adam who seems to live in the back of his own mind. And perhaps he does. For if nothing else, Fritscher's work is an effort to suggest that this personifi-cation of male homosexual libido is what pushed men to gather and connect in the streets and bathhouses. Men allowed themselves to go mad for this man. But if this figure was a man, why was it so hard to find him in a bathhouse?

chapter four

trouble in
paradise

the age of experience

the hunger of angels

Wearing his 501 jeans and tight white T-shirt, Ron Hardcastle jumped on his ten-speed bike and headed east from Westwood. He passed through Century City with its brightly lit towers and through Beverly Hills with its off-putting designer stores. Hardcastle chained his bike behind the Third Street building and then, with a prayer that the vehicle might remain when he returned, he walked to the side of the large old building facing Cedars Sinai Medical Center. The white paint on the metal door was rough and chipped, but the numbers showed all right—"8709": the name of one of L.A.'s hottest sex clubs in the late '70s.

With his heart racing, Hardcastle spotted about fifteen young men in their twenties and thirties lined up along the stairway. "This was just the place I wanted to be on a weekend," he reminisces, "and as I stood there, looking up at the faded Levi's clinging to round but firm asses, I found myself wondering how those bodies looked out of their jeans and if I would have sex with any of them before the night was over."

Once inside, Hardcastle tossed his clothes into a locker and wrapped the towel around his waist "after folding it lengthwise so it was like a short toga rather than having it hang nearly to my feet like a skirt." His next stop was the large open shower room, which, "depending on the hour, one could find empty or jammed with wet shiny bodies, sometimes in singles and sometimes in couples." Often two men shared a nozzle as they washed and nuzzled each other.

It was a calm night, so he repaired to the orgy room, even though it was not his favorite haunt, to ease himself into a state of mind for dispensing with boundaries:

> The orgy room was bathed in a murky red haze, with a huge square custom-built bed on a platform in the center covered by a tight white sheet. I called it "The Bed" and in that light it had been turned a soft pink and it dominated the room. The moment I walked in, I was hit by the smell of lube and poppers and soap. I didn't mind the lube, and soap for me was an aphrodisiac, but I was repulsed by the poppers. I rarely did anything on The Bed, since I didn't relish audiences, but occasionally I'd get an offer I couldn't refuse, and when that happened, I would try to shut everyone else out as I sucked and got sucked, fucked and got fucked.[1]

The no-holds-barred sexual greed that Hardcastle discovered entertained him more than it turned him on:

> Mostly I was amused by the three-ring circus spectacle of the orgy rooms. It was fun to watch the wordless catfights over particularly monumental cocks, and neither finders-keepers nor possession-is-nine-tenths-of-the-law seemed to apply there with one fellow brazenly yanking a cock out of someone else's mouth and immediately stuffing it into his own mouth, and then fighting off the original sucker who was just as determined to get the prized cock back. Girls!

While Hardcastle knew better than to imagine he'd find a lover at this sex club, he knew what he liked—"bathhouse monogamy":

> There were guys who liked to have dozens of hands all over their bodies, caressing and exploring, while others sought but rarely found bathhouse monogamy amid the mass madness. It was surreal, the orgy room clearly the perfect setting for indulging any voyeuristic tendencies you might have been harboring. Since I was more of a one-at-a-time-guy, I was usually one of the dozens standing around, pausing just long enough for a quick peek while on the way to somewhere else.

But meeting a man to fuck around with was easier said than done. It took too much time; entailed rejection. Determined to have as much sex as possible, Hardcastle situated himself in the club's glory hole cubicles. Just then a sabotaging thought attacked him. He hungered for involvement that felt less mechanical. How could he try to find a lover, he'd ask himself, in a glory hole cubicle?

But as soon as the first attractive man pushed his cock through the large hole, second thoughts gave way to second helpings:

> It was only 10 P.M., but the glory hole rooms were already busy and full. Timing being everything, I managed to grab one of the favored rooms just as someone left, but not knowing what had gone on there before I arrived. I carefully wiped the edges around the large holes to sop up any residual mystery juices. What a din. Even the loud rock and dance music pumped nonstop into the area from overhead speakers couldn't drown out the constant slamming of plywood doors as guys came and went, came and went. There were nights when I would bring cotton to stuff into my ears to lower the volume and if I forgot the cotton, I'd use tiny wads of toilet paper.

Hardcastle had a lot of fun collecting his tricks of the bathhouse trade. But even in paradise, a certain demanding quality—a hierarchy of size, for example—set in. "I had become quite a connoisseur," he describes. "And eventually my nights at the 8709 made it difficult for me to truly enjoy sex with anyone whose dick wasn't to my mind near perfect." He wouldn't look twice at cocks that were "skinny or had heads that were pointed or tiny or slick and slimy red or had an unretractable or in any way bothersome foreskin." Choosiness did not hamper Hardcastle's opportunities. At least not at the 8709. That club seemed to draw not just "magnificent young men, but also magnificent young men with equally magnificent cocks."

While Hardcastle was mostly "oral," and could depend on cocksucking as a way of receiving and giving pleasure, he did go through stages where anal fucking appealed too. In the early '70s, for example, he often got fucked at the Corral Club in Studio City. He did so with as many as half a dozen guys in a single night, "sometimes while standing in the showers, but more often while lying on my stomach in private rooms." Fun at the old 7661 club on Melrose Avenue meant "sitting on an incredibly large cock in the dark." He had no idea if the owner of that "heavenly monstrosity" would turn out to look more like "a Paul Newman or a Richard Nixon."

By the time he started frequenting the 8709 club, he'd reserve getting fucked for only the most special of occasions. Hardcastle describes meeting a man who corresponds to his fantasy of the wiry, tough guy with a soft, wounded look. In this account, Hardcastle shows the ways in which two men ass fucking each other can mirror the masculinity they lack yet crave:

> Tonight there was a familiar fellow in his late 20s with a brown military crewcut, a gorgeous body, and a cute face. I had been with him a number of times before,

although we rarely spoke to one another in those tiny dark cubicles or the few times we chose to get a little more civilized in a regular room with a bed. Over 6'8", he was much too big for those rooms, was so tall that in the glory hole rooms he had to crouch down just to get his cock through the hole in the plywood, and even then it would sometimes scrape on the top edge of the hole, especially when he really got moving.

Physical discomfort and mental vulnerability go by the wayside when the man's a hunk:

I made up my mind the first night I met him that I just had to have that huge cock inside me, so I took his hand and placed it on my ass so that it would be his decision whether or not to screw me. "Go for it," he had whispered in a deep masculine voice, making it clear that he was more than happy to oblige. It was awkward, but we managed it and I could feel his hot breath blowing over the partition, could feel every tremor as Mt. Vesuvius erupted inside me.

Fate provided Hardcastle with even more pleasure. While he was bending over and getting his ass pounded by Mr. 6'8", someone else stuck his cock through the other side: "So there I was, bending down like a contortionist to suck this other fat cock which I could just barely reach while the tall stud continued to fuck me from behind. It seemed to go on for an hour."

The two men are given license to go over the top in terms of how much sensation their mind and bodies can take and integrate. They give over to nature, becoming the tools of libido, as if the individual is the object, not the subject of such processes. "Finally," Hardcastle recounts, "as if by an exchanged signal, both of them came at the same instant, shooting inside me toward each other to stereophonic gasps of pleasure that echoed from room to room. And then the three of us went gleefully to the showers together, proudly parading our sweaty bodies and our swinging hard-ons with towels tossed casually over our shoulders, boisterously laughing all the way down the hall."

This time there would be three men under the single shower nozzle Hardcastle noticed when he first entered the club. How fun! And freeing. But only for a time. But while Hardcastle loved the camaraderie, he intuited that in a flash it would be over and he'd be alone again.

on loneliness

If gay pride and the sexual revolution were meant to bring gay men out of the shadows of loneliness, often a hot scene left a person more lonely then ever. The drive to connect with the gay-soul-complex often confronted a man with his gay-shadow-complex. The clone look, and the pose that could accompany it, hardened men and the feeling capacity; the fear of rejection was deferred by the act of rejecting. Seymour Kleinberg sees the armor as a mere persona, with the underlying dilemma hardly addressed: "The problems are the old, familiar ones: misery when in love, loneliness when one is not. . . ."[2] Or put Paul Goodman's way, "What we need is not defiant pride and self-consciousness, but social space to live and breathe."[3] Hardcastle wanted a hug as much as dick. Michael Callen once declared that sometimes anal penetration was the only way he allowed himself to receive touch.

Writer George Whitmore assailed the commercial-driven sex culture as an "unexamined life" that pushed one to extremes of alienation and loneliness. He saw the notion of the "rebel" pushed by John Rechy as an extension of a gay man's oppression, not a way out of it. ("If society tells him the only way he can be gay is to crawl around on his hands and knees in a sewer five nights a week, the Rebel will oblige.")[4] Whitmore believed that men lost themselves in this process, becoming one with the gay ghetto and its dehumanizing codes of sexual tyranny (not to mention distasteful uniforms). If gay lib began as a tearing down of defenses to find the kernel of gay spirit inside each homosexual, the sexual revolution made that pursuit into something merely collective, merely persona.

The truth is, many experienced sexual dysfunction—or confusion or just boredom. Some men were only able to cum with men they didn't know. Others wanted physical companionship—touching, kissing, petting—but got turned off the minute they felt pressure to get a hard-on. In a culture that saw cumming together as the finest expression of sexual athleticism, Whitmore's main character in *The Confessions of Danny Slocum* feels a louse: "In the past two years, I've cum exactly twice—in company, as it were—with two different men. I don't know how many men I've 'failed' with in two years. . . ." The solution is to find a man, Joe, who suffers—and thus mirrors—a similar problem ("Joe has never cum with another person in his life"). With the prompting of their shrink, Virgil, they try to turn each other on vis-à-vis a little sex therapy. "It's clear to me now," confesses Danny, "that what we're engaged in is nothing less than a complete restructuring of our sexual responses. . . ." In a word, the two men can't live up to the demands of the typical gay lifestyle. Of course, they're not alone, but they don't know that. They treat sex as if it were no different from passing the most grueling of tests, overdetermining its importance in their lives and thus ruining their lives:[5]

> With all the ritual concentration of bullfighters suiting up for the ring, Joe and I prepare for our first night of "sex."

As usual we are going to massage. But we have also preselected and set close at hand our porno—pictures for Joe, stories for me. When we finish massaging, we are to begin to jack each other off. Then, when we get hot, we're to finish the job in separate rooms.

The theory, as Virgil's outlined it for us (and as we've read in The Joy of Gay Sex *half a dozen times by now), is to approach each other gradually, over a series of sessions from the other room, from across the room, with our backs to each other, then side by side—and eventually arrive at mutual (if not simultaneous) orgasms.*

We are giggly and self-conscious. I can't look Joe in the eye. I get hard immediately. Joe takes a little longer. As he pumps me, I feel . . . if he . . . does it just a bit longer. . . .

The idea that I might cum then and there is terrifying. I ask Joe to stop for a while. I felt that I could have cum, but I have thrashed around on that particular plateau many times before. Was it an illusion this time as well?

Joe's eyebrows rise on his tanned forehead. He is thinking. I find out later, that I am less fucked up than he. He must struggle for a moment to remember that not cumming is my problem too. Feels faintly betrayed, a sinking disappointment. Will I pass him up? What kind of game have I been playing all these weeks? He falls back on the quilt and closes his eyes.[6]

The two begin their sexual maneuvering again, this time from separate rooms, with Danny in the bathroom and Joe in the bedroom. Each listens to the other turning pages, almost competing as who can cum first.

Finally the relationship based on seeming covenience, sputters. "We are, after all, in this lover-like position only in order to seek out our own lovers freely. If our love achieves its purpose, it will no longer be needed."[7] The world based merely on adapting to the sexual playing field feels desiccated to these men who are plagued by an unremitting paralysis of feeling. These two men weren't trying to become something they could never be: a sexual athlete, a stud, a sexual connoisseur, a slab of meat, a hot property. All they were trying to do was to learn how to get a hard-on with another man. Their dysfunction stands in apparent contradiction to a community of men sport-fucking at the Barracks who thought they were living out a dream of utter individuality. But Danny and Joe are true individuals, for individuality is gained as little by adapting to the social world as it is by merging with it through sex. In fact, Danny and Joe attempt to bring their individual eccentricities to bear on their intimate sex lives. For this heroic effort to learn how to fuck with their humanity intact, they are made to feel "fucked up." The failure on the part of the gay community to see the lesson in Danny's and Joe's struggle, and to look inside during the first militant detonation of gay lib, forced gay radicals to declare the "revolution over."[8]

the return of the repressed

The untamed dance with sexual extremes is not new. As early as the thirteenth century B.C., the worship of Dionysus had spread across Europe and Asia. His cult received state approval by the ancient Greeks during springtime festivals. But the law-abiding Romans and Jews rebelled against the world of sensation in favor of the world of thinking. Violence to the body and soul thus took place through the triumph of reason. But the process of strengthening the ego at the expense of unconscious life seems to some psychologists as developmentally necessary.[9]

Christianity emerged as an antidote to the prevailing polytheistic chaos of the times. Judging by the numbers of its converts, it was a welcome relief. The body had previously been so utterly degraded. The sexual instinct had pressed the spiritual into its service. Oppressed by the body-phobic values of the New and Old Testaments, we don't realize how refreshing Christianity must have felt to people two thousand years ago. Little did they know how relentlessly the spiritual would press the sexual into *its* service.[10]

During the Renaissance, a swinging back to Dionysian licentiousness swept over Europe, where the anarchy of flesh was depicted in "religious" paintings—and acted out in various wars between Catholics, Protestants, and heathens. This heat of Catholicism was cooled by Protestantism and its more literal way of looking at symbols like the Eucharist. Locke led to American-style democracy.[11]

But the latent desire to lose one's mind in sensation could not be laid to rest. It exploded once again in the twentieth century when feminists, civil rights activists, gay liberationists, and free speech advocates saw an egregious suppression of life. When an archetype is not experienced with either consciousness or dignity, it loads up with energy and becomes inhuman.[12]

Historians D'Emilio and Freedman argued that "higher standards of wealth, the expanded opportunities that came with urban living, and the mobility provided by the automobile all pointed in the direction of more sexual experience. . . ."[13] But another argument, just as valid, can be made that psyche itself harbors a need to individuate itself: the creation of an ego with strong defenses and the eventual necessity to dislodge those so the ego can make a relationship to its unconscious contents are historical facts, facts that have contributed to our religious, scientific, and sexual lineages and struggles.

the sexual design

A study of sexual histories from the '70s shows at first a random design—some compulsiveness, some bliss, some dead ends. But if one watches this meandering design over a long period of time, an onlooker can observe an almost hidden or regulating tendency at work. For some men, this pattern reveals almost a directing quality at work; some call this regulatory process "the self." To chart a sexual history of any kind, a person must know whether a man was elated or depressed at one point of his sexual life or another. It is difficult to say anything rational about sex without acknowledging its emotional—irrational—undertones.

The '70s seemed like a rocket ride up in the first half of the decade and a slow emotional descent in the second. There was an attempt to cushion the coming down with the engineering of drugs—a little marijuana, some mescaline, mixed with a quaalude or a Valium. But even the presumably "high" places began to rub the wrong way.

This up-and-down quality can be seen throughout all sexual and romantic life—sometimes during the same evening. This ping-ponging between inflation and deflation (between romantic love and romantic estrangement) is how a person becomes conscious of what psychologist Edward F. Edinger calls "the ego-self axis."

Andrew Holleran's *Dancer from the Dance* is a sourcebook for the way in which opposites bring both bliss and suffering to the urbanites of the Flamingo and Fire Island. The main character, Malone, falls in love with Frankie and, of course, has no clue that his "up" is soon to crash in an inevitable deflation.

"At the beginning," writes Holleran, "Malone could not even allow Frankie to sit down opposite him without getting up and going over to embrace him." Malone couldn't see his friend standing at a window or taking a piss without "enfolding him from behind in his arms." Malone took to wearing identical clothing—sneakers, jeans, earring, and a crucifix. As opposites, who also both looked like pirates, "they began to look like each other—except for that unmistakable difference, when they lay tangled in each other's limbs by day or night, the pale, golden form and the swarthy, dark-eyed one, the northern and southern race joined at last." As Holleran puts it, "Malone lived only for Frankie now."[14]

Frankie seems to return the affection, kissing his friend on the eyelids and holding him for hours "in their window above the harbor." The merger seems magical; both assume it will last forever. "He felt a perfect peace as he lay there on Sunday afternoon in the shadows, his face laid on the cool, smooth depression of Frankie's stomach." Holleran goes on for pages writing about their perfect fit. ("The touch of Frankie's body against his own was so soft, so delicate, when their legs were intertwined after making love and Frankie was drifting off to sleep. . . .") The characters grow intoxicated in the superhuman elixir of love; they get a taste of what every popular song promises and what every gay romance is based on. Frankie gazes at Malone when they make love with "an expression of mild curiosity, and wonderment, at Malone's passion."[15]

But, as Holleran implies, the love each man has for the other isn't based on anything human. It is nothing but a projection, emanating from each of their unconscious psyches, and it just so happens that vibrationally each manages to be a convenient screen. But projections ebb and flow. Extroversion of libido becomes introversion. If an individual does not consciously recollect his "hero" projection, then chances are the unconscious will do him the favor behind his back. And Malone, one day, falls for another boy. And then another. And then another. Then, when returning to Frankie, "It was as if he had fallen from a tree." And then, in making love to Frankie, he feels as if he is drowning in the waters of the unconscious, in inertia, in the clawing, treacherous yawn of the Great Mother. "Was Frankie a trap?" Malone asks. "As viscous as the sticky glue on the No-Pest strip that hung above them like the streamer of a Chinese lantern?" All the things that Malone had loved about Frankie—his TV-watching, his cussing, his blue-collar persona, his temper—now tire Malone. The affair ends violently when Frankie finds out that Malone had been cheating on him. In this way, the opposites of romantic love get revealed in any full experience. But men addicted to only the "light" side of things, flee when a lover shows his shadowy (and thus human) side.[16]

In a 1979 *Advocate* interview, Holleran named this failure to humanize love as being at the core misery of gay life. "So we're looking for the Superman, we're looking for this person better than ourselves and at the same time working to be the superman. We seem to be going farther and farther away from the old human context of love, which is loving a man for his humor, for his character, for the way he deals with the world."[17]

And yet the *superman* seems to exist as an inner phenomenon, despite the way one's unexamined personal shadow disowns or obscures it. How to separate the inner Superman from the outer Frankies of the world so as to avoid contamination and too many failed loves?

If there were a way to honor one's inner superman without imposing his qualities on mere mortals, by making a conscious encounter with the inner soul complex, gay life had yet to come up with such a technique or strategy.

Arnie Kantrowitz also suffered through the opposites of the sexual revolution. What was once "blissful" became "oppressive."

The sexual veteran describes the sex of the late '70s as both a phallic experience and a womblike one, with a protective quality that, in the end, stultified him and went against his impulses to be an individual. "In all these [bathhouses] there was a kind of dorm room where a group of guys could sleep and have sex in total darkness. Once I felt as if I lost my identity there because everyone was sucking and fucking everything that came near them. We were like a pile of warm puppies. I had to stagger out into the dim light of the hallway just to reassure myself that I existed as myself."

Despite the comfort Kantrowitz found, he also discovered that, on a community-wide level, sex had become more and more impersonal and more and more about immediate gratification. "It got to the point where even going to the baths was too much trouble. You had to wait in line to get in." Because the bathhouse life got too predictable, Kantrowitz found himself gravitating to the more earthy side of things. So he frequented the Everhard. With a hint of nostalgia, Kantrowitz remembers that "there were people that you met there almost every time you went, and you kept thinking, could it be a coincidence that we always come at the same night. You began to think that there were some sewer rats who never emerged into the daylight."

Ultimately, Kantrowitz turned to backrooms, in part because you didn't have to get totally undressed in them. "I found it more convenient and less threatening to have mass impersonal sex," he recalls. "During my more social period, I'd meet people and take them home for the night. You'd have a fantasy person you were sleeping with, and then in the morning you're dealing with this little twerp who's late for work, instead of the Lord of the Universe. Besides, I hate making breakfast for people."

So he'd don paratrooper pants ("in their big pockets you could keep books, sunglasses and equipment"). He'd wear a tank top ("Black, because it was more slimming"). Over that, he wore an open flannel shirt with the sleeves rolled up ("I know, so butch"). Then he'd go to the infamous Mine Shaft.

mind shaft   You enter from a lower level and walk up stairs to check your clothes and pay four dollars for two drinks. You pass through an archway into a large dark room. Along one wall are cubicles. Slings hang from the ceiling. Another wall offers glory holes. Two staircases take a person down to pitch-black rooms with icy cement walls. Human *pissoirs* lounge in bathtubs.

The place is located on Washington and Little West 12 in New York City's wholesale meat district. You know the district, because as a kid, during a hot New York City summer, you made money for college there. But that was by day. During the day the area bustled with butchers in blood-stained white aprons spiriting decapitated animals out of gasping trucks into refrigerated storage. Now it's night, and the streets, smelling of blood, look empty. A man exits a cab. He looks anywhere between twenty and fifty, dressed in leather and Levi's and wearing a policeman's cap.

Even with its dress code (no alligator shirts or cologne), the Mine Shaft attracts too many tourists on weekends and poseurs to be of any use to you. You need to be around men like you, men who care for nothing but to be taken down, hard and fast. At its peak, traffic reaches 400, with people from the "bridge and tunnel club" chatting too self-consciously near the two pool tables in the first room for you to lose your mind in cum. So you seek your dance with the slimy homo deity of this place on a weeknight.[18]

You're hungry tonight, thirsty too. Your dick gets hard just thinking about a man's pissing streaming in your mouth, a funny odd piece of cannibalism—at least, that's how it feels to you—that you've gotten into this year, this year being 1978. Last week, it didn't go so well, with the "top" being a bit more of a sadist than you tend to like, forcing you hard on your knees. (You like your rough sex to have a sentimental quality to it, for there to be a touch of sweetness in all the play-acting.) "You want it fresh, pig?" the man asked. You generally like the stuff only when it's watered down, when the men follow the unspoken etiquette of golden showers, and piss out their first piss, so the rest, which is the part you get, is clear, waterlike. It's not piss, in-and-of-itself, that you like, but rather the fact that fluid emerges out of a cock you're loving. For some drinking piss is the ultimate form of cock worship.

So that's why you go to the one place you know works for you: The Mine Shaft, where there's no shame in getting wet.

A fair amount of mythos hangs around the now defunct legends known as the Mine Shaft. And while venues in San Francisco catered either to more esoteric or specialized sexual habits, and while New York City had the St. Mark's Baths and The Saint,[19] it's the Mine Shaft that almost every survivor from the '70s points to as a symbol of the fearlessness with which some gay men broke sexual taboos.

Descriptions show a hypermacho boy's club with a touch of sweetness thrown in for good measure:

In the front, there is a mob costumed in macho fantasies: faded Levis (501's, no underwear), Dago-tees dangling from back pockets, scruffy cowboy boots and hats, chaps, handcuffs, riding crops—the jewelry and props of primal play. Several men wear only shoes. A basso crowd of voices battles with the music, gossiping or telling jokes. One man asks another for a date. Couples, trios pet. Two men hug in celebration of their fourth anniversary. Some men lean against a raw wood wall alone and stare.[20]

At the Mine Shaft, a man swings in slings, with an ethylchloride-soaked rag stuck in his mouth, a bottle of poppers under his nose, as a chap-wearing top sticks two fingers in a tube of Crisco and then smears them on the ring of his still tight asshole. A naked, shaved "slave" stands, chained to a wooden St. Andrew's Cross, while a whipmaster lines his toys—a paddle, a strap, a feather-light whip, a heavier black leather whip, a cat-o'-nine-tails, and a knife—on a towel to the left side. A man lays naked in a bathtub, awaiting either a community sacrament or a community degradation—depending what your state of mind is—from men who had drunk too much water on purpose.

Most of the folklore about the Mine Shaft reveals gay men demonstrating an open attitude to the psyche and its function as fantasy-creating machine. And while there were casualties, most of the time the men seemed more interested in stimulating their imagination more than anything else. Edmund White reports that one night he watched "two middle-aged men, obviously lovers, enact their fantasy." One played dog, in his birthday suit except for his dog collar, crawling around in a corner named the "dog house." The "dog," according to White, was "a truly vicious mutt," who fled the dog house to chomp on the leg of his master "who, in turn, was forced to whip the slavering beast back into his quarters." When the exhausting "training" had been completed, "hound and human packed up and returned to the bar," where they downed some beers and watched a pool game "with vacant, bored eyes."[21]

As White explains, the actual quality of the sex club is "hazier" and "more Brownian" than the comedic mutt scene reveals. For example, you meet a friend at the bar and "gossip with him for a few minutes." Then you walk into a back room, adjusting to the darkness. "You touch, with your blind hands, something that feels like a—could it be? Yes, it is—a shoeshine stand. A man dressed as a cop is having his shoes polished." You shuffle next to someone without the right degree of "stoned, entranced conviction." The man, picking up ambivalence, splits. Action takes place in a corner. Everyone goes toward it: "The other men are too tall for you to see past them, but the spectator beside you gropes you, you him, and something about his timing, his body heat, even the tenor of his voice as he clears his throat and the line of his profile seen against the light awakens a response." After some kissing during which the new friend removes his shirt, then yours ("his is a healthy, firm body with an appealing bit of wobble at the waist, his neck scented—no, his hair—with the antique charm of Vitalis"), the men grab a beer at the bar. After chitchat about weight lifting, "then a new round with him of half-clothed sex in the back room," White sees a friend he's lost touch with: "You both agree that the Mine Shaft is 'tired' (failing to mention it's five in the morning and you've each come twice)." Apparently few will stand up for a dive devoted to lust once the lust has been appeased.[22]

Telling a similar story about the sobering effect of too much sex, Kantrowitz remembers a particularly troubling party. Tearing off his clothes, he was surrounded by a group of guys and pleasuring all of them. "I don't know who they are, but together they are mankind and I am there to serve them." It makes sense that Kantrowitz, a professor of English at the College of Staten Island, would sing the body electric. Even the dirty talk—"Take it, cocksucker"—is all in good fun. But at some point, the verbal gymnastics take a wrong turn. One man orders Kantrowitz to say that he, Arnie Kantrowitz, writer, professor, and gay activist, is "nothing." The strange man repeats his strange demand to Kantrowitz: "Say you're nothing."

Kantrowitz cannot say the words. He lifts himself up from the center of the group and storms off. He refuses to be a nothing.

And he also refuses to continue to play by some of the more rigid scripts men had begun following. Toward the peak of his sexual career, he went into a room in the Everhard and a man, all geared up in leather, blindfolded him. "I want to play a game of truth," the man said. "I want to ask you questions, and I want you to tell me the truth." Kantrowitz was ready to enter this scene: "So he's asking me stuff. He says to me, 'What's the worst thing you ever did in your life.' Now, he probably meant, what's the farthest out sexual thing you ever did? But my mind clicked elsewhere. And I got very serious. I answered, 'I let my cat be taken to the ASPCA.' That was the worst thing I ever did."

It was true. But, as a rule, humor and hard-ons, never easy bedfellows, were an awful match in the late '70s.

when ritual needs more lighter fuel to keep things cooked   Scat parties, attracting socialites of every gender, are chronicled in Jack Fritscher's biography on Mapplethorpe. "The group," writes Fritscher, "was terribly civilized and urbane, or at least most were. Three young men . . . had been hired in as feeders to insure the invited guests would have enough primary material." Fascinated by the "escalating urban perversatility of liberated gay men," Fritscher disputes the claim that fisting is the great last frontier of gay male sport-fucking:

"Scatology, from ritual anointing to communion, is the latest rage among sexual sophisticates who pay Robert court."[23]

Fritscher leaves most of the account to the reader's imagination, but he does try to demonstrate some of the elements that are being brought to conscious perception: the secret craving for infantile experience; the ways in which ancient cultures attributed magical, mannalike properties to bodily functions; how the need to be humbled by transcendent experiences can be contaminated by the need to be humiliated; how cruelly separated the modern man and woman are from any sense of initiation so that only extremes can return him or her to a more primal state of surrender; how hungry men and woman are for an experience of primitive affect; how elementary and undifferentiated most peoples' psychological relationship to this affect remains so only the smearing of shit on one's body can awaken it; and how men would go to great lengths to dismantle the defenses that kept them from relating to their personal shadows. Fritscher gives only a taste (as it were) of the party. But it's plenty. "Under the looming presence of the Grossman totem sculpture," he reports, they devolve back to "incantatory words to grunts and growls."[24]

growing jaded

Kantrowitz began to lose interest not just in sexual extremes, but in sex:

I would take an expensive cab ride downtown, go to the Mine Shaft and stand around for maybe fifteen minutes and say, why am I here? And I was looking at a scene that very few people were ever privileged to see, this level of sexual supermarket. You could watch someone being fisted up in a sling, you could watch people being pissed on in the tub. You could do all kinds of things. I just understood then that all I needed was to get out of my apartment. It had nothing to do with the Mine Shaft. And less to do with sex.

Ritual has a way of exhausting itself when it doesn't become replenished by meaning, or rather, when it is not yet understood how the meaning conferred on it by the past might fuel the future.

Outwardly, it looked as if men had become jaded. "For the longest time," wrote Edmund White, "everyone kept saying the Seventies hadn't started yet. There was no style for the decade, no flair, no slogans. The mistake we made was that we were all looking for something as startling as the Beatles, acid, Pop Arts, hippies and radical politics."

What actually took place, he adds, was a working through of the ideas and values the '60s had easily presented. "Street cruising gave way to half-clothed quickies; recently I overheard someone saying 'It's been months since I've had sex in bed.' " Back rooms supplanted the romance of the hunt and the delight of negotiating terms—whose house to go to; what kind of sex ought to take place. According to White, "Everyone knows that after all (or nothing) is said and done, there's a free blow-job waiting for him at the back of the Strap."[25]

Despite the jaded feeling most men experienced around sex ("A fuck here and there, a blow job, a jerk-off: once you've been to the White House, where's left to visit?" asks a character in Larry Kramer's 1978 novel *Faggots*), inwardly, the psyche remained active.[26] The symbol—in this case, the worship of a man—had hardly lost its power. What happened, rather, was that instead of latching onto an outward form, the libido had turned inward. The symptom might resemble depression or inertia—what some ancients called "loss of soul."[27]

Some men claim that they went to the Mine Shaft not to hunt for dick but to exist in a kind of mediative state. Kantrowitz went there to write:

> I have found these places very creative and I ended up writing there. I'd go to porn films and take out my notebook and write by the light of the movie. And often to the dismay of the guy in the next seat. I'd go to the Mine Shaft and stand by the cigarette machine and write in the light of that. Or I'd go to the roof in the summertime and be alone. I'd go to the baths and lock myself in a little cubicle by the incredibly dim light they provided and write there. Some of all this energy became spiritual stuff. The sex-spirit nexus became important to me.

Here sexuality is not mere instinct, but an implacable creative force, the spokesperson of the other instincts.

David Stein of New York speaks of sex and spirituality not as antagonists, but rather as partners in the effort to transcend ego, "to get beyond the limitations of being a separate self in a separate body." But perhaps that partnership only comes after great struggle, coming after the repressed side of things finds expression. It's as if the two opposing parties must have their say before the third thing—a new way of seeing the world—can take place.

warring parties

When Sigmund Freud made his contribution on the key role of sexuality in the development of psychological health and neurosis, he did not give credence to other instincts, or what he called drives. Only late in his life did he propose an additional drive besides Eros, what he called Thanatos, the death instinct, or the aggressive drive. He saw sexuality as an instinct at war with society.

For Freud, happiness and freedom are incompatible with civilization. Herbert Marcuse, who tried to marry Freud with Marx, questioned and affirmed Freud's views. The pleasure principle must give way to the reality principle—productive renunciation—for civilization to move forward.[28]

Other psychologists, however, such as William James, and other philosophers, such as Friedrich Nietzsche, saw many more instincts existing in a person than just the sexual. Nietzsche saw the impulse to spiritualize life, even sexual life, as deriving from instinct—not culture. He called that spiritualizing force a "consuming fire." Moreover, contemporary depth psychologists, such as James Hillman and Mitch Walker, understood the sex instinct and the spiritual instinct as quite linked—dependent on each other, as a matter of fact. Of course, C. G. Jung and his followers believed in dozens upon dozens of instincts, which they defined as "typical modes of action," regularly recurring, so regular they might not be recognized as special. Each instinct is determined by a primordial image—an archetype—and vice versa.[29]

Where would the spirit be, in other words, if it had no peer among the instincts to oppose it? An empty form? "For us, sex is still problematical," writes Jung, "which means that on this point we have not reached a degree of consciousness that would enable us to do full justice to the instinct without appreciable moral injury."[30] By consciousness, C. G. Jung means not just knowledge, but a feeling "relationship." By linking feeling with thinking, one comes to life in a new way.

The kind of relationship gay men have to this instinct suggests that there was (and continues to be) the attempt to do full justice to it. Obviously, one cannot know something exists without experiencing it. Empathy for an alien person or force can't be cultivated until its acquaintance is made.

no pain, no gain

David Stein was kinky before he was homosexual—a primitive kind of S&M had seized his imagination even before his homo eros did. Born in 1948 and raised in a small town in Pennsylvania, he remembers finding ingenious ways to tie himself in bed at night when he was a mere child—six years old. At eight, he'd stare curiously at cops; they had, after all, handcuffs hanging from their belts. "I got turned on by a pair of pajamas that had tight vinyl cuffs around the wrists and ankles," he reminisces. He tied his cock up and whacked it back and forth long before he could orgasm.

Precocious in school, Stein was somewhat misunderstood at home. "I was a pudgy, pushy, gabby, and grabby little boy, too smart and articulate for my own good or other people's comfort, desperately needing to be liked and almost incapable of making myself likable." Stein was briefly attracted to girls before puberty and invariably to boys afterward, but without any sense of what his feelings meant or what he could do about them. "My head and my heart weren't on speaking terms." Was it a feature of repression? Or just another way to be sexual? Who can say? "Throughout my childhood, I'd spin these elaborate bondage fantasies for myself," he recalls, "and there were no other people in them except certain shadowy figures who'd chain me to a wall and go away."

His experiments with self-bondage periodically recurred, usually followed after a time by an impulse to purge his "pathological" desires and trash his secret collection of homemade "equipment."[31] Despite a liberal education at New York University, where he majored in philosophy, he managed to keep his secret from roommates, friends, classmates, and teachers alike and to avoid stumbling across any evidence that he wasn't uniquely perverted. His youth helped keep him closeted, as he started college at 15. It wasn't until he went to graduate school at Northwestern in 1967, and lived by himself for the first time in his life, that he felt safe enough to check out a porn store. Discovering the tiny supply of kinky gay pornography then available showed him finally that he wasn't alone. But though his fantasies were now plentifully supplied with hunky, dominate men who teased, tormented, and eventually, loved him, he had never met any such men, didn't know where to find them, and was terrified that if he did, they would either reject him or hurt him more than he would like.[32]

During a 1976 trip to a New York City convention, one of his former roommates from NYU—who had come out to Stein in a letter the previous summer— offered to show him around to the gay bars of his choice, and the friend didn't even raise an eyebrow when Stein admitted that it was the leather bar circuit that attracted him. "So he and his lover—who are totally vanilla—took me to the Eagle and the Spike, but they were so far beyond what I was ready for that I was overwhelmed and asked for something a little 'lighter.' They took me to the Christopher Street bar Boots and Saddles—Spike regulars dismissed it as Corsets and Girdles, but it seemed more my speed at the time, so my friends left me there." A burly man in a leather jacket—almost the *only* man in a leather jacket in that "leather bar"—came on to Stein, who incautiously took him back to his hotel room. No danger materialized, but no satisfaction either. The first-ever sex partner of Stein's (who turned out to be an accountant from Brooklyn) was too drunk even to get it up, let alone provide the kind of dominant guidance in the erotic arts Stein was looking for. "He offered to fist me instead! I'd never been fucked. I'd never sucked a dick, and he was offering to fist me?" That unhinged Stein, who found the erotics of this city so lacking pedagogy and real community.

Several years later, Stein did decide to take the bull by the horns. He purchased his first leather jacket; wore it to the Spike; a good-looking man in full leather took him back to his apartment: "The man, named Alan, wasn't into serious bondage or anything involving pain, just temporary role-playing with a heavy leather fetish. He liked having his boots and leather licked, and his cock and nipples sucked. He wasn't really into anything but S&M-lite, 'no pain or anything,' but he did like getting his cock sucked and his boots licked. And he could *talk* a good scene, some verbal abuse and spinning fantasies of things he'd do to me, except I soon learned he'd never do them." As far as role-playing was concerned, the two *were* compatible:

> At first, it was so exciting. I'd be home alone reading, say, and Alan would call at about 11:30 and say, "Get your ass over here." "Yes, sir!" I'd say and rush over to his place for one of our little scenes. He actually bought me my first pair of leather pants, and either I'd wear them over or change into them there. Mostly I would start by licking his boots and then lick his pants and his crotch while he would be calling me names, usually animal names. The one way in which he was into heavier stuff than me was that he started getting into breath control. A lot of rubbing his glove over my mouth and nose so I couldn't breath, squeezing my neck. Manhandling me, moving me around to put my mouth on different parts of him. Sometimes he'd tie my hands behind my back. I loved it when he did that, which wasn't very often. I also really liked hoods and I was able to get one made with an open mouth so I could still give him the oral service he wanted. During the climax, I'd be sucking his cock, and if my hands weren't tied maybe playing with his tits, which was one reason he didn't like to tie me, and that's how he'd get off. And sometimes he'd let me jerk off, and sometimes not, and then usually he'd put me to bed, in his bed. If I was still hooded or tied he'd let me sleep that way if I asked him. Then he'd go out in the kitchen and have a snack and then we'd sleep. Next morning, it was a hello, and some coffee, and it'd be all over.

The scenario satisfied Stein for almost two years. But the leather rough-housing with Alan merely whetted his appetite for his true S&M coming out later on when Alan accompanied him to the Whitewater Weekend "run," sponsored by the Pocono Warriors, a fairly kinky gay club based in Northeastern Pennsylvania. An entire floor in a Howard Johnson's had been made into a dungeon, and Stein managed to realize a dozen or so fantasies in two days:

> I met this guy Chuck Barrow, a full member of the Chicago Hellfire Club. He wasn't particularly my physical type, but he exuded self-confidence and a kind of gleeful expertise, so when he asked if I had ever been on a rack and said, "Trust me, you'll love it," I followed him like a lamb to slaughter. He strapped me onto this ungainly contraption and stretched me out and then started torturing my tits with emery boards. And I'm moaning in ecstasy, and he says, "Did you realize you were into pain?" I said, "I do now, sir." After that there was no holding me back: I wanted to try everything. Alan's jaw dropped open when he saw what I got into. I mean, his idea of a heavy scene was to twist somebody's tits hard, or slap their ass a few times, and here I was in a pillory being flogged for an hour. He said, "I thought I should go over and rescue you, but you seemed to be enjoying it."

Both at that Whitewater Weekend and in later encounters, such as at the Chicago Hellfire's Club's infamous by-invitation-only annual "Inferno" event, Barrow initiated Stein into a then-esoteric S&M art form known as "abrasion." In this process, one slowly rubs away the top layers of dead skin so that the nerves become closer to the surface. "Chuck had an incredible 'armamentarium,' mostly bought from hardware stores," Stein reminisces. "Brushes of all kinds, everything from little plastic kitchen brushes to steel wire brushes used to scrape old paint off pipes or heavy equipment." There were also files, toothpicks, tracing wheels, and little spiked wheels used to mark leather or cloth for cutting.

It sounds torturous, but Stein experienced transformation. The rather aspiritual philosopher discovered in himself a place where mind and body met. He differentiated three conscious levels of the "pain" experience. "There's the first level," as he puts it, "where it's just pleasurable stimulation that looks painful from the outside, but you're getting into it, like the first ten minutes of being lightly spanked." But at some point, as the sensation builds, it *does* hurt: that's the second level. As a result of that, magically, painkilling endorphins are released. That announces the mind-altering "third level":

> In a really good pain scene, when it's really working, the two people seem to know what each other is thinking. There's a sense that each is paying attention to the other in a really intense way. When I'm topping in a scene like that, I'm not thinking about anything except the man that I'm working on and how it's going to affect him.

The top has a real responsibility in this scene: not to allow the bottom to get distracted. This way a "trip" can take place, in which the bottom steps through the veil and the separation between spirit and matter vanishes. At this moment, the internal "judge" or "censor" in each person's mind becomes oddly disabled or flooded:

> I'm one of those people whose internal monologue is virtually nonstop, and it's very judgmental and very critical. It's as if in the back of my head there's this little person who's a part of me analyzing and criticizing everything I say or do or see or feel. And virtually the only time that gets shut off is in a really good S&M scene. The scary part is that it can take quite a bit of pain to get there, and it can be hard work. When I was younger, that was the main attraction, breaking through to this level where that little voice would shut off and I would feel as if I were floating on a sea of sensation.

Hungry for a safe place to talk about S&M, and to meet others interested in it, Stein joined fellow activist (and fellow bottom) Brian O'Dell and others in forming Gay Male S/M Activists, or GMSMA. At first GMSMA met in people's apartments. For two years a hundred men gathered at the Church of the Beloved Disciple.

As an example of how stigmatizing it was to say you liked S&M in the late '70s and early '80s — "as opposed to the '90s, when every little gay boy wants his ass slapped," offers Stein — GMSMA literally had to buy its way into acceptance at New York's Lesbian and Gay Community Services Center by buying chairs and providing other services. But everyone, including Stein, was amazed at how fast the group became a fixture at the Center, one of the largest and most stable organizations meeting there. By its fourth birthday, GMSMA boasted hundreds of members and offered not only workshops and programs on the nuts and bolts of knot-tying, bondage, and flogging — but also on issues in S&M relationships as well as help and advice for novices to the scene and outreach to other groups concerned with expanding and protecting sexual freedom.

While the organization faced problems — it wasn't as politically in-your-face as some would have liked, and not as politically indifferent as others would have preferred — it proved how crucial it was that gay men participate in a continual effort to differentiate through their thinking function their erotic practices.

In this way, gay men wrestled with the opposites of logos and eros (or Apollo and Dionysus) for the purpose both of community-making and individual growth. Sure, films like *Cruising* gave S&M a bad name, which it often deserved, but some men fought hard to establish it as a site where learning was passed on and love could flood a person's hard heart and crack it open with tears.[33] Mark Thompson would put such efforts this way in his *Leatherfolk*, "Liberating erotic potential from the dour puritanical ethics that still rule our culture, and our libidos, is prerequisite to establishing a more sane and forgiving society. S/M practice, composed of highly potent sexual games, increases awareness about ourselves and others. It is not unusual to find leatherfolk who are members of the clergy or the New Age movement, or who have explored psychoanalysis or various recovery programs."[34]

s&m grows acceptable?

By the '80s, you could attend a sleaze party at Paradise Garage or an underwear party at The Saint and watch a muscle leather dude act as if he were about to sit on a prodigious dildo—wrapped in latex, of course.[35] The growing acceptance of S&M—encouraged in part by GMSMA and similar groups around the country and by the commercialization of Tom of Finland imagery—allowed writer John Preston to assail both the S&M support groups (for institutionalizing "outlaw" sexual behavior) and the mainstream gay community (for corrupting its youth through commercialization).

Criticism is nothing new to S&M. Throughout the twenty-five-year period of gay experimentation since the Stonewall Riots, S&M practice—defined once by Ian Young as "any inventive sexuality involving spoken or acted-out fantasy, psychodrama, domination and submission, sex toys or conscious role playing"—went through unyielding scrutiny as far as gay people's attitudes to it were concerned.[36] In the '70s, feminist men like John Stoltenberg lambasted S&M as an "acquired compulsion" and argued that "it would be difficult to imagine an erotic impulse more inimical to justice, personal dignity, or reciprocal caring than sadism."[37]

Meanwhile people like Preston argued that S&M practice served as a good—and loving—way in which the pedagogical nature of homo eros could find a home. In a *GCN (Gay Community News)* essay on S&M, Michael Bronski analyzed people's interest in S&M as coming from a deeply felt need for the mystery of masculine romance.

But the truth is sobering: more people thought about S&M than did it, a fact confirmed by the 1994 *Advocate Sex Survey*, where only one-tenth of thirteen thousand respondents engaged in S&M. They absorbed the gist and fashion of S&M from porno and pop culture without being into whips and dog collars, all the while secretly suspecting that such powerful imagery sprang not just from nutty pornographers but from the living psyche. "Because of the psychological and sexual charge of such extreme masculine imagery for gay men," writes gay Jungian Robert Hopcke, "and because of the obvious shock value such unbridled collective masculinity holds for most conventional heterosexuals, the imagery of S&M has become among the most visible and influential among urban gay male communities."[38]

Is there any surprise that in a patriarchal culture that loathes homosexuals—and expresses its own homo eros through violence in sports arenas, police forces, and hostile corporate takeovers—that gay men would feel the lack of initiation in their lives? Is it any wonder that some would construct a technology for sharing sexual secrets? Although many gay men secretly feel resentment toward John Preston for writing *Mr. Benson*—"Mr. Benson is too perfect a daddy," argues one daddy—there is no question that Preston believed that young gay men deserved love through sex. But given the self-hatred so many gays inherit, Preston thought young men needed to be taught firmly how to open their hearts. Firmly.

Sure, people asked plenty of questions about S&M in the '70s—"Was the leather worn during '70s just a fad, a piece of dispensable urban armor used in search of daddy?"; "Why did it take gay men to create this highly technical and elaborate art of erotics and ritual and not some other group?"; "Did men wear leather to compensate for their faggotry or to amplify it?"—but asking questions is one thing and knowing the answers because one is an experienced pro is another. Studies simply don't exist that let anyone know what percentage of gay men got tied up and which remained militantly vanilla. As everyone knows, there is a huge gradient between those extremes, a fact that the *Advocate* sex survey, which came out in the '90s, does little to dispel.[39]

Of course it's easy to criticize S&M, especially when it's practiced carelessly, or when it's used as a way to act out aggression. But many S&M practitioners *do* seem rather responsible and rather more savvy than most gays who have never explored their aggressive or passive sides about how to communicate about power, submission, and limits.[40] Those who live an S&M lifestyle, and those who just like an extra tug of the hair now and then, admit that modern life too often sanitizes powerful feelings—rage, shame, anger, sadism—and that opening up to these feelings in a consensual sexual relationship is better than not opening up to them at all. As the shrinks say, whatever is repressed returns.

But S&M is not the only way to bring masculine or initiatory experiences into lovemaking. Author Brian Pronger sees the gay interest in athletics—sport as fetish—as coming from the same masculinist impulse. "Although it would be quite wrong to say that all homosexual men are attracted to a certain type of man," declares Pronger, "that is, attracted to the same degree of masculine expression, masculinity *is* the source of homoerotic desire." He implies that despite the myth that gays are more loving than straights, the attraction to masculinity always implies some form of aggression.[41]

Whether the underlying motives behind gym culture are ways to avoid confronting the shame of being a gay man or ways to amplify one's crippled masculinity, the emergence of gay gym culture coincided synchronously with the growing acceptance in the gay community of S&M. (This happened just as gays and straights tried to stigmatize fisters as the principle agents behind the spread of AIDS.) Hard bodies and hard sex became "normalized"—equated as "straight-acting." In Matt Sterling's film *Like a Horse*, three accomplished wrestlers indicate that the hurling to the mat has sexual resonances when a wrestling grip dissolves into some good-spirited and deeply athletic ass slapping. ("Ooh, I heard him say ouch," one wrestler says.) Jeff Stryker's staccato sexual commentary—"Stick that big cock all the way up his ass; pound it in him, pound it in him"—are ruthlessly masculinist but, oddly enough, devoid of humiliating or derogatory implications.

Not everyone thought of S&M sex as rough. The 1980 publication of a book that equated fist-fucking and piercing with tantric sex—the yoga of cosmic erotic energy—made an impact on spiritual gays of all stripes. The book, called *The Divine Androgyne*, written by Purusha Larkin, tied together Eastern mysticism, with the human potential movement, and kinky sex. Attempting to exorcise guilt and shame around the much-reviled asshole, it gave elaborate instructions in the art of anal massage and tantra. Purusha saw "hand-balling" not as S&M but as an act of pure love—"the most reliable ecstatic ritual of our time." The man receiving a fist revisits the primal womb-birth-nursing states of consciousness whereby he can "return to our present everyday consciousness bathed in the glow of that earlier ecstasy and unified consciousness."[42]

Fisting could offer another kind of free fall, a pleasurable one that took hours to prepare for. The cleaning out itself—bags and bags of douche water because, as one man put it, "You always wanted a hand to go in further than it went before"—amounted to a powerful ritual, as did the fasting beforehand, not to mention the taking of some methamphetamine. With the right man—a combination of aura and hand size—a man's ass opened slowly to take in a finger or two by the prostate, then a few more fingers, until, maybe an hour later, a man collapsed his fist in a cave and began to turn the knuckles a hair's breath this way and that until moans turned into cries of a nongenital orgasmic variety.

The most infamous of the fisting emporiums was the Hothouse, located inconspicuously South of Market Street near Harrison, in one of the buildings used as a boarding hotel for workers who came to clean up San Francisco after the 1907 earthquake. The site wasn't marked; you had to know where you were going to get to this fuck palace. People preferred this venue to the garden variety bathhouses—"where your walked around in these little towels and fucked in these cheesy little cubicles on this mattresses only to be out in a couple of hours," in the words of one man—because at the Hothouse, for anywhere between $25 and $30 a night, you could check into a woody, black-painted room the size of a large bedroom with framed beds from which one could hang shackles and slings. The place was so popular you had to book it a week in advance.

a little help from the golden ass

An ancient myth can shed light on a current one, and some of the stories in Lucius Apuleius's *Metamorphoses* (sometimes called *The Golden Ass*) are chock full of insight for anyone interested in the interplay of consciousness and sexuality. There is, for example, a moment in the story "Amor and Psyche," in which the ability to "differentiate" saves the main character from the snake-eating tail of too much carnal collectivity. The myth is helpful in understanding the changes that took place during the '70s. The ancient myth tells a story of how a wobbly ego begins to create an attitude about its world, a world teeming with energies that threaten to overwhelm the emerging "I."

The star of this particular tale is Psyche. The most beautiful maiden in the world, she represents a new symbol, an evolution from the regressive Matriarchal Age. Psyche stands for a new kind of thinking, whereas Aphrodite, who has ruled unchallenged as The Great Mother, comes more from an irrational feeling place.

Wherever she's coming from, Aphrodite, a jealous fertility goddess, does not like to be challenged in the looks department. So the bitch-goddess, gunning for Psyche, imposes harsh labors on her, one of which is to sort out a huge mound of barley, millet, poppy seeds, peas, lentils, and beans. "Separate out," Aphrodite screams at Psyche, "or die." (A similar predicament takes place in other fairy tales, including Cinderella.) Of course, the labor is next to impossible to perform. Psyche is asked to do nothing less than counter Aphrodite's promiscuity with an instinctual ordering principle. Psyche tries to appeal to Aphrodite. But Miss Thing won't listen to reason.

Aphrodite represents the intoxicating fecundity of the swamp stage of humanity. Psyche awakens to the fact that in her unconscious is an innate ability to order, sift, and evaluate. Alone, Psyche is distraught. But with help, she can live.

Help comes in the form of the animal world—symbols of the world of instinct. In this case, it's ants. They come to her in droves. Together they all sort out the puzzle.[43]

Gay men eventually brought a similar organizing principle to their sexual lives, albeit unconsciously:

> Clubs formed: Chubbies and Chubby-Chasers; Uniform-fetishists founded the Pacific Drill Patrol; Country-Western types two-stepped the night away at the Devil's Herd bar wearing cowboy clothes from Ed Wixson's Worn Out West; Rollerskaters, every Tuesday night, chartered a bus from the Castro to a well-poppered rink in South San Francisco. The Goddam Independents of the plaid-flannel-shirt-and-workboot-Logger crowd, and the Bears, older, hairy men with beards, bellied up to the Ambush Bar. Disco Queens found their way to Alfie's, the End Up, Trocadero Transfer, The Stud, and the I-Beam. Biker Leather roamed the Miracle Mile bars on Folsom from FeBe's to the Black-and-Blue, to Folsom Prison, to the Leatherneck, to the Arena, to the Ramrod to the orgiastically slezoid No Name Bar which became the Bolt, which became the Brig, to the afterhours pigpiles of the Covered Wagon and the Bootcamp. . . .[44]

Likewise, Edmund White speaks of an uncanny kind of sexual specialization he began seeing in the late '70s. "Money, status, hobbies, politics and obsessions sort themselves out in New York in bewilderingly original combinations," he writes. "On Fire Island I once met a whole household of bearded he-men who had evolved a group predilection for *silent drag*. The first summer they were together they'd giggled on stoned evenings and donned bits of tatty finery." Sometimes the specializations cross-fertilized: "Take the leather man who works in a leather bar but used his tips to finance his own theater. . . . Or take the S/M tapdancer who between his admittedly *recherche* engagements teaches dance or does secretarial work and hangs out with performers from Al Carmines's Judson Church."[45]

Not every part of this classification was pretty. The sexual revolution evolved its own noxious version of "gay attitude." San Franciscans speak of the "Manhattanization" of San Francisco, by which New York City refugees, intent on glitzing the Bay Area, threw invitation-only sex parties, thus balkanizing the city into sexual cliques that separated the beautiful from the plain, the socially powerful from the ne'er-do-well Castro-nauts. The rate of real estate transaction jumped 700 percent between 1968 and 1978. Leases on Castro rose and destroyed small businesses, a trend that troubled people like Harvey Milk. (Milk was infuriated that his landlord, a gay realtor, had kicked out an elderly woman who lived not far from the Castro to make space for an insurance company.) "Gays no longer came to the Castro to create a new lifestyle," according to Randy Shilts, "they came to fit into the existing Castro Street mold."[46]

"Attitude," writes Fritscher, "assassinated more characters, reputations and motives with more venom than Dan White ever knew." If gay men made fucking their main sport, dishing became their main job.[47] In this way, gay men began to identify the gay shadow.

faggots

A few years before men started to die from immune dysfunction, Larry Kramer wrote a novel in which he diagnosed gay sexual life as pathological and antirevolutionary. Kramer actually named a basic gay psychodynamic, one that could be alternatively called "the gay shadow," or the "narcissistically wounded gay self." In *Faggots*, he broke the no-talk rule on the shadow side of gay sex, characterizing it as a world of half-men, refusing to grow up, inclined to fall in love with role players instead of role models, engaging in love affairs that were nothing but "one cock tease and one doormat," drawn to people "afraid of love" who used their "bodies as barter instead of our brains as heart," settling for the minimum—"humiliation and pleasure"—because of both the woundings and the coverups that no one could see behind the parade of Fire Island Adonises.[48]

The main character is Fred Lemish, "your average, Standard, New York faggot obsessive kvetch"—the perfect counterpart to Jack Fritscher's hypermasculine Tom-of-Finlands. For Fred is nothing but nice. He can't make up his mind whether or not he ought to get pissed on. Why can't we just kiss?[49]

Fred Lemish tries his best to compete in the Meat Rack, even as he watches the world of gay sex descend to the world of toilet sex from which it emerged in the '50s (the newest bar to open, The Toilet Bowl, is all the rage). During the '60s, gay men had placed the emphasis on supportive affirmation. Now that impulse turned on its opposite: rejection. If Fritscher tried to paint a picture of the "gay soul figure," Kramer balanced that equation by exposing the shadows that hid such erotic wisdom from view. The younger, more desirable ones would have cum several times, "while older soldiers, passing tin-walled moans and groans, would by now have received approximately forty-nine rejections as they heaved pasty white frames from cubicle to cubicle." In the end, they settle for one as prosaic as them, "take ten minutes to get an erection and two seconds to come," and then jet, bound for home.[50]

There are men who want love but who can't say that in any other way than with a slap. There are men who want a slap who can't say it in any other way but through a passive-aggressive act. So much sex floods the system with *so* much feeling and *so* much stimulus that it can't be understood in a human and differentiated way. Sighs Laverne: "Yes, sex and love were different items when he wanted them in one, and yes, having so much sex made having love impossible. . . ."[51] Kramer ranted that no one was listening to the lonely cries at night, the increase in STDs, the incessant drug cocktails, the fatigue, and paralysis of feeling. "We have the ultimate in freedom," screamed one character, "and we're abusing it."

He argued that sexual irresponsibility was giving gay men a bad name, that gay men were using sex to run away from self-examination and social responsibility. For this, the author was condemned by the gay press. Men considered him militantly Puritan, shame-based, and Old Testamentarian. No one imagined that, despite his occasional barbs, his writing would prove to have a prophetic edge.

sex, disease, politics: the closing of an era

In the late '70s, the epidemic of sexually transmitted diseases in the gay community prepared men to equate sex with danger. And while the STDs of the '70s were, for the most part, less life-threatening than AIDS, they could be terribly aggravating. (At its worst, the epidemic of Hepatitis B *was* fatal; at its symptomatic best, a person could be laid up weakened and nauseated for months at a time.) Coping with the hazards of gay sexual life, many men developed a familiarity with STD clinics, such as the San Francisco city clinic on Clementina. A veteran recalls:

> It started in early 1978, when I was twenty-one and newly arrived in San Francisco. Going to the city clinic for the first time was like a straight boy's pilgrimage to a prostitute. It was a rite of manhood, you earned your spurs. You took the six-inch cotton swab up your dick or your butt and the two fat hypodermics or the pills like a man; you drank Calistoga for five days and caught up on your reading—and you hit the ground running again by the next weekend at the 'N' Touch or the Stud. It had a seedy location, the doom smell of Lysol and rubbing alcohol and the name of a Gold Rush whore: Clementina.[52]

Sometimes you might be summoned, "having been reported as a contact by some ungentlemanly sex partner." If you were diagnosed with gonorrhea, let's say, you had to sit in a "sour room with a counselor" tracing the men with whom you'd had sex in the previous ten days. This was no easy task in the late '70s when men equated being gay with free love:

> In May of 1979, I came stumbling home drunk one evening and tricked with a previously unmet neighbor in the building's narrow and jerky elevator. We rode to the roof with our pants around our ankles and took turns fucking each other in the gravel, fired up by the smoky tumult and sirens of the White Night riots at Civic Center several blocks away.[53]

The "White Night riots" were the gay community's reaction to the jury's manslaughter verdict for Dan White. Crowds of furious queers marched on City Hall and torched police cars, angry that the assassinations of gay San Francisco supervisor Harvey Milk and Mayor George Moscone could be dismissed so easily. Although empowering at the time, the flames and screams signaled to some that troubling times threatened the gay community in a way no one could have predicted, although trouble brewed in other cities, especially New York City.

No one, for example, could have predicted the uproar a stupid movie—in this case, William Friedkin's 1979 film *Cruising*—could provoke in the gay community. With its obsession with grisly mutilation murders within the city's gay community (not to mention the seamier side of leather sex), the film did do damage to the image gay men wanted to portray of themselves as professionals and law-abiders.

For, after all, hadn't there been a great deal of law-abiding? By 1973, for example, almost eight hundred gay and lesbian organizations had formed. Gay men sang in gay choruses; gay lawyers gave gay legal advice; gay rabbis sermonized in gay synagogues; gay politicians ran for gay political office. In July 1975, The United States Civil Service Commission struck down the policy of refusing gays and lesbians civil service jobs in this country. In 1977, a gay delegation of a dozen leaders met at the White House with presidential aide Midge Costanza, the first such meeting at the executive mansion.[54] Harvey Milk, an openly gay man, ran for the highly visible office of San Francisco supervisor and won, becoming a gay icon over night. In 1978, the San Francisco Board of Supervisors passed its gay rights law. New York City Mayor Ed Koch issued an executive order that forbade discrimination against gays and lesbians in government. Add this victory to the Supreme Court's liberal decision on abortion and, from a moral conservative's point of view, it seemed as if gays and feminists led the cultural and political agenda.[55]

Exciting developments took place on the spiritual front too. As historian Jim Kepner put it, "Gay faeries began to assemble and cross-fertilize in scattered rural and urban sanctuaries and communes during the early 1970s, following hippie models. . . ." The Iowa magazine *R.F.D.* also "became a formative center for the new movement." In 1979, Harry Hay, Don Kilhefner, and Mitch Walker called a conference of "Radical Faeries," in an Arizona desert campground that drew more than two hundred men.[56]

But for every gay political gain, however, a new conservative campaign to roll back reform sprang up. The year 1977 presented a terrible challenge. In Dade County, Florida, the passage of a gay rights ordinance inspired singer and orange juice–pusher Anita Bryant to go on a crusade to repeal the bill. With the help of her husband—and Miami's daily newspapers—her group, Save Our Children, succeeded in repealing the initiative on the ballot. Her success had the backhanded effect of mobilizing gays out of their sexual slumber. "Anita's going to create a national gay force," Harvey Milk predicted. Unfortunately, Dade County marked the start, not the end, of organized opposition to gay civil rights causes.[57]

Bryant's success inspired other conservatives. California State Senator John Briggs placed the infamous antigay measure known as Proposition 6 on the California state ballot. The Briggs Initiative, as it became known, went after gay employees in public schools. When the measure looked sure to win, several gay California checkbook activists appealed to former California governor, Ronald Reagan, to assail the measure on the basis that it violated free speech. That's how desperate they were. (Reagan did come out against Briggs, in the end.) After Dade County, most gays were so pessimistic about stopping Briggs that *Advocate* publisher David Goodstein told his people to slip into the background and let campaign managers handle the next-to-impossible-to-win effort. It seemed so hard to counter the national outcry from right-wingers who screamed that children needed protection from homosexuals. It seemed so hard to get homosexuals organized unless they were attacked.

While gays won the fight against Proposition 6, the necessary effort stole gay political energy from other sources, proving to many leaders that most gays were unprepared to deal with the harsh political realities lurking around the corner. For many, Milk's death and the violent demonstrations that followed the lenient sentencing of Dan White called the end to an era.

chapter five

the great depression

The steamroom, crowded with naked black and white men, mesmerized Ross H. Farley, a tall, athletic African American man in his early thirties. He saw a spitting image of Mr. Perfect there. The man stood six-feet-two inches, like him: slender, beefy, tattooed arms, short-cropped Afro, impish grin. The black man smiled at him and his heart ached. *Just go for the dick,* he told himself. *No smiling. No trust.*

Yeah, years ago Farley *had* trusted men—Latino men, black men, white men, Asian men—and each had, in a matter of speaking, dropped him. At first, Farley-the-businessman survived the dismissals okay. His first relationship with Tom seemed permanent; then one day, after a tiff, Tom declared that he loved Farley but wasn't "in love" with him. The words stung. No, they shredded. But Farley played it cool. Billy, who pledged love-sweet-love, turned out to have a long-term secret lover with whom he apparently lived. (No wonder Farley and Billy never did the nasty at Billy's pad.) George had moved in, but within a few weeks that SOB was discovered going down on a certain Miss Thing on Farley's couch.

To cope with these fickle men, Farley became the *very* person who had hurt him: a sexual outlaw who kept his emotions to himself. He wasn't proud of the decision. But monkhood didn't appeal and certain aspects of being gay—the hunt, the hoping, the hankies—filled him with a longing so deep he almost dared not name it. He needed something, someone, but what? Touch disguised the pain. Or did it? Men, it seemed, wanted men like their dads: cold, calculating, to the point. Men who didn't need them. Men who could reject them. Men butch enough to pass as straight. The moment Farley acted that part, the tricks took the bait. His treat.

"I broke one man's heart, which I regret," he says. "But frequent anonymous sex made me feel good about myself for the first time."

The chilling emotional strategy ended one night in the infamous 8709 bathhouse. Farley, reaching for the pole of a certain black Adonis, was promptly interrupted. The man wanted to know how many sexual contacts Farley had had that night and what, precisely, the contacts had done: fucking, sucking, or just JO? Before Farley was about to say, "It's none of your goddam business," he heard news that changed his life. The fellow reported on a strange, new "gay cancer" in New York City and San Francisco that had really destroyed a few of his friends in a matter of months with tumors and pneumonia. While Farley hadn't done any fisting, hadn't done anything too kinky, in terms of frequency, Farley felt himself a candidate.

What to do? Storming out of the club, his heart racing, Farley resorted to a version of celibacy to cope with his panic, his fear, his concern over the fate of gay men. "I just put the brakes on all my nightly encounters," he says. "If I did meet someone I liked, I limited the sex to mutual masturbation." He remembers that frottage was very adventurous in those days.

traumatic sex

The New York Native had only been on the stands for six months when its July 27, 1981, headline blared: "Cancer in the Gay Community." Dr. Lawrence Mass, a medical writer and veteran of the sexual revolution, broke the news to the gay community in a way that they could hear it—nonjudgmentally. "What is it about male homosexuals," he asked, "or a subgroup of male homosexuals, that distinguishes their susceptibility to this disease?" The photographs accompanying the thorough article disturbed anyone who dared page past them.[1]

One doctor believed that genetic deficiencies caused the purplish raised KS lesions. Others proposed noninfectious agents: amyl nitrate, MDA, ethyl chloride, certain lubricants? Still others saw correlation between immune dysfunction and a past history of other sexually transmitted diseases. One doctor worried that the drug to treat amebiasis—flagyl—caused KS.

What was clear was that the men who suffered from the infiltrative tumors—some leprous-looking pictures were printed in the *Native*—died quickly from the fulminating disease. Underneath the infection lurked a greater problem: suppression of the body's complex immunological mechanisms.

Mass suspected that the pathogens that caused the "gay cancers" were sexually transmitted. This posed a quandary for the new medical writer. "Sexual freedom was essential to being gay," he later said. "And we were making headway in our progress for acceptance. I didn't want to go back to where we had been." He put the "behavior theory" in another person's words (and at the end of the article), quoting *Village Voice* columnist Alexander Cockburn: "Subsequent inquiries seem to support the view that KS is associated with traumatic sex, or in less elevated parlance, such activities as fist-fucking."[2]

There. He said it.

During 1982 and 1983, the *Native* drew a collection of fine AIDS writers such as James E. D'Eramo, Ph.D., and Dr. Harold Ross, among others.[3] But it was Mass who almost single-handedly gave the gay community some of the strongest news it has ever received about the intersection of medical information and sexual behavior. As a gay doctor with a strong activist streak—and a writer's mind—he knew that he simply had to reach readers. A short list of his stories gives an idea of how the epidemic, and attitudes about it, got shaped: "The New 'Anti-Sex' Drug"; "Cancer as Metaphor"; "Do Poppers Cause Cancer: Links Seen to Drugs, Genetics"; "The Epidemic Continues: Facing a New Case Every Day, Researchers Are Still Bewildered"; "New York Physicians Organize At Last"; "Handballing and KS: Is There a Link?"; "Another Infection for the Immune Deficient"; "Creative Sex, Creative Medicine"; "Time for Prevention: Devising Ways of Evading AID."[4]

The idea was to startle readers into changing behavior without startling them into hysteria. That was a hard balance, especially with Mass's pull-no-punches approach. "It hasn't gone away," went the first line of an early article. The disease had already "claimed more lives than the combined tolls of toxic shock syndrome and Legionnaires' disease." What to call the syndrome? Some labeled it grid, or gay-related immune deficiency, while others went for ACID, or Acquired Immunodeficiency Disease. "Unfortunately," writes Mass, "there is little good news to report."

Unable to locate a single pathogen—the Center for Disease Control's James Curran said there was no "smoking gun"—meant that scientists would be a long way from finding a cure. Already Mass was suspecting a single agent, in this case cytomegalovirus. Already he was calling for mobilization by the community. (He and a group of men who had also lost lovers and friends to the disease—Larry Kramer, Enno Poersch, Mel Chernin, Donald Krintzman, Felice Picano, Paul Popham, Edmund White, and Nathan Fain—planned to host the first benefit of Gay Men's Health Crisis at the Paradise Garage in April 1982.)[5]

Mass understood that you could not change sexual attitudes if you repudiated sex. Gay men had enough trouble respecting medical authority. This meant finding new ways to meet the substantial responsibilities of sexual freedom. Mass quoted doctors (such as New York's Dr. Yehudi Felman) who suggested wild solutions. An organization of men who attempt to alleviate the problem of VD through a variety of new rules and strategies? (Sounds bizarre, but people were trying to do something more creative—and effective on a public health level—than just say no. Already, however, an onlooker can recognize a certain shift of attitude taking place around sex.) Not a few writers suggested that sexuality should no longer be understood as a right, but as a privilege, one that could be somehow, if not literally, then morally revoked. Dr. Felman's notion—that gay men carry a gay variety of a sexual driver's license, "a list of agreements about VD testing, avoiding nonmember exposure and freedom from disease symptoms"[6]—struck Mass as not so terribly unthinkable.

How simple the solutions seemed in those days.

did we do something wrong?   The trauma of the health crisis stood to alter more than just gay sexual behavior. It threatened to destroy a decade's worth of consciousness-raising, gay pride parades and political lobbying that went into building self-esteem, civil rights, and a place at the table (and sitcom). Hadn't the movement sought to refute unconditionally that being gay was anything but good? Now it seemed certain that AIDS demonized homosexuality as a perversion of nature. "AIDS provoked fear, anguish and soul-searching," wrote sexual historians D'Emilio and Freedman. "Gay men woke in the morning to check their bodies for the appearance of lesions that signaled Kaposi's Sarcoma."[7]

For despite what everyone had wanted, AIDS implied the opposite of what the sexual revolution had promised. If pleasure had been seen as a birthright one could claim without considering responsibility, AIDS called that into question, as Michael Callen put it.[8] If the body had become the seat of one's strength and identity, AIDS inverted that, as Simon Watney put it.[9] If gay men had thought that they had gained power over the dominant culture through fucking, then they had to learn that the power structure willed this fucking-discourse as a way to stir capital, technology, and science—as Foucault put it.[10] If gay life questioned the spiritual truth that attachment to the flesh resulted in suffering—i.e., Christianity, Buddhism—AIDS suggested that too much pleasure inevitably brought a certain degree of pain—not because pleasure was bad per se, but attachment to anything spelled trouble, as certain women AIDS leaders—Louise Hay, Marianne Williamson, and Sally Fisher—put it.[11] "AIDS seemed to be a cruel outcome of the freedom that gay liberation promised," add D'Emilio and Freedman. "It also shook the pride and confidence that the 1970s had gradually built." AIDS made Anita Bryant's attack on gay self-esteem seem mild by comparison. Some gay men wondered that "maybe we *are* wrong—maybe this is a punishment."[12]

That psychological vulnerability didn't crush the gay spirit completely, but it had some damaging results. Feelings of shame about being a homosexual conspired with the society's impulse to shame homosexuals. "I was involved in trying to change my sexual inclination in the early '80s by attending a change ministry," recalls Tom Cendejas. "AIDS reinforced all the bad things I inherently thought about being gay. It made me think: 'I'd better change fast.'"

More than a few bisexual men who felt a deep kinship with the values of gay letters (and gay bodies) retreated to the sidelines. The great opportunity and even pedagogy that gay liberation offered to all men, regardless of orientation, ended—to some prematurely and thus tragically. While some gays felt the retreat by family members and friends as another awful betrayal—"We're living in a war-zone and everyone else is acting as if nothing's changed," Atlanta's Duncan Teague said—the AIDS epidemic also had the effect of deepening and strengthening the gay survivors. Feelings of grief pervaded gay life. Feelings of abandonment and rejection characterized candlelight marches and middle-of-the-night phone calls. Feelings of isolation and loneliness colored the lives of men who lost their life partners after just a few short years of domesticity. Feelings of shame entered into the simplest of JO scenes with a friend. Feelings of paranoia destroyed the possibility of enjoying a wet kiss. For those not crushed by the weight of so much feeling—no wonder some depth psychologists call feelings rising from the unconscious "shadow"—a new kind of selfhood and strength could be seen developing. Gay men built AIDS organizations and helped bury whole networks of friends with a valor and work ethic that shocked everyone but them.

For the truth was evident to every gay man, especially those who mobilized to stop AIDS: the government wasn't lifting a finger. This much also seemed clear: AIDS wasn't just a gay disease. Unfortunately, AIDS seemed a distant threat to many people—straights and gays, "the misfortune of people who fit into rather distinct classes of outcasts and social pariahs." This kept the government from taking its share of blame for doing little to warn about precautions, little to speak publicly about public health, little to mention the word AIDS, little to appropriate funds.

Gay visionaries felt compelled to fight this unequivocal linkage between homosexuality and immune dysfunction even as they felt crushed by their own paranoia and night sweats. Arnie Kantrowitz knew that gay sex was a beautiful thing. But how could gay sex be defended now? Felice Picano asked the same question. So did Ross Farley. So did just about everyone. The answer occurred to men slowly, in the midst of great suffering and in the midst of well-reported political events—Rock Hudson's diagnosis, Elizabeth Taylor's support, the benefits for Gay Men's Health Crisis—that changed the public face of AIDS. And the answer seemed simple enough: those people trying to change the erotophobia that lay at the heart of patriarchal Western culture were the most vulnerable to attack.

This didn't undermine the fact that many gay people had used sex as a way to cover up their secret vulnerability, just as the patriarchy covered its vulnerability with a violence that seemed destined to destroy modern life. All coverups seemed to expose themselves as destructive in the end. "Those most hurt by the culture would be the ones most eager for redemption," mentioned D.C.'s Greg Scott. "But they had to have the courage to look at their hurt more honestly than anyone if they were to be new kinds of heroes." Like many activists, Scott saw being gay as an important calling.

Calling or no calling, simply put, the whole responsibility of AIDS could not be laid on the doorsteps of gay people. AIDS did not need to have spread as quickly as it did. Had the government responded as quickly to AIDS as it had to Legionnaires' disease, the transmission of the virus could have easily been contained. An array of institutions conspired to leave a legacy of suffering. The government's silence murdered thousands as Reagan administration officials dismissed requests from scientists for research funding. Public health authorities murdered thousands when they put political brownie points ahead of public health policy. Journalists and editors murdered thousands when they refused to run stories because gay sex unhinged conservative advertisers and readers. Thousands died while scientists competed over who discovered which virus, wasting thousands of dollars on protocols that duplicated other protocols. Thousands died while gay men, unable to face the truth, stuck their heads in the sand. According to Randy Shilts:

> But from 1980, when the first isolated gay men began falling ill from strange and exotic ailments, nearly five years passed before all these institutions—medicine, public health, the federal and private scientific research establishments, the

*mass media, and the gay community's leadership—mobilized the way they
should in a time of threat. The story of these first five years of AIDS in America
is a drama of national failure, played out against a backdrop of needless death.*[13]

When it came to nailing gay people, not everyone bought Shilts's way of
looking at the crisis. "A good deal of that book is a distortion," cautions Picano,
referring to the infamous *And the Band Played On*. "Shilts never investigated
carefully or checked his one source well enough. If AIDS had happened to any
other group, AIDS research would be ten years behind what it is now. The fact
that this happened to professionals and that we could raise money to build organizations from the ground up so rapidly shows that, in retrospect, we, as a gay
community, moved very quickly to recognize that a single disease was striking
people. Of course it wasn't perfect, but we moved."

No one moved fast enough to handle the grief. No one moved fast enough
to explore how grief contributed to sexual dysfunction and how feelings of loss
resulted in celibacy or irrational sexual need. No one could put a finger on the
crisis that seemed to lay behind the crisis. For on top of the galloping health epidemic emerged another dilemma: a lack of feeling, an actual refusal of difficult
feeling by means of ever-strengthening defense mechanisms. Defenses can help
a person survive, but ultimately they keep out new life. This world of neglected
feeling loaded up as a hidden power. Some saw this numbness, matched by
covert agendas to circumvent its thawing, as the true pathology, perhaps the one
that assisted in providing the conditions for AIDS to take hold. Sex, like food or
alcohol, can be used as a defense against feeling. Eric Rofes draws attention to a
passage by Susan Griffin to explain the "state of emotional shut-down" that is so
often a feature of modern life, whether gay or straight:

> *There are many ways we have of standing outside ourselves in ignorance. Those
> who have learned as children to become strangers to themselves do not find this
> a difficult task. Habit has made it natural not to feel. . . . But this ignorance is
> not entirely passive. For some, blindness becomes a kind of refuge, a way of life
> that is chosen, even with stubborn volition, and does not yield easily to visible
> evidence.*[14]

And yet how, in 1981 and 1982, was one not supposed to seek refuge? As
Rofes put it, "The corpses had mounted beyond our most extreme nightmares."
But he sees the death toll as only a portion of the larger problem: "Our intimate
relationships, erotic response, and sexual subcultures were becoming freakishly
deformed by the epidemic."[15] Putting feeling and sexuality on the back burner,
gay men did what gay men had done best over the last twenty or so years: they

mobilized. "Formerly apolitical gay men," write D'Emilio and Freedman, "found themselves furious at the callousness of the Reagan administration, whose tepid response to the epidemic suggest a cavalier disregard for the lives of homosexuals." Not only did gay men build service organizations and advocacy groups, they also taught the world a thing or two about behavior modification. D'Emilio and Freedman report that a certain study of homosexual men in cities from 1984 to 1987 found that those who chose celibacy rose from 2 to 12 percent. Gay men opting for monogamy rose from 12 percent to almost 30.[16]

new york state of mind

Horny, jilted, lonely, bored, half-high on cheap dope, you slip into the St. Mark's baths off Second Avenue at St. Mark's Place in Manhattan. You want to take your mind off your debt, your mother, your broken heart. A shiver shakes through your newly pared *twentysomething* waistline even though it's a sweltering August night and the East Village populace fans itself on stoops and by store fronts: the Ukrainian folk and Pyramid punks on separate sides of Stromboli's Pizza. A line of freshly talced NYU/Cooper Union/Tompkins Square Park/Harlemite guys line the stairs, wearing cutoff jeans. No one speaks, but you know you've had a couple of the funnier-looking ones in Mohawks and they're looking as savory as ever.

As if they read your filthy mind, each turns away, chilled by a chill—or is a premonition, a worry, a phobia? The well-built dark Irish lug in his late forties mutters in a Bensonhurst accent: "They say we're committing suicide." Another snorts. No one wants to believe anyone, but everyone's been reading the *New York Native*, which just started printing stories about a strange "gay cancer." An olive-skinned man in blue-collar drag, puts it this way: "They'll do everything to take our last freedom from us ever since that freak Reagan got elected."

He was right and everyone knew it. Last week, during your last trip to St. Mark's, you realized that an era was about to end. You took a hit of acid and allowed yourself not to worry about these punitive, shaming voices that came at you when you sucked dick. All the same, you found yourself sucking a little less dick than usual and refusing entry to one man's probing tongue. You found yourself checking for sores and discovered, to your amazement, that you did not gravitate to the skinny boys, who, generally, amazed you with their tight rib cages and bad posture. The thought occurred to you that it made no sense to discriminate on the basis of surfaces. But you did. You opted not to go into the dark orgy room (which was a secret fetish of yours because you stopped feeling ugly for a moment or two), and found, to your shock, that most men inspected *you* for tell-tale signs of lesions, wasting syndrome, and fatigue. After just a few forays into one or two (or was it three?) men's rooms for some mutual spanking (now that was a new adventure and terribly harmless!) and lots of necking (who knew how harmless? but how sublime!) and then a little frottage (not a first choice among most, but an oldie and goodie for you), you spent the entire night with a sweet, cuddly, crew-cut man your age, your size, and your class background with whom you fell in love while giggling into the whirlpool.

For a week afterward, you dreamt you were going to die.

The thought now occurs to you: *Get a boyfriend and get out of Berlin before it's too late.* You aren't sure whether the simple things you've always loved—some kissing, some rubbing (and okay, some cum dripping into your mouth)—aren't going to get you 86-ed from life. Look, you've never been the douching and fist-ing type; poppers give you a migraine; you loathe tobacco; and if you never got another prick up your butt again you wouldn't die—you mean—complain. But last night, which *was* hotter than hell, you woke up to soaked bed sheets. . . .

Stop: You remind yourself that your doctor has gotten annoyed already palpi-tating your throat to tell you what you already knew: you have a swollen gland—nothing to buy an urn over. He did ask you, however, to return in six weeks and to "limit your sexual partners." That unhinged you. And to make matters worse, everyone on this staircase seemed more interested in disputing the snowballing "*Native* hysteria" than in checking each other out, thus ruining the cruisiest part of Saturday night bathhouse ritual. Still, a part of you does enjoy the debate raging on the stairs. (Was sex a privilege or a right, after all?) The thrill of philosophizing about the politics of erotics *did* make you wonder just why the gay community could never bring sensation and thinking together in one room.

For the *Native* was doing just that, through the spoken word. The paper checked the pulse of gay N.Y.C. and gave it sexed-up octane back. No publica-tion or venue—or, for that matter, a single individual, to your recollection—had ever done that for gays. Not only was the *Native* calling the government on its shit, it was calling the gay community on its shit too, boasting a refusal to buy the line that being gay is merely a sexual matter. Many writers refused to have their individuality erased by the anonymous sex cult dominating gay life. They per-ceived the luded-out butt munches at the Fire Island Meat Rack as reminiscent of a primitive matriarchal merge with natural forces—a necessary, freeing process of gay life, but not its permanent goal.

One such Young Turk was Neil Alan Marks, known by many as the dark-haired Jewish intellectual half of the star-crossed couple interviewed in Michael

Denneny's amazing book *Lovers: The Story of Two Men*. Marks repudiated the attitudes of the '70s that "turned everything in the ghetto into a virtue."[17] He railed against the pattern whereby otherwise intelligent homosexuals "feel the need to describe clone-like behavior as almost heroic and turn sexual hysteria into grotesque self-justification." He saw AIDS as but one symptom of a need for change. "It is out of this small-townish community organization and dichotomous sex club semi-anonymity that the new Gay Man emerges," he said, arguing on behalf of the sharp lines and articulated boundaries of Apollo. "Whether he chooses to view the past as Dresden after the bombing or the Expulsion from Eden, he is, by most accounts, a changed man, a more sober man, an individuated man."

You thought about sobriety just as the cute black man behind you on the crowded staircase began to not-so-meekly rub his crotch against your butt. You remembered reading an article by Drs. David M. Sloven and Jeffrey M. Leiphart that analogized the attachment to pleasure as a kidlike state of mind, one that a person ought to learn how to regard objectively but never repress in a Puritanical way.[18] Sloven and Leiphart insisted that sexual gratification is a natural part of creating a strong gay identity. But, like adherents of Eastern religions, they saw a difference between self-assertion and self-realization. They made sexual addiction sound less like a disease than an eccentricity of youth. They counseled that gay men begin a *literal* conversation with their inner sexual personality, as if it were a "kid" mesmerized by chocolate. Did that mean that maybe you should turn around, face the black man, and ask him home for some coffee? He'd be nice to date, or so said your "kid."

Boy, did many *Native* writers encourage dating—courtships, even! In 1981, borrowing a line from F. Scott Fitzgerald, Thomas Garrett maintained that "Sex is not recreation; it changes things between people."[19] You thought about those lines as the black guy grabbed your hand. *Something did change.* Sweet. Maybe this is what Garrett meant—why he mounted a "justification for staying home, for saying no, for resisting the impulse to fritter away yet another evening in fruitless pursuit of Mr. Maybe." As the guy behind you began to kiss your neck, you wondered: Is there something unique in homosexual libido that men worship? How could that be seen better, understood, valued, not so quickly processed like American cheese, but contained?

There were so many essays to read. But reading was one thing, and applying the information was another. You felt torn between two opposites: you wanted to build a barrier to the tides of a vast inner ocean but you didn't want to keep the ocean out of your life. You thought of Ulysses on his homebound journey being seduced by the Sirens, tempting the sailors with undreamed-of bliss. Ulysses exhorted his sailors to stop up their ears so they would not follow the enchanting music to their deaths. So many of these writers, especially Marks, encouraged readers to stop up their ears too.

You heard the disco music of the bathhouse now, just as the line began to move forward into the bathhouse. The man behind you held your hand, as if holding you back. Your heart opened to him. You wondered what to do.

before condoms, common sense

Supported by the words of Michael Callen and Dr. Lawrence Mass, Richard Berkowitz, Dr. Joseph Sonnabend, David M. Sloven, M.D., Jeffrey M. Leiphart, Ph.D., Thomas Garrett, and Charles Jurrist, gay men did their best to adapt to the crisis situation using a variety of ingenious means. Tom Cendejas, for one, used the classifieds to screen men, to tame his sexual instinct through dating, and to find out in a more slow-and-sure method what kinda Mr. Maybe he maybe liked. Because he was a well-built Latino man with a quirky way of writing an ad, and because he was smart, and because he didn't take himself too seriously, and because he didn't sound too desperate or too distant, he had a lot of callers.

The courtships proved more interesting than the results—but that wasn't so tragic. "It was a wonderful way to keep your energy up and to be thinking about men," Cendejas discovered. "Every now and then you listen to a man talk about himself and you whisper to yourself: 'Yes, yes, that's the one.'"

Many resorted to porn. "The anti-sex backlash of the '80s," writes gay porn impresario Dave Kinnick, "had a devastating effect on the nation's bathhouses and X-rated theaters, but it fueled profits in the video industry. People may have stopped *having* sex, but they certainly hadn't stopped *wanting* sex. Like bathtub gin during Prohibition, the popularity of videos soared. . . ." (Profits weren't the only thing that went up in the porn business. So did AIDS cases among porn stars. It wouldn't be till 1987 that some porn producers began using condoms on camera. In William Higgins's *Hot Rods*, produced by Catalina, Allan Fox sticks a Conceptrol tube up Eric Radford's ass before fucking him doggy-style. "Hey, what's that?" Radford asks. "It's to protect both of us," replies Fox.)[20]

Some men chose celibacy. "The enormity of the devastation hit me in 1981," Picano remembers, "when I was in Fire Island walking around and I bumped into Paul Popham [the first president of GMHC, profiled by Randy Shilts in *And the Band Played On*, who died from AIDS in the '60s] on Sky Walk. We had begun talking and we realized that so and so was sick with pneumonia and that so and so had this symptom and that so and so had nightsweats and that so and so had these lesions. At some point, we just stopped talking and looked at each other and said: 'We're dead.'" So Picano just gave up sex.

Celibacy may sound too drastic a response in retrospect, but the trauma resulting from the early deaths did much to sap people's sexual urges. A thousand men had already died by 1983. Besides which, the condom hadn't yet become the bulwark of AIDS prevention. AIDS agencies were cautioning different measures, which in retrospect seemed foolish, but were not so foolish: the reduction of partners, staying clean, getting to know your partner, asking questions about VD. To most, sexual sobriety wasn't such a sacrifice—especially to the New Yorkers and San Franciscans who got hit hardest and earliest. Some men, like Eugene Sachs, struggled to find a new definition of "discipline" that wasn't moralistic or heterosexual. "For so long," he said in a *New York Native* article, "discipline has been equated in our minds with the repressive forces of law, medicine and religion which have imposed their anti-sexual morality upon us from the outside." He called for a new kind of inner discipline arising from gay hearts and minds to set up new sexual strategies for coping with the new disease.[21]

As early as 1983, gay men mounted an effort now known as "behavior modification." For many, it wasn't fast enough or modified enough, but for others, it kept AIDS at bay. That's why Picano bristles at the suggestion in Randy Shilts's *And the Band Played On* that gay men fucked when they knew better. "We were so busy caring for sick friends," acknowledges Picano, "that who had the time to think about sex? My friend and I did a lot of cuddling at that time."

Others stayed put—away from New York City. "There was minuscule coverage in the local press, and nothing approaching a citywide welling of fear and protest," writes Paul Monette in *Borrowed Time*. "The most constructive thing anyone seemed to be doing was avoiding all travel to New York and San Francisco, which were now perceived as 'over,' not to mention a bummer."[22]

Of course, such a fear of the body—never mind such fear of the urban homosexual—was exactly what those who loathed homosexuals wanted homosexuals to feel. This hatred filtered down into even the most liberal of outposts. Not since the '50s had gays faced such out-and-out hatred—sanctioned by the media and by many middle-class Americans who secretly resented the gay man's privilege, spending power, and alleged lack of social responsibility. The power of the religious right grew in the mid-'80s, and in "mellow" California, Christian Fundies mounted proposition after proposition trying, in one way or another, to quarantine those suspected of having AIDS or to include mandatory reporting of HIV or to stop anonymous testing or to compel those convicted of crimes to mandatory testing. Those measures ultimately failed, but only after the affected gay communities threw enormous time and money into those efforts, resources that could have been better spent on AIDS.

The Christian Right used AIDS to wage a cultural war against homosexuality. And it succeeded—as the Reagan Administration's refusal to deal responsibly with the health crisis proved. Even after Rock Hudson came out with AIDS, and there was a public shift in the attitude of the disease, with celebs like Elizabeth Taylor virtually glamorizing AIDS, all the Reagan administration could propose in its 1986 budget was a reduction of AIDS funding by 10 percent. This led to wealthy gay men getting behind the fight against AIDS with a dedication they had not previously offered gay politics. The '80s saw the flowering of the "checkbook activist."

But the resounding call within the gay movement to fight Reagan's recalcitrance and to build from the ground up a multibillion dollar AIDS infrastructure around the country, did not address the question of sex, how to have it, who to do it with, and when it should be done. For the most part, sex, whether J-O or sucking (most avoided mention of the ass as a favored erogenous zone) took a back burner to CBO—AIDSspeak for community-based organization—building. The same could be said for the psychological backlash created by the health crisis. Although organizations like Shanti and Northern Lights Alternative did much in the mid-'80s to help gay men cope with grief, dying, and bereavement, the gay interest in twelve-step programs, therapy, and psychological thinking was more a feature of the '90s, what some people erroneously call "post-AIDS" life.

retroactively psychological

The feelings of loss that overtook the gay community took a decade before they could be assessed. After all, it is only survivors who can have feelings, and it is only survivors who can synthesize feeling and thinking. A variety of books would come out in the '90s—Walt Odets's *In the Shadow of the Epidemic* and Eric Rofes's *Reviving the Tribe*—that would serve to fill in the colors around sexual dysfunction and emotional grief, colors too unbearable to be seen clearly in the early '80s.[23] To more than a few onlookers, it took time for certain feelings to enter the psychic body, fill the empty shell with blood, as it were. Some say that one can't record the subjective experience of a trauma but retroactively. Even that fails the historical record. For those who suffered the most are dead.

In his book, Walt Odets parallels Paul Monette's and Andrew Holleran's literary gaze on gay life. He sees AIDS not as the cause of the feeling of loss, but rather as an amplification of an already existing situation: "In my experience with adult gay men there is an unusual level and frequency of sadness, nostalgia and longing."[24] This loss may come from childhood. It may come from developmental challenges around first trying to "pass," and then coming out. Wherever it comes from, its presence—loss's fullness of feeling—reduces many a gay man to tears, especially around feelings of either intense erotic or romantic need or, paradoxically enough, profound gratification. One psychotherapy patient—Odets calls him "Bob"—experiences a feeling of loss after the moment of orgasm:

> It's been so much a part of my experience ever since I started masturbating that I've never noticed it before. But I just realized a few days ago that right after I have an orgasm, I feel terrible grief. I just never noticed it, but when I think back, that's always been the case.

Odets asks if this loss occurs only during masturbation or during sex with another. Bob answers that the sadness comes only when he's alone; he cries after he comes. "It's just this intense sadness," he says, "really a feeling of loss, and I may attach it to something else going on, but I think it really comes from my sexual fantasy somehow." As Bob explains it, it's the disappearance of the masturbatory fantasy that flattens him:

> And when I was a kid, it was only when I was masturbating that I could have him. I mean, I knew I could never really have sex with a man, and I had this relationship with this beautiful man in my fantasy, which was the only one I could have, and when I came, he would be gone.

As Bob puts it, he's "died a thousand times by now." Odets presses him to see that this feeling of loss goes beyond what Bob experiences in connection with orgasm during masturbation, that Bob has a "long-standing experience of feeling sadness and loss in connection with homosexual intimacy."

While Bob admits that the feeling of loss is less severe when he "really trusts someone," he also admits that the thought of HIV sometimes shatters even the most loving of experiences:

> Well, I started to say that I didn't feel the loss if I was connected to the person, and I realized that there was something else in there—that sometimes when I come, I think about AIDS, and about how it is spread, and when I come that's what I think of, and I feel very depressed about that. I thought of that once when Dan and I were having sex, and afterwards we were cleaning up, and he said, "Let's wipe up this killer cum," or something like that. And I got very angry, and I said, "Why did you say that?" And he said, "I was just making a joke, like killer

kum, you know, K-U-M." And I thought, "Well here's a new reason to get depressed after sex."

Odets is a profoundly insightful psychologist. His suggestion that the loss Bob feels around cumming comes from a deeper problem than AIDS is revolutionary. But like most post-Freudians of the school of object relations, he does not touch on the archetypal dimension—only the personalistic. In part, he is right to focus on the personal, the loss gay men experience around parental issues and coming out, not to mention the grief surrounding AIDS. But there is a cosmic connection that Bob refers to vis-à-vis his fantasy—especially just as the fantasy disappears—that represents both the real loss and the real potential of gay psychic transformation. One could see it as a connection to his unconscious gay Self, his soul connection, which is both so close yet so far away. Depth psychologists call this "soul connection" the "anima" in a man and the "animus" in a women. But in a gay man, maybe it is altogether different. A masculine double?

Observing the lives of gay men, according to psychologist Mitch Walker, it'd seem as if one is born with a "soul-buddy." He writes that "the idea of one's soul as a 'double' is ancient and can be traced to Sumerian and Egyptian writings." Walker recounts the story of Gilgamesh, a man who is "redeemed from a purposeless life by a strong man named Enkidu." He quotes from a translation of the text to show that it was the gods who created a "second image of Gilgamesh: may the image be equal to the time of his heart." With a love that is likened to that between husband and wife, it is the paradigm of many social relationships (husband and wife, brother-to-brother). "Ultimately," adds Walker, "it is through passionate love for manly Enkidu, a figure too grand and bright to be a shadow, yet too weak and mortal to be the Self, that every-inch-a-man Gilgamesh finds maturity."

In this vein, the loss experienced by Bob may not be derived from pathological causes, or even AIDS. It may have its roots in this connection to the "soul double," and the powerful feelings of emptiness that often send a person on a journey to find his missing half.[25]

fags without facial hair

Popular folklore suggests that, without AIDS, the sexual revolution would have continued apace—that gay life in the '90s would have been one big Valhalla. But long before the health crisis, some younger gay men had rejected the hedonism that came with a heavy emphasis on pleasure.

"There were a bunch who spray-painted 'Clones go home' on the streets of Lower East Side," recalls performance artist Tim Miller, who had cofounded

Performance Space 122 on Ninth Street and First Avenue. He was part of the short-lived "Fags Against Facial Hair" mini-movement that sprouted in the Lower East Side at the start of the '80s. "This [spray-painting] was a tangible representation that young gay guys resented the imposition of the West Village mentality on bohemian East Side values," he says.

The new group was made up of punks, New Wave music adherents, Tom Robinson fans, Pyramid-club habitués, anarchist-intellectuals, contact improvisation types, and performance artists. This de facto clique wasn't merely focused on style differences: black jeans, skinhead hairdos, and black-dyed hair versus 501s, mustaches, and bomber jackets. With its motto—"disco sucks"—the group summed up its attitude toward the marketed sexual culture of the '70s.

"Class had a lot to do with our rejection of the clone routine," Miller adds. "A lot of poor artists couldn't afford to spend the weekend at the Pines, even if they wanted to. But the big difference was that some younger men didn't see the appeal of anonymous sex."

Some of the youngest gay refugees to New York City felt burnt and used by the older set. "Isolated gay boys from small towns," writes Ian Young, ". . . arrived in the Village or the Castro lacking the discernment and abilities necessary to maintain real friendships or meaningful ties. Alienated and adrift, they formed an excellent target group for the marketing of a new kind of urban lifestyle that was economically and culturally a lucrative expansion of the illegal drug market and the quasi-legal sex industry."[26].

Visual artist Keith Haring was one such "kid." A few days after his arrival in New York, he fell into the illegal drug world and quasi-legal sex market Young lambastes. "The scene," recounts Haring in John Gruen's biography of him, "was still that you went from bar to bar, and little by little I discovered where the interesting gay places were, including the back-rooms bars, like The Stud, where they had porno movies playing and a more or less dark room with people groping and having anonymous sex." Haring found the nightly cruising at first strange, but then he acclimated. He thought he was unattractive and the sex became a way for him to fit in.[27]

Along with other bohemians of the East Village, Haring grew resentful and pissed off about the delusion that being gay meant being sex-crazed. It was Ronald Reagan's election as president that radicalized younger gays—turning them off to what they perceived of as the previous generation's inability to prevent the political disaster. To be sure, by the end of the '70s, New York gay life was terribly politicized. But there was a reason for this—gay life's complacency resulted, in part, from successes GLF and GAA radicals had had in changing attitudes. But the youngest of New Wave New Yorkers rejected even the terms of the free love liberationists. If the GLFers of the early '70s renounced wedlock in the hopes of revolutionizing life, the New Wavers pinned hopes on a boyfriend to keep themselves from spinning off into hyperestrangement. Anvil habitués fucked men to get to know them; some of the boys from HeBeGeBees tried it the other way around.

Not everyone came out explicitly against promiscuity in the year or two before AIDS validated their misgivings. But in one form or another, many younger men did what they could to live a different way. "Of course we were reacting," reminisced African American writer Steven Corbin, who came out in the late '70s in Jersey City, but found himself settling down with a lover in Los Angeles in the '80s. "But serial monogamy had a radical tinge to it. At the very least, I wanted to know the man I was fucking."

Corbin, and others like him, saw the collective pressure to fit into the sleazy gay world as anti-individualistic and anti-eccentric—and they questioned the commercialization of gay spirit just as often as they questioned its unrelenting racism. The ghetto was far from perfect, it seemed. Sex had become the social mask of the gay man, not a conductor any longer of unique and vital energy. "What was homogenizing the gay community," writes John Lauritsen, "was fragmenting the individual." The problem could be stated another way. A certain brainwashing had taken place that designated hard-core sex as the ticket to gay identity, not, as Lauritsen puts it, "learning the ABCs of love." Some younger men revolted.[28]

young turks

Lauritsen wasn't alone in his assessment.

The years before the discovery of HIV—and before the development of safer-sex AIDS prevention—show an outpouring of intellectual conjecture on the role of sex in gay life.[29] One *New York Native* cover after another posed controversial questions in 1981 and 1982, such as "Is Promiscuity Dead?" The *Bay Area Reporter* followed in the *Native*'s footsteps and finally, even the *Advocate* ran articles questioning the equation of sex with wholeness in gay life. Many writers saw that pleasure had become so addictive that the addictive quality of sex grew painful. When getting fucked in the ass lost its edge, a fist was needed. When pot didn't bash down defenses, a quaalude was in order. "What was next?" Arnie Kantrowitz wondered. "Necrophilia: not interested." Sexually jaded men like Kantrowitz and Ross Farley mused that when you've done *everything* some times *nothing* is the more radical act. But since American life valued *doing* over *being*, "nothing" seemed to come to "nothing."

cancer as curse

What does it feel like to be young, attractive, hitched with a handsome lover, and successful at the office only to face a fatal cancer? In the summer of 1981, Dr. Mass published the first interview with a PWA, from the first study group of Kaposi's sarcoma patients. That person was Donald Krintzman, the former lover of GMHC cofounder Paul Rapoport, who himself later died of AIDS. Mass found out that Krintzman was terrified of dying. But more than anything, he feared being crushed by critics, social ones as well as those within his own mind.[30]

In January 1981 Krintzman noticed a lump in his neck that didn't go away. He suffered no symptoms; his internist told him not to worry. But when a Fire Island pal suffered a rare cancer and subsequently died, he noted that man had had a similar lump. Healthy, he tried to put the bogeyman out of his mind. A *New York Times* article a few months later unsettled him. The short piece reported on the Center for Disease Control's announcement that forty-one gay men in New York and California had been diagnosed with KS and/or Pneumocystis pneumonia. The report, which featured no gay spokespeople, seemed to curse him personally:

> *Even though they [the* New York Times*] didn't precisely state that all or most of the victims were promiscuous to the extremes that were stated, the implication was there. As one of the victims, it made me feel terrible, as if I had been doing worse things than normal or respectable people do, as if I had gotten my just desserts. And that's not the case. I've intermittently enjoyed recreational sex, just as I've occasionally taken drugs. But I also have a lover and I'm a fully employed, tax-paying, law-abiding contributor to society. . . . I may have the cancer, but I haven't the slightest doubt that I'm a lot more moral than many people, gay and straight, who have no disease.*

So this is how, after ten years of defending public sex as the expression of their identities, gay men were so easily crushed by the culture's inherent distaste for sex. Mass refused to give in to the shame, but he was in a minority. "I've always been impressed," he argued, "by the Catch-22 situation that American society offers homosexuals. It says that because homosexuals are promiscuous, immature and incapable of forming stable relationships, they are therefore forbidden the legal, theological and social opportunities to establish them."

AIDS revealed that gay men had to do more than fight for civil rights. Individually they had to investigate how they had internalized the culture's shame so as not either to be a victim to it or to act out from it. This amounted to an added burden. But the inquiry also deepened the personality.

tin man   Like Dorothy Gayle, Eddie Mohr came from Kansas. But once arriving in San Francisco's Oz, he had no interest in utilizing his Ruby Slippers. The sexual hunt cauterized his already frozen heart. He cared little for his Auntie Em or Uncle Henry or the blistering hot summers, the wind, and the monotony of the plains. He'd toss letters from his family. "I had no feelings for anybody," he told an interviewer in 1986, "all I had feelings for was sex and more sex and drugs—that Saturday night high."[31]

The barricades that keep an ordinary man from being swallowed up by the existential problems around love and rejection often get dismantled by AIDS. With AIDS, Eddie suffered dementia, memory loss, and a blurring of realities. Like the onrush of instinctual life flooding his resistances, a host of split-off inward personalities emerged during his dying days. The most potent voice was that of a child, a child who misses his father, a child who hungers to set foot in his father's symbolic *and* literal home:

> To me, to be in my father's home is to feel such security. It's like being home. . . .
> It's like God's in the room. Even though we have never been that close, there's
> something about my dad; he's such a responsible man. Being in his home . . .
> [is] like going back to being a child and being [laughs] in his home.
>
> I feel that if it were just him, it would be okay. But the fear for the children has
> been a little block there. It'll either go away, or if it doesn't, I know my father will
> come see me wherever I am—to be with me.

When Eddie visited Kansas, his father neglected to extend an invitation, frightened that his grandchildren would contract Eddie's illness. The mother kept her distance too. Eddie died alone in a city-owned house.

the role of the father in sexual life

To see Eddie's symbolic wish for a father as connected to his desire to have hot compulsive sex may seem too simplistic to some. But one cannot easily overlook the way in which the need for sex and the effort to heal archaic rejection fit so nicely together. If one assumes that a homosexual baby is born thus, then it makes sense that the father receives potent love projections. Whether the father is a homophobe or not, chances are he'll deflect the attention. This agonizing deflection coincides with the birth of awareness. Men are attracted to men in part because these vibrations remind a guy of his first great romance. In this way, the archetype of the double that forms the foundation of many gay romances has something of the father in it.[32] One wants, if not a soul buddy, then a sex buddy. The man providing touch is for a moment one's most valued connection.

Many gay men intuit a profound connection between themselves and their fathers, despite the fact that their dads secretly, and not so secretly, dislike them. Pillars of gay literary and activist society, such as Steven Corbin and Michael Callen, were, in their final moments, reduced to tears at the way in which the love from father (or father surrogates) seemed so out-of-reach. "Were we looking for our fathers through so much sex?" Callen once asked an observer as he approached death.

As depth psychologists put it, this level of incestuous longing ought *not* to be understood literally. It is meant as a vibration, a symbol, an inner switch turning on. Things that happen in the first years of life resonate not just in the present; they also shape the future. If one follows Plato, then love is always a pursuit of what one lacks, but secretly already has.

To be sure, the rejection of the boy by the father does *not* cause homosexuality. Rather, a boy is born with a special, erotic, twin "brother," who is felt to be the source of life, and it is *this* soul-complex that gets projected onto the father. So the wish for father-incest becomes the original nostalgic call to union with a primal homo source, and thereby the father (and father-complex) becomes the first filter through which love-hate shines. What are those dozens of ads in the gay classifieds asking for in a search for the "straight-acting"? Why do Tom of Finland and Jeff Stryker make such good fantasy figures?

Men as diverse as Arnie Kantrowitz, David Stein, Steven Corbin, Alan Bell, Ross Perlie, and Rob Campbell agree that while relations with father were always tense, some reverberating fascination lurked there. Thinking further, they agree that there must be two types of fathers in the mind—the literal schmoe, but also an inner voice of wisdom about whom most gay men remain unconscious (in part because to reach him, one must process many horrible feelings around the literal "Dad"). So his form is aimed out into the social world.

It comes as a shock to most people that falling in love is one of the most profound projections we ever engage in.[33] To look for one's father in the outside world is a necessary way to awaken to the fact that things found on the outside are really projections coming from the inside. Like all complexes, it tends to get personified. But because the "separate personality" may be too hard to feel, or because modern people are not taught the tools by which this inner personality would be felt, it is projected on a suitable person—in a gay person's case, another man. Of course, few people buy this analysis. "The individual from whom such a personification emanates does not, as a rule, recognize it to be a factor within his own psyche," according to an early writer of analytic psychology. Historically speaking, the world of psyche is not yet honored as a living reality—only the world of unconscious projections.[34]

changing behavior

Larry Kramer was still smarting from his rejection by the Fire Island set that followed the writing of *Faggots* when he started to lose friends with AIDS. He had argued that gays had never achieved social power and respect because they seemed more intent on creating a better disco than a social movement. Now history intervened, calling not only hedonism into question, but political hubris also. But if AIDS vindicated Kramer, very few were willing to say so.

For the truth is that by 1982, only the deadly ill dared question the equation of promiscuity with gay identity and liberation. And they were dismissed as demented or guilt-ridden. Kramer was written off the same way—at first, because of his alarming rhetoric. "It's easy to become frightened that one of the many things we've done or taken over the past years may be all that it takes for a cancer to grow," he wrote. Why not go one step further and ask philosophical questions about sex? "Yes, I think that people should not fuck in the IRT or in the streets," he screamed. "How long must we remain so small-minded and reductionist that we are still fighting for the right to be judged solely by our sexual appetite?"[35]

Kramer was tarred and feathered for his first *Native* jeremiads. But at least he got people to listen. Being offended is an indication that something has not been integrated, as the slew of letters pouring into the *Native* proved.

"If it's toilet sex *per se* that Kramer finds so distasteful, then it would be better if he reacted with a little compassion. . . ," wrote one man who accused Kramer of sounding too much like the Moral Majority, and who suggested he make a sociological inquiry as to why some men only feel safe in an IRT john. Wrote another, "If Kramer thinks we shouldn't be having sex in the IRT, that's his privilege. But when he says we shouldn't be allowed to, and makes it clear he approves of our being 'nabbed by policeman,' he aligns himself with fag-haters and queer-bashers."[36]

Playwright Robert Chesley accused Kramer of antieroticism, guilt, and the desire for punishment, moralism, and adulation of authority. "I think the concealed meaning of Kramer's emotionalism is the triumph of guilt: that gay men *deserve* to die for their promiscuity. . . . Read anything by Kramer closely and I think you'll find the subtext is always: the wages of gay sin is death."[37]

Kramer volleyed back in several letters of his own: "But *something* we are doing *is* ticking off the timebomb that is causing the breakdown of immunity in certain bodies and while it is true that we don't know what it is specifically, isn't it better to be cautious until various suspected causes have been discounted, rather than reckless?"

Few doctors had taken public stands; now some admitted that. "There can be no equivocation," railed Dr. Joseph Sonnabend, himself a gay man. "Promiscuity is a considerable health hazard; this is not a moralistic judgement, but a clear statement of the devastating effect of repeated infections."[38]

Sonnabend saw the ways in which his medical authority and gay men's relationship to authority were ridiculously intertwined; he also understood AIDS as a disease of many factors. "Gay men have been poorly served by their medical attendants during the past ten years," he said, including himself in the criticisms. "For years no clear and positive message about the dangers of promiscuity has emanated from those in whom gay men have entrusted their well-being." He believed that the accumulation of STDs in the early '80s together created the conditions that led to the breakdown of people's immune systems, questioning the single agent line. At this early historical juncture, Kramer's concern over promiscuity from a moral point of view and Sonnabend's from a medical point of view intersected in a few people's minds. Michael Callen, and early AIDS patients like him, began speaking out against promiscuity. It would be several years before the single-virus-theory dominated gay community life—and hence several years before the "condom-every-time" mantra became the community standard of sexual life. For the time being, the frequency of sex and number of different partners became the modality around which leaders and doctors coalesced and fought.

sex changes things between people While many gays saw AIDS as stemming mostly from societal homophobia, a few thinkers saw the transformation it effected in gay life as announcing a bridge from a dying era to a new one. In other words, the creation of consciousness could not come without the integration of the most troubling of feelings. "Now that's why getting into the unconscious, into the shadow, makes the descent, is something to do," said Mitch Walker, who in the early '80s helped found a "gay soul making" group called Treeroots. "There is something that comes from inside to pull you in, because there's a treasure! It's within that inner crucible, through this work of coming out inside, that you find the treasure. The alchemists called it the 'royal gold.'"[39]

While not everyone cared to speak about AIDS in alchemical terms, everyone agreed that the crisis was quickly transforming gay life. These social critics, which included Neil Alan Marks,[40] Michael Callen, Don Clark, and later on, Camille Paglia,[41] tried not to condemn the way gay men transformed sexuality into an art form. They did gently question, however, a certain naïveté about the downside of bliss, a certain too-easy fearlessness around sex, a certain hubristic approach to nature—all of which, of course, have been the bane of people since mythological times.

Oedipus, for example, thought that he had banished a plague at Thebes merely by answering the Sphinx's riddle. But in trying to find the source of the plague later on, Oedipus realized that it was his incest that was responsible for the plague. Overestimating his intellect in a typically masculine way, Oedipus fell into a trap. Anyone who thinks he can outsmart the Sphinx Herself is maliciously stupid; for a deeper riddle lies lodged in the overt one. The riddle of the Sphinx is Herself: the Great Unknowable and Inscrutable matrix that cannot ever be fully apprehended or even seen by the rational mind. Of course, man must wrestle with the force. The case of Job shows a man gaining insight from this terrible struggle. But he will always be humbled by that which he does not yet know. Certain riddles cannot be answered.[42] To think one has found freedom in sex is to think one has answered a certain riddle.

Many sexual athletes understood this mysterious aspect of sex. "Some people," maintains Christopher Wittke, " 'experts mostly,' would call my attraction to the kind of public sex I pursue an 'addiction' at worst or a 'compulsion' at best. I prefer to consider it an ever-evolving fascination."[43]

One thing remained clear to everyone who loved sex: Christian myth was dying a slow death as far as feminists and gays were concerned (this despite the vigor shown by the right wing and its attacks on gays). Of course, Christianity had served an important psychological purpose. Through the establishment of institutions like the Church and marriage, the "Age of the Fishes" helped to "control and harness the energy of primitive sexuality and to permit creative use of it in spheres not directly sexual," according to psychologist M. Esther Harding.[44] But this harnessing did great damage to the spiritualizing properties of the body. According to Harding, the repression became "so excessive as to foreshadow a danger that modern man might be cut off almost entirely from this source of energy."

The repression became so great in puritanical countries that the individual suffered a terrible split inside himself. He became alienated from his passions, his best and worst. To stay a "good" person, many people projected their "bad" feelings onto the weak and undesirable. Homosexuals were often used as a screen for people's shadow projections. It's no wonder that to shrug off those projections, homosexuals also created a new myth, a new value system about the centrality of sexual expression and Dionysian abandon.

Those who challenged the prevailing repression in this way suffered a serious backlash. Reagan reigned supreme; so did family values. How refreshing monogamy looked by 1983, even to gays. Only the most courageous—those willing to risk attack even in their own communities—could do what was necessary: defend gay sex while also showing where the fascination with pleasure had produced its opposite.

we know who we are

Michael Callen retained a clear image of himself on a subway platform at rush hour, "frozen in place, reading for the first time about a new, lethal, sexually transmitted disease that was affecting gay men." The world had changed utterly and forever. By late 1981, he suffered mysterious fevers, night sweats, fatigue, rashes, and diarrhea. Although he didn't get his official AIDS diagnosis until nine months later, his doctor told him he had what was being called GRID, gay-related immune deficiency. He suffered a disease—cryptosporidiosis—found in livestock.

Trauma had the effect of forcing a new attitude:

> Like some rabid animal, AIDS picked me up by the scruff of my neck, shook me senseless, and spat me out forever changed. I am today a totally different person than I was when the decade and the epidemic began. AIDS has been a cosmic kick in the ass—a challenge to finally begin living fully.[45]

Raised in a small Indiana town, he knew that "a homosexual must be *the* most horrible thing anyone could ever be—so horrible no one had ever spoken of it in my presence." Dr. David Reuben's *Everything You Wanted to Know About Sex But Were Afraid to Ask* informed him that all gays, pathetic psychopaths, stalked toilets. "At first," he says, "I had been promiscuous because the only information I had about gay men was that we were all promiscuous *by nature*. But after discovering gay liberation, I proudly and defiantly celebrated the promiscuity that mainstream society so disapproved of." He bought the line about the radical potential in brother lust. "Where else . . . could a Wall Street stockbroker and a Puerto Rican delivery boy, each divested of the costumes and privileges of rank and class, 'come together' as equals?" he asked.[46]

Edmund White, coauthor of *The Joy of Gay Sex*, proposed that "gay men should wear their sexually transmitted diseases like red badges of courage in a war against a sex-negative society."[47] Callen, nodding his head in agreement, thought that every time he got the clap he struck a blow for the revolution. But, with AIDS, Callen saw that the clap-as-badge principle didn't work:

> Unfortunately, as a function of a microbiological, not a moral, certainty, this level of sexual activity resulted in concurrent epidemics of syphilis, gonorrhea, hepatitis, amebiasis, venereal warts and, we discovered too late, other pathogens. Unwittingly, and with the best revolutionary intentions, a small subset of gay men managed to create disease settings equivalent to those of poor third-world nations in one of the richest nations on earth.[48]

Although statistics documenting the galloping rate in epidemics of sexually transmitted diseases among gay men were available before AIDS, Callen wondered why "no one asked what the cumulative consequences might be of continually wallowing in what was, to put it bluntly, an increasingly polluted microbiological sewer."[49]

Writing with the moral authority of two "AIDS victims" (they, with San Francisco's Bobbi Campbell, would later coin the term "people with AIDS"), Callen and Richard Berkowitz in 1983 published with Richard Dworkin's editorial assistance a groundbreaking piece, "We Know Who We Are: Two Gay Men Declare War on Promiscuity."[50] (It's important to keep in mind that this discussion took place before the discovery of HIV and the basic agreement that HIV causes AIDS. It's also important to keep in mind that Callen never accepted the single-agent theory.) Arguing that a series of pathogens caused AIDS, and not a single agent, Callen said that the chances of getting a sexually transmitted disease from an encounter at a bathhouse in 1983 were much greater than a decade ago: disease had spread exponentially. From this logical position, he and Berkowitz charged that promiscuity was killing gay men. "We are not suggesting legislating an end to promiscuity," they wrote. "Ultimately, it may be more important to let people die in the pursuit of their own happiness than to limit personal freedom by regulating risk. The tradition of allowing an individual the right to choose his own slow death (through cigarettes, alcohol, and other means) is firmly established in this country; but there is also another American tradition represented by the Federal Trade Commission and the Food and Drug Administration, which warns people clearly about the risks of certain products and behaviors."[51]

All the same, the authors insisted that the gay community could no longer tolerate knee-jerk defensiveness to any discussion of promiscuity. They didn't understand how difficult changing behavior would be. "We need to support each other's search for sexual alternatives," they declared. "Certainly the future holds more options than phone sex! The epidemic of AIDS need not result in abstinence or even monogamy for everyone. Perhaps the concept of 'fuck buddies' can be modified to become circles of healthy individuals who can be trusted to limit their sexual contacts to members of that closed group."[52]

But gay men who saw their civil rights being tampered with were not interested in "closed groups." Outrage greeted "We Know Who We Are."

Despite the attacks, or because of them, Callen raised some money and, along with Berkowitz, put out an even more inflammatory piece. The pamphlet, "How to Have Sex in an Epidemic: One Approach," would become a classic of early AIDS paraphernalia, forming the basis of the sexual creed of the '80s: safer sex.[53] Edited by Dworkin with a foreword by Dr. Joseph A. Sonnabend, the authors presented the pamphlet not as a permanent solution, but as an emergency measure. They did not think safer sex was more effective than abstinence. The basic advice is simple enough for the short term: *limiting what acts you choose to perform to ones that interrupt disease transmission.*

Callen, a multifactorialist, never bought the line that a single agent caused AIDS. His fundamental position remained that frequent innoculations of cytomegalovirus into the body—as well as the presence of other pathogens—contributed to the immunological collapse known as AIDS. "No-risk sex" meant eliminating the sharing of bodily fluids through creative means such as masturbation and the use of dildoes.

The pamphlet promoted an ethical relationship to oneself and one's partner and, as such, ushered a new level of boundary-making into the Dionysian sex world. This meant taking precautions, using rubbers, planning ahead, staying sober, talking about boundaries, and learning how to select a partner who might be healthy. The authors suggested a simple question—"Been here long?"—to figure out how many contacts a potential partner might have had on a given night: "Discussing precautions before you have sex might seem like a turn off, but if you enjoy staying healthy, you may eventually come to eroticize whatever precautions you require prior to the sexual encounter."[54]

The habit some gay men had of going to the baths, despite the warnings about disease, alarmed the authors. They suggested guys jerk off *before* going out; they recommended limiting contact to only one or two men. They insisted on washing, condom use, an effort to exchange phone numbers and to avoid losing control. "The party that was the '70s is over," they insist. "Taking ignorance to the baths and backrooms is not sexual freedom—it's oppression."[55]

Most curious of all, these former sex pigs counseled that love make a come-back in gay life. "Men loving men was the basis of gay male liberation," they write, "but we have now created 'cultural institutions' in which love or even affection can be totally avoided." To them, affection is the best protection: "If you love the person you are fucking with—*even for one night*—you will not want to make them sick."

creating the community standard

Callen's call for a more thoughtful and sensitive approach to sexuality won out, but only in part. Many criticized guidelines to restrict sexual relations to a limited number of healthy partners. How is one to know who is healthy? If someone had a cough, would you shun him? Sex radicals wanted hard data before they took vows of celibacy.[56]

Charles Jurrist defended promiscuity as the last refuge of the lonely: "So not having a husband or a steady beau, I trick. I engage in casual sex on the lookout for non-casual sex. I am, if you like, promiscuous, hoping always to find someone with whom I could be monogamous. (I also trick because I need to get my rocks off once in a while. Celibacy would drive me nuts.)"[57]

His point is a powerful one: gay men were told by the dominant medical culture in the nineteenth century that they were "homosexual"—that what defined them was deviant behavior in which men had sex with men. In one way or another, twentieth-century gay culture has been a response to these myths. It had evolved into a world of *doing* more than *being*. To order a change, to order that men find something anything but sex—a husband; a true love; a mediational practice; a shrink—without providing a clear-cut paradigm as to how to do so was almost as inhuman as the repression that had colored life before Stonewall.

Major scientific and political events in 1984 actually helped people like Jurrist out. Dr. Robert Gallo announced in April 1984 that he had discovered what he had considered to be the causal agent behind AIDS. It was a single virus and it was called HIV. (In 1985, Secretary of Health and Human Services Margaret Heckler announced the licensing of the HIV antibody test.) This new discovery had profound implications for gay sexual life. If it was a virus that made people sick, and not sex *per se*, then maybe people could have as much sex as they wanted, as long as they could know that no virus was being transmitted. A lightbulb went off in many gay minds: condoms. At this point, Callen's suggestion to use a barrier during sex made enormous sense to almost everyone. Use of the condom became an effective strategy that essentially said to most gays that they didn't have to change their lives, they just had to wear latex. Armed with a condom, the gay community tentatively tried to reexperience a wholesome attitude around sex.[58]

Something apparently was working. A certain San Francisco Men's Health Study showed big changes in the sex lives of gay men. "Comparing the 6 months between January and June 1984 with the same 6 months in 1986," writes Edward King in his seminal *Safety in Numbers*, "there was a 60 percent decrease in the number of men who had over ten or more partners during this period." By late 1987, HIV-negative men had reduced the times during which they got fucked with two or more partners from 14 percent to about 3 percent; seropositive men had reduced insertive anal sex with two or more partners from about 40 percent in 1985 to about 5 percent in late 1987.[59]

In 1983, the California-based AIDS Behavioral Research Project studied 655 gay San Franciscans. It was shown that between 1984 and 1988 condom use became significantly more common. Those who had unprotected anal sex dropped from 50 percent in 1984 to 12 percent in 1988.[60]

In 1985, the CDC reported on a telephone survey with five hundred men from the San Francisco area. Writes King, "The proportion of men who said they were monogamous, celibate or performed 'unsafe' sexual practices only with a steady partner increased from 69 percent to 81 percent over this period."[61] Likewise, cases of rectal gonorrhea plummeted, representing, by 1991, a tenfold decrease over a seven-year period.[62] A similar drop in rectal gonorrhea—the only way to track unprotected anal sex—took place in other centers of gay life. It has never been clear, however, what conditions resulted in the drop in new infections. AIDS prevention leaders have often touted the success of their safer-sex campaigns. But AIDS leaders as diverse as King, Walt Odets, and Greg Scott say that the reduction of AIDS cases has more to do with the fear of sex men developed in the '80s than how often they used condoms. According to King, "It appears to have been more usual for men to stop anal sex altogether, rather than to continue fucking but start to use condoms."[63]

This isn't to suggest that gay men didn't use condoms or that condoms weren't at least part of the reason why the gay community saw a reduction in the rate of rectal gonorrhea. But condom use had at least as much to do with what relationship an individual had to his sex partner as his resolve to stay healthy. For men who had come out before AIDS, and for couples who had had sex before AIDS, the imposition of condoms seemed like a bad joke.

In 1985, for example, a group of men from Black and White Men Together/ Atlanta began putting together an AIDS education committee, which became affiliated with AID Atlanta. One of the live wires from this group, Duncan Teague, saw the psychological hurdles in changing sexual behavior:

> I had a lover—R—when I started working for AID Atlanta and we had not been practicing safer sex and I wanted us to go to a workshop. The three-day retreat—a kind of AIDS 101—was so intense and upsetting that my lover got physically sick and had to leave. When I came home, I was all ready for us to have safer sex. I was very young, in my early twenties, and R was 34. In his mind, condoms were a heterosexual thing. Condoms prevented pregnancy. Condoms didn't have any place in our lives as far as he was concerned. He kept implying that by my asking him to wear a condom that I didn't trust him. I saw then that there'd be this huge generational divide for AIDS education to work through. That the youngest might resist condoms the least. I never had had to prove myself as a heterosexual. I guess I had an easier time coming out because of people like R. But that also meant I had no associations—either good or bad—to condoms. I never had straight male friends who bragged about condoms. I never felt oppressed by condoms. I saw no reason to start using them. Whereas R had been subjected to all this education from the '50s about condoms, that you used them with "bad" girls or your wife. Also I don't think they had these ultra thin condoms in the '50s.

In the end, Teague's story illustrates the way in which condom use accomplished two important sociological feats: it reduced the transmission of virus and it allowed gay men to feel good about gay sex again via an "approved" sexual practice. A terminology of piety entered the vernacular around gay sex. In a word, condoms helped to de-shame gay sex—to take the AIDS out of it by taking the cum out of it.

But the wear-a-condom line that won out in the late '80s never did answer the still lingering problem of the epidemic of other venereal diseases. Their link to AIDS was rarely discussed and those doing so were marginalized as quacks. Sex became compartmentalized: some things were okay to do, some weren't. As long as you didn't get fucked in the ass without a condom, you'd probably be safe—or so the word on the street went. (Oral sex would remain a bone of contention. No one could prove unequivocally that it caused infection and no one could prove that it definitely didn't.)

And while safer sex served to return the joys of gay sex back to gay men, it also interrupted a profound conversation, and thus served as a mere Band-Aid. A philosophical opportunity was lost about the role sex played and did not play in gay identity formation.

The volatile debates of the early '80s that showed gay men struggling to transform and differentiate their relationship to instinctual life gave way to the necessity of politics: how to stop the dying, how to get the government to start dealing with the medical health crisis, how to get drugs approved. The preoccupations with sex—the differences between love and lust, let's say—were abandoned until the '90s, when it became clear that condom use for anal sex no longer prevented so neatly the spread of HIV. (The jury is still out on whether or not oral sex results in seroconversion, a debate that would explode in the '90s.) Simply put, until reports shook the gay community in 1993 that AIDS cases were rising all over again, especially among the young, the community virtually stopped asking provocative questions about sex.

eroticizing latex

Condoms solved the problem—for a time. Men returned to Dionysus, but this time with an Apollonian intervention. The intoxicating merger with one's hidden depths could no longer take place with utter unconsciousness.

"I've actually managed to fetishize rubbers to the point of not seeing them as an intrusion," wrote Christopher Wittke. "I like to suck lots of cock and I like to feel the shaft pulsing against my tongue as the cock spills its seed into the rubber." Wittke's well aware that many men suck without condoms and make the choice either to swallow or to not. "But when you suck as much prick as I do," he continues, suggesting he sometimes goes through two twelve-packs a week, "the safes seem like a great way to have a no-worry no-mess explosively sexual time in an otherwise worry-filled and messy era."[64]

In his case, the use of condoms is no turnoff to the men he attracts:

> He pulled out his cock and started stroking furiously, not six inches away from my eager face. To my delight, his pecker got much bigger than it had appeared to be through the glory hole. I started blowing hot and cool air on his shaft and though I could tell he didn't want me to touch his prick, I really wanted it in my mouth, I kissed his balls lightly, which alternately disturbed and aroused him. After a few minutes of this I decided he was sufficiently turned on for me to interest him in something else. Plus, I'd lose him when he had another panic attack.

He extracted a condom from his pocket and held it up for the man to see. "When he focused on it and realized what it was (it probably went through his mind that it was a badge), he nodded." Wittke notices how "accommodating" some tricks can be, "while others get all straight-acting," and protest. Not this guy. Wittke unrolled the rubber on his "hardening shaft" and took the "rod in one gulp." Had it been the first cock of the day, Wittke would have gagged like an amateur. But it wasn't:

> *I took his hands and placed them on the back of my head. I wanted him to fuck my face. Hard. Why is it that you have to do so much work to convince people that you want to be treated roughly? Finally he got the idea and started vigor-ously thrusting his hips. Soon he was pounding away so hard that it seemed al-most involuntary, like he couldn't stop if he wanted to. Personally, I love being on the receiving end of such an experience. It's as if you've become part of a well-oiled cocksucking machine set on perpetual motion.*

The guy pounds Wittke's mouth so hard that his eyes water and his nose runs and Wittke finds himself quite enjoying the act of choking on this cock. He asks for a rare treat: for the guy to stick his becondomed dick in his ass. Being extra "safe," he slides on a "second rubber" (a practice not encouraged by educators who say there is more chance of tearing with two condoms than one). Wittke gets "fucked to Nirvana." He sees stars in the "perimeter of my field of vision" and feels the man's "hip bones bounding off my ass cheeks as he held me roughly by my soaking wet armpits." The condom becomes a site for the redemption of pleasure that comes with one man receiving the seed of his another, an archetypal practice where the "manna" of one man is transferred to another in an act of enormous symbolic significance not yet undermined by AIDS. The Egyptians believed that an invisible being existed in each person—the idealized image of the person him-self—and they called this the "*ka.*" Sex seems to shake this *ka* alive in Wittke.

"I could hardly wait for the throbbing sensation as his dick delivered billions of sperm into the rubber," Wittke says, proving how possible it is for Apollonian thinking to join up with Dionysian excess. This joining of opposites is a "her-maphroditic" way of looking at life. Through the intersection of the field of plea-sure with the field of safety he does more than keep himself alive. He shows a new attitude. This new consciousness both includes and erases distance between men. It fights the natural tendency to sleep with the drunken delirium of unconscious-ness, a return to primal unity that is the goal and prize of every orgasm.

boundaries—as a minus   The imposition of boundaries around sex did not always, however, make for easy camaraderie. Although an HIV apartheid never really picked up speed—in fact, most gay men, regardless of their HIV status, were taught to identify as "AIDS affected" and never discriminate on the basis of serodiscordancy—a new level of circumspect did enter into the bar and dating scenes which, as Simon Harvey's story explains, left people feeling more lonely then ever:

> He's very cute. Maybe too cute. Probably leaves here with a different guy every night. A guy this cute has probably slept with all of West Hollywood. Remember what they say: "You're having sex with everyone your partner's had sex with." Maybe I'm jumping the gun. He does have an adorable smile. I'll ask him where he's from. From a small town in South Carolina? Very nice. I love a southern gentleman. Wait! He moved to New York when he was 18? New York!?[65]

Harvey calculates the man's age to find out that he lived in New York in 1979, "four years before ANYONE used condoms. Four whole years in the big HIV apple." Harvey notices all of sudden that the fellow looks thin and wonders: "If I could just see his pants from behind I could tell if he's lost weight recently." At some point, Harvey insists he stop thinking the worst. First off, the man's a lawyer—his mother would like that: "Used to be a corporate attorney but took some time off to travel and now he's working part-time for a not-for-profit agency." That worries Harvey who knows of many stories of HIV-infected men who leave the rat race to do something good in their lives before it's too late. Harvey thinks to ask but stops himself. After all, you're not *supposed* to ask. And besides, you're supposed to assume everyone is positive. Harvey thinks to ask what the fellow eats. "If he mentions wheatgrass juice or macrobiotics, I'm outta here. And that goes for Marianne Williamson and Louise Hay." But thank God the fellow likes Burger King! It's Harvey's lucky night. No lesions and the fellow's nicely aggressive—masculine. That must make him a top, which means he's less likely to be infected.

But then the dialogue takes a wrong turn:

"Well, it's been nice talkin' to you. I'll see you around."

"Yeah! Same here. See ya! Damn! He seemed like such a nice guy. I've got to stop being so negative."

As Harvey explains it, AIDS destroyed some romantic opportunities through the mutual fear so many experienced in trying to get closer to each other. While it would become more acceptable in the '90s to ask a potential sex partner whether or not he was HIV-infected and whether or not he practiced safer sex and whether or not he'd agree to take a test with you, such directness had not yet become a community standard in the mid-'80s. Everyone was supposed to presume his partner was infected and proceed accordingly. The notion that "We're All Living

With AIDS" lumped positive and negative together and kept men from venting their genuine needs to ask specific questions—no matter how irrational or paranoid they were.

musical s&m

The drug-induced fisting and flogging that was a feature of Folsom Street S&M had receded as the baths and backrooms catering to esoteric tastes shut their doors. Nevertheless, some younger gay men turned to S&M playacting as a relatively safe way to make connections with men while also opening themselves up to some of the initiatory death and rebirth experiences that are often unconsciously part of sexual encounters. "In the early '80s," maintains Doug Mirk, "when everyone was so freaked out about what caused AIDS and if sex caused it, you could bottom to a really cool, hot top and never once worry that you had exposed yourself."[66]

"It must have been a very long time ago [in the early days of AIDS]," writes Mirk, "because I remember when he tried to put the butt plug up inside me, when he put my wrists in handcuffs and guided me over the side of the bed blindfolded (if I were on the edge of a diving board, I would have scored a perfect ten from this position), the butt plug wouldn't go in. It must have been a *very* long time ago."

It must have been a long time ago, because Mirk was impressed that his friend was in a New Wave band and wore skinny leather ties, spiked hair, and mascara. Mirk's hair was spiked too and he wore Converse tennis shoes. Mirk met his friend, "Rip Shredder," through a personal ad in the *Detroit Metro Times*: "GWM big brother seeks littler brother for S&M scene, bondage, whipping, shaving, call (313) blah blah blah." At the time, Mirk lived with his mother, so Mirk asked for discretion and a six o'clock call on the dot on a Wednesday, when it was Mirk's turn to do the dishes:

> I walk in and Rip leads me to one of the vinyl seats. I nestle myself as far into the couch corner as I can and tap my knees with the pads of my fingers. He offers me a drink. I believe I take a coke. Rip is old, probably at least thirty. He wears tight black jeans and a T-shirt cut above the belly button, intriguing tufts of hair spiraling downwards. He has the worn look on his face of someone who had enjoyed his twenties, someone who understands what punk rock had been all about, now that it was almost over. I'm sure that my dick is perfectly visible to him as he reached across me to set my drink down on the glass end table.

Out from the corner of the room pokes an older gentleman on the heavy side. Jim, Rip's roommate, is an organist. Rip escorts Mirk into the dungeon/bedroom, whacking Mirk's butt hard in the process. "Out of nowhere, titillated, excited," Mirk hears the sound of organ playing: "Jim has begun to play." As Rip cuffs Mirk and places his hands over his head, chaining him to the doorway of his closet, Jim cranks out show tunes.

Not only was the sex safe, but it was musical.

As Mirk explains it, the fantasy level of S&M sex—where the hard-on takes place as much in the mind as on a sensation level—would come in handy during AIDS, where the individual needed to detach himself from the equation of gay sex with the exchange of cum. Add to this the relatively few bodily fluids exchanged during a flogging or a spanking, and it's easy to see how S&M would grow popular during the health crisis. Safer-sex manuals of the '90s promoted dog collars, pinching, and "sensuous slapping" as safer-sex alternatives. "The only perversion is unsafe sex," declares Peter Tatchell in his British-based and safer-sex glossy manual: *Safer Sexy: The Guide to Gay Sex*. As long as bodily fluids weren't exchanged, nothing could be too taboo.

bathhouse bathos

"If this article doesn't scare the shit out of you," Larry Kramer railed on the cover of the *New York Native*, "we're in real trouble. In this article doesn't rouse you to anger, fury, rage and action, gay men have no future on this earth. Our continued existence depends on just how angry you can get." Kramer pulled no punches about the enormity of the crisis: "I repeat: Our continued existence as gay men upon the face of this earth is at stake. Unless we fight for our lives, we shall die. In all the history of homosexuality we have never before been so close to death and extinction." The five-thousand-word story wasn't just a rant. It offered solutions as to how to create an AIDS movement, with suggestions about getting serious about what was causing AIDS and the warning that all gay men were susceptible ("All it seems to take is the one wrong fuck"). The article encouraged gays to question the CDC's manner of surveilling the disease, talk more actively about treatments, educate health care workers and hospitals about dealing with the new disease, lobby for gay tax dollars to go to gay health care, examine health insurance and welfare problems, and criticize the then-mayor's reluctance to deal with AIDS. Kramer ended his *cri-de-coeur* with a list of twenty men who had died who were Kramer's friends.[67]

The impact of the piece was felt in gay communities throughout the country. In some cases, it set off a fierce national debate around public sex—perhaps the most divisive fight the gay community had ever seen.[68]

A civil war emerged in San Francisco between gays who wanted the bathhouses closed and those who saw the venues as places to dispense safer sex education. Radicals saw bathhouse closure as infringement of civil liberties. (During one protest, bathhouse owners and patrons, naked except for towels, carried signs that screamed: "Today the tubs, tomorrow your bedrooms.") Conservatives lambasted the bathhouses as agents of suicide. (Larry LittleJohn, a former president of the Society for Individual Rights, screamed that "the bathhouses couldn't go on as they were without killing thousands of gay San Franciscans.") In the middle sat San Francisco Public Health Director Mervyn Silverman, who refused to close the bathhouses without community support. As he told then–San Francisco Mayor Dianne Feinstein, "It's not the bathhouses that are the problem—it's sex. People who want to have sex will find a way to have it."[69]

The debate evolved into a political sludgefest. Political pressure coming from pro-bathhouse gays forced leaders to withdraw their support for closure. The ugly confrontation pitted gays against the health department—precisely what Silverman wanted to avoid. The gay press was discredited because it benefited from bathhouse advertisements. (Throwing a lighted match onto the explosive situation, the *Bay Area Reporter* printed an enemy's list of the leaders advocating closure on April 4, 1984: "These 16 people would have killed the movement, glibly handing it over to the forces that have beaten us down since time immemorial. . . . The gay community should remember these names well, if not etch them into their anger and regret.")[70] The vacillating Silverman was ridiculed as a wimp by conservative gays and straights alike. The Stonewall Democratic Club, which supported the bathhouses, was suspected of political opportunism. The Harvey Milk Club, which supported closure, was mistrusted as assimilationist. Sex radicals lost all respect when they argued that no compelling medical evidence existed to prove that bathhouses spread AIDS.[71] The National Northern California Bathhouse Owners Association, seeking $100,000 from sex club owners around the country to start a legal challenge to closure, looked idiotically self-serving. The mayor, who wanted the baths closed for the Democratic Convention, was held off by Silverman who insisted that political necessities and public health needs conflicted.[72]

Despite the mess, or perhaps because of it, gay community support for the bathhouses waned. Most gays, freaked out about the death of friends, saw the issue as a losing battle. By June 1984, more than two thousand Americans had been killed by AIDS, and quite frankly, their survivors found their own libidos flagging. Their political allies got exhausted too. ("I have too many beloved friends in the gay community who have died or who are dying of this," moaned Supervisor Richard Hongisto. "I'm going to too many funerals. It's time the bathhouses be closed.") As Shilts put it, the decline in business proved lethal to private sex clubs such as the Hothouse, Cornholes, and Liberty Baths: "The cells at the Bulldog Baths were locked for the last time. The Cauldron announced 'the Last J-O Party' and threw in the sling." Bisexual patrons at the Sutro Baths engaged in a three-day Farewell Orgy during which the five people losing their jobs burnt AIDS brochures over the barbecues—an image burnt into the public's imagination.[73]

Still, the issue didn't die easily. First Silverman banned all risky behavior; then he changed his mind and closed down fourteen establishments. Even though a Superior Court told the bathhouses they could reopen as long as they hired monitors and threw out those who engaged in high-risk sex, the issue died on the vine. Some bathhouse owners filed for appeal in 1985, but most sold their buildings. On December 11, a beleaguered Dr. Silverman resigned.

The uproar did, however, raise the level of AIDS awareness in the gay community. The sexual complex got differentiated by a stronger and stronger ego and thus lost some of its domineering control over the individual. Leon McKusick of the AIDS Behavioral Research Project conducted a study that showed that sexual behavior had shifted dramatically. A San Francisco AIDS Foundation study found that of the five hundred men interviewed, 62 percent reported having no unsafe sex and nine out of ten reported having altered high-risk sex. Safer-sex advertisements revealed a sharp change in attitude, with political discretion appealing less than straightforward messages, such as "There is no longer an excuse for spreading AIDS."

It wasn't a happy time. One of the main strategies gay men had for dealing with crushing social oppression was sexual release. However, that release—that "sexual complex"—was now denied them. A psychological complex is nothing but a cluster of images, ideas, and memories that form around a particular archetype. The ego tends to merge with a complex, especially one as strong as the "sex complex." Only the strongest of egos can fend off such a merger. And even that comes after a hard-won inner battle (one part of the mind says, "fuck his ass," while another part says, "get some sleep"). During the bathhouse and safer-sex controversies, the grip of the sexual complex on gay men lost some of its domineering control, paving the way for psychological differentiation and freedom. In this way, the AIDS crisis tended to undermine the "Myth of the Homosexual" within the gay community. But the effect so far was mainly negative. New consciousness about the different possibilities had not yet occurred to the conscious mind.

the soul murder of dionysus

The bathhouse controversy lanced a certain contentious boil among gay men and contributed to making some of the ensuing political crises less vicious. With the discovery of HIV came a test for tracing HIV antibodies in the blood. The potential civil liberty issues made the bathhouse controversy seem like small potatoes. How could the test results be kept confidential? Would people lose their insurance? Their jobs? Would an HIV diagnosis lead sooner rather than later to death? "But the gay leaders and the gay press generally discussed these issues in a rational manner without discovering 'enemies' and building up factions," writes FitzGerald. Following the bathhouse civil war, the community seemed less torn apart.[74]

In cities all across America, sex establishments shut their doors for good. Reagan's henchmen and the mainstream press launched both implicit and vicious attacks on gay sexuality. Michael Bronski says that the times succeeded in causing "many men to react with fear and guilt rather than inventiveness of expression" about the attack on Dionysus.

"Urban renewal," he maintains, "has also played a part, and many of the bars, bookstores, and theaters where sex was so easy and plentiful have been destroyed by developers. Some have argued that the advent of the VCR was the primary cause of the peep shows and porno houses closing. But this is untrue. These places existed not only so that men could watch the films but so that men could meet one another—socially and sexually. They were community gathering places."[75]

What would emerge in their place?

introversion gives back libido

AIDS organizations   The gay community witnessed a new investment in spiritual and political organizing during the mid-'80s. It experienced what Bronski calls the "undeniable recognition that AIDS was the most crucial problem our community had ever faced." But with the political priorities in place, the community also saw the reemergence of a gay sensibility in popular culture. Some of the cultural production was escapist; or else it was an effort to keep the sexual fires burning. But everyone agreed that despite the work's content, it could not be viewed outside of the AIDS experience. Indeed 1984 and 1985 saw accelerated change and bizarre culture clashes: Rock Hudson's diagnosis, Keith Haring's Lower East Side gay pride logos, Dennis Cooper's slash novels, Robert Mapplethorpe's objectification of black men, the Gay Games' queer jocks, Larry Kramer's *Normal Hearts*, the prancing of *La Cage aux Folles*, and the social satire of Ethyl Eichelberger. Reacting to the overwhelming grief and loss, thousands of West Coast gay men flocked to New Age gurus Louise Hay, Marianne Williamson, and Sally Fisher in Southern California. Fisher founded Northern Light Alternatives, which offered workshops to teach people how to "live powerfully with HIV."

On the East Coast, AIDS activists drafted the Denver Principles, the magna carta of the Persons with AIDS Empowerment movement ("We condemn attempts to label us as 'victims,' which implies defeat, and we are only occasionally 'patients,' which implies passivity, helplessness and dependence upon the care of theirs. We are 'people with AIDS.'"). PWAs created journals, conferences, buyers' clubs, social clubs, and changed the way the gay community saw itself and its so-called "victims." On both coasts, AIDS service organizations grew to become million-dollar-budget agencies. With all this activity, sex no longer seemed the most important thing gay men did with each other.[76]

Libido was channeled into the AIDS activist movement, which had the result of legitimizing sex all over again, but in a new way. "The twin effects of the epidemic and the Reagan administration's neglect," writes Neil Miller, "strengthened the gay community as a political force during the period."[77] Previously, the gay mainstream thumbed its nose at gay politics; national organizations were weak; lesbians identified more with other women than with gay men; few visible national leaders had emerged; external threats (Anita Bryant, Dan White) galvanized only for a short time. But AIDS forced wealthy checkbook closet cases to become checkbook activists; lesbians began to feel they could identify with gay men. And young gay men got so pissed off they were ready to listen to someone who demanded that the only answer was to take to the streets.

In fact, ACT UP was begun by the gay community's most controversial figure: Larry Kramer. On March 10, 1987, Kramer gave a speech at New York's Gay and Lesbian Community Services Center that changed the way gay politics would be talked about for a long time. "If my speech tonight doesn't scare the shit out of you, we're in real trouble. . . . We have sat back and let ourselves literally be knocked off man-by-man — without fighting back."[78]

Several weeks later, on March 24, approximately three hundred young men and women flooded to a Wall Street corner to rail against the Food and

Drug Administration policy of keeping life-sustaining drugs bound up in their nine-year approval process, in which half of the terminally ill get the effective treatment while the other half get a placebo and die. The group called itself the AIDS Coalition to Unleash Power—ACT UP. The demonstration made the evening news. A few days later, when FDA chief Dr. Frank Young talked about speedier drug releases, Dan Rather credited ACT UP with the change. The following Columbus Day weekend, when hundreds of thousands marched in Washington, gays and lesbians from around the country met to learn how to set up dozens of ACT UP chapters around the country.[79]

ACT UP demonstrations did more than create some interesting logos (SILENCE = DEATH) and fashion statements (crewcuts, Doc Martens, whistles). Men with "Fuck you" attitudes made sure that all the bumping and grinding that took place as men got hauled off into paddy wagons was followed up by bumping and grinding when they were released by the cops. The motto "ACTION = LIFE" took on a new twist.

ACT UP proved that Dionysus could not be murdered, that his presence revitalized life, and that youth culture would not tolerate repression. In fact, ACT UP *was* a sexual environment, according to some observers like Michelangelo Signorile, and it channeled libido into political rage reminiscent of the early GLF and GAA days and proclaimed queerness and not just AIDS as the overriding juice behind the new movement. "If in the first years of the epidemic," writes Frank Browning, "many gay men found that they could win greater social acceptance by presenting themselves as people who had a disease rather than people who *were* homosexual and thus suffered *from* a disease, by the end of the eighties a new generation of gay men came to insist upon and celebrate the fact of their queerness—whether they had AIDS or not."[80]

high camp

The three-day "AIDS vigil" outside of L.A. County/U.S.C. Medical Center began ceremoniously toward the end of the '80s against a black backdrop sporting fang-enhanced portraits of county supervisors Pete Schabarum, Deane Dana, and Mike Antonovich. ACT UP members heard testimony from HIV-infected individuals about visits to a hospital famous for its heroic staff and inadequate facilities. (ACT UP's charges of county AIDS neglect were many, but the major "crime" was the absence of an AIDS ward; PWAs lay in gurneys in corridors. Homophobic roommates taunt patients; Christian fundies coerce queers to renounce homosexuality.) For one entire week, about fifty men and women wrapped their chilled bodies in blankets and parkas, and snuggled into sleeping bags at two in the morning.

The enemy was nowhere in sight, so Connie Norman, in her sassy red winter boots, started up a Marlboro and regaled the curious with anecdotes about being neither man nor woman, but a transsexual—or as she prefers to call it, a "transy." She dispelled many a sex-change myth: "Nooooo, it works, darlin'—I get horny as fast as I used to get hard." While she spoke, a group of men and women gathered in a circle, "consensus making," for tomorrow's press conference. Meanwhile two swarthy young men, condoms in hand, ducked into a small tent. But rumor caught on. And like a group of gypsies on the night following a wedding, a gaggle of ACT UPers rooted them on.[81]

act up, fight back, make out

ACT UP made at least as great a contribution to the evolution of gay sexual culture as it did to educating America about the AIDS crisis. Of course, promoting safer sex among members wasn't its rationale. ACT UP came into being in chapters all around the nation in the late '80s because, as activist Bruce Mirken said, gay groups were not combative enough. ("I don't think you can work in the AIDS bureaucracy and be an AIDS activist," added the late Mark Kostopoulos in 1987.) The explicit debate involved how to respond appropriately to the crisis: to be part of the system or step way out and threaten the fabric of the system itself. To put it another way, ACT UP (and later on Queer Nation) reinvigorated the questions that shaped both the Mattachine Society and the Gay Liberation Front, the Gay Activists Alliance, and the Radical Faeries. It made gay men go to the core of their identities and ask, in the manner of Harry Hay, "Who are we gay people? What have we been for throughout the ages? What might we be for?"

Of course, implicit in the philosophical questions was the matter of sex. ACT UP chose not to get in the middle of moral questions about how much or how little sex ought to be part of a gay identity. But taking the matter as already settled—simply put, gay sex was a wholesome part of street activism—marked an enormous step forward. "Kiss-ins" became a staple of every street action. While some guys gave a peck, others refused to separate until horseback cops charged the crowd.

What surprised ACT UP newcomers wasn't merely its anger, or its stylizations, but its emphasis on creating a joyful definition of community. (In L.A. that entailed a spiritual dimension; San Francisco saw a clash between hard-core left energy and a pretty gay boy mentality; New York grew famous for its near-thousand person meetings and superior attitude about how it handled the press.) To be sure, ACT UP was based on the conviction that AIDS would never have spread had it not been for homophobia. But on a day-to-day level, ACT UP helped break down the psychic damage and cult-of-coolness that kept gay men from imagining themselves as belonging to something larger and more powerful than Fire Island—thanks in large part to ACT UP's celebration of participatory democracy and human eccentricity. ACT UP exploded the nonsense about what gays and lesbians look like. "We are not only fighting every battle and venting every rage," ACT UP founder Kramer said. "We are Mickey and Judy putting on a show."

civil disobedience weekend

Tonight's show featured ACT UP member and performer Tim Miller. Synthesizing a prosex ethic with a street activist one, the monologue told the story of a bunch of diverse, buff ACT UP activists about to be arrested by the cops. "This was the big moment," Miller bellowed into a microphone during an AIDS vigil, "the time where all our careful training, our split-second organization, our carefully honed message, not more rehearsing or nursing a part, we were about to enter—CIVIL DISOBEDIENCE WEEKEND." In his fantastic tale, politics and porn blend in a Whitman-like revelry. Once in the holding room, for example, one activist says to another, "Boy, these ACT UP civil disobedience anticensorship actions sure get me all hot." And the orgy has indeed begun—in jail, no less:

> Hands began to move underneath "Action Equals Life" T-shirts, and that message took on a whole new meaning. One of the boys from Highways [Performance Space] reached into the pants of one of the boys from the L.A. County Museum of Art and they began to kiss big wet sloppy larger-than-life tongue kissing. . . . The semiotic instructor from Cal Arts has now pulled his dick out and is demonstrating the Theory of Signification to the graduate student from the Inland Empire. . . . The pants are dropping. . . . Shirts are pulled over heads in a practical arabesque. . . .[82]

In a flurry of "safer activist sex," the men don't just cum for cumming's sake. It's quite revolutionary: "One after another we cum on the face of Jesse Helms. On a banner with the word "Guilty" burned across his forehead. He is now awash in the semen of twenty-four pissed-off artist fags . . . defiant even in the slammer." Screaming "No" to antisex, antilife, anti-art Nazis, Miller envisions the jailhouse sex leading to a new day where a cure for AIDS is found. Imprisoned queers take to the streets as the L.A. Philharmonic plays Beethoven's Ninth. A telegram from

Boris Yeltsin insists the activists create a new government to address global warming, nuclear disarmament, economic restructuring and, of course, a cure for AIDS.

Instead of demonizing cum as disease-ridden, Miller saw the jism as fertilizer. A transformation of libido was occurring. "Though the state may chain us," he insisted, "our crazed and juicy bodies and imaginations will not be imprisoned." Miller, like many ACT UP artists—David Feinberg, Douglas Crimp, Steven Corbin, John Weir, and David Wojnarowicz—put a lot of value on the power of gay men to change the world through eros. Their work could be seen as a militant effort to fight right-leaning attempts in both the gay and straight communities to crush radical queer men right where they were both most vulnerable and most strong: their need for and attachment to each other.

a holding pattern

But despite ACT UP's—and later on, Queer Nation's—success in putting the "sex" back in homosexual, the philosophical debate about the role of sex in gay life remained largely unexamined. Harry Hay's questions were never sufficiently tackled vis-à-vis sex. Queer theorists at the academy, arguing that gay identity was nothing but a social construction, dismissed such questions as essentialist. The spiritual approach that, for a time, served many gay men's needs came from New Age women who *did* do much to get gay men to look at the poor self-esteem that led, in some cases, to the meatracks. But it did not offer a deeper way to reclaim phallos as a galvanizing symbol of gay life.

With new AIDS cases galloping, the sexual question took a back burner to other issues: how to take care of the dying; how to fight the government for more money; how to get the president and the press and the politicians and the medical establishment to start treating AIDS seriously; how to get gay people to be more politically active. With the discovery of HIV and its wide acceptance as the cause for AIDS in 1984, the whole issue of how many sex partners one had diminished in importance. All one had to do was wear a condom. As AIDS researcher Dr. Joseph Sonnabend put it, "One should take an aggressive view. The rectum is a sexual organ, and it deserves the respect that a penis gets and a vagina gets. Anal intercourse is a central sexual activity, and it should be supported, it should be celebrated."[83]

Or as safer sex cocreator Michael Callen stated it, "Simply put, those who enjoy getting fucked should not be made to feel stupid or irresponsible. Instead, they should be provided with the information necessary to make what they enjoy safe(r)! And that means the aggressive encouragement of condom use!"[84]

So the moral, ethical, philosophical, and psychological ramifications involved in thinking anew about the sexual instinct no longer obsessed minds in the
same way it had in the earliest days of the '80s. After the initial shock and shame
of AIDS subsided, many gay men returned to their sexual lives. Most found a fairly
empty and even dessicated playing field. An entire world vanished step by step;
popular bathhouses no longer existed, peep shows closed their doors, backrooms
went on hiatus. It was up to younger gay men to try to reclaim the healthy and re-
demptive qualities of gay sex.

chapter **six**

the second
sexual
revolution?

gay history redux

A mini-version of gay sexual history got played out during the '90s, to everyone's surprise and then dismay. In the early '90s, gay men equipped themselves with latex and safer-sex guidelines and felt confident that it was good to have gay sex again. Some even experienced a replay of '70s-style one-night stands and safer sex orgies. But AIDS invaded the condom-covered Eden. By 1993 and 1994, reports suggested that AIDS cases were rising anew. Some dubbed the crisis "The Second Wave." Gay men, unhinged by the news, called for '80s-style sobriety, monogamy, and just-say-no attitudes. Condoms, it seemed, helped to ward off pathogen. But they were never meant as a permanent solution. Some trotted out new solutions. What, after all, was so terrible about two HIV-negative men pledging sexual monogamy and ditching rubbers? Nothing—so why didn't AIDS agencies advocate such an option? New paradigms and new sexual strategies emerged, shocking everyone.

The drama began innocently. Encouraged by early Clintonmania, the decrease in sexually transmitted diseases and presumably flawless condom usage, safer-sex radicals—Joseph Kramer, Michael Callen, Scott O'Hara, Jöel B. Tan, Alan Bell, Marshall, and Alan O-Boy!—announced a second sexual revolution. The second sexual revolution was predicated on the moral belief that everyone in the gay community engaged in safer sex—another word for "approved" sex, polite homosexual sex. As psychologist Walt Odets put it, "For many men, safer sex—indeed AIDS in general—has provided the opportunity to experience a respectable position in the world that does not rest on concealment or denial of one's homosexuality."[1]

Odets didn't like the moralistic tone characterizing safer sex. He saw the new piety as a brand of internalized homophobia. Not only did he *not* believe that everyone engaged in safer sex, he didn't think that condom use was the only way to stave off infection, especially among sero-similar couples. But where were the psychological nuances in AIDS education? Why was there no safe place to talk about "slippage"?[2]

All the same, the PR coup around safer-sex workshops, condoms, and water lubricant did make men feel good about having sex again. "My impression," rhapsodized Michael Callen in a 1992 QW article, "is that public forms of group sex were largely dead from about 1985 through 1989. There was palpable shame. It was 'cool' to stridently denounce any form of gay sexual expression which was neither completely safe i.e., masturbation, or which was not monogamous—serially or otherwise. . . . Only an asshole like me defended the asshole in those dark days."[3]

In 1989, as Callen explained it, "the sex-funk fog lifted" and "life-affirming, sex-positive sunlight reappeared" and with the birth of street radicalism, "a generation of post-AIDS babies seemed to rediscover the lost joys of gay sex."[4] The trend was promoted by a slew of new publications devoted to analyzing sex in a hip, provocative manner. With its cum-from-the-hip approach, *Steam* characterized itself as something between an academic journal and a travelogue (it rated alleys, tearooms, and clubs nationwide *and* put them in historical perspective). Bringing writers as diverse as *Steam* publisher and ex-porn star Scott O'Hara together with Michael Bronski, Pansy, Dave Kinnick, and Allan Gassman, it married porn with panache and fathered *Wilde*, a brainy sex magazine that made fun of beefcake glossies. Cut from a similarly boho cloth as the sassy *In Touch* in its New Wave heyday, *Wilde* tried to woo the Generation Xers and bi-boys away from *the* most thumbed through porn mag of the '90s: *Freshmen*. *Wilde* tried to tap the pulse of rejuvenated sex radicalism by bringing in more diverse depictions of sexy men boasting body hair and other signs of maturity. But after two issues, it folded. *Freshmen* could not be beat, not with its college-aged boys with made-up lips and Brazil-like complexions—not to mention smooth-as-silk arms ornamented with muscle and tendon to die for. (*Freshmen* also had going for it William H. Henken's sex column, which, second to Pat Califia's, provided some of the sanest advice to guys flirting with crystal methe, unsafe sex, compulsive love, and death rock.)

Diseased Pariah News gave HIV-positive men the skinny on poppers, rejection, decay, and survival with smartass pieces, such as the infamous, "How to Tell If Your Loved One Is Dead." The 'zine ran photos of naked HIV-positive beauties, listing their age, height, CD4 count, and medications. "Delectable pinup boy" Jose Sequiera, diagnosed in 1988, told *DPN* in the manner of a *Playboy* bunny that, "I'm very Catholic; I love and eat the body of Christ every Sunday. If it hadn't been for His nakedness, I probably would not have felt drawn to Him—even with the wounds." Slews of calorie-rich recipes were printed with the admonition, "GET FAT, don't die!" Aunt Kaposi provided advice for the Lovelorn.

In addition to these "alternative" sex journals, the 1977 classic *Joy of Gay Sex*, out of print and woefully outdated with its pre-AIDS exuberance, saw a masterful revision by Felice Picano and Dr. Charles Silverstein. Picano's experience as gay publisher (Seahorse Press) and chronicler of gay life and love (*The Lure, Ambidextrous, Men Who Loved Me, Like People in History*) combined with Silverstein's medical credentials to celebrate sex-positivity without skimping on the warnings about the dangers of viruses.

To their credit, they saw sex as completely altered—but hardly destroyed—by AIDS. They knew that if the straight world of the '70s revolted against the open celebration of gay sex announced by *The Joy of Gay Sex* with book burnings and court rulings that homophobic society would bristle even more at the updated version. So much more the reason for printing it.[5]

With evocative illustrations by F. Ronald Fowler and Deni Ponty, Silverstein and Picano underscored the advantages of latex, sobriety, nipple play, S&M, and the increasingly popular phone sex. Of course, phone sex existed long before HIV. But with the epidemic, cumming with a little help from Ma Bell did away with condoms and anxiety-filled talks about sero-status. The authors provided practical tips about phone dating ("Goose it up with a very sexy-sounding voice") and offered sociology (why gay men are allowed a five-year discount when disclosing their age) as well as nurturing advice ("The phone is no substitute for cuddling so if you want to meet someone for real, don't describe yourself as a Tom Cruise lookalike when you bear more resemblance to Henry Kissinger"). Acknowledging every possible strategy toward pleasure that didn't put the sexual parties at risk, the book tried to reassure gay men that their bodies and sex practices were, quite simply, okay.[6]

The '90s also saw a new outpouring—and legitimizing—of porn as gay male vernacular. "Pornography is the first place a lot of gay men are exposed to sex," said Frank Browning, author of *Culture of Desire*, in *Out Magazine*. "It functions as a kind of cookbook for sexual technique and allows us to build a catalog of images of how it can be when males touch each other. . . . This may be true heterosexually, but if so, to a far lesser degree." Author John Rechy explained that while the straight world holds porn stars as "questionable figures," gay men endowed these figures with a certain "respectability and accomplishment."[7] Someone profited. In the early '90s, the gay porn industry produced anywhere from between fifty to seventy videos a month, with magazines like *Gay Video Guide* and companies like Falcon and Catalina accruing big talents and half-million-dollar budgets.[8] You had writers like Dave Kinnick, one of the most famous journalists in the gay adult industry making waves with his sweet yet naughty book of interviews *Sorry I Asked* ("I just hope people remember me as a nice person," said Jason Ross of *Bedtime Stories* and *Open House* fame).[9] You also had former porn stars that made unusual names for themselves as personalities, such as Joey Stefano, Jeff Stryker, and Scott O'Hara, known at one point as "Scott the Biggest Dick in San Francisco O'Hara" (who, by the way, also distinguished himself in videos as the guy who sucked himself off). O'Hara, an intellectual sex slut, left the porn business when he began suffering HIV symptoms and threw every last penny into publishing *Steam* and *Wilde*. He used his career as a porn star to give back to gay sex its revolutionary good spirit.

Stefano, whose real name was Nicholas Anthony Iacona, was something of the Marilyn Monroe of the gay-underground-porn-glam crowd: a manufactured porn icon whose career was masterminded by Chi Chi La Rue. Stefano was "the first bottom in the history of male porn to become a major star," according to *Out Magazine* editor Kevin Koffler, who wrote the quintessential rags-to-riches-to-overdose article on the tattooed porn celeb in *Out Magazine*. The rise to stardom that resulted after *The Buddy System II* may have been too much for the once-awkward, always-needy young man. As Koffler puts it, "The party boy with a Peter Pan complex" appeared more obsessed with fun than money (unlike the sexually ambivalent Jeff Stryker, who put business before pleasure). By the end of his life, Stefano chose drugs over sex, buying one hundred hits of Ecstasy at a time. After repeated efforts to clean up his life by attending twelve-step programs and trying to leave the porn scene, Stefano died from an overdose that some considered suicidal.

To everyone who took an interest in porn, Stefano symbolized all that went wrong when sex and money mixed. Meanwhile, O'Hara, who had left the money changers and cameras behind and moved to rural Wisconsin to write and edit, epitomized all that was right in a gay sex culture that rejected the money market as its highest calling. In this context, in an effort to further differentiate gay erotic life, emerged John Preston's *Flesh and the Word* series. It gave a new prestige to porn writing. It equated "nasty" with "good taste," and implicitly suggested that gay literature that didn't speak the authentic truth about gay eros was, if not a sham, then a bore. Preston's handsomely edited and packaged anthologies legitimized writers like Aaron Travis and Will Leber and D. V. Sadero, expanding their audience to fifteen thousand–plus readers.[10] To be sure, the three *Flesh and the Word* volumes—a fourth is in the works by Preston's sex radical heir Michael Lowenthal—offered a slap in the face to rarefied gay literature, proving that it's in *Honcho, Drummer, Freshmen,* and *Advocate Men* that gay writing could truly thrive, grabbing its audience by the balls in a way that would strike envy even in the most precious of novelists.[11]

This axis point between the production of culture and the production of hard-ons—an axis point one could call, for lack of a better word, "gay-centeredness"—became more palpable as the gay movement blossomed and also splintered. For, after all, wasn't gay-centeredness at the heart of Queer Nation's success? "The year 1990," wrote Randy Shilts, "was not one during which the gay movement evolved. Instead, the movement transmogrified into something new, barely recognizable and somehow threatening even to the seasoned veterans of gay organizing in years past."[12]

Queer Nation began in New York in 1990, and almost immediately attracted hundreds of burnt-out ACT UP members, community leaders and self-proclaimed "baby dykes and fags" who wanted to organize around something besides AIDS. To be sure, the emphasis was more on polis than eros, with the group defining itself as a "militant and uncompromising group dedicated to subverting compulsory heterosexism in all its political and cultural manifestations through direct public actions which will celebrate and flaunt sexual diversity."[13] Yet despite the unwieldy rhetoric, the basic idea—people marginalized through gender orientation, uniting on a national basis to "promote homosexuality"—gained celebrity status fast. "In the late '70s, you couldn't get a handful to meetings," observed the late film critic Vito Russo. "Where are all these people coming from?" The answer was as simple as it was implicit: Dionysus had many guises. Whether the effort looked like GLF, Stonewall, Wigstock, the March on Washington, or the Fire Island Meat Rack, it could be said that the powerful phenomena emanated as much from something within as without.[14] By the summer of 1990, Queer Nation boasted sizable chapters in Los Angeles and San Francisco, with other groups springing up in fifty cities, including such unlikely places as Salt Lake City and Dallas.

Like ACT UP before it, Queer Nation thrived on the politics of panache—following one activist's imperative, "Go Out There and Be Fabulous." A movement seeking to synthesize eros with polis should be art-directed, as the "Every Tenth Jesus Is a Queer" poster demonstrated. The organization's very name was conceived as a crafty marketing ploy that showed lesbians and gays redefining a term of oppression with an in-your-face, media-savvy élan. True, the ruse did alienate lesbians and gays who cringed at calling themselves by an epithet. But aversion was far from unanimous. Queer Nation tapped into a growing distrust within the gay community of its mainstream institutions, questioning the ability of polite lobbying, checkbook activism, and electoral campaigns to effect political change when it so militantly sanitized gay life. If AIDS had taken all the fun out of being gay, queerness redeemed it, suggesting that there was life beyond AIDS, a politics beyond ACT UP and a dress code beyond Lacoste. Queer Nation was nothing if it wasn't sex-positive. Like in the early days of GLF, rage against the system was often channeled into lots of making out and safer-sex jerk-off sessions.[15]

And the libidinal explosions fed the rage. Hence Queer Nation/SF's banner's over Castro Street ("Straights Behave or Be Gone") or Queer Nation/N.Y.'s manifestos (the most famous being "I Hate Straights"). Not since GLF and GA did gay groups seek to organize simply on the basis of creating indigenous culture, separate from the hetero myth.[16]

California queers experienced a resurgence of libidinal energies that brought political life and sexual life together when the center of gay life turned to Los Angeles and San Francisco in 1991. That's when Governor Pete Wilson vetoed A.B. 101, a bill that would have protected California lesbians and gays from employment discrimination. True, Los Angeles could always boast a feisty, if small, activist community. The place, after all, was known for its domestic pleasures and work life. But after the veto, thousands of heretofore tame—and semi-closeted—women and men flooded the long boulevards of West Hollywood.[17] According to Village Voice editor Richard Goldstein, "A broadside pasted up along Santa Monica Boulevard at the height of the disturbances said everything about the new queer consciousness in Los Angeles and across America: 'WE'RE EVEN ANGRIER THAN WE'RE FABULOUS.'"[18]

Activists as diverse as Judy Sisneros and David Mixner referred to the city transformed as "Stonewall II." The California flag was torched; so was Wilson's effigy. Wayne Karr smashed a glass door at the Ronald Reagan State Office building; John Heilman, a gay West Hollywood city councilman, alerted the sheriffs that he was marching and not to disturb him; as many as fifteen thousand gays and lesbians stopped traffic and business on city streets almost daily for one week. The "gym dudes" sprinted alongside the Queer Nation crowd. Most important, people of color refused to take a backseat and saw to it that issues around race, sexuality, and cultural diversity would never again be considered subordinate to the mainstream movement's paltry civil rights agenda again.

If the gay white world's inability to speak to people of color has proved to be its biggest failing so far, almost everyone agreed that the '90s showed a change in both the sexual and political culture of California's queer citizens. Many men of color felt as horrified as they felt exonerated by the beating of Rodney King. The ensuing rebellion would expose the gay movement's much-vaunted rhetoric of multiculturalism. The irony, of course, was that the fires that spread from Korea Town to Long Beach actually linked neighborhoods. Even to the white gay in West Hollywood—a bit more conservative and Midwestern than their counterparts in Silver Lake or Venice—the fires blazing a few miles away were also the fire next door. For African American queers like former L.A. City AIDS coordinator Phill Wilson, who lived and organized and made love within the white gay world, many alliances and allegiances—both sexual and political—had to be reexamined and reformed.

And they were. Jöel B. Tan, a Philipino man, usurped the floor from a white "organizer" at Creating Change West, a national conference held after the A.B. 101 Veto, and this rightful grasp at leadership became the catalyst for the founding of Colors United Action Coalition—a group of African Americans, Latinos, and Asians specifically formed to address the Wilson veto and the segregation of queer life in L.A. Although no study correlates the founding of Colors United with the recrudescence of dance clubs, community venues, and sexual trysts created for and by men of color in California, it's clear that gay men of color had become leaders in arenas once dominated and compartmentalized by white gay life: sex and politics. In the '90s, a dozen dance clubs—including the Buddha Lounge, Escandalo, Catch 1—catered to the Asian, Latino, and African American gay dance crowd, respectively.

Like Queer Nation's antics, the A.B. 101 riots and the universal symbolism of Wilson's slap to the gay community showed many white gay men and gay men of color that there was a reason to organize outside of AIDS. Of course, the riots built on a decade of unchanneled AIDS grief and sexual frustration. But, at bottom, the consciousness raising groups, performance art projects, and sexual orgies that took place after A.B. 101 indicated a need to create a gay male culture that would synthesize the lessons of the '70s and '80s and not stay overly attached to either polarity. What would a new culture look like? Would it be a culture of power and influence—what most gays, whether right- or left-leaning wanted—or a culture of thoughtfulness and new directions, one that paraphrased Harry Hay's questions ("Who are we?" "Why are we here?" "Where do we come from?").

Whether the new gay world was about self-assertion or self-realization, there was no question that, every now and then, its manner of synthesizing eros with politics took everyone by surprise. "The gay community is the new Jewish community," said the national finance director of the Clinton campaign. "It's highly politicized, with fundamental health and civil rights concerns. And it contributes money. All that makes for a potent political force, indeed."[19]

The reconfiguring of gay power and influence on the East Coast couldn't help but trigger explosions in Hollywood. In 1991, queers forced the industry to reconsider its relation to gays and lesbians as never before. Everything from the "outing" of stars, to the *Basic Instinct* and Oscar protests, to Madonna's tell-all interviews—shook up an industry that viewed itself as tolerant. *The Advocate* published this warning: "The unwillingness of Hollywood's major studios—Twentieth Century Fox, MGM-UA Paramount, Warner Bros., Universal, Disney and Columbia—to take chances on gay themes or positive gay characters in films can't be explained away by the absence of homosexuals in power-broking positions. The heads of at least two of those studios are gay, as are the production executives of at least two others."[20]

The sociology behind the closetedness was obvious. Some argued that it was the inadequacy too many gays feel about themselves that made success in material terms such an imperative. Like the Jews who came to Hollywood in the '20s and '30s, gays found the industry an extraordinary contradiction: an opportunity to exercise enormous influence over American culture and to reap extravagant financial rewards while, at the same time, being forced to deny their cultural identities. Gay activism of the '90s called an end to this psychological prison, even in the world of illusion, false smiles, and coverups known as Hollywood.

This optimism about the new gay influence came on the heels of real progress on the electoral level, with the Democrats trotting out a candidate—Bill Clinton—who not only might win, but who seemed supportive of gays. Moreover, some gays, like "Friends of Bill" Bob Hattoy and David Mixner, figured prominently in the campaign.[21] Meanwhile the Republicans had tried to make gays into the Willie Horton of 1992 during their August convention, but the attack didn't take.

The Democrats' embrace and the Republicans' repudiation of gays resulted in two unprecedented phenomena: the emergence of a one-party gay voting bloc and huge sums of gay-identified money directed to that party. Until 1992, gays had either been too closeted, too Republican, or too culturally diverse to be counted on when it came to support a candidate like Clinton. Forty percent of the gay vote had gone to George Bush in 1988; more than twice that amount went to Clinton. The mainstream media began to note the transformation of gay and lesbian—American—politics. *Newsweek* addressed the development in its "Gays Under Fire" cover story, complete with polls showing 78 percent support for equal rights for gays in job opportunities.[22] Other articles proclaimed the failure of the Republican crusade against gays and reported that the Republicans could not so easily wage their cultural war by scapegoating gays.

The discourse around the role of homosexuality in the American psyche—both within the gay community and outside of it—only accelerated further with the gays in the military crisis. First Clinton asserted that he wanted to press forward in an expeditious way early in his term to end the ban on gays serving in the military.[23] Then he endorsed a lame compromise on ending the ban on homosexuals, emphasizing that the government should not "appear to be endorsing a gay lifestyle."[24] In between his flipflopping, thousands of news stories clogged the airwaves on issues related to masculinity, homosexuality, patriotism, and equality. While the debacle did little to improve the political condition for gays, everyone agreed it gave new meaning to "visibility." And horniness. Allan Gassman, a member of a network of gay men who held safer-sex orgies at each other's homes, said that O-Boy! membership almost doubled during the gays-in-the-military crisis. "People wanted to meet as much to talk about the brouhaha as to make out with each other," he says. You could get away with making gays into second-class citizens, it seemed, but you could no longer do so without rousing a lot of angry second-class citizens.

Extroversion, visibility, and securing a place at the table grabbed the attention—and purses—of gays and lesbians as never before. Some considered this burst of social frenzy as the last burst of an old "materialist" myth—with self-assertion winning the day yet again over any hint of self-realization. Others saw such exhibitionism as the only way to demand change—America understanding only soundbites, money, and the way the two go together. The efforts culminated in the huge coming out party known as the 1993 March on Washington for Lesbian, Gay and Bi Equal Rights and Liberation. To be sure, most gays didn't come to D.C. to seek acceptance from elected leaders; they came to see themselves.

During the weekend, there was no lack of sexual élan. GQ-style boys danced bare-chested in Dupont Circle while Radical Faeries in beads and feathers drummed. Occasionally, the two groups did more than cruise each other.

The party atmosphere paid off in a country that likes rage almost as little as it likes queers and people of color. Unlike the 1987 march, out of which emerged groups like ACT UP and Llego, a national gay Latino group, the 1993 march was inundated by the press, with USA Today putting a pink triangle on its front cover. Hundreds of lesbians marched to the White House in a Dyke March. Two thousand gay and lesbian couples were married at the Internal Revenue Service building. Sergeant José Zuniga, a highly decorated veteran of the Persian Gulf War, announced his homosexuality at a celebration luncheon hosted by the Victory Fund, the Emily's List of the gay community. A half-dozen closeted elected officials used the occasion to come out.[25]

As if to prematurely honor this new extroversion, many gay men threw themselves into sexual exploits with a renewed frenzy—and naïveté. With the bathhouses shut down, the community witnessed a fresh new phenomenon: backrooms. In urban meccas, a host of New Wave, safer-sex mazes appealed to men who really had no place else to go to get immediately touched. "Safer sex clubs," wrote John Preston, "because they only facilitated orgasms, couldn't fulfill the real demands that had made the Mine Shaft such a success. However, they were a necessary transition." Preston understood that men continued to come out and meet each other through the intensity of anonymous sex and that safe venues remained an important community institution, moralists be damned. "The gay world hasn't been good at providing this sense of bonding, this kind of belonging, for its members."[26]

In addition, gay men set up household parties in the manner of the '50s-style network of private dinner parties and social clubs. Jerk-off clubs, insisting on no sucking or fucking, saw a new recrudescence. Many men found no trouble in adapting to the new constraints. "Grown men found themselves thrown back to their romanticized memories of innocent adolescence," added Preston, "jerking off in groups in settings that often were designed to look like their high-school gymnasium. Even the little bits of clothing that were allowed in these clubs were throw-backs to teenage years: sneakers and sweat socks, athletic shirts and jockstraps, sweat bands and Jockey shorts."[27]

To be sure, the new trysts seemed so innocent that few would have predicted that this new embrace of safer-sexual freedom—the word *promiscuity* no longer seemed to fit into the safer-sex lexicon—would result in yet more AIDS cases.

But it did. Victory over the sexual problem proved short-lived. Eden had come and gone, with great dispatch. "In 1993," writes Eric Rofes, "two events jolted us collectively into Kubler-Ross's stage-four depression." Scientific reports at the International AIDS Conference in Berlin implied a cure was far off; and anecdotal reporting confirmed that many men engaged in anal intercourse without a condom: "Thus the dual foundation of our collective hope—no new infections and the imminent development of a cure—eroded from under our feet, and a thick veil of depression which for years had hovered just overhead, dropped over the community."[28]

The second sexual revolution thus failed to live up to its hype. Activists looked for someone to blame. And while it could be argued that a lifetime of latex use offered a built-in recipe for failure, many heretofore sex radicals argued that they had no choice but to become conservative—moralistic even—at the news of rising cases of AIDS among gay men. Almost every gay man seemed to know someone who seroconverted.[29] Almost everyone knew someone who seemed buff and bold one day, and then got sick the next. Almost everyone knew someone who said he never got fucked in the ass—with or without condoms—and simply tested positive, to his and everybody else's surprise. The fact that most of the reports were anecdotal, and that the few researchers studying the correlation of sexual activity with seroconversion were few and far between, was lost on those who grew immediately hysterical.

Statistics backed up the worst fears. Although the avalanche of studies reporting the new rise of AIDS cases wouldn't hit the gay community till mid-1993 and early 1994, early reports alarmed a few health care workers. As early as 1990, *Village Voice* reporter Robin Hardy reported on a 1988 UCSF School of Medicine study in which one-quarter of the 686 men interviewed reported unprotected anal intercourse in the previous twelve months. Meanwhile, epidemiologists from Seattle announced a 400 percent increase in anal gonorrhea among men who had sex with men. The San Francisco *Sentinel* published this story: "Study: Young Gays Returning to Unsafe Sex."[30]

Some lambasted safer-sex education and its failures to reach gay men, especially men of color, in a street-savvy way. Others took their anger out on the gym culture that insisted men could—and should—reward themselves for all their hard pumping with hard fucking. Some went after urban gay life as if it had soured or poisoned itself.[31] Men like Michelangelo Signorile, Greg Scott, and Gabriel Rotello asked hard questions about the negative side of modern gay life—deploring promiscuity, lookism, drug addiction, gym culture, and narcissism. Gabriel Rotello blamed multi-partner unsafe sex in sex clubs for the new rise in

AIDS cases and he also invited gay men to question the complacency that led many to see oral sex as safer sex: "The truth is that nobody knows how risky oral sex is."[32]

The second sexual revolution ended as quickly as it began. To cope with the new despair, some young gay men turned to drugs—in particular, a cheap variety of speed known as crystal methe. Designer drugs appeared in so many homes, the community seemed more split between "tweaked" and "not-tweaked" than HIV-positive and HIV-negative. To psychologist Walt Odets, "Substance abuse and addiction, and the compulsive use of sex have always been prominent responses to the inevitable developmental stresses of growing up gay."[33]

The AIDS epidemic only exacerbated the problem. Concomitant with the rise of substance abuse the gay community saw the rise of twelve-step programs. While no doubt constructive and even life-saving to many, some activists—many of them psychotherapists—dared to suggest that the programs didn't dig deep enough into the personality; moreover, they kept the "higher power" as a projection rather than as something to find in one's own heart; they furthermore added to the "Just-say-no" ethos that made people act out in the first place. To these critics, the programs had become substitutes for truly indigenous gay social settings. Argues Odets: "But the programs have also become a force in gay communities that is sometimes used to support emotional isolation and the abandonment of genuine intimacy and, unfortunately, new and subtle feelings of internalized homophobia." In other words, "abstinence may be used indirectly and directly to avoid psychological conflict." Seeing twelve-step programs and sex clubs as not intrinsically destructive, some psychologists all the same view them as subject to compulsive use by its members, as a way to avoid examination of feelings and greater intimacy.[34]

In the midst of this polar struggle among those men who threw themselves into sex and those who became sexually abstinent, those who tried to settle down with a boyfriend, those who just compromised with their loneliness, those who sprinkled their loneliness with an affair here and a date there, and those who looked for quickies, an altogether new attitude about homosexual libido emerged. A third group of men chose to try something new with their sexual hungers. They introverted them. That is, they looked at their sexual pursuits symbolically and tried to contain the impulse to find a man on the outside in order to try to find his humpy likeness on the inside.[35]

To some, the approach sounded overly mystical, to others it made perfect sense. For weren't gay men always looking for something that existed in their imaginations, but knew, in their heart of hearts, they could never find in the "outer" world? Although few would believe that this approach had any value in gay life—"It sounds too much like more repression to me," argued one man, "I happen to love dick,"—those men who did try to do what they called "inner work" on their lusts found that a new world had opened up to them. Comments gay activist and clinical psychology student, Matt Silverstein: "Inner work from a gay-centered perspective isn't very glamorous. It's not like this emphasis on orgiastic sex. Neither is it about abstinence. It's about taking as much time to look inside as to look on the outside. On the inside it's like suffering through some of my complexes to separate unfinished family business from a romantic intimacy. At first glance it doesn't have nearly the lure, but it does provide liberation from basically feeling doomed to please everyone else in the world. And that's a relief. Eventually you get a gay sense of self, the source of eros."

Psychology, in a stark turnabout from its earlier oppressive status toward gays, had, by the '80s and '90s, become an important tool by which gays have peeled off the projections of sickness laid on them by society. But garden-variety psychology—that which addresses issues like self-esteem or even the psychological "injury" many gay individuals experience growing up in straight families—didn't go deep enough for some gay men. It didn't address enough issues related to gay political life nor did it touch sufficiently on collective symbolism and archetypal patterns. According to some gay-centered depth psychologists, if we are to inquire more deeply into our natures, we must investigate our personal injuries not as the final goal, but as an important step along the way to something even meatier. Ultimately, these thinkers asked questions about soul, gay soul. To do so, they parted company with contemporary gay academics who say gay identity is a fiction or a "social construction."

The point was not to talk about "God" or "higher power," whether of the ancient or New Age variety. The interest went rather to each man's personal life—where he feels the greatest values inside himself. For gay men (like most men) this was seen as the arena of sex and love. Traditionally religious people don't view their romantic needs as being a mystical path. But depth psychologists argue that love, in particular erotic love, is the first place to start if one wants to know oneself.

According to men like Mark Thompson and Mitch Walker, and psychotherapy patients like Hassan Moinzadeh, Chad Mitchell, and Leng Leroy Lim, the gay movement has yet to catch up with the implications of gay-centeredness on a day-to-day level. After all, many gays desire to fit into the fabric of American life and not be so unique. But, these men argue, the conscious mind may demand one thing and the unconscious another. For after all, the unconscious produces the hunger for love for a man in the first place. And, it can be argued, love and desire are central and centralizing feelings. But desire may also be motivated by a host of other feelings, such as need and incompleteness. If one argues that at the core of every person lies a primal love and resulting childhood injury when that love is inevitably frustrated by the incest taboo (in the manner of the Oedipal and Uranian Complexes) and that primal love and its core wounding are the engine behind which every person makes a life, then one can argue that love and love's frustration make the world turn. From this opens a psychological way of understanding "gay-centeredness" as the birth and transformation of homosexual libido in the wish for father-son union and its frustration. One can trade stocks and bonds, or write books like *Virtually Normal*. But if such a person dreams about riding off into the sunset with a stud or youth or daddy who feels just like himself, he is essentially gay. That is, from the ground up, his libido is organized, and thus will transform, in a gay way, according to homosexual desire, a desire indigenous and primal in the gay psyche. The center of his total personality, these men argue, is gay. To reflect on this gay-centeredness in a regular way, and with the assistance of a certain psychodynamic technique, is what is called "gay inner work."

While inner work didn't solve the problem of how to cure AIDS, it did suggest that there was as much political and sexual value in introversion as extroversion and that not every solution had yet been tapped. Taken together with all the events of the early part of the decade, the '90s showed themselves to be a decade not so much of new developments or new social revolutions but a new synthesis of the events characterizing the previous twenty-five years.

black jacks

AIDS hit just as Alan Bell had gotten tired of being rejected by white guys. He had begun to observe the mating patterns with a certain detached humor. He had, for example, a favorite glory hole haunt not far from Christopher Street where two rows of rooms were separated by a single corridor. He'd always notice that the same man who shunned him in public had nothing against sucking his black dick once it poked through the hole. "It's like they didn't want their white brothers to notice that they were lowering themselves by making out with a black man," he recalls, laughing. "You grow up with this kind of nastiness and discrimination," he adds. "It's never been new to me, even among my so-called white gay brothers. You know it and develop a thick skin."

But the racism takes a toll. "Over the years," he says, "it does drive you back to black institutions." It was hard, however, to find sexual places that were mostly black. "And I noticed that I really only wanted to have sex with black men. I found it so much more of a turn-on." So, once he moved back to his native L.A., the ex-New Yorker had the idea of creating Black Jacks in 1986, an all-black gay sex party that continues to meet in the mid-late '90s.

Other black men followed suit around the country: "If you walked up to someone [white], you were pushed away, recalls Kobi, who along with Lidell Jackson, created Jacks of Color, a New York jack-off and safer-sex club for blacks, Asians, Latinos, and gay men of color. Author Max Smith brought a black-on-black club to the Windy City in 1988.

These clubs helped provide a black gay man a safe harbor from two vicious and linked enemies: AIDS and gay racism. In the process they showed gay people's ability to adapt creatively to hardship in the creation of a new kind of community. They also had a good time.

Bell, who himself doesn't miss anal sex now—"I never enjoyed it, whichever way it went"—seems as sexually happy now as he was in his promiscuous New York City days when he managed to cum at least once a day with a different man. "Frottage, rubbing, kissing—these are all very pleasurable," he says. And while he spends must of his time manning the parties—"No monitoring here," he says, "we're all big boys and we know the risks"—he does allow himself to have some fun too. Still, he is HIV-negative and wants to stay that way. "As I've gotten older my libido isn't so raging, but if there's a nice energy between a gentleman and myself, I will go down on him. I don't think it's a terrible risk but I live with the fact that there is a risk, however small."

orgy-boys

A naked man stands in a West Hollywood living room. Another lingers close by, wondering aloud whether or not Clinton will lift the military ban on gays. In fact, the room is filled with about thirty naked men between the ages of twenty and thirty-five. Jesus and Mary Chain erupts from a CD player. Party fare abounds— dip, Bud, diet Coke, Evian—as well as party favors: condoms, lubricant.

Large signs posted around the room blast messages about AIDS and etiquette, including "WEAR CONDOMS" and "BE FRIENDLY"—the mantras of the O-Boys! We are at an O-Boy! party. The "O" refers to "orgy." Party organizers Alan Gassman and Randy Marshall, known as Alan O-Boy! and Marshall O-Boy!, circle the room, making sure participants have all the favors they need.

Lying naked on the bed in his studio apartment, Vince O-Boy! answers some questions. It's an unusual way to engage an interviewer, but he says it makes him feel more natural and comfortable. The twenty-nine-year-old reveals weariness in his Italian eyes—and that Little Rascals' charm that makes him popular among the hip, sexually active set of West Hollywood. Vince is a cofounder of the O-Boys! "The gay community is no less hypocritical in its sexual values than the dominant culture," Vince says. "We send out potent sex symbols in ads, marketing, the gym and bars, but then we get all upset when someone has sex."

The revolt began in 1990 when Vince began going to underground clubs and West Hollywood parties—such as Sit-n-Spin—where he was paid to dance in his underwear. Later, Slam Glam threw infamous "underwear parties." As Vince tells it, guys would show up, check their clothes except for their briefs, and drink. "Of course," adds Vince, "they'd get aroused. But the moment anything sexual occurred, the bar management strongly discouraged the behavior. So I invited a few fellows to my home."

Vince's primary mode of "communication with God and people," he says, "is through mind, soul and body, with an emphasis on body." He says he knew that such a philosophy was not shared by the men he invited home. So he established a system to keep the attitude he saw too often in West Hollywood from recreating its muscular aristocracy at his home. He made each man remove his clothes upon entrance, kept lights on, and schooled participants in the etiquette of safe-sex orgies: egalitarianism and rigid codes of safe sex. "An orgy," says Vince, "is nothing without hospitality." His recipe clicked. For Vince, who became known as the "impresario of orgies," to leave the bar and retire to his home was to leave the barbarity of sexual persecution.

Enter partygoers Alan and Marshall. "These orgies had the feeling," Marshall declared, "of a true, [grass-roots] revolution." Marshall and Alan saw the makings not just of a libidinous circle, but a political network. ACT UP members, artists from L.A. performance spaces, mainstream lawyers, and gay politicos showed up. In a matter of months, Alan O-Boy!, who by trade is a publicist, turned Vince's, Marshall's, and his own black book into a hot political mailing list. They created posters promoting safe sex and fashioned a sexual sensibility promoting a new way of life. Parties mushroomed; O-Boys! had to begin charging $5 admission to pay for overhead. While some problems ensued—the O-Boys! became more of an institution than Vince would have preferred and even created two porn movies and one "cockumentary"—the essential spirit remained throughout the group's four-plus-year stint. To Vince, this meant "having sex and being nice about it, realizing that it is wonderful to have sex with your friends."

promoting ethical sexual culture   The room is filled with laughing men—all handsome. At tonight's party, nearly all the men are between the ages of twenty and thirty-five; at least two-thirds are white; few have any facial hair; forget body fat. Admission is also based on political attitudes. To become an O-Boy! you must fill out a legal release; later on a questionnaire is sent to you. Questions range from how you'd respond to a man who touched you when you'd rather not be touched to your AIDS activism. (The O-Boys! have conducted safe-sex orgies after marches and demonstrations. During elections, the group advises members "to vote as if your dick depends on it.")

The hand-picked quality of the party does have the effect of calming the men down, creating what Marshall O-Boy! calls "a level playing field." In sex clubs, the young can be ruthless in their rejection of what are so impolitely referred to as "trolls." The behavior borders on demeaning. By the same token, the less physically fortunate can be seen to paw young men to the point of disrespect. It's not a pretty sight. As politically incorrect as it may sound, not a few men seem relieved to be spared what O-Boys! refer to the "trolls versus Adonises" split.

At this evening's party, Alan provides newcomers with the O-Boys! safer-sex rules: "One: No fucking without a condom. Two: Don't come in his mouth. Three: Be clear about where you draw the other lines, and respect his. Four: Assume that everybody is HIV positive. Five: Be friendly. Directive number five caught one man off guard, so Alan explained: "There were four incredibly hot men with great bodies at our last party who will not be invited back. You're not posing at the bar or at the gym. You're expected to share your incredible body and your smile. If you don't want to play with somebody, be nice about it."

And the rules seem to work. The atmosphere is remarkably comfortable: introductions are easily made. It is okay, within reason, to touch; a simple smile implies, "No thanks." Two blonds hug in a shower. A few onlookers, stunned by a scene one only sees in porn, freeze. "Don't just stand there," the older blond calls out. Another, the Howard Cosell of sex, cheers his friends on with commentary. ("These boys are going, going, gone!")

the freeing power of touch

All around the country, young gay men, resentful that they were deprived the free love of the '70s, took the lead from the O-Boys! and organized similar safer-sex parties. Few boasted the O-Boy! blend of grassroots political organizing and the promotion of an ethical sexual culture. Most catered to a mostly white gym culture. But even the elite felt called upon to rebel. In this account, Rob

Kindred meets a "cute little muscle boy" at a certain party and struggles to find some individuality in the collective merge:

> We toured the [apartment] . . . and not much fucking was going on yet. Good, because I needed to be among the first to get it up the ass, instead of taking the crowd's lead and waiting for some appropriate moment. We sucked face for a while and then I asked him if he liked to fuck. Yes. If he'd like to fuck me. Yes! And we went to the other, brighter bedroom where the packets of lube contained nonoxynol–9. It was crowded but we found an empty spot on the bed. I readied myself with my fingers, lay on my back, rested my legs on his shoulders, and let him ease himself in.

Kindred notices that, despite the fact that fifteen guys are fucking like animals, no one makes much noise. Silence during hard-core sport-fucking, thinks Kindred, shows signs of *machismo*, uptightness, and homophobia. Verbal commentary happens to loosen him up. Politically speaking, he doesn't feel inclined to hide what he refers to as his "bottom pride." So, taking a deep breath in, he takes the plunge, and starts to scream out obscenities in the manner of a Jeff Stryker flick, belting out, "Fuck me hard!" He is promptly shushed by the party host. But to no avail. The harder Kindred gets plowed, the more he has to say by way of appreciation. Rather than experiencing the shame reminiscent of the '50s or the wasted feeling of the '70s or the celibate "Just-say-no" caution of the '80s, he feels a new, synthesized series of feelings that don't cancel each other out. He's able to integrate his inferior feelings without being crushed by them:

> By breaking the silence around me, by declaring myself while in a state of absolute vulnerability, I set myself free and prove to myself, in that moment at least, how little my shields are needed. . . . I have this private belief that strikes me so powerfully it's taken on the dimensions of legend in my mind, a tentative uncertain faith that the portion of myself that I hide, that I keep underground for fear of mockery and ridicule, that I hold trapped partly because I actually fear the strength of it—it's this part of me that holds my greatest strength, that contains the power to conquer my fear, that is the source of whatever depth is to be found in my work. . . .

Sex seems like an effort to connect with people on the outside. But in reality, sex returns him to the deepest part of the personality, one that could be said to speak to him with its own autonomous intelligence. As Kindred explains it, this "portion of myself that I hide" is not to be confused with the conscious personality, which is but an effect of this larger Self. Of course, the question automatically occurred to Kindred: How to experience more of this Self? For a long time the answer seemed simple, perhaps too simple: Have more sex, safer sex.

It is that idealistic assessment by many young men that led Michael Callen—the creator of safer sex and himself monogamous through the '80s—to announce "the second sexual revolution" in a series of articles in New York's *QW* magazine. He wasn't entirely unjustified. After the bathhouse controversies ended and only a few lone dives remained, backroom radical sex clubs sprouted up it cities around the country. They did so as if to react against the jackboot attempt to stamp out desire.

"Even in the face of a deadly AIDS epidemic," declared John Preston in the early '90s, "public sex clubs are popular because these places present an arena in which men can undergo these transformations publicly. Their almost religious music, reliance on symbolic posturing and clothing and ability to define stages of development produce a codification of gay male sexuality against which the applicant can measure himself." And while Preston may have overemphasized the need horny men have in "the gathering congregation of a tribe of men," he was correct in identifying the irrepressible need gay men have to honor eros as the seed of vital energies.

Of course, the clubs that arose hardly served to integrate eros into daily life, succeeding rather in further compartmentalizing it. But for a few short years in the early '90s, a new appreciation of safer sex brought with it a spurt of innocence and good feeling.

Some clubs, like L.A.'s Zone and San Francisco's Church, did try to implement rules to keep men from treating each other like cattle and more like friends. In addition, the national gay community saw queer-centered indigenous spaces— 848 Divisadero in San Francisco; 2 Spirit Salon and Black Jacks in L.A.; Jacks of Color in New York City—that held sex parties. (The West Coast venues specialized in tantra, healing, touch, breathing.) AIDS agencies held consciousness-raising groups promoting safer sex, intimacy, and massage. The Body Electric School of Massage provided workshops around the country to teach queer boys an approach to eros that attempted to displace the Western eat-and-run technique with something more intimate and prolonged; it emphasized holding one's cum to prolong sex and contain one's energy—one's chi—rather than shooting one's load right away. And one of the best-selling gay erotic videos in the gay community was Neil Tucker's *Hin Yin*. Utilizing porn-perfect models, it subverted porn's cum-driven ethos by emphasizing the use of massage and meditation.

For those gay men who survived the trauma of the '80s, sex had become once again fair game. "My impression," wrote Michael Callen in an article announcing the so-called second sexual revolution of the '90s, "is that public forms of group sex were dead from about 1985 through 1989. There was palpable shame. It was 'cool' to stridently denounce any form of gay sexual expression which was not monogamous—serially or otherwise." Then, as Callen saw it, "Around 1989, for reasons which remain mysterious, the sex-funk fog lifted; life-affirming, sex-positive sunlight reappeared, and with the birth of that uniquely obnoxious but effective form of activism known as ACT UP and Queer Nation, a generation of post-AIDS babies seemed to rediscover the lost joys of gay sex."

"From my perspective," he insisted, "the new sex radicals have a more realistic sense about the body and its limitations. *All* sex these days is group sex—it includes the participants *and* the palpable presence of AIDS and death. The sexual ethic of the '70s was every man for himself. The new sexual revolution is built upon hard-won microbiological interconnectedness of us all—men perfectly willing to be their friend's keeper, enforcing safer-sex standards among their peers."

the political problem with orgies: not everyone is invited

The O-Boys! made a controversial name for themselves in the early '90s as the most creative effort on the part of a few visionary gay men to marry sex, politics, and community. With its sex-positive approach, these "orgy-boys" caught the attention of the national media. O-Boy! cofounder Alan O-Boy! appeared on a half-dozen talk shows, including Phil Donahue and Joan Rivers, to talk about "the healing power of frequent safer sex" as a way to fight AIDS and create consciousness around sexual persecution. But they also pissed off many in their own community who felt their policies excluded men who didn't fit a certain look. (Truth be told, the O-Boys! were the least exclusive and most politicized of the orgy organizers around the country, galvanizing what Michael Callen called "Gay Plain Janes.") On November 14, 1992, Alan O-Boy! and Marshall O-Boy! presented their views at the annual "Creating Change" conference organized by the D.C.-based National Gay and Lesbian Task Force.

The other panelists were Jim Curtan, representing the Body Electric School of Massage, and African American novelist Steven Corbin. Curtan spoke to the more inclusive approach of Body Electric. ("I'm fifty years old, thirty pounds overweight, and probably have the smallest dick of any man in this room and I'm sure I have the hottest sex.") Corbin talked about the segregation in the gay community between HIV-negative and HIV-positive as well as the color line that divides the community into GWM and POC.

But most men gave their apt attention to Gassman and Marshall, who began the panel "Male Sexuality: New Awareness, Hot Action" with an installation: three naked O-Boys! having sex inside a cellophane cage. The O-Boys!' speeches synthesized two decades of feminist "My-body-is-myself" thought with the renegade spirit of young turk AIDS prevention educators. Gassman's presentation marked a refusal to choose between marriage and promiscuity: "Our *major* point is that, while certainly fun and somewhat liberating, completely anonymous sex is ultimately degrading to me. . . . I don't find the message behind statements like 'I don't want to know your name, just shut up and fuck my man-pussy!' particularly liberating." As he put it:

> On the other hand, an obligatory declaration of undying monogamy between lovers tends to develop into a series of petty jealousies, minor infidelities, major lies, and debilitating breakups. It's just plain selfish, rude and stupid to expect one person to fulfill all of our sexual and emotional needs. It seems to me, that by rejecting monogamy as a societally enforced lie and accepting and communicating our human needs to relate socially and physically with others, we can form healthier, more honest, primary relationships.

Marshall echoed Gassman, separating the need in the gay psyche for friendly eros in a gay-friendly "tribe" from the need to use the tribe in an autoerotic manner, as an extended Phallus who never became human. Three denominators linked the O-Boys!: (1) love of sex; (2) the concern for survival in the fight against homophobia; and (3) the social aspect of the group. The basic need of kindred spirits—friendship and communication. Pillow talk on a group level.

But the O-Boy! recipe for a more friendly, sex-positive gay community based on indigenous values and grassroots political concerns—not to mention, an encouragement of an ethical conscience—did not last for long. Rising AIDS cases among young gay men did little to boost the morale of organizers. Neither did the selfishness of the younger O-Boys! who lacked the social consciousness of Marshall and Alan and preferred hot dick to hot debates. But perhaps the most painful slap of all came from the political left in the gay community.

At the November 14, 1992, Creating Change conference, for example, anger filled the room when Alan and Marshall finished giving their speeches. Word had gotten out that the O-Boys! had rented a room in the hotel and were planning an orgy later on. Typical O-Boy! panache. Not everyone in the room was impressed. Not everyone in the room was invited. And why not? Well, Marshall stated his point clearly: Not all were "in shape." He couldn't understand why he, as a man in his late thirties, managed to take care of his body while others let theirs go to pot. He meant his comment as a call for gay men to see the links between body image, persona, and self-esteem, but audience members accused him of sexual apartheid, lambasting the O-Boys! for participating in the very cult of beauty with which the culture oppresses women. "This horrible disease has already driven a wedge of mistrust against us," railed one man, suggesting that the O-Boys! only dug the wedge in deeper. Marshall attempted to empower people. "It's easy to create a group of your own. If you don't like how we do it, make your own rules."

The notion that all sexual desire is based on some measure of exclusivity could not reach the crowd. "If you want to throw around words like *brotherhood* and *tribe*," declared former Los Angeles AIDS Coordinator Dave Johnson, "that means that everybody gets to come." Foreshadowing a town hall meeting several years later during which the first reports of the "second wave of AIDS" were made, the audience projected its frustration onto the panelists.

As one of the men in the room with the most advanced cases of AIDS, Michael Callen had the moral force to call a truce:

> There is an aristocracy of beauty: get over it. . . . I am not prepared for the alternative, which is to create a politically correct "I must find everybody equally sexually attractive" [environment]. I would like to declare our sexuality to be the last natural preserve where we are not required to justify in any sort of public way why we are sexually attracted to somebody and not to somebody else. . . .
>
> I'm a person with AIDS. I don't expect everyone to be willing to have sex with me. I don't judge them harshly. I will talk to them about why and maybe if there's some education there and some movement that can happen, that's fine. I'm not prepared to define the central politically correct act as having sex with me. That would be nice. But not likely to happen anytime soon.

Callen's wisdom didn't defuse the yelling and screaming. Deep divisions around color, race, and class have never gone away; they have rarely been addressed. The controversy demonstrated how much work gay men have to do to get at the underlying and painful feelings behind the sexual drive. "Gay men simply don't process about sex enough," moaned Gassman. To his mind, gay sexual life—indeed, gay life in general—can hardly advance itself unless people learn some basic tools for venting their feelings at least as often as they vent their libidos.

a defense of sex

During one of his last public talks on the subject of sex, Callen lay on the floor of his West Hollywood home. He was nauseated from the chemotherapy he received to resist the AIDS-induced Kaposi's sarcoma lesions in his lungs. A fever raged. A Latino nurse provided Callen with an aspirin suppository. "Yes," he joked, "that is the best sex I've had in months." The sight of a man so racked by a sexually transmitted disease celebrating sexuality made poignant sense to onlookers. A few couldn't help but see a certain Einstein-like quality in the discoveries of sexual pioneers like Callen. With the atomic blast of a scientific discovery, too many forces—some good, some overwhelming—have been unleashed for most to have survived in one piece.

Callen spoke with enormous authority as Mr. Safer Sex and Ms. Pre-Madonna. More than anything else, his warning about protective sex became an emblem of how swiftly the gay community responded to the onslaught of AIDS and the threat to gay identity the epidemic presented. But in the intervening years, Callen became convinced that the rules he called for were too stringent.

"Of course," he added, "we cannot pretend that unsafe sex isn't happening. We can't pretend that some commercial sex establishments aren't fire traps. We can't pretend that every gay person has all the necessary safe sex information that he needs to make rational, informed choices." But all the same, it bothered him that AIDS agencies advocated condom usage for sucking when the word on the street was that oral sex presented relatively low risk. For Callen's part, this "rift between what people do and what agencies tell us to do" created a "cognitive dissonance" in most peoples' minds: "People feel guilty and ashamed by their behavior—believing themselves to have 'slipped.'"

Antisex attitudes in the gay community upset him too, needlessly feeding ammunition to their enemies: "I frequently hear gay men cluck about 'all the unsafe sex' that goes on in backrooms and the few bathhouses still in existence. When I press them for specific details, which I always do, it almost never turns out that they mean unprotected anal intercourse in which the man cums inside his partner's ass. No, they usually mean they witnessed the sucking of un-be-condomed dicks. Big sucking deal. And when I ask them if they observed anyone swallowing cum, they hesitate and almost always say, "Well, no . . . but."

It angered him that the first impulse of many gay men when responding to heterosexual confusion over gay sex was to apologize for the radicals: "Well, most of us really want to have our equal rights and to fight in the military and not talk so much about sex." But Callen aligned himself with the "in-your-face" school of sex radicalism that said to reproving gays and straights: "All the terrible things you say about us are true, we want to suck dick and so do you, we want to have sex all the time and so do you, only we'll do it and talk about it and are that much healthier for it."

It was a provocative point, but it went to the heart of the emerging discussion on gay sex. "Gay people are at the forefront," added Callen, "on calling the central bluff on Western culture that uses sex to sell everything from toothpaste to cars but heaven forbid you should admit to actually having it." For Callen, "We are back to where we were pre-AIDS. We had sex without a theory about it. Then AIDS came and we stopped having sex. Then we started again—but as yet still have no theory that we can use to defend ourselves from the inevitable attacks. Rarely does a movement get a second chance to create itself."

Sitting up in bed, Callen grew so passionate about developing a theory and defense of sexuality that he read from one of his latest manifestos. Callen worried that if the gay movement failed to come up with a clear defense of sexuality, "then our enemies will be much savvier about preemptively explaining our sexual activities for us than we have so far been." It broke Callen's heart that "the vast majority of gay men and lesbians appear to be in essential agreement with their oppressors. The 'average' monogamous queer couple, virtually indistinguishable sociologically from their conservative suburban heterosexual counterparts, do not appear to grasp the obvious fact that the same heterosexist power structure that feels it has the right to close down backrooms and bathhouses is precisely the same power structure that keeps any form of consensual adult gay sex illegal in twenty states. You may not think it's a good idea to suck dick or eat pussy in some orgy, but your right to engage in tasteful oral sex with your lover in the sanctity of your bedroom is very much linked to an implacable defense of the inalienable civil right which each individual possesses to make consensual sexual choice."

Callen argued that gay men had never been given permission to talk openly about the role sex played in their lives. He proposed a feminist model: "Call a truce and allow people to talk about what gets them hard now, even if the behavior seems initially politically incorrect. The next step would be to give people permission to say what they'd like to do sexually but are too frightened to admit that it turns them on." Only then, he added, could one construct a vision of sexuality that would be as "humbly respectful of where people actually were" and that was as inclusive of sexual diversity as possible. Callen's point: "I don't believe we can get there through shaming people, even in the service of saving lives."

Callen wanted the gay community to rethink sex and disease—in a word, to take in the lessons about the sanctity of the body while trying, at the same time, to tease out the social silence and personal shame that not only led to the spread of AIDS, but was further exacerbated by AIDS. It's a paradox emblemized by the messages Callen wants on his tombstone: "Less shame" and "Shoot this load in memory of me."

breathe!

Fuck fucking. A group of thirty men—ages ranging from nineteen to seventy—stand in a circle, clothed. Each man bows to a partner. Each is taught how to "breathe consciously" while gazing into another's eyes. New circles develop. In an hour's time, each man will have his clothes off. No one will reach orgasm, at least not in the conventional sense.

Standing in the center of the circle is Joseph Kramer. A graduate of the Jesuit School of Theology at Berkeley, he founded the Body Electric School for Massage in 1984 and became a professional sex healer. No pinup figure, he's big-bellied, mustached, and frumpy. That's the point—to dislodge some of the addiction most people, including most gay men, have to Madison Avenue's take on beauty and sex. "Most Western sex is necrophilia," he tells the crowd, "one dead body having sex with another. This is in contrast to the Chinese concept of sex-as-energy—as Chi, as a charge that can take you to ecstatic states." Kramer refers to the West's focus on orgasm as "balloon sex." One tenses; one pops. Kramer speaks of "ecstasy" as if it's one's birthright, as if it's bigger and better than what passes for sex in Western culture.

This is one of Kramer's last workshops; he's taught hundreds around the country. There is a young Latino man in the circle. He looks worried he'll be pounced on. Later, participants confess that before the session, they fretted over their body fat, baldness, and dick size. That's where Kramer's panache comes in. He casts a spell with down-to-earth language, stating his intentions for the afternoon. He teaches names for erogenous zones: the perineum, located between the testicles and anus; the "magic wand," his preferred name for "penis." Kramer tells people not to worry if they have an erection or not, to "gauge your discomfort levels," and to let your partner know that "something doesn't feel right."

During this afternoon, the men will engage in bouts of conscious breathing, shamanic drumming, simultaneous heart-and-genital connection—all toward the goal of building greater sexual excitement without orgasms. The idea: the genital-based energy that leads to ejaculation can be spread throughout the body like an elixir; within the context of ritual, that elixir can teach important lessons about selfhood. "You will relearn sex as sacred, playful, nonaddictive, noncompulsive and nonstop," Kramer says. "The idea here is to flood your resistances with body awareness, to flood the stuff that holds you back in life. Therapy is one way of working with the resistances. The therapist 'respects' your resistances. Here, with your permission, we will disrespect them."

Sounds so California. But on day two, much of the bowing-to-your-partner and blindfolding gives way to a day of intensive touch: two and a half hours of massage by seven different men. Each rubs the heart area and the "magic wand" in a series of involved strokes that were taught the day before. Kramer and assistants goad the men to "Let yourself feel!" The result is an orgasm that obliterates; it blasts the ego from its crutches of anxiety. Kramer says he wanted to call his workshop on Taoist erotic massage a "rehearsal for death." He might as well have. The only difference is that one comes back rather alive.

No bodily fluids, no rejections, no apologies.

In the early '90s, Kramer's workshop sounded a tad New Agey to most gay men, who shivered at the notion of breathing intimately with men they didn't know and didn't find automatically attractive. From a psychological point of view, however, Kramer's work represents an Apollonian way of developing mind-fulness—remove, tension, and differentiation—around instinctual drives. The sexual drive says to the person, "I want," an expression of the fact that that life wants "in me." Although Kramer hardly saw his work as psychological—it was a body-first approach to spirituality—it encouraged anything but sheer obedience to shooting one's wad. The idea was to develop intimacy with "self" and others.

Of course, in a more literal sense, Kramer's work came as a result of dealing in a healing way with the trauma of AIDS—a way, as journalist Don Shewey put it, "to emphasize massage as a way of restoring a healthy attitude toward sex and intimacy among gay men threatened or afflicted by HIV disease." Shewey is the journalist who helped make Joe Kramer accessible to East Coast readers in a profoundly beautiful *Village Voice* article.[36] He's also become a "sacred intimate" and massage worker himself. Like many writers with finely tuned thinking functions, Shewey has found Body Electric a useful way in which to explore his sensation and feeling functions. Like most gay men, he knows the truth: despite the stereotype of sex-crazed homos, gay men often don't have a clue as to how to be naked in a room. So few see sex as a birthright. Shewey refers to the Marvin Gaye song "Sexual Healing" when talking about the power of tantra, massage, and breathing into a hard-on: a decade of death and grief have made the body a minefield. That's a tragedy, considering the wisdom the body can provide, including that it can teach a man how not to be overly identified with it. Shewey underscores the need to acknowledge that

the fun and the pleasure, the vitality and the divine mystery of sex have nourish-
ing properties in and of themselves—a message that can easily get overwhelmed
in a culture where "sex appeal" is routinely exploited to sell products but sexual-
ity (read: actual fucking) is usually discussed only in the context of abuse, ad-
diction or AIDS transmission. The sex negativity of the culture creates its own
damage and alienation. For some people, their sexuality—their juiciness, their
comfort with their bodies, their talent for intimacy—is a gift they're not asked
to share often enough; when they act on it, they run the risk of being viewed as
pathologically compulsive, promiscuous, or somehow perverted. How often do
we encounter public discourse that treats sex as something other than a sin or
*a joke?*37

It's a philosophy that appealed to those who tended to feel excluded by the
values of Chelsea or West Hollywood. And although Body Electric was never
known for its cultural diversity, those people of color who could afford the workshops found a new world there. Leng Leroy Lim, a gay Christian man of Chinese descent, says he fought all his life against his homosexuality. When he
came out to his Singapore parents, he was met "with a torrent of prayers, with
laying of hands and the casting out of demons." (His parents had converted to
Christianity as a result of his evangelizing.) The experience filled him with complex feelings: self-loathing, guilt, fear. At a Body Electric retreat, the laying-on-of-
hands had a difference result:

I was in a spacious wooden hut with twenty-five other naked men, our ages rang-
ing from twenty-nine to seventy-four years of age. Our bodies told stories of ad-
diction, operations, accidents, age, work, grooming, leisure, and "race." To see
men in each age bracket was to witness the life-cycle, and to feel myself a part of
an unfolding future. Aging had become less frightening because I now witnessed
*embodied meanings/being to it.*38

Lim's description shows the ways in which the body holds the pain of the
mind. Lodged inside him remained hurt feelings about being an Asian man in
America, being seen as effeminate, unattractive. He had fought these feelings
many times in his life, especially during herolike treks in nature, in the American outback, leading younger men through torrential rivers. But all the same, in
the United States he had been "vexed by the racism and the right-wing Christian
homo-hatred that was passing as moral revitalization. In the sexual hierarchy of
America, Asian women (and some gay men who fit the androgynous, feminine,

youthful type) are exoticized, while the majority of Asian men (gay or straight) are rendered invisible." As he puts it, he needed the healing to work through Eros:

> *A soft tune with a steady drum beat was played in the background. Somewhere the voice of the leader said, "Wake up the body of your sacred brother, be with him in your breadth and touch." I took a deep breath, and the sound of a common breath coursing through the room joined us together as interconnected beings. Two pairs of hands, warm, gentle and firm touched me on my heart and genitals and I was gently rocked from side to side. Breathing into the touch, I realized my whole body. "Open your hearts, say yes to life and love." I shuddered at the words. As the warm oil was spread on my torso and genitals, and then on my legs and arms, I found myself drenched in painful sensations of pleasure. Strong hands kneaded my aching muscles, so long untouched: and my aching heart, so long yearning. I took another breath and let out a long moan, the sum of a whole year's pain and disappointment.*[39]

Unlike many "sacred intimates" who find tantra a body-first approach to spirituality, Lim doesn't stay overly attached to the hands-on experience. "Buddhists are therefore right to say that powerful experiences of ecstasy and union should neither be sought after, nor refused, nor clung to." In this way, the body becomes material for realization, but not the realization itself. Such wisdom often eludes practitioners of sexuality.[40]

the trouble with looks

Rather than develop a healthy lack of attachment to the body, gay men, shamed and abused during AIDS, found themselves more hungry for bodily perfection than ever. "Think for a moment," challenged William J. Mann, "of the images of gay men in the '90s. What comes to mind? The hunky boys tossing streamers from the deck of the RSVP cruise ship. Ryan Idol. Bob and Rod. Big, buff, young, white. So perfect that their sexiness . . . becomes muted." He argued that in fifteen years the image had not predominated over the human: "The image of a gay man was overtly sexual: the Village People, in all their assorted sexual stereotypes; the Castro clone, with his over-emphasized basket and buns; the phallic supermen of Tom of Finland. It was a radical revolution from the limp-wristed pansies of the '50s and the androgynous flower children of the '60s."[41]

The '90s saw the triumph of the image—it had almost been raised to the level of pagan worship. This "symbol" of homo eros—this buff dude one sees on every porn magazine and every gay advertisement—confused gay men who naturally felt they could never measure up to these standards. It did not ease anyone's minds to suggest that these porn-perfect images were reflections of the archetypal: the gay version of graven images—gods. In our antimyth culture, people lacked the conceptual tools to differentiate the archetypal from the personal. All men could do was shake their heads at the primacy of the Marky Mark images and feel oppressed by it or enslaved to it. And gay thinkers assailed this enslavement as oppressive.

"It's true that there have always been paradigms in the gay world," adds author Michelangelo Signorile, "but it seemed in the past there were more choices, more leeway about what was considered a gay stud." Signorile argued that the current cult of "body fascism" epitomized by the advertisement of the David Barton Manhattan gym ("No pecs, no sex") is worse in the gay world than the straight world, in part because of the already existing inferiority gays inherit for being gay. As a compensation for this inner worthlessness, a man becomes a "great beauty" or find himself attracted only to Adonises.[42]

Not everyone was down on "body fascism." While ex-porn star and *Steam* publisher Scott O'Hara found the parties that excluded men on the basis of looks boring—"They all had a homogenous quality"—he refused to lambaste them. "The word *discrimination* has gotten a bad rap. It used to mean you had taste." Even so, few could deny that current trends were being driven by fear of AIDS. "People are trying to prove they're healthy," explained Victor D'Lugin. Body hair became suspect. It suggested maturity. And didn't maturity suggest that a man had lived through the decadent '70s and might have AIDS?[43]

In addition, racism fueled the imagery. "The premium placed on young white boys," author Steven Saylor says, "is really high. The cachet they carry is apparently what everyone is looking for." The situation burdened many gay men of color, especially Asian men who suffered from stereotypes of being "nerdlike" or undersized. Norman Wong explored the problem in his novel *Cultural Revolution*. The main character, Michael, a Chinese American, discovered a porn magazine in his parents' house:

> His eyes froze upon the next couple of pages. A group of white men stood together shoulder to shoulder, wearing only tight bikini briefs of different colors. Michael examined each one, but his gaze fell upon one man in particular. This man was unlike his father or any other Chinese man he'd ever seen without his shirt on; the man in the magazine seemed stronger and bigger. But most amazing to Michael was the brown hair racing all over his body, over his chest, entering into his briefs and reappearing on his thighs, a flow of hair that ended near

his ankles. After a good part of the afternoon, he returned the magazine to the top shelf of the closet. But his eyes were not convinced that he had replaced the magazine in its original position. His shaking hands touched it, then took hold of it again. In a matter of minutes his mother would be returning home from work. But the imagined sight of the hairy man dared him to open the pages once more.[44]

To make matters more complex, the rigid roles of gay looks encourage straight-acting behavior. Psychologists say that there is both a personal and archetypal way of looking at this problem as well. On one hand, it refers to feelings of internalized homophobia by valorizing straight-acting over "gay-acting." (It also shows a secret romance with father or fatherlike figures, who, after all, were straight.) But on an archetypal level, it calls up what Jack Fritscher calls the image of the "masculine homosexual," which, like it or not, seems at the core of many gay men's fantasies.

But even this notion oppresses gay men who are, quite positively, fey or feminine or just simply mildly androgynous. Duncan Teague, an African American psychologist and AIDS activist from Atlanta, Georgia, positively bristles when anyone asks him when he came out as gay. He was so effeminate all his life that he never had to come out at all. "I was always a sissy," he says. "I was also the minister's son and one of the smartest boys in class, so it was best not to mess with me." As someone who has learned how to mediate beautifully between his own masculine and feminine sides he has little patience for men who equate masculinity—true tests of courage—with brawn.

desire is an unconscious manifestation

A few gay men argued that before burning our porn mags, it might benefit us to wonder how powerfully these images do work in the first place. Of course, they don't seem to work the right way—at least according to the PC ego. "We need to empower people who don't feel attractive," Signorile said. "The range of what's attractive needs to be expanded." Of course, he was right. Not every gay man's soul image corresponded to a white, buff, hairless, straight-acting clone. This image, imposed upon the many by group psychology, was oppressive. But who would disagree that almost every gay man, no matter what his color, is looking for an idealization? Whether white or black or brown, gay men worship beauty—there can be no denying it. Is there a place inside that's human and another that's archetypal? If so, only the former can be found in the world.

Sure, once in a while a guy snared his incarnated god, for a night. But most remained hunters. Reasonable fellows found a nice person, albeit one with faults, to love. But because *few* gay men were taught that the doll-faced pinup boy was an inner symbol of something that is not yet conscious *in them*, men looked for this replica in the outside world, disappointing everyone, including themselves. Few made distinctions between the transpersonal, with its grandiosities, and the personal with its inferiorities. Contaminating each with the other, one appreciated neither.

This is why the marketplace remains successful. Sellers know how to go to the most private and vulnerable places in the imagination for the purpose of cajoling people into buying. But some gays argued that the sale was less likely if gay men honor first that there were at least two realms in the mind: the archetypal, with its idealizations and compulsions to worship, and the personal, with its nasty habit of tripping a person up on the unfinished business of shame, rage, and hurt. (This is why a man can see a beauty and send him projections of a divine nature as well as those of a resentful hue.) Because modern life teaches a person only how to adapt to the human, marketing experts have an open playing field when it comes to the archetypal. But through a subjective process, through a conscious and consistent encounter with the unconscious, everyone can have access to both realms. This way, one becomes an activist not just in the social world but in the inner world, too. For years, activists claimed that the highest calling in gay political life was to fight the authorities. In many cases, they were right. But few entertained the possibility of waging another fight, one in which a person relates to a deeper place in his own mind and confronts the authorities (or angels) there. One doesn't have to find or become a Marky Mark if, in one's heart, one has some relationship to the unconscious power that gives representations of him power.

This fact of nature didn't jive easily with the current facts of PC culture. A more responsible relationship to the forces of psychological life had not yet dawned on people. It may be easier to confront foes in the world, rather than those in the psyche. The man who is too cowardly to wrestle his morally problematic archetypes will be less inclined to admit that he has them.

sex individuates

To learn more about sex, one might approach it from the attitude of the unconscious. Sure, armchair social constructivists speak of the "unconscious" often, but by their tone one surmises that they can reason the nonintellective parts of the mind away. They approach the unknown from a reasonable attitude. But what other recourse is there? To look at life from its backside seems impossible. But depth psychologists suggest that genuine access to the living psyche is available — through one's inferior function, one's gay shadow.

The few gay men writing today who have undertaken the difficult path of gay individuation demonstrate that to let old attitudes go about sex and identity, one experiences a kind of death. Learning how to *feel* itself is a kind of death; for at first, the repressed feelings are overwhelming and sad. But in joining thinking with feeling in a lifelong cycle, the gay personality widens, and two previous stages of Western thinking, religion and science, are united. The instincts become not just places to wrestle, but places by which psychological truths can be experienced for the sake of the development of personality.[45]

chapter **seven**

condom meets crystal meets individuation

crisis in AIDS prevention

In this bedroom scene, taken from life in D.C. a few years ago, latex is conspicuous by its absence. The same can't be said for testosterone. The top is a Tom of Finland clone, or as close to those leather-jacketed "blond beasts" as any human form comes. His name is Greg Scott. As he takes a drag of his Marlboro, he looks sweetly at the younger, thinner man, who earlier alleged he was a connoisseur of love when Scott picked him up at the Pop Stop, a gay cafe in Dupont Circle. And this fellow wasn't lying.

Not one moment into Scott's apartment, and the dark-haired, olive-skinned youth tumbles seductively to a sitting position on the couch. He looks up at Scott, who now stands in front of him. Scott caresses the fellow's hair. With his eyes, Scott orders his friend to stop chatting (i.e., "You're gorgeous"; "Do you have any pot?"). To pay real attention in sex, one must be silent, at least at first.

Scott bends down and, face to face now, pulls the twentysomething-year-old into a hard kiss. Lips open delicately. Tongues click. Men moan. Bingo! When the bodies and minds fit like so, it's as if a nuclear voltage passes between two forms. Who's to say what's love and what's lust? Right now, the fullness of passion and the emptiness of need seem like two sides of the same coin.

Scott unzips his leather jacket, and then pulls off his skintight T-shirt to reveal the quintessential "smooth, hard chest," sought in so many gay personal ads.

And truth be told, with his ex-military swagger, crewcut, Ivory Boy complexion, and mid-thirties aplomb, Scott is a certain gay boy's dream come true. This former TV writer has been in the forefront of AIDS activism in both ACT UP and Queer Nation. But rarely have the warrior stripes paid off so well before.

"You're such a stud," whispers his friend. Little does the boy-toy know how hungry Scott is to be hungered for. Life, after all, sucks. There aren't many gay men who haven't been kicked around as kids. There aren't too many who haven't buried a few friends as adults. Touch redeems. Especially when you consider that gay men have what a lot of straight men don't avail themselves of: the ability to be taken. And the young man makes clear what he wants. With each presuming the other shares the same sero-status as himself, both men having earlier admitted that each was "in the same boat," there is no talk of condoms. Odd; but these dudes have made each other into angels. Funny how feeling immortal always entails some form of denial.

"Cum inside me," the young man whispers. A stick of dynamite goes off in each man's primary sex organ — the psyche — where the worlds of spirit and matter come together in the realm of the imaginal. With the release into animal dynamism, and the dissolution of boundaries, someone (or is it both of them?) lets loose the notorious L-word. In a world that vilifies male-to-male intimacy, whether gay or straight, sometimes it does take the very intense emotional overload that comes with anal sex to flood a man's defenses about getting close to another.

beyond condoms

AIDS education teaches everyone to presume that each and every partner is infected and to use a latex barrier with each sex act. For the most part, the line, pioneered by safer-sex cofounder Michael Callen in 1983, seems to have worked. In dance clubs and workshops all over the country, gay activists from AIDS agencies teach men and women how to apply condoms to bananas and how to work miracles with dental dams. But gay men have brought their own brand of street folk wisdom to the safer-sex discussion. On occasion two men who are HIV-positive *do* do away with condoms, in part because some studies suggest that the possible damage caused by reinfection is low. Some HIV-negative men abandon condoms when having sex together too. It's not an altogether senseless form of safer sex. It actually works — that is, if each person knows (as well as anyone could know) his partner's HIV-status.

Greg Scott, for one, always loathed the emphasis the gay community put on condom use as the bedrock of safer sex. To him, the motto "Safer sex is hot sex" always seemed disingenuous. As an uncircumcised man, he found condoms irritating. But more important, it seemed patently clear that the exchange of bodily fluids went to the sacramental heart of gay sex. To demonize the fullness of intimacy seemed not only unnaturally penalizing to Scott, it made little sense as a permanent prevention technique.

So in the late '80s, Scott eschewed usage, instead pledging to "serodisclose," that is, to tell every potential partner that he was positive. At first, Scott found it oddly romantic to talk about his health status, and then to reestablish the appropriate boundaries before diving into bed. But not every queer found the talks comfortable. Scott spent many months celibate.

"Why bother disclosing?" a lover finally asked him. "Everyone takes his own risk. What difference does it make whether we're positive or negative, because we're going to wear condoms anyway." In a minority, and hungry for touch, Scott adapted to the imperfect community standard, armed himself with condoms and vowed he would never exchange bodily fluids without them unless he could be sure his partner were positive too. Then came the inevitable night when Scott thought it was safe to engage in ordinary sex because the person shared the same HIV-status. But in retrospect he worries that he may not have stipulated his concerns firmly enough. (Being tipsy didn't help.) "If this guy were negative, he'd ask me to put on a condom," Scott reasoned. And the reverse reasoning must have been similar. Something like, "Greg seems responsible. Since he didn't put on a condom, he must be negative."

That night, and one or two others like it, now haunt Scott, who worries about those he may have inadvertently infected by not only sleeping with HIV-positive men like himself, but by not "seroseparating," as he puts it. "We have held up condoms as the foundation of safer sex," he says. "And that has allowed us to think we are all the same regardless of sero-status. But the truth is condoms are not foolproof. There is a huge difference between the HIV-negative and positive."

untamed youth

A rise in cases among gay men signaled to men like Greg Scott that the *second* sexual revolution had ended as quickly as it was announced. By 1991 AIDS had become the fifth-leading cause of death among youth aged 15–24, according to the 1992 AIDS report given by the Select Committee on Children, Youth, and Families. Young gay men were many times more in jeopardy that older gays. In fact, the younger the men, the riskier the behavior.

The reasons? A national distrust of talking to youth about homo sex. Assaults on sex education by the right wing. A myth that new AIDS cases are primarily among heterosexuals. Confusion over safer-sex guidelines. A failure of the

Stonewall generation to reach out to Clinton-era queers. Twentysomething gays who haven't felt the grief that's shocked an older generation into radical changes of behavior. An AIDS educational system that gives support services to men if they're infected, thus implicitly sending the message that HIV-negative men are less deserving. A rapid rise in drug and alcohol use. The ostracizing racism gay men of color continue to suffer. The failure of AIDS prevention to effectively reach people of color.[1]

A 1993 San Francisco Department of Public Health seroprevalence survey of 425 Bay Area gay or bisexual men aged 17–22 interviewed at street locations and social events found that the percentage reporting unprotected anal sex in the prior six months was 28.1 percent among whites, 38.5 percent among African Americans, 40 percent among Latinos, and 27.1 percent among Asian/Pacific Islanders. Other cities showed a similar rise. In a study published in the *Journal of Acquired Immune Deficiency Syndrome and Human Retrovirology*, ethnic minority men were three times more likely than white men to test HIV-positive in the study of an ethnically diverse group of 174 New York City gay men aged 18–24. The study found an HIV rate of 40 percent among African American men and 30 percent among Latinos compared to a rate of 2 percent among white and other ethnic groups.[2]

Safer-sex guidelines were established with the expectation that they would be temporary, that a cure would make them obsolete. An increasing number of gay men found by the '90s that unfailing condom use was impossible to maintain for a lifetime. It just so happened that many HIV-positive men did take enormous responsibility about who and how they fucked. Some dated only HIV-positive men; others chose celibacy; others branded tattoos of positive signs on their arms or butts (warning labels, as it were). Some men mummified themselves in latex or leather, making some kinds of S&M the safest of erotic highways. To be sure, most gay men mastered the art of condom usage. Witness the sharp plummet in cases of rectal gonorrhea (the best way to trace unprotected anal sex) in American cities in the '80s, when gay men taught the world a thing or two about peer norms and behavior modification.[3] (In 1984, 1,299 cases of rectal gonorrhea were reported to the San Francisco Health Department; in 1987, 197 cases; in 1991, 134 cases. This represents a remarkable "ten-fold decrease over a seven-year period," maintains Edward King in *Safety in Numbers*.)

While all that was true enough, some gay men, either exhausted from more than a decade of unrelenting barrier sex, or overcome by the heat of the moment (or the buzz of being tweaked on crystal or Southern Comfort), or simply confused about what's safe and what's not, did slip into what prevention experts dub "ordinary sex." Ordinary sex is, after all, natural sex. Why should that seem so unreasonable? If you asked heterosexuals to give up raw sex forever, not only would they not stand for it, you'd put an end to the species.

Some men, like Greg Scott, wanted to bring ordinary sex back to gay life as a safer-sex technique in a process he (and Australian AIDS educators) call "negotiated safety." (A process in which gay partners can, through regular testing, engage in full-on sex as long as both men agree to get tested often and set up rules that allow for slips, which would then be followed by condom use until such time as the men reaffirm each is HIV-negative.) But, to Scott, ordinary sex and negotiated safety only worked if it included seroseparation. Perhaps the most provocative point of Scott's message was that HIV-positive men should not have sex with HIV-negative men under any circumstances. Logically speaking, as he put it, HIV can be transmitted only where HIV is present. The position provoked cries of viral apartheid. Scott and others were accused of further stigmatizing an already stigmatized group. But they certainly started discussion.

the journalist outs the community

The debate accelerated at the hands of a few gay community journalists, former sex radicals who felt that there was no excuse for rising caseloads of AIDS among gay men. They felt a renewed sense of panic—and responsibility. Their critique of AIDS prevention transcended AIDS.

Many attacked the community standard that equated (safer) sexual freedom with gay identity. Even some lesbians got into the act. In an *Advocate* column former National Gay and Lesbian Task Force director Torie Osborn railed that "Clearly we won't survive as a community without an articulate public community ethic that goes well beyond sex-positivity and without a politics of meaning well beyond the AIDS rage that sustained us for the first decade of the epidemic."[4]

Perhaps the most vocal and eloquent of those writers was Michelangelo Signorile, a former editor of *Outweek*, a columnist for *Out*, and the author of *Queer in America*. There is a tradition in new (now old) journalism for the author to make news from his own story. After all, all perception of objective life is subjective, so why not start with the personal? Signorile used his venue as national queer spokesperson to bear ethical witness to the inhuman pressure that demands men seek approval as sexual toys and muscle technocrats. As such, he helped alter discussion of gay sexual mores by waving a red flag that the community could hardly ignore.

In his now classic *Out* article, "Unsafe Like Me," Signorile told *the* gay '90s story. After a grueling work week on assignment in Hawaii, he wrote that he had met "your classic gay hunk" with "razor-sharp cheek bones, a body of granite and a Texas drawl" at a Waikiki gay bar. When the guy promised to make Signorile see God, Signorile decided he needed a religious experience. The line is tossed off as tongue-in-cheek, but it reveals a search for wholeness—one so needed that certain sacrifices get made. As Signorile puts it, "As usual, one thing quickly led to another. But not as usual, he didn't put on a condom before we had anal sex, and I didn't demand he use one."[5]

The next day, Signorile was seized by guilt and anxiety:

> I'd had a couple of Absolut Citrons. And I had made a quick decision—inside of 10 seconds—based on heat-of-the-moment rationalizations that at some distance seem absurd: 1) Since he did not put on a condom, he must be negative. 2) He is a Navy petty officer and therefore is a responsible "good" boy. 3) Since he's in the military, he must be tested every six months and would be discharged if positive. 4) He's absolutely perfect—the gay male ideal—and I don't want to do anything to make him blow off the whole night. 5) I'm sure it'll be OK, as long as he doesn't come. 6) This is Hawaii, and the AIDS problem can't be like it is in New York. 7) I'll only do it this one time.[6]

As Signorile explains it, a funny "I've survived" way of thinking *had* entered the minds of men not yet infected that sometimes amounted to a more liberal attitude around condoms. "As ridiculous as it sounds," he declares, "I felt I'd gotten far away from HIV." His oldest friends were infected a decade ago; it seemed that few were newly seroconverting. These facts provided a "little archipelago of hope carefully mapped out in an ocean of illness, fear, uncertainty, and grief."

Then friends, seemingly overnight in the '90s, began to seroconvert—one after another.

The archipelago disintegrated.

This forced Signorile to investigate the psychology behind seroconversion. What he found disturbed him. Libido had not been fully transformed by the events of the '80s and '90s; in some cases, the transformation was only at a midpoint; in other cases, it had received a mere Band-Aid called "condoms." Often the Band-Aid fell off. Signorile talked to many men who felt so bad about their looks and personality that, with the help of alcohol or drugs, they would probably have ditched the rubbers if the man in question was a stud. "What worries me," said one man, "is that I feel so beneath guys like that, I'd allow them to do *anything*."

Signorile found that some gay men felt they had nothing really to live for: "Far too many gay men say they actually *fear* growing old in a gay world that puts the young and the buffed on a pedestal while treating the over-35 crowd like lepers."[7]

The charge that the gay community's sex culture is not liberating—but is, in fact, a recipe for failure—isn't new. It echoes Larry Kramer's position in *Faggots* and George Whitmore's in *The Confessions of Danny Slocum*. But those critiques on the commercialization and reduction of gay life to sex could not have reached gay men of Signorile's younger generation had they not first undergone certain key stages of the '80s: trauma, humbling, and the reappreciation of eros. By the time Signorile wrote, social transformation had already taken place through the efforts of safer-sex radicals, Queer Nationals, and ACT UP kiss-ins. In a decade's time, the libido had been assessed, contained, and then acted out—because of AIDS, in response to AIDS, in reaction to AIDS, respectively. And, as such, the symbols of the libido had been changed, if just a little.[8]

To be sure, Signorile's attack on the "Stepford Homos" would piss off many sex radicals as well as those who interpreted any reflection on sexual life as an attack on it. But others intuited what Signorile made explicit: this breakdown of self-esteem around one's looks contributed to an attitude in which slips into unsafe sex practices could take place through the desperate effort to get touched at all. Signorile made a connection between the emphasis to be beautiful and the unspoken desire to die inside when that beauty failed you. Because there are so few tools to deal with this symbolic dying, it often gets literalized.

going public

It was standing room only at the New York City Gay and Lesbian Community Services Center on the night of November 16, 1994. Leaders from sixteen AIDS prevention agencies had called this emergency meeting to announce "the second wave" of AIDS. The place was packed with leather-jacketed young gay men and lesbians flirting and nursing old grudges—and exchanging bets on how politically volatile the panelists would be. There was no lack of luminaries (Tony-Award winner Tony Kushner; African American novelist Steven Corbin) but, for the most part, the crowd was made up of guys in their thirties—the ones who had put so much faith in the tenets of safer sex.

So much for blind faith.

There had already been scattered discussion of the emerging crisis in AIDS prevention. A few months earlier, at a conference in Dallas, Texas, the news that gay men were again having unprotected sex shook the national prevention community.

Tonight's New York City Town Hall meeting had more riding on it. This gathering would mark the first announcement to the general public—and New York's status as media capital makes any report on sex and AIDS politically inflammatory. The buzz in the room was reminiscent of a meeting in this same auditorium seven years earlier when Larry Kramer gave his rousing jeremiad demanding that his audience start a "new organization devoted to political change." Out of that meeting, ACT UP was born. Who knew what might happen tonight? Already people like Town Hall moderator (and veteran street activist) Ann Northrop were predicting an in-your-face, ACT-UP-style movement to form around AIDS prevention after this meeting.

What happened instead left many reeling. Where Kramer had lambasted the government, tonight's panelists turned their anger on the gay community.

Dr. Walt Odets, a Berkeley-based psychologist and the country's leading spokesperson for change in AIDS prevention, argued that "our AIDS work to date has been responsible for much psychological damage."[9] He expressed anger that current models don't differentiate between negative and positive men. "In the first nine months of 1993," he said, "the annualized incidence of new HIV infections in San Francisco was about four times that necessary to sustain a 50 percent prevalence of HIV infection in San Francisco's gay community—indefinitely. Such figures leave no doubt that there has been some sort of failure." The failure stems from the refusal to differentiate between positive and negative men in AIDS education and prevention, lumping the two populations together as the same.[10]

He explained the historical factors behind the reluctance to differentiate. The 1985 ELISA HIV test was developed at the height of Reaganomics. Gay leaders, fearing discrimination from the insurance, medical, and political establishment, blurred differences between negative and positive. Furthermore, in the '80s, long-term AIDS survivors argued that it was possible to "live and thrive with HIV." Meanwhile, AIDS research promised better drugs just at the time the HIV test was created. It was estimated that almost half of the gay community was infected. Sending the message to the uninfected that HIV was a "deadly virus" conflicted with the more hopeful one being constructed for the thousands living with the disease. As a result, it became virtually impossible for the fortunate members of the community to explicitly hope for something that was impossible for the less fortunate. "They [HIV-negative men] were never singled out as the—and the *only*—*outcome* population for primary prevention." In fact, as he put it, HIV-negatives became *personae non grate*. Most AIDS pamphlets in the '80s and early-to-mid-'90s did not explicitly mention the needs of uninfected men. The one important reason HIV-negative men remained uninfected, according to Odets, is because the gay community, stunned by AIDS, just stopped having sex.

Which is to say, uninfected men in 1986 abstained from sex, largely out of fear—and not necessarily, as many people believe, because they had become proficient at using condoms.[11] But, as Odets explained it at the Town Hall meeting, as men started to have sex again in the mid-and-late '80s, HIV-negative men entered a sexual culture that did not make explicit their particular quandaries:

> *Any explicit assertions of the needs of uninfected men—including the assertion, in occasional whispers, that it was not always easy to remain uninfected and men needed to talk about that—were experienced as an affront to men with HIV or AIDS, because they, after all, had undeniably pressing needs.*

Being PC about AIDS had the effect of creating the conditions that allowed for the transmission of virus. "If we continued to explicitly assert—as we *had* done early in the epidemic—that it was *better* to remain uninfected, were we not implying that there was something 'wrong' with being infected, and perhaps aggravating already powerful, if unutterable, feelings that infected men were somehow culpable for their infection?" Why, asked Odets, was it so hard for the fortunate members of the community to hope for something—a long, healthy life—that was impossible for the unfortunate? Was it possible to assert that it was better to be living without AIDS than with it?

For Odets, the solution is simple. Differentiate the message between the two groups. Target these two radically different groups so that the HIV-uninfected get an explicit message that hits them right at the center of their sexual lives:

> *Implorations like* "We can do something about AIDS, instead of letting AIDS do something to us" *will become* "You don't have to become infected simply because you're gay"; "It's about our future. It's about our community. It's about commitment" *will become* "Staying uninfected is about *your* future, *your* community and your commitment to both"; *and* "AIDS has affected every one of us in one way or another" *will become* "If you are HIV-positive, you can make a big difference in the *life* of an uninfected man."[12]

His views provoked outrage. "Stop blaming the victim," came a scream from the audience. "Sounds like apartheid to me," bellowed another, as a contingent of young men stormed out.

The additional panelists participated, with Odets, in tearing down the already fragile edifice of AIDS prevention. African American AIDS educator Colin

Robinson put the blame for the current AIDS fiasco on the sociology of the men who created it in the early '80s. ("These white gay men went for a temporary Band-Aid solution instead of creating a vision of social change that addressed the needs of the entire personality.") Youth activist Andy Montoya criticized the lack of places in which queer youth can meet that don't have as their primary goal serving alcohol on one hand or providing AIDS services on the other. Still others screamed about the lack of more racially diverse speakers on the panel.

Carmen Vasquez, director of public policy at New York City's Gay and Lesbian Community Center, tried to put the brawl in perspective: "The community heard a message that made them angry. They need some time to sit with the news before we can do any serious organizing. We all felt overwhelmed and overloaded."

Odets's direct approach to life, and his rejection of mainstream gay cant, has made him something of an underground hero in the AIDS movement. He's no number-crunching AIDS researcher. Rather he's a psychoanalyst who really enjoys being a gay man and has, by force of charisma, attracted a large gay clientele. He sticks to his position—By being too PC, AIDS prevention has failed America—with an unwavering simplicity, a characteristic he attributes to growing up as the son of someone who often experienced himself as a failure. Clifford Odets was one of the playwrights and screenwriters hurt by the McCarthy era and spurned by both right and left. The determination not to be broken himself has forced the younger Odets into learning everything there is to learn about AIDS statistics, and research methodology, along with the Machiavellian world of gay politics. He's become quite the public speaker in the process.

"We have literally not allowed HIV-negative men to name themselves," he says, arguing that, rather, being positive has become a real identity—predominating, in many respects, being gay. "Young HIV-positive men do receive more attention, support, and social services within larger gay communities than their HIV-negative counterparts," Odets says, referring, by way of example, to Pedro Zamora, the former twenty-two-year-old MTV actor who became an AIDS spokesperson and hero before his death.

This outlook has lent Odets's writing moral force—and controversy. "Feelings about 'sickness' because one is homosexual become entangled in feelings about being sick with AIDS," he writes. "Feelings about an invalidated and hated form of life because one is homosexual become feelings about living in a semiprivate plague; and feelings of guilt about being gay become feelings of guilt about having AIDS, not having AIDS, or not doing enough for those who do have it."[13]

"The incentive to have AIDS," Odets adds, "may be enhanced by the sometimes liberating nature of such lives."

The idea is to make it more compelling for HIV-negative men to secure their future. This is no small feat. All of the social containers that at one time offered people a sense of meaning—church; family; state—are cracking, so that people are loading all their libido up in sex. Gay people, who have traditionally lacked indigenous spaces, have turned to sex as the finest gradient in which to experience the wholeness of their lives. The experience returns people back to themselves in an existential way.

Alienation can offer either the greatest of possible opportunities or the most devastating of catastrophes. Sometimes, both. "Psychologically," writes depth psychologist Edward Edinger, referring historically to classic symbols of alienation, "this means that the experience of the supporting aspect of the archetypal psyche is most likely to occur when the ego has exhausted its own resources and is aware of its essential impotence by itself."[14]

There have been scattered attempts to create indigenous community spaces that had as their main purpose an effort to connect Eros with Culture: to invite gay men to see the meaning in love, to ask the fundamental questions Harry Hay catalyzed the movement with: "Who are we?" "Why are we here?" and "Where did we come from?" In the early '70s, Gay Activist Alliance members created the Firehouse—a coffee house meeting place—but it was burnt down. 2 Spirit Salon, a queer-centered venue, closed in 1994. While Gabriel Rotello was editor of *Out-Week*, he dreamt of converting a bathhouse into a place for gay men to go to have sex with the lights on and to gather politically and culturally. But when the magazine went defunct, so did that idea. Likewise, Queer Nation and ACT UP galvanized people—but only for about three years. At the moment, gay and lesbian community centers try to offer programs, but have their hands filled with trying to provide services—the same for AIDS organizations.

in the meantime . . . tweaking

We're doing our "sashay, shantay" thing on the runway of the world at the Probe disco. But we might as well be making voguing fools of ourselves at New York's Tunnel or Miami's Paragon. There's a metallic red buzz on the dance floor and in the eyes of the guys that crowd it, but only a fool would mistake the heart racing, the run-on sentences, snaps-in-your-face, and boys-will-be-boys shoulder punches as health signs from young men high off the endorphin rush you can get from humping and bumping on the dance floor. Just look at their bug-eyes, vascularity and dry mouth, and "Aren't-I-fabulous?" sneers.

These guys want more than Robin S. In fact, they want more than mere sex. And they want more than mere drugs—poppers, dope, coke, and even X being dissed as passé. The drug of choice in the twentysomething parts is a highly refined version of speed called crystal—methamphetamine. Sniffing or snorting crystal has become so popular, in part, because—as one twenty-five-year-old Marky Mark-in-a-dog-collar clone put it: "Nothing makes you as completely horny as crystal." Sex while tweaked, he says, equals nirvana.

If the early years of the '90s saw accelerated progress in gay mainstream politics and more favorable media coverage, the period also saw a corresponding rise in sex clubs and an increase in drug use. Far cheaper and longer-lasting than cocaine, and more available on the streets than Ecstasy, crystal methe raised sexual cravings to superhuman levels. "Crystal is the perfect drug for gay men in the '90s," comments psychotherapist Guy Baldwin. "Crystal disables the mind's tendency to run subroutines that inhibit sexual impulses." In other words, if you want to get dressed up in leather and tied up, but you're afraid of what your mother or society will think, "crystal quiets those inner voices" and defense mechanisms "to let you freely do what you want to do."

For the gay man who feels nervous about his looks, charisma, penis size, or susceptibility to HIV, Baldwin says that crystal seems, at first, like a magic bullet. The gay guy too scared to ask the most beautiful man in the disco to dance turns suddenly courageous: "All of a sudden, there you are, ripping off your shirt to be the world's hottest go-go dancer."

"Yes," confesses the thirty-two-year-old Doug Mirk, "crystal does make a shy person seem rather outgoing. But it also makes you very, very aware." As he tells it,

> There are those who say they don't need drugs because they want to feel everything, every sensation—but crystal is not like that. It does not hold back anything. It makes you feel every nuance of every slap, every ridge of that big cock going down every ridge of your throat . . . the friction on your ass . . . the whole world being swallowed into you.

Mirk doesn't just kneel at the crystal cathedral. He lays prostrate, as he describes his first time slamming (or mainlining) it: "Quickly he reaches for the tourniquet and yanks it off my arm. Immediately I feel a rush to my chest and give a slight cough . . . and then, the waves, the waves all around me." He sits on a chair to watch TV with the friend who helped him shoot up and as he moves his head, the side of the room moves too—a phenomenon the friend calls "framing."

Later on, Mirk is alone, watching porn video:

This has become the perfect setup for a crystal experience . . . the ultimate form of ecstasy: unattached fantasy. The television near the ground, blanket laid out on the floor in front, lube, cum rag, dildo, bottle of poppers all laid out like the Holy Sacrament beside me. I am the priest of Virtual Reality and I am also the entire congregation. Nothing exists beyond this world of porno and crystal and dicks and fantasy. I don't usually like myself when I do crystal. I see myself as pathetic, paranoid. Early tonight, I had smoked about half my quarter. This is how you do it: you take a piece of tin foil, fold it in half, dump the stuff . . . into the crease, and put a flame underneath. The crystal burns and disintegrates almost immediately. Up above, you have a tube in your mouth, probably an empty pen holder or a straw, and you suck suck suck in all the smoke. When you smoke crystal, the rush is almost exclusively in your head.

After he takes his hit, Mirk shakes and the granules fall to the floor. He spends time crawling looking for the "two little specks of crystal methe," but finding mostly dust. Finally, he resolves his problem just as the fucking on the screen starts. "Yeah, oh fuck me, oh fuck me," the characters say and

I lean forward with my upper body, stick my ass into the air. "I'm ready," — and I stuff the dildo up inside me at exactly the right moment. Yes, yes, this is all really happening: for this instant that cock really is going up inside my perfect ass and I have nothing, nothing, nothing to worry about: no life aside from this sex. No guilt. No notion of sin or the harm that I could be doing, may have already done, to my body. This is holy, this is great and I am alone in the world at this instant, am the only one experiencing perfect and utter, utter bliss. Everything else can wait until tomorrow. . . .

While some experts bemoan the new epidemic of drugs as a backsliding of safer-sex education, some crystal users themselves tend to find the theories too reductionist. If the '80s saw a backlash against a certain disco-induced delirium — in part because the shell-shock of AIDS inured gays to what they perceived of as "clone" indulgences — the '90s showed that not everyone could find love and dates at a twelve-step program — especially those younger gays who felt less susceptible to AIDS by virtue of their youth and stash of condoms, and sense of entitlement to ecstasy.

During one long Saturday night at the L.A. disco Probe, two tweaking men, royalty in the hierarchy of nightclubs, make distinctions between themselves and the "speed queens." Mark is a young professional weighted down by packs of gay muscle. Robert is a slightly older "career boy" who is more naturally attractive, a skinny Latino Brad Pitt. They snort crystal through straws or vials on a casual once-a-month or so basis. Their muscles boast a certain diamond-cut shape under their skin which they attribute to weekend speed use. Only once has Robert injected it. Mark likes the practice of breaking off the needle and shooting the liquid up his butt. Mark speaks of using the drug like a tool "to expand horizons." Yet he says he can't wake up in the morning without doing a line. And Robert admits to being unable to enjoy sex without the drug: "My boyfriend doesn't approve, but having an orgasm on crystal is incredible, lots of aggressive sexual contact." Robert, who says he is mostly a top, says crystal "opens up the butthole like you wouldn't believe. You can stick an entire hand in there if you want."

But scratch the surface and even Mark and Robert haven't been spared their horrors. Mark seroconverted last year; Robert is dealing with "some pretty heavy nightmares" where he is "screaming, nonstop, in a rage." They chalk up their problems to "personal shit." But it's not merely personal. Call the Hardcore 976 line on any night of the week and "partying dudes" leave messages that reveal something unfinished about the collective gay psyche. It's as if peoples' father complexes and inferiority complexes come together with speed, with Eros as the messenger. One "foot bitch" wants to be "used like a toilet" by a "straight-acting man." Another man announces himself as "hot muscular white toilet looking for a dude into kink and sleaze—Latins preferred, partying a must."

When the archetypes demand a person bash down the defenses that keep life boring, inhuman, manageable, and superficial, nothing short of Dionysian madness ensues. This madness, a necessary part of development, as Ian Young makes clear in his book *The Stonewall Experiment*, leads to suicide if it is not partnered by Apollo. It is possible to make an objective encounter with autonomous (and irrational) psychic imagery, as long as reason is not too outraged and the creative play of images is not suppressed. But too few gain the courage or will to marry religion and science in their own souls, and one or the other generally wins out. To leave the childhood psyche, one needs to surrender to Dionysus— but not forever, otherwise pleasure becomes like another overbearing mother who won't let her son grow up and transform. As the legend of Parsifal shows, no man can leave his mother's home and enter the King's castle without tearing off the protective homespun garment she made for him. But sex can sometimes be another way back into this "garment." Here the mother isn't so literal but symbolic, representing fear of change. The gratification gained through some transcendence-seeking sex can be a symbolic return to wholeness represented by the inward mother which, because it's unconscious, can manifest as fierce and destructive. Sometimes a drug experience can give a person a momentary hit of the union of the World Parents inside the soul, a union that disintegrates all too quickly if the ego has no tools or inclination to relate to its fiercesomeness in a conscious way.

Larry Cain, a screenwriter in Los Angeles, says that the fascination gay men have with drugs comes as a compensation for the lack of depth in the rationalistic, me-first gay community. Cain, a recovering crystal addict, explains his dance with the drug this way:

> Gay men are looking for something in taking crystal and to say that they are merely numbing out, which is in part true, is not addressing fully what they find. The drug cracked me open. It changed my energy. In a strange way, it enabled me to discover who I am. Snorting speed was a spiritual experience. I felt connected to something bigger than myself, even if I lacked the tool to integrate that into conscious life. It eliminated my blocks, which had kept me stilted all my life. It made me love men in a new way. Of course, crystal is no way to go about getting in touch with God on a regular basis. I had four amazing months and then I almost died.

As some experts explain, a low-functioning person with a serious depression problem takes to crystal because it gives him motivation for the first time in his life. But some reject that pathologizing approach. Jöel B. Tan, a Philipino activist and writer, talks about crystal use as a "tool" to learn about the parts in his personality that exist once some aspects of the superego's (social voices of judgment) "self-hatred" and "body-shame" are eroded by the drug. He doesn't see crystal as a substitute for "good old fashioned Western psychotherapy," or "plain old soul searching," which he supports. Tan found out about the drug from house parties in particularly black and Latino communities. For him, the drug served as a way to recontextualize the "racializing" of roles that often plagues him—people see him as a large Asian man and peg him as top. To complicate matters further for Tan, Asians are often seen as small, passive bottoms. "To be a large, Asian top is an oxymoron," he comments. In a lovemaking situation with an African American man, Tan found that drugs helped to wear down all the resistances to each of them getting fucked *and* closer. In the end, Tan says, "I fucked him with everything I had."

To be sure, Tan, who is an AIDS activist and has been a point person in organizing cultural events and even organizations for people of color, is *not promoting the use* of drugs to work through racial problems or intimacy crises. His point is simple: short of profound psychological or philosophical solutions in the gay community, young gay men are going to be attracted to strategies that help them cope in a culture that asks that they dissociate themselves from their most difficult feelings. Tan is one of those people who like to examine feelings as he's having sex and as he courts another man. To him, sex is merely one of the vehicles for communication. And while he likes sex for sex's sake, he also likes to employ sex to dig deeper into the mystery of personality, race, color, and male-to-male bonding.

He says he likes to have as much information as possible from people before he decides how close to get to them. "I like to be fascinated with someone emotionally," he says. "I like to find a way to ask them questions in one form or another":

> *"What do you want from me sexually?" "And what gets you hard?" "How do you feel about disclosing your sero-status?" "Are you looking for a lover or a sex buddy?" "Do you think talking about sex robs the sex from the experience?" "Do you hate your body?" "Do you like large men?" "What's your thing around rough sex?" "How do you resolve the contradiction that you're in a love relationship of X years with another man and I'm sticking this huge dildo up your ass?"*

Tan wants to make his attitude on drugs perfectly clear: he does not wish to abuse his body or mind through the use of substances. Rather, he wishes to employ whatever tools he can to explore the different levels of consciousness.

on ritual death

Some gay men see compulsive drug use as stemming from a failure of modern life to provide precise outward rituals that mark, provoke, and name inward ones. Thinkers as diverse as Ian Young, Joseph Kramer, and the Italian psychologist Luiji Zoja see America's fascination with drugs—and fireworks sex—as stemming from its repression of the "archetype of dying." "When the initiatory process is not a satisfying and complete enough an experience," writes Zoja, "one can be tempted to persist in it with increasing fury. This insistence can at times lead to an intensification of the material process without necessarily augmenting the psychic one." In other words, drug use—and the drive for repeated nuclear sex—is both a symptom and a corrective; the subject wants a relationship to symbolic life but has no means to attain it. Or he senses it, a bare hint of it, and that hint makes him hungry for more, for the Holy Grail that some drugs, when mixed with some sex, can instantly provide, and then dissipate. "A need," Zoja writes, "which is not expressed symbolically always tends to become literalized."[15] The question put forward by both Young and Zoja is how to meet up with the intoxicating energies of instinctual life with a more sober and consistent attitude, so as not to be bored on one hand or sizzled to death on the other.

on conscious introversion

It's 10 P.M. at a San Francisco cafe and the two men—both in their late twenties—read and smoke cigarettes alone. One is a dark-skinned New Mexican, the other a dirty-blond Italian. Their friends are preparing for an evening at Blow Buddies or Eros but they have decided that such dives do little for them. Each wants a boyfriend, someone to court, to fall in love with, to make meals for. Having spent most of their adult lives falling in love the moment they fall into bed, only to find out a week later that the lover-boy has dumped them (or vice versa), they have decided to be more circumspect. After hours of glances, one man picks up his papers and sits himself at the table of the other.

"I thought you'd never make the move," the darker one says.

"I usually think I'm too good to make a pass," the lighter one says. "But you looked so cute, I ate my pride."

"I'm glad you did."

There is nothing easy about the chat, which has the charge of sex all over it. One can read so much in the eyes alone: animal lust, a need to repair a narcissistic injury, a defense against depression, an affirmation of self-worth, a way to repudiate homophobia, a love of the body. One knows, if one is human, and especially if one is gay, that so much psychological *materia* can be swept under the rug with a hard-on; by the same token, so much can be amplified—intensified. Does it make sense to light fireworks one more time?

Maybe yes, but maybe no. Through a new social contract, one that has been silently written up in cities across the country, these two agree to hold off on the firecrackers of a kiss, the M-80s of a moan. Neither do they leave the scene. The men decide to contain their sexual instinct—that is, they don't bash it, but they don't let it lead the way. Through "containment," they bring a more virginal touch to the new meeting. "I'm trying not to give it all away," one man says.

Meanwhile, in L.A., Rob Vargas, a handsome Latino writer, gives the brush-off to another handsome writer—which is strange, considering the obvious vibrational connection the two men experience when in the same room. They can barely look each other in the eye. Their voices quiver—just barely. They rearrange things from their pants pockets. But Vargas won't have anything to do with the man because the two are "sort of dating" other men. "In the old days," Vargas explains, "I would have thrown caution to the wind. So what if the guy has already given his heart to someone else. If he was cute, sweet and available—do him! I mean I had a lot of sex back then, just like a lot of gay guys. But now that I am inching towards forty, I just won't have sex with someone I'm not sure is boyfriend material."

In other words, he just doesn't feel like giving it all away.

How virginal. How antithetical to the tenets of the gay sexual revolution—everything one's forebears stood for. What would the pioneers of the revolutionary spirit who saw sexual freedom and psychic freedom as one and the same—people like Charles Shively, Michael Bronski, Jack Fritscher, Mark Thompson, John Francis Hunter—say about such an Eisenhower-era ethos?

"It's partly out of fear of AIDS," Vargas explains. "But I was actually growing quite unhappy with gay sexual life even before AIDS. It was when I finally fell in love with a man—a man with whom I wanted to have sex—that I saw there was no substitute for getting fucked by someone you loved." Now, AIDS has only solidified his resolve to keep sex an exclusive part of his gay "marriage." To him, the waiting and courting period around romantic love is also a good way to keep oneself free from sexually transmitted disease, especially HIV. In fact, Vargas makes every potential boyfriend take an HIV test before they get too terribly intimate. But his interest in courtship extends past disease—he wants love to be the causal element behind sex, not just the man's hot appearance. "After the first few dates," he says, by way of explaining his romantic-erotic practice, "we kiss":

> Then, if we continue to like each other, we take off our shirts. Then there's a period of heavy petting. This could go on for several weeks. Meanwhile, we're getting to know each other, getting to see if each other is boyfriend material, if each wants to cohabitate on some level. By the time he puts his dick in my ass, it's an involvement—we're intertwined. This ain't no joke. Of course, there's never a guarantee. But we've become so intertwined at this point, that the fucking is a way to cement the intimacy, not to create it. The idea of "sex as a birthright" is so trashy to me. Of course, I have animalistic needs. But if I give in to them, what does that make me?

Vargas expresses a relationship to sex—"I won't make love to a man with whom I've not already shared a great deal of intimacy" that is antithetical to the one explored during the '70s—"I won't love a man who I've not yet fucked."

On the other end of the spectrum is someone like Dredge Byung 'chu Kang, a queer Asian Health Outreach Worker, who, at the age of twenty-four, represents a contingent of young sex radicals who believe sex represents a profound way to meet men without the bourgeois trappings so often laid on relationships. "There is a freedom to having sex with men, especially Asian men, and Latino men, that makes me feel fully in my life. It also allows me to give appropriate AIDS prevention information to young men of color for I know where they are coming from." Dredge argues that every generation—no matter whether or not it faces a health crisis—will find itself rocking back and forth from Apollo to Dionysus for the purpose of finding a middle, self-regulating energy.

sex as persona

For all the cumming that ACT UP, Callen, the O-Boys!, and the Black Jacks experienced in an extroverted manner, a few things began to change on the unconscious and introverted level.

Some gay men squarely confronted the fact that sex had become their persona—the way they were seen socially. (Robert Hopcke wrote a book on the subject—*Persona*—and Ian Young's *The Stonewall Experiment* makes a similar analysis.)[16] The persona is another way of saying our "social self," a collective way of adapting to the world. A man overidentified with his persona as the *only* place he feels alive can become two-dimensional. If there is a place of individuality stewing in his unconscious, and it is being neglected, chances are that it loads up with energy and becomes a shadowy place. This is why some depth psychologists refer to this place as "the shadow," a negative double to the ego-personality that includes qualities we find painful or regrettable. Too much overidentification with one's persona results in an opposing reaction on the side of the unconscious, resulting in moods, irrational rages, and depression.

Of course, the creation of a sexual persona was not the goal of the sexual revolution. But in an effort to destroy the false masks of straight white patriarchal culture through an orgy of cum, and to bash down the defenses that kept a man from coming out, gay men succeeded in creating a persona of their own. This was part of what was called "gay pride." But as thinkers like Robert Hopcke and Mitch Walker explain it, this was not a culture in the indigenous sense of the term, which would be based as much on spiritual and psychological internals as much as outward signs of success. The community looked "gay" but the psyche had not yet been brought out. It existed but in a collective manner, what some anthropologists call "participation mystique." The psyche can only be brought out—which is to say, individualized—through a process of voluntary or forced introversion on the part of the individual. To reflect on his life he must stop giving it away completely to the world. Such simple awareness poses problems for the person who is set apart from his most everyday feelings, for the first repressed feelings to come up can be overwhelmingly difficult. Gay men reeling their libidos home often find that the material gets blocked around issues relating to "father." A diary entry from Chad Mitchell shows how gay identity can necessitate a struggle with paternal history:

> I put my father's letter back in the envelope and noticed that he had misspelled my last name. We don't share the same last name. How odd, and he misspelled it. He is such an enigma, half Mussolini and half Norma Desmond. I look in the mirror and see my father's son, Buddy's boy, a Fontaine through and through. But he will never know. . . . I look in the mirror and the man I see shows no sign at all of the boy who still wonders where the truth lies. The man I see knows his childhood never will be solved. Other men will teach me what those in the past have failed to do. Nameless men have mirrored me far more than Buddy's boy, I see grown up, in the mirror when I shave.

A relationship to the "father imago"—or the place in the unconscious that contains a great many feelings and images about father—is understood as hotwired. According to Mitchell, this is because the first love relationship a gay boy has is with his father, "a wounding that leads to the process of ego-formation." Seen this way, love relationships offer a way to either redeem or recreate that primal romance which is also an old injury to the self. "Completion would not be necessary were there not a breach," says Mitchell.

gay-centered men

A community of gay-centered, psyche-based psychologists and writers interested in finding the subjective truths of hard cocks is shaping up on the West Coast. These Californians, claiming links with Harry Hay, are rooted in the origins of the American gay movement. Today, figures like Mitch Walker (author of *Men Loving Men*), Mark Thompson (*Gay Spirit, Gay Soul, Leatherfolk*), Don Kilhefner (cofounder of L.A.'s Gay and Lesbian Community Services Center), Chris Kilbourne (therapist), and Robert Hopcke (author of *Jung, Jungians and Homosexuality* and coeditor of *Same Sex Love*) speak often of gayness and homosexual libido in-and-of-itself as a source of wisdom and satisfaction. What separates this new spiritual outlook from gays going to their Jewish and Hindu temples or Christian and crystal churches is that the power of gay psyche as these thinkers see it is rooted specifically in gayness and the latent divinity said to reside there; it needn't borrow from institutions with a history of persecuting gays. While these thinkers say they aren't Jungian so much as "gay-centered," it's obvious that they borrow from the theoretical tools of analytic psychology.

Walker holds that the AIDS epidemic has accelerated the meeting with inner archetypes or complexes—that it's a pulling down into the underworld to unleash the latent powers in the unconscious that no amount of Louise Hay affirmations can wish away. The questions these thinkers ask are simple: How is it possible for people to develop real, life-sustaining empathy for their most crippled places? How can a gay man see his attraction to hunks as "symbols of illumination"? How can the ego become a partner to the unconscious? How can a person learn to take his fantasies as facts and not as annoyances or distractions from life?

These simple questions have been asked in analytic circles for over a hundred years, as well as in popular books written by heterosexuals. But depth psychology has remained out of reach to gays due to its hetero-bias and history of pathologizing homosexuality until not long ago. In addition, so much gay energy has been spent in building a community that could sustain itself against attacks that gays have put aside the spiritual question from a gay-centered perspective. But "public visibility" seems, according to Walker and Hopcke, only one-half of the coin. A seeing of the very dynamic underlying inner relations has not taken place.

As Hopcke and Walker explain it, introversion of libido entails a confrontation with what they call the "shadow," a mythological way of understanding the part in the psyche that we don't yet know. The shadow can sometimes be personified in dreams as the ego's nettling demonic twin. The failure to embrace with this "doppelgänger" can be seen in the desperate search for romantic embrace in the outside world. If a person falls in love without "owning" his shadow, soon enough quarrels and finger-pointing taint every seemingly perfect union.

It's no secret that gay life, already difficult, avoids embracing such notions. "The gay male American community," argues Leng Leroy Lim, "in its effort at reversing the pathological psychological designation of homosexuals as inherently depressed and sick, had chosen 'gay' as a politically liberative self-designation. But once the equation is made between gay = happy, then what kind of space is left for someone experiencing and working with unhappiness or existential pain." Lim says that gay people of color are often bewildered by this gay = happy "flattening" of culture. "Because the experience of racism is by definition an unhappy feeling, and since white-American culture (gay or otherwise) is set-up not to mention racism, let alone the pain, non-whites can feel doubly negated. The real problem here is America's obsession with light . . . trying to cast out shadows with light is a self-defeating game that leads to paranoia, because the shadows (of loss, mystery, rejection, sadness, imperfection, uncertainty, emotions, sex, body, ecstasy, surrender, vulnerability) are everywhere."

As strange as it sounds, inner work and new consciousness, at least the way Jungian analyst Robert Johnson defines it, seem to arise from one's inferior place, one's shadow, whatever is unknown, and not from the manageable and rational side of things. To Johnson, being offended is a sign that something has yet to be integrated. Withdrawing projections—from those one hates as well as from those one loves—is very embarrassing work.[17]

Yet it paradoxically offers the beginning of what Mark Thompson calls "the pursuit of a unique and personal path," a conscious encounter with the unconscious, an effort to follow the inner experience and become aware of the hidden regulating or directing tendency at work. This creates a slow, imperceptible process of psychic growth, which Jungian theory calls "individuation." The organizing center of this regulatory effect is called the "Self," an archetypal and altogether different center of life than the "ego." To develop what Walker calls the "ego-Self" axis when it comes to libido may be the prime joy and potential of sex, for sex and romance bring thinking and feeling together in an explosively fecund marriage of the opposites.

This depth approach to gay sex offers a way to take the gay love of men to a new personal level as it rescues the symbolic from the semiotic. It offers a way for a gay man to honor his feelings for a lover—or a sex object—in such a way that each encounter creates consciousness, creates an ever-deepening meaningfulness around the riches of symbolic life, even if the encounter hurts.

Heterosexual depth psychologists speak of an erotic "inner figure" who arises in dreams and fantasies after the initial shadow work is done. They refer to this as the "soul figure," meaning the source of life and inspiration. They call it the "Anima" for a man and the "Animus" for a woman. These figures are experienced as initially poisonous, but if one approaches them without prejudice and completely naïvely they can turn into guides and mediators to a world within.

While traditional depth psychologists suggest that gay men, when they are in love, simply experience the anima in male disguise, Walker has, through an obvious look at gay male life, put forward a far more phallic and satisfying symbol: the masculine double as the child of symbolic father-son incest. Whether it's Mr. Benson or Yukio Mishima or Marky Mark, the man provoking the crush is no mere man but also a screen for the projection of soul, with all the weight and potential that loaded word implies. We are throwing onto our lovers the best and worst part of the Self when we fall for them. Romantic love is nothing but a projection, but a fabulous one. To become more and more aware of this psychic phenomenon is not to stymie love, but rather to become a more artful player in the steamy cycles of projection and recollection, falling in love as well as owning that feeling as one's own and seeing how that could take one into new dimensions of being.

While only time will tell if these West Coast gay-centered thinkers will reach a larger audience, their main point can't easily be overlooked: Gay men have so far put the majority of their energies behind projection and extroversion. But if the laws of nature and physics apply as well to the laws of the psyche, chances are a little swinging back to the opposite pole could bring new energies to the sexual question. "The liberation movement that has been carrying gay people collectively forward through the last half of the twentieth century is about to run out of gas," cautions Mark Thompson. "What is needed to refuel our progress is not more spirit but a deeper understanding of soul."

Introversion does not suggest celibacy or enforced loneliness. It does suggest that at least as much energy is given to the subjective valuing of an experience as to the hunting for that experience itself. But for those who hate owning feelings, pursuing Mr. Right may remain the foremost goal.

All the same, gay men seem to resist inertia. Just as a person can be said to have a sexual instinct, observation shows that there is also an instinct to individuate. While everyone has a definition of what individuation is, few would disagree that the development of personality is an important goal, or that sex lies at the heart of it, in part because sex won't be banished, and will punish any efforts that seek its banishment.

"The history of trying to stop any pleasurable behavior is abysmal," said Michael Callen just before he died. "Look at Prohibition, gambling, dance halls. You cannot stamp out pleasure with a jackboot, so the second best alternative is using what you know about yourself and your society."

There simply is no question that gay people have an enormous role to play in transforming libido. "I feel that homosexuals," writes Edmund White, "now identified as the element of our society most obsessed with sex, will in fact, be the agents to cure the mania. Sex will be restored to its appropriate place as pleasure, communication, an appetite, an art; it will no longer pose as a religion, a reason for being. In our present isolation we have few ways besides sex to feel connected to one another; in the future there might be surer modes for achieving a sense of community."[18]

For all the men who have given their lives in the struggle to figure out what it means to be a gay man in modern times, we are still in the earliest stages of consciousness—a fact that both humbles and emboldens. "When we look back on this time," explains Greg Scott, "we will be judged on how valiantly we tried to prevail against forces that extend beyond our conscious control. I'd like to see us return to the full intimacy of sex but that means learning how to talk to each other well enough that condoms don't become a crutch for poor communication of feelings, fears and needs. Some young gay men seem to be one step ahead—courting each other, treating male-to-male love as a gift. I think this is part of a process of creating a new culture. We are evolving still. The amount of self-examination that is required of all of us at a time of so much pain is mind-boggling."

Self-examination? For too long, moralists have equated wisdom with the renunciation of hot sex. What a scam. The odyssey of gay life over five decades proves at least this much: that a magical thread links one's third eye with one's cock. Yes, a man must go out of himself to find the stud he dreams of: *Whenever I'd touch Chris, I felt safe, at home: he showed me how two bodies could become one.* And yes, often the search throws the person back into his own unfathomable depths: *When I think of the men I loved, I feel terribly lonely and yet oddly at peace.* Whatever the dangers in sex, gay men's innate drive to make love to other men (one or many) corrects, redeems, and intervenes on a world gone mad with man-to-man violence. There may be a greater intelligence in Eros than we can grasp—for now. Desire seizes that man whose soul has been brushed by another man's kiss and, holding him by the collar says: This is your existence—and it is natural, it is positive, it is good, and it is spinning a new way to be. Developing greater and greater mindfulness about this powerful inner call seems likely to become the emergent gay myth for the future.

notes

introduction: foreplay

1. See Gayle Rubin, "Thinking Sex: Notes for a Radical Theory of the Politics of Sexuality," in *Pleasure and Danger: Exploring Female Sexuality*, ed. Carole S. Vance (Boston: Routledge & Kegan Paul, 1984), p. 275. "A radical theory of sex must identify, describe, explain and denounce erotic injustice and sexual oppression. Such a theory needs refined conceptual tools which can grasp the subject and hold it in view. It must build rich descriptions of sexuality as it exists in society and history. *It requires a convincing critical language that can convey the barbarity of sexual persecution*" (emphasis mine). No serious study of sex or sexuality is complete without this book, which originated at a feminist conference at Barnard College in 1982 called, "Towards a Politics of Sexuality." See also Pat Califia, *Public Sex: The Culture of Radical Sex* (San Francisco: Cleis Press, 1994).

2. For statistics on the rate of infection in the gay male community, see Edward King, *Safety in Numbers: Safer Sex and Gay Men* (New York: Routledge, 1994).

3. See Jeffrey Weeks, *Sexuality* (London: Tavistock Publications, 1986), p. 11. "The strong emotions [sex] undoubtedly arouses gives to the world of sexuality a seismic sensitivity making it a transmission belt for a wide variety of needs and desires: for love and anger, tenderness and aggression, intimacy and adventure, romance and predatoriness, pleasure and pain, empathy and power. *We experience sex very subjectively*" (emphasis mine).

4. See Plato, *The Symposium*, trans. Walter Hamilton (New York: Penguin Books, 1951), p. 78. "So after all Love lacks and does not possess beauty?"

5. Henri Corbin, *Creative Imagination in the Sufism of Ibn 'Arabi*, trans. Ralph Manheim (Princeton, New Jersey: Bollingen Series XCI, 1969), p. 279. Ibn 'Arabi (1165–1240) was one of the great mystics of all time. Not only did he make a unique contribution to Shiite Sufism, but throughout his life he recognized what can only be called homosexual Eros as a key path toward wisdom and gnosis. In the walk around the Mystic Kaaba he encounters the mysterious being whom he recognizes as his eternal companion: an "Evanescent Youth, the Silent Speaker, him who is neither living nor dead, the composite-simple, the enveloped-enveloping."

6. John Preston, *My Life as a Pornographer* (New York: Masquerade Books, 1993), pp. 62–63.

7. Gabriel Rotello, "Watch Your Mouth," *Out Magazine*, June 1994, 153. "At any rate, the fact that HIV has been detected in 52 percent of pre-come samples, compared with only 30 percent of semen samples and 20 percent of cervical/vaginal samples, indicates that if oral sex is safe, it is probably no thanks to pre-come."

8. See Ian Young, *The Stonewall Experiment: A Gay Psychohistory* (London: Cassell, 1995), p. 53. Young refers to the psychotherapist Paul Rosenfels's warning to gays that compulsive promiscuity and compulsive repression were not opposites but effects of the same oppressive cause.

9. For a provocative early discussion of the role of AIDS in gay spiritual and psychological life see "A Group Interview—Gay Soul Making: Coming Out Inside," in *Gay Spirit: Myth and Meaning*, ed. Mark Thompson (New York: St. Martin's Press, 1987), p. 241. Thompson talks about AIDS as a wake up call: "I think the horror of AIDS has served as a trigger for a lot of gay men, signaling that something is obviously not right in their own society but also on the planet as well. . . . For many people, AIDS hastened the awareness that perhaps gay culture—as popularly defined in the 1970s—was headed for some kind of awful distress. I'm not being moralistic here, either. It's just that during the 1970s, when most of us were coming out . . . we were somehow being artificially contained—like being put on a reservation. And, as I've heard it expressed, we were given 'the booze and the pox.'"

10. See Camille Paglia, *Sexual Personae* (New York: Vintage, 1991), pp. 88–89. "The Apollonian Olympians . . . are eye-gods. Dionysus represents obliteration of the western eye. Heir to the Great Mother of chthonian nature, he is, with Osiris, the greatest of the dying gods of mystery religion. Out of his worship came two rituals of enormous impact on western culture, tragic drama and Christian liturgy."

11. This focus on the symbol is an intervention on the single-mindedness with which contemporary cultural theory focuses on the materiality of the "sign." (See Julia Kristeva, *Desire in Language: A Semiotic Approach to Literature and Art* [New York: Columbia University Press, 1980], p. 39, for a cogent discussion of how the symbol was weakened by the sign from the thirteenth to fifteenth century.)

12. See C. G. Jung, *Freud and Psychoanalysis*, trans. R. F. C. Hull, *Collected Works*, vol. 4 (Princeton, N.J.: Bollingen Series/Princeton, 1989), p. 291, for the distinction between Freud's emphasis on reading the symbol semiotically, as a sign or token of certain primitive psychosexual processes, as opposed to Jung's way of "amplifying" the symbol to get at its unconscious meanings. For Jung, "the symbol is not merely a sign of something repressed and concealed, but is at the same time an attempt to comprehend and to point the way to the further psychological development of the individual." See Judith Butler, *Bodies that Matter: On the Discursive Limits of Sex* (London: Routledge, 1993), p. 10, for the academy's "materialist" arrogance: "To claim that discourse is formative is not to claim that it originates, causes, or exhaustively composes that which it concedes; rather, it is to claim that there is no reference to a pure body which is not at the same time a further formation of that body." Of course, the minute one writes down a dream, one changes its representation from "pure" to "written" form. But so what? One could argue that the symbolic *feeling* one has in working with the dream is *pure*, is *essential*, is *experiential*. The nightmare gets the heart beating, it incarnates a certain truth. Butler argues things on the level of "concepts" but what if one brings feeling to bear on thinking? What if the imaginal world, the world of psyche, is more real than the world of discourse? What if the unconscious originates, causes, and composes?

13. Depth psychology postulates an autonomous world of the living psyche, of which the ego is merely the handmaiden. See Robert Johnson, *Inner Work* (San Francisco: Harper & Row, 1986).

14. I have found it useful to compare Freud's use of the term *libido* with that of Jung's. Freud defines *libido* as a "quantitative variable force which could serve as a measure of processes and transformations occurring in the field of sexual excitation." He adds that libidinal sexual energies are "*distinguished from the nutritive processes by a special chemistry.*" Sigmund Freud, *Three Essays on the Theory of Sexuality*, trans. James Strachey (New York: Basic Books, 1975), p. 83 (emphasis mine). Jung, on the other hand, sees libido as informing all life—eating, lovemaking, thinking. It's simply where one puts one's attention: "Libido is intended simply as a name for the energy which manifests itself in the life-process and is perceived subjectively as conation and desire. . . . It brings us into line with a powerful current of ideas that seeks to comprehend the world of appearances energetically. Suffice it to say that everything we perceive can only be understood as an effect of force." Jung, *Freud and Psychoanalysis*, p. 125.

15. The emphasis here is on withdrawing some of the bias from the sphere of the external world so as to begin to value the reality of feelings and values that exist in each gay man's *subjective* experience of his

life. This, in other words, is another kind of science: one can only know something because one knows it at the bottom of one's heart.

16. See Friedrich Nietzsche, *The Birth of Tragedy*, trans. Francis Golffing (New York: Anchor Books, 1956), pp. 22, 65. Although Nietzsche would at the end of his life embrace Dionysus, he now calls Apollo the "marvellous divine image of the *principium individuationis*."

17. Mitch Walker, "Jung and Homophobia" (Putnam, Conn.: *Spring*, 51, 1991, p. 57). Jung wrote little on homosexuality, but various schools of gay Jungians have developed in recent years. Robert Hopcke, in San Francisco, is perhaps the best known — in particular for his exhaustive review of Jung's writings on homosexuality. (See Robert H. Hopcke, *Jung, Jungians & Homosexuality* [Boston: Shambhala, 1989].) Also see *Same-Sex Love: And the Path of Wholeness*, ed. by Robert H. Hopcke, Karin Lofthus Carrington & Scott Wirth (Boston: Shambhala, 1993). The L.A. school, with ties to Harry Hay, branches off from Jung and puts more of the focus on "gay-centeredness." Psychologist Mitch Walker has laid the intellectual groundwork for this process of gay-centered inner work. He has identified the central gay archetype (the Masculine Double) and has labeled the basic gay psychodynamic as "the Uranian Complex" (the boy, born gay, wishes incest not with his mother, but his father). Also see Walker, "The Double: An Archetypal Configuration," London, England, *Harvest: Journal for Jungian Studies*, 1976, pp. 165–175; Walker, *Men Loving Men: A Gay Sex Guide and Consciousness Book* (San Francisco: Gay Sunshine Press, 1987); Walker, *Visionary Love: A Spirit Book of Gay Mythology* (San Francisco: Treeroots Press, 1980). Also see Walker's interview in Mark Thompson's *Gay Soul* (San Francisco: Harper San Francisco, 1994), pp. 248–263. For the more Freudian-psychoanalytic approach, see Richard A. Isay's groundbreaking *Being Homosexual: Gay Men and Their Development* (New York: Farrar, Straus, Giroux, 1989). For the most recent contribution from the field of self psychology, see Carlton Cornett, *Reclaiming the Authentic Self: Dynamic Psychotherapy with Gay Men* (Northvale, NJ: Jason Aronson, 1995).

18. Jung believed that there were many more instincts than Freud's Eros and Thanatos. He called these archetypes. Archetypes are not inherited ideas; nor are they common images. They are rather "molds" into which personal experiences are, as it were, "poured," and, as such, are distinct from symbols. These archetypes are said to function autonomously, almost as forces of nature. See also Jung, "Instinct and the Unconscious," *Collected Works*, pp. 129–38; Thomas Moore, *Care of the Soul* (New York: Harper Collins, 1992).

19. See Joseph Campbell, *The Hero with a Thousand Faces* (Princeton, N.J.: Bollingen Series XVII, 1968), p. 3. "It would not be too much to say that myth is the secret opening through which the inexhaustible energies of the cosmos pour into human cultural manifestation."

20. In addition to the papers generously donated to my by hundreds of gay male students over the last five years, as well as the sexual library and stash of personal papers left to me by Michael Callen, I must point to the following texts as primary sources without which I could not have written this book. They are as follows: Frances FitzGerald, *Cities on a Hill* (New York: Simon & Schuster, 1986); George Chauncey, *Gay New York: Gender, Urban Culture and the Making of the Gay Male World, 1890–1940* (New York: Basic Books, 1994); John D'Emilio, *Sexual Politics, Sexual Communities: The Making of a Homosexual Minority in the United States, 1940–1970* (Chicago: University of Chicago Press, 1983); Alan Bérubé, *Coming Out Under Fire: The History of Gay Men and Women in World War Two* (New York: Free Press, 1990); John D'Emilio and Estelle B. Freedman, *Intimate Matters: A History of Sexuality in America* (New York: Harper & Row, 1988); Martin Baum Duberman, Martha Vicinus, and George Chauncey, Jr., eds., *Hidden From History: Reclaiming the Gay & Lesbian Past* (New York: New American Library, 1989).

21. "The Advocate Sex Survey," *The Advocate*, August 23, 1994; Edward Laumann, Robert Michael, Stuart Michael, John Gagnon, *The Social Organization of Sexuality* (Chicago: University of Chicago Press, 1994); Gina Kolata, *Sex in America: A Definitive Survey* (New York: Little Brown, 1994).

22. "Now for the Truth about Americans and Sex: The First Comprehensive Survey Since Kinsey Smashes Some of Our Most Intimate Myths," *Time*, October 17, 1994, 68.

23. Ibid., p. 66.

24. Alfred C. Kinsey et al., *Sexual Behavior in the Human Female* (Philadelphia: W. B. Saunders Company, 1953), p. 477.

25. D'Emilio and Freedman, *Intimate Matters*, p. 286.

26. Martin S. Weinberg and Colin J. W. Williams, *Male Homosexuals: Their Problems and Adaptations* (New York: Oxford University Press, 1974); William H. Masters and Virginia E. Johnson, *Homosexuality*

in Perspective (Boston: Little, Brown and Company, 1979); Karla Jay and Allen Young, *The Gay Report: Lesbians and Gay Men Speak Out About Sexual Experiences and Lifestyles* (New York: Summit Books, 1977); Lawrence D. Mass, *Dialogues of the Sexual Revolution*, 2 vols. (New York: Harrington Park Press, 1990); also see *Gay Relationships*, ed. John D. De Cecco (New York: Harrington Park Press, 1988).

27. See Helen E. Fisher, *Anatomy of Love: The Natural History of Monogamy, Adultery, and Divorce* (New York: W. W. Norton and Company, 1992).

28. Richard Fung, "The Trouble with Asians," in Monica Dorenkamp and Richard Henke, eds., *Negotiating Lesbian and Gay Subjects* (New York: Routledge, 1995), p. 129.

29. Luis Alfaro, "The Land West of La Brea," *Frontiers*, October 20, 1995, 66.

30. Alfaro, "La Brea," 67.

chapter one: what did you do in the war, daddy?

1. Donald Webster Cory, *The Homosexual in America* (New York: Greenberg, 1951), pp. 44–45, 278–79; see also William C. Menniger, *Psychiatry in a Troubled World* (New York: Macmillan, 1948), pp. 221–31; *Newsweek*, June 9, 1947, 54.

2. Keith Vacha, *Quiet Fire: Memoirs of Older Gay Men*, ed. Cassie Damewood (New York: Crossing Press, 1985), p. 25.

3. Vacha, *Quiet Fire*, p. 26.

4. D'Emilio, *Sexual Politics*, pp. 26–28.

5. Gore Vidal, *Palimpsest* (New York: Random House, 1995), p. 101.

6. Bérubé, *Coming Out*, p. 40.

7. Alan Bérubé, "Marching to a Different Drummer: Lesbian and Gay GIs in World War II," in Duberman et al., eds., *Hidden From History*, p. 384.

8. John Nichols, "The Way It Was: Gay Life In World War II America," *QQ Magazine*, July/August 1975.

9. Ibid.

10. Vacha, *Quiet Fire*, p. 48.

11. Bérubé, *Coming Out*, p. 37; Vacha, *Quiet Fire*, p. 171.

12. Vidal, *Palimpset*, p. 101; Vacha, *Quiet Fire*, p. 49.

13. Bérubé, *Coming Out*, p. 198.

14. Ibid., p. 197.

15. Robert Peters, *For You, Lili Marlene: A Memoir of World War II* (Madison, Wis.: The University of Wisconsin Press, 1995), pp. 38, 82.

16. Vidal, *Palimpsest*, pp. 101–2; Mitch Walker, "The Double: An Archetypal Configuration," *Harvest*, 1976, p. 169.

17. Peters, *For You, Lili Marlene*, p. 87.

18. For a particularly good example of such World War II nostalgia in gay porn fiction writing, see John W. Rowberry's "Coastal Cocksucker," in *Flesh and the Word 2: An Anthology of Erotic Writing*, ed. John Preston (New York: Plume, 1993), pp. 124–26. Also see Andrew Holleran, "Sleeping Soldiers" in *The Violet Quill Reader: The Emergence of Gay Writing After Stonewall*, ed. David Bergman (St. Martin's Press, 1994) pp. 142–51.

19. Vacha, *Quiet Fire*, pp. 48–49.

20. Bérubé, *Coming Out*, pp. 41–42.

21. Vacha, *Quiet Fire*, p. 59.

22. *Walt Whitman's Civil War*, ed. Walter Lowenfels (New York: Plenum Publishing, 1960), pp. 111–12.

23. Jim Kepner, private papers.

24. Randy Shilts, *Conduct Unbecoming: Gays and Lesbians in the U.S. Military* (New York: St. Martins Press, 1993), pp. 4–6.

25. Chauncey, *Gay New York*, pp. 207–11; Eric Garber, "A Spectacle in Color: The Lesbian and Gay Subculture of Jazz Age Harlem," in *Hidden from History*, Duberman et al., eds., p. 318.

26. As quoted in Chauncey, *Gay New York*, pp. 182–84.

27. As quoted in D'Emilio and Freedman, *Intimate Matters*, pp. 223–24. Also see Jonathan Ned Katz, *Gay/Lesbian Almanac: A New Documentary* (New York: Harper & Row, 1983), p. 312.

28. Paul Robinson, *The Modernization of Sex* (New York: Harper & Row, 1970), pp. 8, 31.

29. D'Emilio and Freedman, *Intimate Matters*, pp. 223, 241.

30. Chauncey, *Gay New York*, pp. 166–77.

31. Donald Vining, *A Gay Diary*, 4 vols. (New York: Pepys Press, 1979–1983), vol. 1, pp. 231–34 (entries for September 12, 14, 17, 18, 23, 1942). Also see *Jeb and Dash: A Diary of Gay Life 1918–1945*, ed. Ina Russell (Winchester, Mass.: Faber and Faber Inc., 1994).

32. Chauncey, *Gay New York*, p. 136; Shilts, *Conduct Unbecoming*, pp. 16–17; Bérubé, *Coming Out*, p. 19.

33. Menninger, *Psychiatry in a Troubled World*, p. 231. "Homosexuals," wrote psychiatrist William Menninger (a relatively sympathetic voice during the war), "have immature personalities which make them and their lives and some of their personal relations grossly pathological. Like any sick person, they deserve understanding instead of condemnation." Bérubé, *Coming Out*, p. 148. (A 1942 article in *Time* magazine showed that a new question, "How do you get along with girls?" was asked during the induction physical.)

34. Bérubé, *Coming Out*, p. 147.

35. Peter M. Nardi, David Sanders, and Judd Marmor, ed., *Growing Up Before Stonewall: Life Stories of Some Gay Men* (London: Routledge, 1994), pp. 151–152.

36. To discharge homosexuals, officials needed ways to identify these men, to distinguish them from others, and to fit them into useful administrative categories. Mounting a bureaucratic apparatus in 1941, the Army moved from a penal to a discharge system based on psychiatric principles, thus transforming homosexuality from a crime of behavior to a pathology.

37. Bérubé, *Coming Out*, p. 148.

38. D'Emilio, *Sexual Politics*, p. 76.

39. *Edward Carpenter: Selected Writings, Vol. 1: Sex*, with an introduction by Noel Greig (London: Gay Modern Classics, 1984), p. 73.

40. Carpenter, *Selected Writings*, vol. 1, p. 75.

41. Chauncey, *Gay New York*, pp. 13, 97.

42. John Lauritsen and David Thorstad, *The Early Homosexual Rights Movement 1864–1935* (New York: Times Change Press, 1974), p. 6.

43. As quoted in Thompson, *Gay Spirit*, p. 153.

44. Carpenter, *Selected Writings*, vol. 1, p. 75.

45. Young, *Stonewall Experiment*, p. 34. Also see Michael Bronski, *Culture Clash: The Making of Gay Sensibility* (Boston: South End Press, 1984), pp. 22–28.

46. Bérubé, *Coming Out*, p. 82.

47. Bérubé, *Coming Out*, p. 92. See also Richard Fawkes, *Fighting for a Laugh: Entertaining the British and American Arms Forces 1939–1946* (London: Macdonald and Jane's, 1978), pp. 112–22.

48. Bérubé, *Coming Out*, p. 92; *New York Times*, October 29, 1943, p. 4.

49. Walter Lowenfels, ed., *Walt Whitman's Civil War* (New York: Da Capo Press, 1989), p. 115. Also see Eugene Monick, *Phallos: Sacred Image of the Masculine* (Toronto, Canada: Inner City Books, 1987), p. 22, for a discussion of "the autonomy of *phallos*."

50. See Hubert Kennedy, *Ulrichs: The Life and Works of Karl Heinrich Ulrichs, Pioneer of the Modern Gay Movement* (New York: Alyson Publications, Inc., 1988), p. 10.

51. Kennedy, *Ulrichs*, p. 57.

52. Ibid., p. 86.

53. While it is fashionable today in gay academic circles to reject Ulrich's views along with any hint that homosexuality is inborn, a person with a little common sense has but to look, on one hand, at gay male pornography (where even the bottoms err on the side of being "straight-acting"—i.e., Joey Stefano) and, on the other, at gay male popular culture (*Priscilla, Queen of the Desert*; Lypsinka; Wigstock) to see these two poles actively at work in our own day and age. Sometimes they are at work in the same person, to one degree or another, as he learns how to express himself sexually.

chapter two: toward democracy

1. An old New York associate, in his seventies, told me this story. He did not feel comfortable allowing me to use his name; neither did he like a pseudonym. These men represent the oldest living generation of gay men. Their reticence is a measure of the shame with which they lived. Part of their discretion comes from the sociology of the time, where the separation between private life and public life was much greater than it was after the revolutions of the '60s.

2. See Robinson, *The Modernization of Sex*, p. 51. Kinsey became a household world with his scientific approach to homosexuality, which argued that homosexuality was neither a clinical syndrome nor a sexual identity.

3. D'Emilio, *Sexual Politics*, p. 205.

4. Cory, *Homosexual in America*, p. 119.

5. Cory, *Homosexual in America*, pp. 25–39. Latter-day militants took issue with Cory's moral inquiry into the sexual appetite, not to mention Cory's use of a pseudonym. While *The Homosexual in America* marked the first time a gay man wrote to gay men, his pioneering work did not provide enough reason to forgive Cory for being as much a victim to the oppressive times as anyone else. In this way, gay activists of the '70s, in their rejection of homophile decorum, rendered the previous generation's work to the oblivion of history. Also see Cory, p. 114. Here Cory points out the unspoken truth of the '50s: "No group has so little recognition and acceptance, is so apparent in its lack of organization, yet exercises so strong an influence and contains so many people who have gained wide public acceptance as individuals."

6. See Laud Humphreys, *Tearoom Trade: Impersonal Sex in Public Places* (Chicago: Aldine Publishing Company, 1970), pp. 14, 44, 47–54 for one of the best sociologies of bathroom sex ever written. Humphreys writes that tearoom sex evolves into an elaborate game where signaling, contract-making, risk-taking, and payoff took place: "Tearoom action is not unlike a great many other gaming encounters. The tactics employed are all aimed at (1) Maximizing rewards and (2) minimizing risks (and other costs such as fatigue)." The following rules preserve anonymity: "1. Avoid the exchange of biographical data; 2. Watch out for chicken [teenagers]—they're dangerous game. 3. Never force your intentions on anyone. 4. Don't knock a trick—he may be somebody's mother [homosexual mentor]. 5. Never back down on trade agreements. ["Trade" are "tricks" who do not, as yet, consider themselves homosexual. This group includes most of the male prostitutes, "hustlers." Trade agreements, then, include paying the amount promised, if a financial transaction is involved, and no kissing above the belt, because most "trade" think kissing is "queer."]"

7. See NYMS *Newsletter*, November 1961, 4–5; D'Emilio, *Sexual Politics*, p. 163. See also Cory, *Homosexual in America*, p. 40; as Cory put it, "Who would dare to question the fact that homosexuals were unworthy of employment by this great government?"

8. Vining, *Gay Diary*, p. 209.

9. Ibid., pp. 123–24.

10. Ibid., pp. 283–84.

11. Ibid.

12. John Kelsey, "The Cleveland Bar Scene in the Forties," in *Lavender Culture*, ed. Karla Jay and Allen Young (New York: Harcourt Brace Jovanovich, 1979), pp. 146–49.

13. Ibid.

14. Cory, *Homosexual in America*, p. 115.

15. James Baldwin, *Giovanni's Room* (New York: Signet Books, 1959), p. 121.

16. Cory, *Homosexual in America*, p. 118. Erich Neumann, *The Origins and History of Consciousness* (Princeton, N.J.: Bollingen Series, 1954), pp. 103–4. Neumann refers to dozens of myths which contain mention of the separation of the World Parents as part of the evolution to consciousness. This is understood as the splitting off of opposites from a preconscious unity. This separates heaven from earth, inside from outside, and most unpleasant of all, light from darkness. His point is well taken: While we must value light as what brings us consciousness—for that is how the ego is developed—what lies outside of the ego in the realm of darkness must not always remain repudiated.

17. Cory, *Homosexual in America*, pp. 116–18.

18. The idea of an inner father, a personification of the self, was lacking in this stage of development. Such an inner sensibility might have been able to intervene when the gay ego felt engulfed by its shadow

inferiority, might have helped the ego to say, "Ah, ha! There is that shredding feeling once again. So let's personify that feeling and work with Him and see what's behind His nastiness so that He does not destroy this lovely sex experience again." The notion that the ego mediates between opposing feelings, much in the way King Arthur mediated between the Knights of the Round Table, is a rather new definition of the ego's role in psychic life. Oppression often cripples the poor ego. Or most people want to see their egos as the dominators inside, at the center of the universe in their life, not as a cork bobbing on a sea of feelings.

19. Evelyn Hooker, "Male Homosexuals and Their 'Worlds,'" in Judd Marmor, ed., *Sexual Inversion* (New York: Basic Books, 1965), p. 97.

20. Humphreys, *Tearoom Trade*, p. 14.

21. D'Emilio and Freedman, *Intimate Matters*, p. 293; see also Neil Miller, *Out of the Past: Gay and Lesbian History from 1869 to the Present* (New York: Vintage Books, 1995), pp. 258–75 for another account of the McCarthy years.

22. 81st Congress Senate Document, 2d Sess., No. 241: "Employment of Homosexuals and Other Sex Perverts in Government," in Martin Duberman, *About Time: Exploring the Gay Past* (New York: Meridian, 1991), p. 183.

23. Adam, *The Rise of a Gay and Lesbian Movement* (Boston: Twayne Publishers, 1987), p. 74; Miller, *Out of the Past*, p. 259; Young, *Stonewall Experiment*, p. 52; D'Emilio and Freedman, *Intimate Matters*, p. 292; D'Emilio, *Sexual Politics*, pp. 41, 77.

24. D'Emilio and Freedman, *Intimate Matters*, p. 271. Also see Daniel Scott Smith, "The Dating of the American Sexual Revolution: Evidence and Interpretation," in Michael Gordon, ed., *The American Family in Social-Historical Perspective* (New York: St. Martin's Press, 1972), pp. 321–41.

25. D'Emilio tells the story of a man called B. D. H., who had been kicked out from the University of Illinois for making a pass at a man. FBI investigators informed the supervisors and coworkers of B. D. H.'s homosexuality for twenty years and in the early 1960s FBI agents tracked him down in his home to get him to divulge names of gay friends and tricks. See D'Emilio, *Sexual Politics*, p. 47.

26. Cory, *Homosexual in America*, p. 12.

27. Stuart Timmons, *The Trouble with Harry Hay* (Boston: Alyson Publications, 1990), pp. 136–37.

28. Ibid.

29. None of Hay's friends or associates cared to risk their lives and reputations to meet informally to discuss anything associated with gay sex. It would be two years before Hay found another person who saw things his way. With fashion designer Rudi Gernreich, the "society of two" created what would become known as the Mattachine Society.

30. Bronski, *Culture Clash*, p. 79.

31. Bronski, *Culture Clash*, p. 75.

32. For point of information, see Charles Michael Smith, "Bruce Nugent: Bohemenian of the Harlem Renaissance," in *In The Life*, ed., Joseph Beam (Boston: Alyson Publications, 1986), pp. 209–20. Richard Bruce Nugent, one of the longest-living figures involved in the Harlem Renaissance, was born in 1906 in Washington, D.C., and was one of the first black writers to deal explicitly with homosexuality.

33. Ira L. Jeffries, *NYQ*, February 23, 1992.

34. Judy Grahn, *Another Mother Tongue* (Boston: Beacon Press, 1984), pp. 51–72.

35. Katz, *Gay American History*, p. 288.

36. Ibid.

37. Ibid., p. 285.

38. Grahn, *Another Mother Tongue*, p. 58.

39. D'Emilio and Freedman, *Intimate Matters*, p. 7.

40. Katz, *Gay American History*, pp. 301–302.

41. "The Story Behind Physique Photography," *Drum*, October 1965, 14.

42. See Tom Waugh, "A Heritage of Pornography," *Body Politic*, January–February, 1983 for a review of the gay film collection of the Kinsey Institute.

43. F. Valentine Hooven, III, *Beefcake: The Muscle Magazines of America, 1950–1970* (Germany: Benedikt Taschen, 1995), p. 22.

44. *Drum*, p. 9.

45. Ibid., p. 10.

46. Hooven, *Beefcake*, pp. 50–74.
47. Ibid.
48. Kenneth R. Dutlon, *The Perfectible Body* (New York: Continuum, 1995), p. 136.
49. Duberman, *Cures* (New York: Plume, 1992), pp. 83–84.
50. Ibid., pp. 84–86.
51. Ibid., p. 87.
52. Ibid.
53. Ibid., p. 91.
54. Ibid., p. 14
55. Ibid., pp. 15–16.
56. Barry Miles, *Ginsberg: A Biography* (New York: Harper Perennial, 1989), p. 95.
57. The following description comes from Miles, *Ginsberg*, pp. 98–105.
58. Timmons, *Harry Hay*, p. 164.
59. Ibid.
60. D'Emilio, *Sexual Politics*, p. 71.
61. Ibid., p. 77.
62. Bob Bishop, "Discard the Mask," *Mattachine Review* (April 1958): 15; D'Emilio, *Sexual Politics*, p. 113.
63. Eric Marcus, *Making History: The Struggle for Gay and Lesbian Equal Rights, An Oral History* (New York: Harper Collins, 1992), pp. 34–36.
64. Marcus, *Making History*, p. 24.
65. Hooven, *Beefcake*, p. 122. "A book cannot be proscribed unless it is found to be *utterly* without redeeming social value," wrote Justice Brennan in 1966, hinting that almost anything could boast social value. By 1965, the total monthly sales of physique magazines reached 750,000. Hundreds of pulp novels were published (such as Richard Armory's *Song of the Loon*, which described a world of gay fur trappers and Indian braves) as well as more literary works with homosexual themes: Jean Genet's *Our Lady of the Flowers*, Hubert Selby's *Last Exit to Brooklyn*, William Burroughs's *Naked Lunch*, and John Rechy's *City of Night*. D'Emilio, *Sexual Politics*, p. 133.
66. D'Emilio, *Sexual Politics*, p. 153.
67. SIR's rhetoric foreshadowed the gay militancy of Stonewall: "We find ourselves scorned, our rights as persons and citizens before the law imperiled, our individuality suppressed by a hostile social order, and our spirit forced to accept a guilt unwarranted by the circumstances of our existence." See *Vector*, December 1965, 2; D'Emilio, p. 190.
68. *San Francisco Chronicle*, January 3, 1965; D'Emilio, p. 193.

chapter three: *so, you say you want a revolution?*

1. Jordi Consentino, private journals.
2. Edmund White, "A Letter to Ann and Alfred Corn," July 8, 1969, in Bergman, ed., *Violet Quill*, p. 2.
3. Martin Duberman, *Stonewall* (New York: Dutton, 1993), p. xv.
4. See Donn Teal, *The Gay Militants* (New York: Stein and Day, 1971), for a comprehensive history of the first two years of gay liberation as well as the sociology of the Stonewall Inn. Teal's book has just been reprinted by St. Martin's Press and is crucial for anyone wishing an understanding of the vibrant politics of early gay lib; p. 17.
5. Lucian Truscott IV, *Village Voice*, July 3, 1969.
6. Ibid.
7. Dennis Altman, *Homosexual: Oppression and Liberation* (New York: Avon, 1971), p. 122; Teal, *Gay Militants*, p. 20; also see Felice Picano, *Men Who Loved Me* (New York: Masquerade Books, 1994), p. 412.
8. Teal, *Gay Militants*, p. 23. See also Edward Sagarin, "Behind the Gay Liberation Front," *The Realist*, May–June 1970, 18: "Protests blossom forth when the oppressed social conditions are slightly ameliorated," writes Sagarin, "when they seem to be on the road to improvement, offering hope and promise for change, but creating frustration in those impatient for change and still suffering under less than tolerable conditions."

9. Kay Tobin and Randy Wicker, *The Gay Crusaders: In Depth Interviews with 15 Homosexuals—Men and Women Who are Shaping America's Newest Sexual Revolution* (New York: Paperback Library, 1972). See especially the chapter on Frank Kameny, pp. 89–134.

10. For a key barometer of the explosion of creative libido during the first three years of gay lib see Carl Wittman, "Refugees from Amerika," in *The Homosexual Dialectic*, ed. Joseph McCaffrey (Englewood Cliffs, N.J.: Prentice-Hall, 1972), p. 158.

11. Steve Dansky, "Hey Man," *Come Out!* June–July 1970; John Francis Hunter, "The Rise of the New Conscience: Gay Pride on Parade," *Gay*, June 29, 1970; Ralph Hall, "Gay Liberation Front," *Gay Power* 5; John Francis Hunter, *The Gay Insider/USA* (New York: Stonehill Publishing Company, 1972), pp. 109–13.

12. "How Sweet (and Sticky) It Was," by Michael Bronski, in Preston, ed., *Flesh and Word* 2, p. 74.

13. Bronski, "Sweet," pp. 76–77.

14. Ron Hardcastle, private journals. Hardcastle has compiled hundred of pages of good writing on his sexual escapades over the last three decades that are of immense value to anyone interested in gay sexual history, especially on the West Coast. He is the Donald Vining of contemporary gay sex.

15. For a sense of the innocence and good feeling of the time, and for a comprehensive opera of voices and impressions and sociology, see Hunter, *The Gay Insider/USA*. Also see back issues of *QQ*, the magazine that put the sex back in homosexual, in particular "Editorial: Plastic Fig-Leaves," *QQ*, January/February 1974, 5. Also see *The Long Road to Freedom: The Advocate History of the Gay and Lesbian Movement*, ed. Mark Thompson (New York: St. Martin's Press, 1994), pp. 17–83 for a superb time line of the early years of gay liberation and the attending sexual revolution. For early sociology on the "crisis of aging" see William Simon and John H. Gagnon, "Homosexuality: The Formulation of a Sociological Perspective," *Journal of Health and Social Behavior* 8: 3 (September 1967): 180–83. Also see Laud Humphreys, *Out of the Closets: The Sociology of Homosexual Liberation* (New Jersey: Prentice-Hall, 1972), pp. 115–20 for a good discussion of aging gays.

16. Craig Rodwell, "Sex: How Important Is It?" *QQ*, May/June 1973, 54.

17. Steven Solberg, private journals.

18. David Wojnarowicz, *Close to the Knives: A Memoir of Disintegration* (New York: Vintage Books, 1991), p. 18.

19. Bronski, "How Sweet (and Sticky) It Was," in *Flesh and the Word* 2 (New York: Plume, 1993), ed. John Preston, pp. 76–77.

20. Ibid., p. 83.

21. "A third problem [between gay liberation and women's liberation] is differing views of sex; sex for them has meant oppression, while it has been a symbol of our freedom" Wittman, "Amerika," p. 160. Also see John Francis Hunter, *The Gay Insider* (New York: The Traveller's Companion, Inc., 1971), pp. 89–94.

22. Charles Shively, "Indiscriminate Promiscuity As an Act of Revolution," in *Gay Roots: Twenty Years of Gay Sunshine*, ed. Winston Leyland (San Francisco: Gay Sunshine Press, 1991), p. 258.

23. Ibid, p. 261.

24. Ibid., p. 262.

25. Barry D Adam, *The Rise of a Gay and Lesbian Movement* (Boston: Twayne Publishers, 1987), p. 78.

26. John Rechy, *The Sexual Outlaw: A Documentary* (New York: Grove Press, 1977), p. 31.

27. Andrew Holleran, *Dancer from the Dance* (New York: Plume, 1986), p. 40. Wittman, "Amerika," p. 271.

28. Jack Fritscher, *Some Dance to Remember* (Stanford, CT: Knights Press, 1990), p. 160. Also see Humphreys, *Out of the Closets*, p. 2.

29. Dansky, "Hey Man"; see also Teal, *Gay Militants*, p. 57; also see Wittman, "Amerika," p. 158: "We want to make ourselves perfectly clear; our first job is to liberate ourselves, and that means clearing our heads of the garbage that's been poured into them."

30. See Sagarin, "Gay Liberation Front," p. 17. "If only society could be convinced that the homosexuals were really good boys and good girls, not promiscuous, very loving, always law-abiding, forever the victim and never the victimizer, they would be accepted. They were loyal, excellent security risks, were not sissies and bull-dykes and would make good soldiers and sailors, if only given the opportunity"; Teal, *Gay Militants*, p. 59.

31. Teal, *Gay Militants*, p. 58; Jonathon Black, "The Boys in the Snake Pit: Games 'Straights' Play," *Village Voice*, March 19, 1970.

32. Adam, *Gay and Lesbian Movement*, p. 80. It's easy, in the PC '90s, to value GLF's revolutionary panache to GAA's more directed approach. But GAA created a powerful camaraderie and democratic spirit among its hundreds of members. For the story of how participation in GAA transformed one man and made him into a gay leader (and GAA officer), see Kantrowitz, *Under the Rainbow*, pp. 128–156.

33. Theodore Roszak, *The Making of a Counter Culture* (New York: Anchor Books, 1969), p. 70.

34. Roszak, *Counter Culture*, pp. 50–51.

35. And while not many gay men spoke R. D. Laing's psychological lingo, how could they not disagree that Laing's recipe for growth applied to their coming out process, life being, "in one way or another, the dissolution of the normal ego, that false self competently adjusted to our alienated social reality: the emergence of the 'inner' archetypal mediation of divine power, and through this death, a rebirth, and the eventual reestablishment of a new kind of ego-functioning, the ego now being the servant of the divine, no longer the betrayer." R. D. Laing, *The Politics of Experience and The Bird of Paradise* (London: Penguin Books, 1976), p. 119.

36. "The Flamingo was our club," adds Picano, "the place for the Fire Island set in the winter. You could not get in unless you were brought in by a member."

37. Thompson, ed., *The Long Road to Freedom*, pp. xvii–xxv.

38. See chapter on Lige Clarke and Jack Nichols in Tobin and Wicker, *Gay Crusaders*, pp. 177–88. A few *Gay* articles included: "The Bored in the Band," "Closets are for Clothes Only," and "Can Psychoanalysis Really Be Cured?"

39. Roger Watson, "Sex Has Its Ugly Side: VD," *QQ*, March/April 1973; "It's Not Nice to Fool Mother Nature: The Folly of Increasing Phallic Size Through Silicone," *QQ*, January/February 1973; Frank Samuels, "Glory Holes: A Piece of Vanishing America," *QQ*, May/June 1974; Alan Diaz, "Sex & Cocaine: The Drug Called 'Powdered Champagne,'" *QQ*, March/April 1977.

40. Angelo d'Arcangelo, *The Homosexual Handbook* (New York: Ophelia Press, Inc., 1969), pp. 45–46 and 106–107. I am indebted to John Hunter Francis for sending and giving me his copy of *The Homosexual Handbook* and for his valuable time in providing insights into the past.

41. d'Arcangelo, *Handbook*, pp. 45–46.

42. Hunter, *The Gay Insider/USA*.

43. John Francis Hunter, *The Gay Insider: A Hunter's Guide to New York and a Thesaurus of Phallic Lore* (New York: The Olympia Press, Inc., 1971), pp. 89–94.

44. For one of the best pieces of historic/autobiographical writing from this period, see Arnie Kantrowitz, *Under the Rainbow: Growing Up Gay* (New York: William Morrow and Company Inc., 1977); also see Arthur Bell, *Dancing the Gay Lib Blues: A Year in the Gay Liberation Movement* (New York: Simon & Schuster, 1971); Dennis Altman, *Coming Out in the Seventies* (Australia: Wild & Wooley, 1979).

45. Arthur Bell, "The Bath Life Gets Respectability," in *Lavender Culture*, p. 77.

46. Bell, "Bath Life," p. 80.

47. Jack Fritscher, *Some Dance to Remember*, p. 159.

48. Ibid.

49. See Humphreys, *Tearoom Trade*. See also Laud Humphreys, "Impersonal Sex and Perceived Satisfaction," in *Studies in the Sociology of Sex* (New York: Appleton-Century-Crofts, 1971). Richard Piro, "The Rich Street Baths: An Alternative to the Alternative," *Vector* 9 (April 1973): 4–6.

50. Martin S. Weinberg and Colin J. Williams, "Gay Baths and the Social Organization of Impersonal Sex," in *Gay Men: The Sociology of Male Homosexuality*, ed. Martin P. Levine (New York: Harper & Row, 1979), pp. 167–69.

51. Fritscher, *Dance*, p. 157.

52. Ibid., p. 158.

53. Altman, *Coming Out in the '70s*, p. 120.

54. Randy Shilts, *The Mayor of Castro Street* (New York: St. Martin's Press, 1982), p. 61.

55. FitzGerald, *Cities*, pp. 42–43.

56. Shilts, *Mayor*, p. 61.

57. FitzGerald, *Cities*, p. 42.

58. Joel Hall, "Growing Up Black and Gay," in *The Gay Liberation Book*, ed. Len Richmond and Gary Noguera (San Francisco: Ramparts Press, 1973), p. 55.

59. Crawford Barton, *Days of Hope: '70s Gay San Francisco*, foreword by Mark Thompson (London: GMP Publishers, 1994), p. 5.

60. Wittman, "Amerika," p. 157.

61. Eric Rofes, *Reviving the Tribe: Regenerating Gay Men's Sexuality and Culture in the Ongoing Epidemic* (New York: Harrington Park Press, 1995), p. 71.

62. Jay and Young, *Gay Report*, p. 466.

63. Bronski, "How Sweet," p. 76.

64. Allen Young, "Out of the Closets Into the Streets," in *Out of the Closets: Voices of Gay Liberation*, Karla Jay and Allen Young, eds. (New York: Distributed by Quick Fox, 1972), p. 13.

65. Bell, "Bath Life," p. 81.

66. *My First Time: Gay Men Describe Their First Same-Sex Experience*, ed. Jack Hart (Boston: Alyson, 1995), pp. 119–20.

67. "Cousin," in Hart, p. 122.

68. Allen Young, "No Longer the Court Jesters," in *Lavender Culture*, pp. 42–47; also see Young, "Out of the Closets," p. 11.

69. Fritscher, *Dance*, pp. 160–61.

70. Ibid., pp. 39–44, 101.

71. Ibid., p. 42.

72. Ibid., p. 93.

73. Kenneth R. Dutton, *The Perfectible Body: The Western Ideal of Male Physical Development* (New York: The Continuum Publishing Company, 1995), p. 133.

74. Adam, *Gay and Lesbian Movement*, p. 95.

75. Edmund White, *States of Desire: Travels in Gay America* (New York: Dutton, 1980), pp. 45–46.

76. See Jay and Young, *Gay Report*, pp. 86–88, for a series of stories about the power of the crush.

chapter four: trouble in paradise

1. "In the Dionysian orgy," writes Nietzsche in the *Birth of Tragedy*, "alienated Nature, hostile or enslaved, celebrates once more her feast of reconciliation with her prodigal son—Man." For an interesting history of sexual license and its divine powers see Walter F. Otto, *Dionysus: Myth and Cult* (Dallas, Tex.: Spring Publications, 1981), p. 30.

2. Seymour Kleinberg, *Alienated Affections: Being Gay in America* (New York: St. Martin's Press, 1980), pp. 190–96.

3. Paul Goodman, "The Politics of Being Queer," in *Nature Heals: The Psychological Essays of Paul Goodman*, ed. Taylor Stoehr.

4. George Whitmore, "After a 'Career' in Suicide: Choosing to Live," *Advocate*, March 3, 1983, p. 25; George Whitmore, "Living Alone," in Allen Young and Karla Jay, eds., *After You're Out: Personal Experiences of Gay Men and Lesbian Women* (New York: Link Books, 1975), pp. 52–61.

5. George Whitmore, *From the Confessions of Danny Slocum*, in Bergman, ed., *Violet Quill*, pp. 101, 108.

6. Ibid., p. 110.

7. Ibid., p. 115.

8. Aubrey Walter, a GLF live wire in London, didn't expect the aims of GLF to be realized overnight. Walter, in fact, expected even more resistance from "the state and other apparatuses of repression." But capitalism didn't fight gay lib quite so much; gay dances took place and gay business establishments flourished. See the introduction of *Come Together—The Years of Gay Liberation 1970–1973*, ed. Aubrey Walter (London: Gay Men's Press, 1980).

9. For the classic book on the history of Dionysus see Otto, *Dionysus*. For a taste of how violent Dionysus can be, see Walter Norris, "The Gay Receiver: The Zip and Zap of Masochism," *QQ*, July/August 1973, 10. Also see Kleinberg's rather exhaustive description of a San Francisco fisting scene: pp. 180–87.

10. See Robert A. Johnson, *Ecstasy* (San Francisco: Harper San Francisco, 1989).

11. For an interesting historical survey about the role of eros in shaping history, see Wilhelm Reich, *The Function of the Orgasm* (New York: Noonday Press, 1973), pp. 8-19.

12. Jean Shinoda Bolen, M.D., *Gods in Everyman: A New Psychology of Men's Lives and Loves* (New York: Harper & Row, 1989), p. 276.

13. D'Emilio and Freedman, *Intimate Matters*, p. 264.

14. Holleran, *Dancer*, pp. 83–84.

15. Ibid., pp. 83–93.

16. Ibid.

17. Thompson, ed., *Long Road to Freedom*, p. 185.

18. For a good piece on the closure of the Mine Shaft, see Pat Califia's essay in Thompson, ed., *Long Road to Freedom*, pp. 275–76.

19. For a good article on the end of an era from a '90s perspective, see Brooks Peters, "The Sexual Revolution Mailman Delivered," *Out*, July/August 1994. Also see Jonathan McEwan, "The Saint Goes On," *MetroSource*, Winter 1994; David W. Dunlap, "As Theater Turned Disco Faces Demolition, Gay Alumni Share Memories," *New York Times*, August 21, 1995, B3.

20. Darrell Yates Rist, "Policing the Libido," *Village Voice*, November 26, 1995.

21. White, *States of Desire*, p. 283.

22. Ibid., pp. 284–85.

23. Jack Fritscher, *Mapplethorpe: Assault with a Deadly Camera* (Mamaroneck, N.Y.: Hastings House, 1994), p. 42.

24. Ibid.

25. White, *States of Desire*, pp. 266–67.

26. "The central concern of such [Greek] celebrations," writes Nietzsche in *The Birth of Tragedy*, "was, almost universally, a complete sexual promiscuity overriding every form of established tribal law; all the savage urges of the mind were unleashed on those occasions until they reached that paroxysm of lust and cruelty which has always struck me as the 'witches' cauldron' par excellence" (pp. 25–26).

27. The argument is that a new symbol might be forming in the unconscious, presenting the subject with a new attitude.

28. For a brilliant read on this problem, the reader is directed to Herbert Marcuse, "Freedom and Freud's Theory of Instincts," in *Five Lectures: Psychoanalysis, Politics, and Utopia* (Boston: Beacon Press, 1970), pp. 1–43.

29. C. G. Jung, "Instinct and the Unconscious," *Collected Works* 8: 129–38. "Just as his instincts compel man to a specifically human mode of existence, so the archetypes for his ways of perception and apprehension into specifically human patterns."

30. Jung, *On the Nature of the Psyche cw*, 8, (Princeton, N.J.: Bollingen, 1970), pp. 57–58.

31. This kind of secrecy is common for people who experiment with S&M. See the profile on Fakir Musafar: Andrea Juno, ed., "Fakir Musafar," *Research: Modern Primitives* (San Francisco: Re/Search Publication, 1989).

32. This search for love through S&M is the basis of John Preston's *Mr. Benson* (New York: Masquerade Books, 1992). Also see Michael Bronski, "S/M Fiction: Isn't It Romantic," *Gay Community News*, February 16, 1985.

33. See the interview between Joseph W. Bean and Fakir Musafar, "Magical Masochist: A Conversation with Fakir Musafar in *Leatherfolk: Radical Sex, People, Politics and Practice*, ed. Mark Thompson (Boston: Alyson Publications, Inc., 1991), pp. 303–19. In some spiritually oriented S&M experiences, the top and the bottom become aware of a larger impersonal energy in each of them and the roles reverse or neutralize.

34. Thompson, *Leatherfolk*, p. xvii.

35. Mark Thompson, "To the Limits and Beyond—Folsom Street: A Neighborhood Changes," *The Advocate*, July 8, 1982.

36. Jay and Young, *Lavender Culture*, p. 85. "Neither sadism nor masochism is inherent in human sexuality," argued John Stoltenberg in a forum on sadomasochism. See pp. 85–117 for entire transcript.

37. Jay and Young, *Lavender Culture*, pp. 99–100. Lyn Rosen argued that there was actually more consent in S&M than in ordinary sex. S&M introduced a new level of thinking to lovemaking because one had to talk through one's fears, desires, and boundaries as opposed to just throwing oneself into bed and wrestling around to find what the other person liked.

38. Robert Hopcke, *Jung, Jungians and Homosexuality* (Boston: Shambala Publications, Inc., 1989), p. 163.

39. Jay and Allen, *Lavender Culture*, p. 103. See also Geoffrey Mains, *Urban Aboriginals* (San Francisco: Gay Sunshine Press, 1984), pp. 103–10.

40. Ibid., pp. 103–5.

41. Brian Pronger, *The Arena of Masculinity* (New York: St. Martin's Press, 1990), p. 130.

42. Purusha Larkin, *The Divine Androgyne* (San Diego, Calif.: Sanctuary Publications, 1981), p. 111.

43. See Erich Neumann, *Amor and Psyche* (New York: Bollingen Foundation, 1956).

44. Fritscher, pp. 299–300.

45. White, *States of Desire*, p. 253.

46. Shilts, *Mayor*, p. 226.

47. Fritscher, *Some Dance*, p. 301.

48. Larry Kramer, *Faggots* (New York: Plume, 1978), pp. 378–99. Young, *Stonewall Experiment*, p. 147. Young quotes psychotherapist Paul Rosenfels warning gays that compulsive promiscuity and compulsive repression were not opposites but effects of the same oppressive cause. I am grateful for Young's pointing out of this text: Paul Rosenfels, M.D., *Homosexuality: The Psychology of the Creative Process* (Roslyn Heights, N.Y.: Libra Publishers, 1971).

49. Kramer, *Faggots*, pp. 27–28, 173–75.

50. Ibid., pp. 173–74.

51. Ibid., p. 44.

52. Kevin Bentley, "My Clementina," *Diseased Pariah News* 10.

53. Ibid.

54. D'Emilio and Freedman, *Intimate Matters*, p. 346.

55. Randy Shilts, *Mayor*, pp. 275, 165, 203.

56. Jim Kepner, *Song and Dance*, personal newsletter, October 1995.

57. Shilts, pp. 155–58.

chapter five: the great depression

1. Larry Mass, M.D., "Cancer in the Gay Community," *New York Native*, July 27–August 9, 1981, 1, 21–22.

2. Mass, "Cancer," p. 20. See also James Kinsella, *Covering the Plague* (New Brunswick: Rutgers University Press, 1989), p. 29. "I never believed that there was any *direct* association between fisting and transmission," Mass wrote me in 1996. "The link would be indirect: Someone getting fisted would be more likely to experience rectal tears, which would then predispose him or her to acquire a blood-borne agent from ejaculate. But there's no conceivable direct connection." See also *Village Voice*, July 15, 1981.

3. Other key *Native* AIDS writers include Brendan Lemon; Wallace Hamilton; Peter A. Seitzman, M.D.; Richard Berkowitz; Michael Callen; Joseph Sonnabend; Michael Quadland, Ph.D.; R. William Wedlin, Ph.D.; and Dan Belm.

4. See also by Larry Mass, "The New 'Anti-Sex' Drug," *The New York Native*, July 27–August 9, 1981, 22; "Cancer as Metaphor," *Native*, August 23–September 6, 1981, 13; "Do Poppers Cause Cancer: Links Seen to Drugs, Genetics," *Native*, December 21–January 3, 1981; "The Epidemic Continues: Facing a New Case Every Day, Researchers Are Still Bewildered," *Native*, March 29–April 11, 1982, 1; "New York Physicians Organize At Last," *Native*, March 29–April 11, 1982, 13; "Handballing and KS: Is There a Link?" *Native*, May 10–23, 1982, 15. "Another Infection for the Immune Deficient," *Native*, July 5–18, 1982, 15; "Creative Sex, Creative Medicine," *Native*, July 19–August 1, 1982, 11; "Time for Prevention: Devising Ways of Evading AID," *Native*, August 16–29, 1982.

5. When Larry Kramer and Paul Popham, Enno Poersch, and a few others stretched a banner—"Give to Gay Cancer"—at the entranceway to the Fire Island Pines, they were sneered at. "This is a downer" and "Leave me alone" were the typical reactions as men leapt off the ferry. The activists raised $124.00, the first official act of Gay Men's Health Crisis.

6. Mass, "Epidemic Continues," pp. 1, 15.

7. D'Emilio and Freedman, *Intimate Matters*, pp. 355–56. See also Ananda K. Coomaraswamy, *The Dance of Shiva: On Indian Art and Culture* (New York: The Noonday Press, Inc., 1957), p. 12. "However much the Brahmans held Self-realization to be the end of life, the *summum bonum*, they saw very clearly that it would be illogical to impose this aim immediately upon those members of the community who are not yet weary of self-assertion." In other words, self-realization is going to make more sense to someone who's fucked himself silly than one who hasn't yet integrated that level of experience.

8. *Native*, March 15–28, 1982; Richard Berkowitz and Michael Callen, with editorial assistance by Richard Dworkin, "How to Have Sex in an Epidemic: One Approach" (New York: News From the Front Publications, 1983), pp. 3, 15, 29, 38–40. Anyone interested in the history of safer sex and gay life circa 1983 must read this valuable publication.

9. See Simon Watney, *Policing Desire: Pornography, AIDS and the Media* (Minneapolis: University of Minnesota Press, 1987), p. 9. Watney's basic notion is this: "AIDS is not only a medical crisis on an unparalleled scale, it involved a crisis of representation itself, a crisis over the entire framing of knowledge about the human body and its capacities for pleasure."

10. See Michel Foucault, *The History of Sexuality: An Introduction* (New York: Vintage, 1990), p. 23. "Toward the beginning of the nineteenth century, there emerged a political, economic and technical incitement to talk about sex."

11. Michael D'Antonio, *Heaven on Earth* (New York: Crown Publishers, Inc., 1992), pp. 66–108.

12. D'Emilio and Freedman, *Intimate Matters*, pp. 355–56.

13. Randy Shilts, *And the Band Played On* (New York: St. Martin's Press, 1987), p. xxii.

14. As quoted in Rofes, *Reviving the Tribe*, p. 8.

15. Ibid., p. 9.

16. D'Emilio and Freedman, *Intimate Matters*, p. 356.

17. Neil Alan Marks, "The New Gay Man," *Native*, April 12–25, 1982, 18.

18. David M. Sloven, M.D., and Jeffrey M. Leiphart, Ph.D., "Coping with the Kid in the Candy Store: Is Promiscuity Dead?" *Native*, March 15–28, 1982, 15–16.

19. Thomas Garrett, "Not Play, Not Recreation: Sex Changes Things," *Native*, June 15–28, 1981, 4–5. Garrett saw that ceaseless extroversion of libido as insulting to nature. He saw the mad pursuit of "recreational sex" as a devotional attitude that had been corrupted by modern life. He spoke of the man who claimed to have fifteen hundred sexual contacts as "a prodigious achievement," one he ranked with those of the "medieval monks who devoted their lifetimes to the illumination of a single manuscript or the carving of a lone iconostasis, going blind or bats in the process."

20. Dave Kinnick, "How Safe Is Video Sex?" *Frontiers*, September 27, 1991, 45.

21. Eugene Sachs, "Talking Love and Sex: Five Voices on AIDS," *Native*, February 28–March 13, 1983, 20–23.

22. Paul Monette, *Borrowed Time: An AIDS Memoir* (Orlando, Fla.: Harcourt Brace Jovanovich, Publishers, 1988), p. 47.

23. There are exceptions to this rule, the most prominent being Paul Monette's *Borrowed Time*, which distinguishes itself as being the one written record that documents the grief exactly as it was happening. Another such book is Andrew Holleran's *Ground Zero* (New York: William Morrow, 1988). Also see Steven Corbin's *A Hundred Days from Now* (Boston: Alyson Publications, 1994); Walter Rico Burrell, "The Scarlet Letter, revisited: A Very Different AIDS Diary," in *Brother to Brother: New Writings for Black Gay Men*, ed. Essex Hemphill and conceived by Joseph Beam (Boston: Alyson Publications, 1991). See also Dan Bellm, "Days of Courage, Nights of Hell: The Story of a Person with AIDS," *Native*, February 27–March 11, 1984.

24. Walt Odets, *In the Shadow of the Epidemic: Being HIV Negative in the Age of AIDS* (Durham: Duke University Press, 1995), p. 67.

25. Odets, *Epidemic*, pp. 68–70. Also see Mitch Walker, "Jung and Homophobia," p. 62.

26. Young, *Stonewall Experiment*, p. 63.

27. As quoted in Young, *Stonewall Experiment*, pp. 63–64. I am indebted to Young for pointing out this material.

28. As quoted in the notes section of Young, *Stonewall Experiment*, p. 84. Also see John Lauritsen, "Political-economic construction of gay male clone identity," *Journal of Homosexuality* 24 (1993): 3–4.

29. See Bronski, "Sweet," p. 75, for a good analysis of why public sex has always been a contentious topic. Also see Califia, *Culture of Radical Sex*, for the most trenchant defense of public sex to date, especially the essay, "Public Sex," pp. 71–94.

30. Mass, "Cancer as Metaphor," p. 13.

31. For a splendid sociology of the first gay men who suffered AIDS see Steven Petrow's *Dancing Against the Darkness: A Journey through America in the Age of AIDS* (Boston: Lexington Books, 1990). See especially the interview with Eddie Mohr, entitled "Fear and Loathing of Oneself," pp. 145–68.

32. See Mitch Walker, "The Double: An Archetypal Configuration." See also Hopcke, *Jung, Jungians and Homosexuality*, pp. 116–20; Mark Thompson, *Gay Soul* (San Francisco: Harper San Francisco, 1994).

33. See Robert A. Johnson, *Owning Your Own Shadow* (San Francisco: Harper San Francisco, 1991) for a good analysis of romantic love as a shadow projection.

34. M. Esther Harding, *Psychic Energy: Its Source and Its Transformation* (New Jersey: Princeton University Press, 1973), p. 135.

35. "A Letter from Larry Kramer," *Native*, December 21, 1981–January 2, 1982, 1, 12–13. See also *Native*, January 4–17, 1982, p 5.

36. For some interesting letters to the editor between Kramer and his critics, see *Native*, October 19–November 1, 1981, 4; *Native*, October 5–16, 1981, 4.

37. *Native*, January 4–17, 1982, 4–5; *Native*, February 15–28, 1982, 4.

38. See also J. A. Sonnabend, M.D., "Promiscuity Is Bad for Your Health: AIDS and the Question of an Infectious Agent," *Native*, September 13–26, 1995.

39. "A Group Interview — Gay Soul Making: Coming Out Inside," in Thompson, ed., *Gay Spirit*, p. 251.

40. Neil Alan Marks, "Narcissism," *Native*, March 1–14, 1982, 16. In the "narcissistically wounded" the self is crushed because the parent didn't properly mirror the child when it was an infant, but rather demanded that the infant satisfy the needs of the parent to receive love. Rather than disappoint the parent with any hint of his own individuality, the child developed a false self. Sometimes sex can be a way to shatter this false self, a feature of coming out that gay liberation put forward as its goal. But sometimes sex, because it offered comfort, and kept difficult feelings at bay, propped up this false self and was used as a vicious defense against being in relationship to the self as it really was.

41. Camille Paglia, *Sexual Personae: Art and Decadence from Nefertiti to Emily Dickinson* (New York: Vintage Books, 1990), pp. 1–3, 28. "Sex is daimonic. . . . Sex is the point of contact between man and nature, where morality and good intentions fall to primitive urges. . . . The search for freedom through sex is doomed to failure. In sex, compulsion and ancient Necessity rule."

42. Some depth psychologists argue that within each person a vibrant self-regulating mechanism exists. But given no role models, an individual can find that site for himself only after he frees his own mind of stupidity, oppression, and pettiness — after, in short, he lives to the fullest. See Harding, *Psychic Energy*, p. 39.

43. Christopher Wittke, "Just Do It," in Preston, ed., *Flesh and the Word 2*, p. 87. One might say that the same energies that used to be projected out toward a "God" image, when the Judeo-Christian myth was still the going thing, were now projected out toward the sex object. The Greek root of *enthusiasm* means "a god within."

44. Harding, *Psychic Energy*, p. 141.

45. Michael Callen, *Surviving AIDS* (New York: Harper Perennial, 1990), p. 2.

46. Callen, *Surviving AIDS*, pp. 2–4.

47. Ibid.

48. Ibid.

49. Ibid., p. 12. Also see *Sexually Transmitted Diseases in Homosexual Men: Diagnosis, Treatment and Research*, eds. David G. Ostrow, Terry Alan Sandholzer, and Yehudi Felman (New York: Plenum Medical Book Company, 1983).

50. Michael Callen and Richard Berkowitz (with Richard Dworkin and Dr. Joseph Sonnabend), "We Know Who We Are: Two Gay Men Declare War on Promiscuity," *Native*, November 8–21, 1982.

51. Ibid.

52. Ibid.

53. *Native*, March 15–28, 1982; Berkowitz and Callen, "Sex in an Epidemic." Anyone interested in the history of safer sex and gay life circa 1983 must read this publication. Significant portions have been reprinted in *Surviving and Thriving with Aids: Collected Wisdom, v.2*, Michael Callen, ed. (New York: PWA Coalition, Inc., 1988), pp. 164–67.

54. Berkowitz and Callen, "Sex in an Epidemic."

55. Ibid.

56. See Letter from Boyd McDonald, "The Hypocrisy of Loveism," *Native*, June 15–28, 1981, 5. Boyd McDonald of *Straight to Hell* fame wrote that "Love is no substitute for sex."

57. Charles Jurrist, "In Defense of Promiscuity: Hard Questions About Real Life," *Native*, December 6–19, 1982, 27–29.

58. Shilts, *Band Played On*, p. 455; Miller, *Out of the Past*, p. 446.

59. King, *Safety in Numbers*, pp. 14–15. King also refers to these key studies: Warren Winkelstein Jr. et al., "The San Francisco Men's Health Study: III. Reduction in human immunodeficiency virus transmission among homosexual/bisexual men, 1982–1986," *AJPH* 76, no. 9 (1987): 685–89; Winkelstein Jr. et al., "The San Francisco Men's Health Study: continued decline in HIV seroconversion rates among homosexual/bisexual men," *AJPH* 78, no. 11 (1988): 1472–74.

60. King, *Safety in Numbers*, p. 14. King also refers to these studies: Leon McKusick et al., "AIDS and sexual behavior reported by gay men in San Francisco," *AJPH* 75, no. 5 (1985): 493–96; McKusick et al., "Reported changes in the sexual behavior of men at risk for AIDS, San Francisco, 1982–4—The AIDS Behavioral Research Project," *Public Health Reports* 100, no. 6 (1985): 622–29.

61. King, *Safety in Numbers*, p. 15.

62. Ibid., p. 16. King also refers to a key article written by Michael Callen on what Callen considered underreported news of the '80s, the decline in cases of rectal gonorrhea among gay men. See Michael Callen, "Your Country Needs You!" *QW*, June 14, 1992.

63. King, *Safety in Numbers*, p. 43.

64. See Wittke, "Just Do It," pp. 85–104 for one of the hottest stories ever written about latex. The following excerpts are taken from pages 93, 96, and 97.

65. Simon Harvey, "Accentuating the Positive," in *Ecstatic Scene Zine* 3 (Winter 1995), ed. Ron Hardcastle, produced out of D. Sadownick's 1990–1995 gay male writing workshops at the Eighteenth Street Arts Complex and the Los Angeles Gay and Lesbian Community Services Center.

66. Doug Mirk, "Nineteen-Eighty-One," in *Ecstatic Scene Zine* 2, ed. Sean Early, produced out of D. Sadownick's writing workshops.

67. Larry Kramer, "1,112 and Counting," in *Reports from the Holocaust: The Making of an AIDS Activist* (New York: St. Martin's Press, 1989), p. 33.

68. Neil Miller writes that even "the city government of New York took notice," with the influence of the article "felt as far away as San Francisco." See Miller, *Out of the Past*, p. 444.

69. Shilts, *Band Played On*, pp. 431, 439. FitzGerald, *Cities*, p. 92.

70. This material is documented in Shilts, *Band Played On*, p. 445. The April 4, 1984 *BAR* editorial, called "Killing the Movement," was written by Paul Lorch.

71. See Shilts, *Band Played On*, p. 443. "Nathan Fain . . . wrote in the *Advocate* that 'there is no proof that even one of the 3,775 cases of AIDS tallied by the Centers for Disease Control had involved sexual transmission.' The gay-backed move to close baths in San Francisco, he wrote, showed that gay leaders were prepared 'to make criminals of their own people.'"

72. Shilts, *Band Played On*, pp. 413, 421–22, 430–37, 439–523; FitzGerald, *Cities*, pp. 88–104; "San Francisco Health Director Bans Sex in Bathhouses," *Native*, April 23–May 6, 1984, 6; Mike Hipler, "And Now, A Word From Your Local Bathhouse," *Native*, April 11–24, 1983; *Bay Area Reporter*, April 4, 1984.

73. Hal Slate of San Francisco's Cauldron was one of the few bathhouse owners to provide information on AIDS to his clientele. He held benefits, a "cum clean party" and also distributed AIDS information. But most bathhouse owners did surprisingly little and did not have the foresight to make their clubs into safer-sex venues or AIDS education sites. The public health climate was such that the bathhouses might have been closed anyway, but one wonders if proactive involvement on their part would have changed their destiny. See Shilts, *Band Played On*, pp. 304–305, 464.

74. FitzGerald, *Cities*, p. 113.

75. Bronski, "How Sweet," p. 82.

76. Max Navarre, "Fighting the Victim Label," and "PWA Coalition Portfolio," in *AIDS: Cultural Analysis, Cultural Activism*, ed. Douglas Crimp (Cambridge, Mass.: The MIT Press, 1989), p. 149.

77. Miller, *Out of the Past*, p. 452.

78. Kramer, "The Beginning of ACTing Up," in *Reports from the Holocaust* (New York: St. Martin's Press, 1989), p. 127.

79. Douglas Sadownick, "ACT UP: And the Politics of AIDS," *L.A. Weekly*, October 6–October 12, 1989.

80. Frank Browning, *The Culture of Desire* (New York: Crown, 1993), p. 21.

81. Sadownick, "ACT UP."

82. Tim Miller, "Civil Disobedience Weekend," *Metroline*, December 10, 1992.

83. Michael Callen, "Media Watch (And It's Still Ticking)," in Crimp, *AIDS*, pp. 150–51. Also see *PWA Coalition Newsline* 7, December 1985.

84. Ibid.

chapter six: the second sexual revolution?

1. Walt Odets, *In the Shadow of the Epidemic: Being HIV-Negative in the Age of AIDS* (Durham: Duke University Press, 1995), p. 180.

2. The language AIDS educators used—"caving into relapse"—criminalized the impulse to have "ordinary" sex, something sero-similar couples could do without grave risk. The language of "recidivism" and "slippage" shamed men who put their lips to a bare dick or who let their sero-similar lovers enter them. Sometimes that shame led to a global disregard of safer sex—but it didn't have to. If only men could process their "slippage," their "shame," a more human and effective gay sexual way of life could take hold. The more educators began asking questions, the more they saw that everyone slipped at one time or another. Yet no one felt safe enough to talk about it. The "Use a condom every time" slogan did not provide psychological freedom for men to talk about what they *really* did in bed.

3. Michael Callen, "Your Country Needs You," *QW*, June 13, 1992. This article serves as the second half of a two-part series on post-AIDS sexuality. The first article, "Wading the Deep, Messy Waters of Sex: Wear Your Rubbers!" can be found in *QW*, June 7, 1992. *QW* can be found in gay archives that store the short-lived New York City gay newspaper that emerged after *Outweek*. The two pieces mark some of the best writing ever on the sociology of gay sexual life in the midst of AIDS.

4. Ibid.

5. Dr. Charles Silverstein and Felice Picano, *The New Joy of Gay Sex* (New York: Harper Collins, 1992), p. xiii. "In 1977, the straight world was not ready to accept an open celebration of gay sex, and the book encountered antisexual, homophobic resistance. French customs had the book shredded; the British burned it." Also: "In the United States, the book created a furor. At the time Anita Bryant was raging against homosexuality. Many bookstores, fearful of offending customers, kept the book out of sight. To buy it, you had specifically to ask for it" (p. xiv).

6. Silverstein and Picano, *Joy of Gay Sex*, pp. 139–42.

7. Kevin Koffler, "The Ballad of Little Joey," *Out Magazine*, September 1995, 94. Grateful acknowledgment is paid to Koffler for his insights—as both a colleague and a writer—into the cutting edge of gay life and gay sex.

8. This information comes from Koffler's article and interviews with O'Hara and porn actor Robert Campbell. According to Campbell, the bottom line emphasis of these companies is also what undermines them morally: some in the industry don't always insist on safer-sex practices.

9. Dave Kinnick, *Sorry I Asked: Intimate Interviews with Gay Porn's Rank and File* (New York: Masquerade Books, 1993), p. 335.

10. *Flesh and the Word* 3, ed. and intro. by John Preston with Michael Lowenthal (New York: Plume, 1995), p. 3.

11. Of course, porn could be terribly predictable. But even in the most trite of cum-zines, talented authors who had to pay the rent could be found doing their best to break down porn's traditional jocks-with-an-itch-to-scratch narrative line. *Flesh and the Word* grabbed those writers up. Preston's books marked the axis-point in the gay imagination where the abstract need to create a culture and the fleshly compulsion to merge through fucking met between the sheets.

12. Randy Shilts, "The Queering of America: Looking Back at 1990 and the Resurrection of the Gay Movement," *The Advocate*, January 1, 1991, 32.

13. Douglas Sadownick, "The Birth of a Queer Nation," *L.A. Weekly*, May 17–May 23, 1991.

14. See Otto, *Dionysus*, for a profoundly important discussion of cult, myth, and Dionysian explosiveness and a way out of purely rational analysis of human history: "There is, to be sure, a mental attitude which we are completely justified in calling 'magical.' It draws all of its power from subjectivity and is aware that it can affect men and things in astonishing ways by a mysterious concentration of the total faculties of heart and soul" (p. 35).

15. This trend would swing back the other way with the rise of more conservative younger gays, announced by the publication of Bruce Bawer's book, which valued the peace of mind that came with social recognition over that which came from inner eccentricity. See Bruce Bawer, *A Place at the Table: The Gay Individual in American Society* (New York: Poseidon Press, 1993).

16. See Nina Reyes, "Queerly Speaking: The Three-Word Title of an Essay Has Hurled the Lesbian and Gay Community into Yet Another Raging Controversy. Why Has 'I Hate Straights' Ignited Such a Furor?" *Outweek*, August 15, 1990, 40, for a trenchant analysis of the anonymously written essay entitled "I Hate Straights," which was distributed as a broadside on the street and was later printed at the end of the above article. Borrowing from the rhetoric of black nationalism, the broadside addressed self-defense, rage, and gay and lesbian self-determination: "I hate having to convince straight people that lesbians and gays live in a war zone, that we're surrounded by bomb blasts only we seem to hear, that our bodies and souls are heaped high, dead from fright or bashed or raped, dying of grief or disease, stripped of our personhood."

17. As Randy Shilts put it in his *Advocate* cover story in January 1991, "Straight strollers on San Francisco's Castro Street were advised by broadsheets to watch their behavior so they didn't alter the ethnic purity of the neighborhood's essential gay character." Shilts, "The Queering of America," p. 33.

18. Richard Goldstein, "1991—The Third Wave: Multi-Culti Queerism Emerges," *The Advocate* (January 14, 1992): p. 36.

19. As quoted in Jeffrey Schmalz, "Gay Politics Goes Mainstream," *New York Times Magazine*, October 11, 1992, sec. 6, p. 21.

20. James Ryan with G. Luther Whitington, "Homophobia in Hollywood," *The Advocate*, March 26, 1991, 33.

21. See Profile on Bob Hattoy, Josh Getlin, "The Speech of His Life: Fate Pushes a Political Insider Into Democratic Convention Spotlight To Talk About AIDS," *L.A. Times*, E1–E2, July 2, 1992.

22. "Gays Under Fire: What America Thinks—a *Newsweek* Poll," *Newsweek*, September 14, 1992.

23. Douglas Jehl, "Clinton Rebuffs Critics on Gay Military Ban," *L.A. Times*, November, 17, 1992, 1.

24. Richard L. Berke, *New York Times*, May 28, 1993, 1.

25. Douglas Sadownick, "Coming Out Party: The Bash that Bill Missed," *L.A. Weekly*, April 30–May 6, 1993, 10.

26. John Preston, *My Life as a Pornographer*, pp. 57, 58, and 134.

27. Ibid., p. 57.

28. Rofes, *Reviving the Tribe*, p. 3.

29. See George DeStefano, "Are Gay Men Having Safer Sex?" *Outweek*, February 18, 1990, 38–43 for one of the first articles to begin reporting that the PR victory touted by the gay movement of total behavior modification was inaccurate.

30. Robin Hardy, "Risky Business," *Village Voice*, June 26, 1990, 35–38; Odets, *Shadow of the Epidemic*, n. 2, p. 294; Charles Linebarger, "Study: Young Gays Returning to Unsafe Sex," *San Francisco Sentinel*, June 28, 1990, 5.

31. For longer pieces on the safer-sex controversy, see Michael Warner, "Why Gay Men are Having Risky Sex," *Village Voice*, January 31, 1995; Mark Schoofs, "Can You Trust Your Lover?: Gay Couples Weigh the Risk of Unprotected Sex," *Village Voice*, January 31, 1995; John Weir, "Blood Simple," *Details*, October 1995; Douglas Sadownick, "Beyond Condoms: Rethinking Safer Sex," *L.A. Weekly*, June 16–June 22, 1995; Douglas Sadownick, "The New Sex Radicals: The Return of Desire," *L.A. Weekly*, July 2–July 8, 1993. For a strange piece on the rise of backrooms, interesting for its internalized homophobia, R. Daniel Foster, "From Baths to Worse," *Los Angeles Magazine*, January 1995.

32. Gabriel Rotello, "Oral Arguments," *The Advocate*, October 17, 1995, 80. Also see Rotello's "Watch Your Mouth: The Word Is In on HIV and Oral Sex, and It Isn't Good," *Out Magazine*, June 1994.

33. Odets, *Shadow of the Epidemic*, p. 135.

34. Ibid., pp. 135, 136.

35. See James Hillman, "The Masturbation Inhibition," in *Loose Ends* (Dallas, Tex.: Spring Publications, 1975), pp. 117–121 for some interesting views on "introverting libido." See Douglas Sadownick, "Me and My Shadow," *L.A. Weekly*, June 22–June 28, 1990.

36. Don Shewey, "Sexual Healing: Joe Kramer Sings the Body Electric," *Village Voice*, April 21, 1992, p. 37.

37. Ibid.

38. Quotations from Leng come from discussions with him in which he shared a variety of his writings, in particular a piece called "Embodying Hybridity." Portions of these writings will appear in an essay of his entitled "Exploring Embodiment," in *Boundary Wars: Distance and Intimacy in Healing Relationships*, ed. Kathern Rapsdale, and in Robert Gosses, *Our Families, Our Values*, both to be published in 1997.

39. Ibid.

40. See Sogyal Rinpoche, *The Tibetan Book of Living and Dying* (San Francisco: Harper Collins, 1992), p. 76.

41. William J. Mann, "Perfect Bound," *Frontiers*, January 13, 1994, pp. 82–86.

42. Ibid.

43. Ibid.

44. Norman Wong, *Cultural Revolution* (New York: Persea Press, 1994), pp. 54–55.

45. For a brilliant story about one gay man's conscious acquaintance with the archetype of evil, see David May's "Hot Under the Collar," in Preston, ed., *Flesh and the Word* 3, pp. 191–202.

chapter seven: condom meets crystal meets individuation

1. William Hamilton, "In San Francisco, Grim AIDS Cycle Poised for Encore," *The Washington Post*, August 29, 1994; David Tuller, "Big Change Urged in AIDS Education," *The San Francisco Chronicle*, October 22, 1993; Jane Gross, "Second Wave of AIDS Feared by Officials in San Francisco," *New York Times*, December 11, 1993; Delthia Ricks, "Safer Sex Is a Subject They're Failing: An Informal Survey Finds College Students Are Still Engaging in Risky Behavior," *The Orlando Sentinel*, December 1, 1994. Printed material from Summit on HIV-Prevention for Gay Men, Bisexuals and Lesbians at Risk, July 15–17, 1994, Dallas, TX., Opening Remarks by Benjamin Schatz, J.D., executive director of The American Association of Physicians for Human Rights; Jim Graham, "Facing the Reality of AIDS: A Guide to Living with HIV Infection Still Overlooks Some Important Issues," *The Washington Post*, September 3, 1991; "Speaking of the Plague," *U.S. News and World Report*, June 17, 1991; Rob Polner, "Safer Sex Leads to Less Disease," *Newsday*, June 9, 1993; Malcolm Gladwell, "Graphic Safer-Sex Ads for Gay Men Often Judged Offensive by Others: AIDS Groups Express Frustration with Federal Funding Restriction," *The Washington Post*, March 17, 1991; Linda Roach Monroe, "Street Smarts," *Los Angeles Times*, May 29, 1988; Douglas Sadownick, "Untamed Youth," *Genre*, March 1994.

2. Laura Dean and Ilan Meyer, *Journal of Acquired Immune Deficiency Syndrome and Human Retrovirology* (February 1994).

3. See King, *Safety in Numbers*, p. 16; Sadownick, "Beyond Condoms."

4. Torie Osborn, "AIDS: Still the Issue," *The Advocate*, September 6, 1994, 80.

5. Michelangelo Signorile, "Unsafe Like Me," in *Out Magazine*, October, 1994, 22.

6. Ibid.

7. Ibid., p. 24.

8. Ibid., pp. 24, 128.

9. For a brilliant piece on the failures of AIDS education see Walt Odets, Ph.D., "Why We Stopped Doing Primary Prevention for Gay Men in 1985," *AIDS & Public Policy Journal* 10, no. 1 (Winter 1995). In this piece, Odets wastes no time getting to his point: "Much of our work to date has not only failed to provide gay men with a foundation for long-term prevention, it has been responsible for much psychological damage and has often inadvertently *supported* the transmission of HIV" (p. 1 in Odets's manuscript).

10. The following material comes from a talk entitled "Why We Stopped Doing Primary Prevention for Gay Men in 1985," which was given at the November 16, 1994 Town Hall Meeting at New York City's Gay and Lesbian Community Services Center. Much of the material was later published in expanded version in the *AIDS & Public Policy Journal* (Winter 1995) article referenced above.

11. Also see King, *Safety in Numbers*, p. 43: "It appears to have been more usual for men to stop anal sex altogether, rather than to continue fucking but to start to use condoms."

12. Walt Odets, Ph.D., "AIDS Education and Harm Reduction for Gay Men: Psychological Approaches for the 21st Century," *AIDS & Public Policy Journal* 9, no. 1 (Spring 1994): 16.

13. Ibid. This is where Odets the AIDS activist shows his real stripes as a psychologist-cum-philosopher. For whatever the new models look like, they have to do more than teach people about water-based lubricant. Odets, the shrink, speculates it may have something to do with a new marriage between thinking and feeling—a union neither gay culture (nor for that matter, Western culture) has yet to get behind. "For a man living in a lifelong epidemic," he writes, "in which intimacy might become assault and love become death, we had no [models], we had only contemplation itself: the internal space for each man to think and feel and thus make for himself the best possible decisions that he might."

14. Edward F. Edinger, *Ego and Archetype* (Boston: Shambhala Publications, Inc., 1972), p. 50.

15. As quoted in Young, *Stonewall Experiment*, p. 116. Also see Luiji Zoja, *Drugs, Addiction and Initiation: The Modern Search for Ritual* (Boston: Sigo Press, 1989), pp. 24–27. Also see Thomas Szasz, *Ceremonial Chemistry: The Ritual Persecution of Drugs, Addicts and Pushers*, rev. ed. (Holmes Beach, Fla.: Learning Publications, 1985).

16. In his *Jung, Jungians and Homosexuality*, Hopcke sees in the donning of the flexible armor of leather a conscious attempt to develop the fullness of one's own gay masculine nature in a society that "robs [gays] of their masculine self through social values and stereotypes which deny that they are men at all." While many condemn S&M for aping the pathology of patriarchal society, Hopcke sees it as representing a hunger for tribalism and collective archetypes. The only problem is that the final third stage of any true initiation—incorporating a person back into the community with his new social status—is missing from gay life (as opposed to the first two stages, "separation" and "transition," which have been perfected). Also see Hopcke, *Persona: Where Sacred Meets Profane* (Berkeley: Shambhala, 1995).

17. Robert Johnson, *Owning Your Own Shadow* (San Francisco: Harper San Francisco, 1991).

18. As quoted in Miller, *Out of the Past*, p. 450.

permissions

The following publishers and individuals have generously given permission to use extended quotations from copyrighted works.

From *In the Shadows of the Epidemic: Being HIV-Negative in the Age of AIDS* by Walt Odets. Copyright © 1995 by Duke University Press. Reprinted by permission of Duke University Press.

From *Dancer from the Dance* by Andrew Holleran. Copyright © 1978 by William Morrow and Company, Inc. Reprinted by permission of William Morrow and Company, Inc.

From *Coming Out Under Fire: The History of Gay Men and Women in World War Two* by Alan Bérubé. Copyright © 1990 by Alan Bérubé. Reprinted with permission of The Free Press, a Division of Simon & Schuster.

From "Why We Stopped Doing Primary Prevention for Gay Men in 1985," a November 16, 1994, talk given by Walt Odets, Ph.D., at New York's Gay and Lesbian Community Services Center. Copyright © 1994 by Walt Odets, Ph.D. Reprinted by permission of Walt Odets, Ph.D.

From "Unsafe Like Me," by Michelangelo Signorile. Copyright © 1994 by Michelangelo Signorile. Reprinted by permission of Michelangelo Signorile.

Excerpt from "The Chinese Barber," from *Cultural Revolution* by Norman Wong. Copyright © 1994 by Norman Wong. Reprinted by permission of Persea Books.

From *Cures: A Gay Man's Odyssey* by Martin Duberman. Copyright © 1991 by Martin Duberman. Used by permission of Dutton Signet, a Division of Penguin Books USA Inc.

From *States of Desire* by Edmund White. Copyright © 1980, 1983, 1991 by Edmund White. Used by permission of Dutton Signet, a division of Penguin Books USA Inc.

From *Gay American History, Revised Edition* by Jonathan Ned Katz. Copyright © 1976, 1992 by Jonathan Ned Katz. Used by permission of Dutton Signet, a Division of Penguin Books, USA Inc.

From "We Know Who We Are: Two Gay Men Declare War on Promiscuity," By Michael Callen and Richard Berkowitz with Richard Dworkin and Dr. Joseph Sonnabend). Copyright © 1982 by Michael Callen, Richard Berkowitz, and Richard Dworkin. Used by permission of Richard Dworkin.

index

Fleischer, Robert, 38–39
Flesh and the Word (Preston), 191
For You Lili Marlene (Peters), 26
Freedman, Estelle, 11, 55, 65, 119, 147, 150
Freshmen (magazine), 188
Freud, Sigmund, 32–33, 127–28, 244n12
Fritscher, Jack, 87, 109, 111, 125–26
Fung, Richard, 16

Gallo, Robert, 169
Gay Activists Alliance (GAA), 88–89
Gay bars, 50–52
"Gay cancers," 144–45
Gay identity: collective soul symbol of, 110–12; during second sexual revolution, 191–92; impact of AIDS on, 146–50; media image of, 66–68, 82, 104–6; myths of, 70; new spiritual outlook on, 238–42, 262n16; psychology as tool for, 119, 199–200; racism within, 65–66, 200–201; slow emerging of, 36, 46–47
Gay Insider, The (Hunter), 82, 92
Gay Insider/USA, The (Hunter), 92
Gay and Lesbian Alliance Against Defamation, 75
Gay Liberation Front dances, 88
Gay Liberation Front (GLF), 79–80, 88
Gay Manifesto (Whitman), 87
Gay Militants, The (Teal), 79
Gay New York (Chauncey), 14, 32, 34
Gay (newspaper), 91
Gay porn, 105–7, 153, 189–90
Gay pride, 237–38
Gay Report, The (Jay and Young), 11, 101–2

Gay sexual liberation: disease and, 139–41; failures of, 120–22, 225; "gay attitude" within, 137–38; Ginsberg's impact on, 70–72; histories of white/black, 61–62; impact on public sex, 81–85; Mattachine impact on, 73–74; militancy of, 87–89; sex as commodity of, 86–88; Stonewall as birth of, 6, 17, 60–61, 77–81. *See also* Bathhouse sex; Second sexual revolution
Gay sexuality: body worship within, 108–12, 214–16; desire and, 216–17; during early 1970s, 89–91; during Roaring Twenties, 32–33; during World War II, 21–44; as effect of libido, 12–13; ethnic/class issues of, 16–17, 200–201, 213–14; extroversion of, 107–12; guilt/difficulties attached to, 53–55; impact of AIDS on, 150–53, 164–75; issues of contemporary, 1–9; masculine/feminine roles of, 41–44; national surveys on, 10–13; of O-Boys!, 201–4; pathology of, 138–39, 224–25; role of father in, 161–63, 238; tearoom, 45–49. *See also* Second sexual revolution
"Gay shadow, The," 138–39
Gay soul symbol, 110–12
Gay-centered psychology, 199–200
Gay-in-the-military crisis, 195
Gernreich, Rudi, 74
Ginsberg, Allen, 70–72, 79–80, 101
Giovanni's Room (Baldwin), 52
GMSMA, 132–33
Goishi, Dean, 62–64
Golden Ass, The (Apuleius), 136–37
Golden showers, 123
Goodstein, David, 141

Grahn, Judy, 64–65
GRID, 166
Grison, Todd, 23
Guilt: emotional impact of, 56–58; of secret sex, 53–55

Haley, Thomas, 31
Hall, Joel, 100
Hardcastle, Ron, 81–83, 113–16
Harding, M. Esther, 165
Haring, Keith, 158
Harlem Renaissance, 60–62
Harvey, Simon, 174
Hay, Harry, 36, 58–60, 73–74, 182, 194, 229
Heard, Gerald, 36
Heilman, John, 192–93
Hillman, James, 128
Hin Yin (porn film), 205
Hirschfield, Magnus, 40
HIV infection, 169, 222. *See also* AIDS
HIV negatives, 226–27
Holleran, Andrew, 120–21
"Homophiles," 49, 67
Homosexual in America, The (Cory), 46–47
Homosexual Handbook, The (d'Arcangelo), 91–92
Homosexual tendency, 27–29
Homosexuality: as acquired illness, 58; cultural attitudes toward, 64–65; political parties on, 194–95
Homosexuality in Perspective (Masters and Johnson), 11
Homosexuals: AIDS and hatred of, 154–55; creation myth on, 36–38; fathers of, 161–63, 238; military crisis over, 195; as security risk, 55–56; segregation of, 65; sociological classifications on, 11–12; as well adjusted, 74–75; World War II experience of, 21–44, 99–100. *See also* Ethnic minority men
Hooker, Evelyn, 55, 74